Activism at Home:
Architects dwelling between politics, aesthetics, and resistance

Isabelle Doucet
Janina Gosseye (eds.)

Architects dwelling between politics, aesthetics, and resistance

Activism at Home

jovis

Stock Orchard Street: Activist project

by Sarah Wigglesworth

A respected senior architect visited Stock Orchard Street not long after we moved in. He had requested a tour because the building had caused something of a sensation and he was curious to find out more. He didn't stay long and didn't say much but his parting comment was: 'It's very crafted.'

This remark surprised me because this architect's work was commissioned by rich institutional clients and was known for its complexity and attention to the details of living. It dawned on me that this was the comment of a modernist whose goal was the expression of machine technology, efficiency, and economy. The slightly willful, hand-built, even unfinished quality of our building seemed to be his problem, although I thought it a virtue. My own view was that our home reflected its self-build roots so there was a certain humble honesty about it. The opportunity to experiment with our own lives and money, to bespoke a building to our vision, was a precious gift begging to be embraced. What is more, it literally was the expression of who built it and how, in line with our original aim to encourage self-builders and greenies to expand the range of possibilities beyond the rural vernacular that was regarded as the authentic ecological canon.

The comment by the reputable architect was, however, one of the more benign reactions that the building elicited. We had approached its design with the deliberate intention of challenging both planning and building regulations but we were not prepared for the onslaught that followed its publication. Used to working under the radar with nobody taking any notice, we were catapulted into the limelight, completely unprepared for the hostility of its reception, which accused us of being publicity-seeking, and of the building as a vainglorious project. Unlike some of the experiments showcased in this fascinating volume, we were not challenging social norms. Rather we were trying rigorously to find other (eco)-logical criteria to guide our decisions, and it was the aesthetics (mess, lack of control, 'too many ideas', uncategorisable material range) that seemed to upset the architects. The greens, meanwhile, condemned its urban location, the aversion to the vernacular tradition, and the use of petrochemical-based products.

We, however, were sure our approach showed how the architect could show agency in confronting the limitations of imagination, orthodox design thinking, real estate value, and the regulatory frameworks under which we labour. Everything about the project was well-researched; we spent months self-educating, addressing the myriad risks pertaining to the project and its realisation. As site-finders, fundraisers, designers, publicists (we were featured in the first series of *Grand Designs*), clients, builders (in part), and occupants, our commitment and embeddedness in this project was total, and demonstrated the potential freedom available to the architect given sufficient determination and resources.

Such resources included fearlessness and a willingness to take calculated risks, be they professional, technical, or financial. I only once felt completely out of my depth. In the UK, one's personal wealth is bound up in real estate, so financial risk plays an expanded role in dictating the ambitions of an activist project. We found that no high street bank was willing to lend to a building with unusual materials, and insurers felt the same way, advising that our elevations should be 'tidied up' by replacing the timber boarding with brickwork(!). In addition, finding a contractor to build it with us proved an obstacle, as perceived risk (that is, unfamiliar building techniques and complexity) sent builders running and costs soaring beyond our means. The financial aspects of activist homes – which determine so much of what is produced in the built environment – is hardly ever mentioned but would make an interesting subject for further research into the governing parameters for design.

Our own 'embodied resistance' has been an ongoing performance enacted through successive mini-completions, adjustments, and a recent refurbishment after twenty years of occupation. The advancing awareness of the circular economy has meant that what was once reviled has been absorbed into architects' consciousness so that, although our project could hardly be called mainstream, it stands for what is possible given enough willpower and risk management. Of particular interest to me, as an architect and feminist householder, is the interplay in our project between themes of work and home that manifest spatially, typologically, symbolically, and through the landscape. The relevance of its themes concerning identity, self-determination, and meaning remain central and resonant with the current debate about inclusion and diversity in architecture.

Current activisms such as Rural Studio's 20K house project attempt to address the financial barriers to deprived American communities getting on the housing ladder. By using self-build and subsidised labour as well as design talent provided by students, a model of modest but experimental housing is emerging that stands outside mainstream funding schemes. While our own experiment is in the tradition of self-builders like Rudolf Schindler and Walter Segal, what is particularly engaging about this book is the range of less well-known projects and architects, each of whom deserve greater recognition for their unique contribution to activism. It shows that the home remains a site of continued interest, fluidity, and experimentation. The authors point the way towards further themes for study and I sincerely hope these emerge in due course.

Activism at Home: Architects dwelling between politics, aesthetics, and resistance

Isabelle Doucet and Janina Gosseye

The architect's own home has long been a source of fascination, as well as fodder for richly illustrated coffee table publications. Examples include Michael Webb's *Architects' Houses* (2018), Bethany Patch's *Architects' Homes* (2017), Stephen Crafti's *Architects' Houses: Twenty Australian Homes* (2015), Gennaro Postiglione's *One Hundred Houses for One Hundred European Architects of the Twentieth Century* (2004), Anatxu Zabalbeascoa's *The House of the Architect* (1995), Michael Webb's *Architects House Themselves* (1994), Miranda H. Newton's *Architects' London Houses* (1992), Walter F. Wagner and Karin Schlegel's *Houses Architects Design for Themselves* (1974), and so on.[1]

All these publications fit into a particular genre in architectural writing that emerged in the late nineteenth century when, in conjunction with the increasing professionalisation of the architectural profession, periodicals such as the *Architects' Journal* and *Country Life* published recurring features on architects' own homes. Such features were generally rather formulaic, both in terms of layout and content. Emphasis was commonly placed on the aesthetic qualities of the house, and the key recurring theme was the veneration of architects and their realisations.[2] The aim was clear: to showcase the superiority of architect-designed dwellings and (thus) promote the services of the architect. In the introduction of *Houses Architects Design for Themselves*, published in 1974, Walter F. Wagner, for instance, unapologetically (and quite bafflingly) writes:

> There is something very special about a house that is special for you [...] This is why some people (bless them) go and find a good architect and enter on the time-consuming, mind-bending, sometimes frustrating, but always rewarding process of having their own house designed and built just for them. Living in an everyday kind of house – compared with living in a house that really fits your way of living – must be like being married to a woman who has never bothered to learn to cook well; you can get used to it, but you miss something every day of your life.[3]

Nevertheless, even in these largely promotional publications on architects' own homes, critical asides were sometimes made. For instance, an article published in *Country Life* in 1936, entitled 'An Architect's Own House', opened with:

> We know what the doctor prescribes for us, but does he take his own medicine? In the same way, we might ask, does the architect live in the kind of house he recommends to others? In secrecy let it be said there are some very modern architects who live in very old houses, and zealous advocates of modern furniture whose own homes are filled with fine old pieces.[4]

More than four decades later, in 1980, architectural theorist Léon Krier formulated a similar critique. In a photographic series entitled 'Vertus Privées et Vices Publics' (Private Virtues and Public Vices), which was published in the *Bulletin des Archives d'Architecture Moderne*, he opined: 'It is remarkable to observe the good taste and restraint with which the most wildly innovative architects choose their own residence and workspace.'[5] In this text, Krier mocked the

1
For publishing details of these titles, see the bibliography.

2
A noteworthy exception is Gonzáles de Canales's *Experiments with Life Itself.* In this publication, the own homes of architects Ralph Erskine, Charles and Ray Eames, Juan O'Gorman, and Alison and Peter Smithson are discussed, in addition to the homes that Catalan architect Germán Rodrígues Arias designed for the poet Pablo Neruda. Gonzáles de Canales qualifies these homes as 'domestic self-experimentation [. . .] [in] the peripheries of the existing social order'. They were, so the author claims, 'located outside of normal civic regulations and were generated as a responsive practice'. Put differently, they were a form of activism at home. Also, architects' own homes figure in a wide range of anthologies discussing new trends, innovations, and experiments in houses, often with thematic focus such as ecological and handmade homes (e.g. Olsen's *Handmade Houses*) or experimental houses (e.g. Pople's *Experimental Houses*).

3
Wagner and Schlegel, *Houses Architects Design*, vii.

4
'An Architect's Own House', xliv.

5
Krier, 'Vertus Privées et Vices Publics', 7. Translated from French by the authors.

6
Krier, 'Vertus Privées et Vices Publics', 7. Translated from French by the authors. In *Experiments with Life Itself*, Gonzáles de Canales includes the Solar Pavilion that the Smithsons designed for themselves in Fonthill (Wiltshire, UK) as a notable example of radical domestic architecture designed between 1937 and 1959. He writes: '[F]rom time to time, Alison and Peter Smithson with their children withdrew from the city to an ephemeral-looking pavilion, where they attempted to "establish a territory under their own control". They felt that the new order of their lives would be compatible with the small everyday things: the mutual belonging of the human, the natural, the memories and imagination.' See Gonzáles de Canales, *Experiments with Life*, 144–65, particularly 156.

different approaches that architects adopt when designing dwellings for others as opposed to designing their own homes. The former, he suggested, was far more experimental than the latter. Krier's critique was largely directed at modern architects who were involved in mass housing projects, such as the Smithsons, who in the late 1960s designed Robin Hood Gardens, but who themselves (in Krier's words) chose to live in a 'sympathetic Italianate villa in Chelsea'.[6]

Activism at Home takes Krier's statement as a prompt. It seeks to demonstrate that architects did not and do not only experiment at the expense of others, but that a long tradition exists of architects designing experimental dwellings for themselves. Architects frequently use their own homes to critique not only the status quo within the discipline, but also to challenge prevailing social, political, economic, and cultural conditions. The architect's own home, one could argue, allows for more far-reaching forms of experimentation than would be possible through commissioned work. This book seeks to study the architect's house from this angle. It showcases the homes of architects that have been consciously designed to formulate social, political, economic, and cultural critiques. In doing so, this book seeks to deepen the conversation between different components of activism in architecture including ideology, aesthetics, domesticity, and lived-in experience.

This book has been developed through two symposia that were held in 2017 and 2018; the first at the University of Queensland in Brisbane (Australia) and the second at the University of Manchester in the UK. It also connects to a research methods elective course that Isabelle Doucet taught at the Manchester School of Architecture in the autumn semester of 2017, which bore the title 'Architecture and Resistance: The Architect's Own Home as Locus for Activism'. Within the frame of this Master of Architecture course, students conducted in-depth analyses of architects' own homes as sites of experimentation and resistance, studying also the role of these houses in the further career trajectories of the architects. The course focused on the UK, and included the homes of Patty and Michael Hopkins, Richard Rogers, Roderick Hackney, Jon Broome, Sarah Wigglesworth and Jeremy Till, Neave Brown, and FAT/Sean Griffiths. As part of this course, Isabelle, along with students, also interviewed some of these architects. Fragments of these interviews are interlaced into this introduction to the book.

Tensions

Throughout the various events that shaped *Activism at Home*, particular emphasis was placed on case studies that examined certain tensions that come to the fore in 'activist' or 'experimental' dwellings that architects design for themselves. One of these tensions is the desire for (radical) experimentation versus the pursuit of commissions. This tension is, of course, also present in the practice of architecture in general, but becomes more pronounced in the design of architects' own dwellings – particularly those designed to formulate social, political, economic, or cultural critiques – as they are often considered a calling card for potential clients, and therefore commonly strive to be aesthetically pleasing.

An interesting example is the Blue House, which Sean Griffiths, one of the founders of the London-based architectural practice FAT (which stands for Fashion, Architecture, Taste), designed for himself and his family. Located in east London, the design for the Blue House began in 1997–98, and the building was completed in 2002. Clad in weatherboards that are painted light blue and with a cartoon-like, billboard aesthetic, the house explicitly sought to question and challenge the orthodoxy of good taste **(Fig. 1)**. When interviewed in 2017, Griffiths noted that even though this house, which was extensively published, played an important role in the success of FAT as a practice, the commissions that they received subsequently were not necessarily for private homes: 'I did see [the Blue House] as a calling card but it failed miserably [chuckles] [...] I don't think we did a single residential project [...] apart from social housing [...] That's what the Blue House did, it ensured that no one asked us ever again to do a residential property!'[7]

For different reasons, Jon Broome, an architect who specialises in ecological design and self-build, drew a similar conclusion. Broome, who worked with Walter Segal and the self-builders in Lewisham (London) in the 1980s, built his own Tree House, which uses tree trunks as part of its structural system, also in London, between 1991 and 1994 **(Fig. 2)**. Although the house was an experiment in eco-housing, Broome did not consider it a calling card, simply because the architectural office he had cofounded, Architype, did not explicitly target commissions for 'big houses for rich clients [...] which is what this sort of thing tends to lead to.'[8]

Another tension that exists in the architect's own home is that between the architect as designer versus the architect as client. By collapsing the roles of architect and client, the distinction between designer and user is also effaced: the architect is both the (radical) social engineer and the one who 'lives' the work. This collapse of designer and user can produce tension, which is aptly described by professor of anthropology and geography David Harvey, who begins the chapter 'The Insurgent Architect at Work' in his book *Spaces of Hope* as follows:

> Imagine ourselves as architects, all armed with a wide range of capacities and powers, embedded in a physical and social world full of manifest constraints and limitations. Imagine also that we are striving to change that world. As crafty architects bent on insurgency we have to think strategically and tactically about what to change and where, about how to change what and with what tools. But we also have somehow to continue to live in this world. This is the fundamental dilemma that faces everyone interested in progressive change.[9]

This tension was strongly felt by British architect Roderick (Rod) Hackney, now director at Kansara Hackney Ltd., who in the early 1970s purchased a house in Black Road in Macclesfield, UK, which

7
Interview with Sean Griffiths, 12 December 2017, Manchester, UK, as part of the Research Methods elective course within the MArch program at the Manchester School of Architecture. Interview by Annabel MacLeod, Aimee Williams-King, and Isabelle Doucet.

8
Interview with Jon Broome, 9 January 2018, London, UK, as part of the Research Methods elective course within the MArch program at the Manchester School of Architecture. Interview by Marco Fedrigo, Meera Lad, and Rossarin Ungrangsee, and Isabelle Doucet.

9
Harvey, *Spaces of Hope*, 233.

was slated for demolition. Hackney soon joined the community effort to save the Black Road terrace houses and took a leading role in the renovation not only of his own home, but also those of his neighbours **(Fig. 3)**. Hackney believes that it was crucial that he, as an architect, was part and parcel of this 'activist' community and that he lived and shared their struggle for social empowerment: 'You must be available [twenty-four hours a day] because people work and they want to see the architect in the evenings and on the weekends.'[10] Over time, the Black Road struggle has become a famous example of community architecture in the UK.

In *Spaces of Hope*, Harvey speaks of the 'insurgent architect', an embodied agent who productively takes part in the transformation and (re)construction of everyday life worlds, one of which is the personal sphere. Harvey states: 'The insurgent architect, like everyone else, is an embodied person.'[11] This figure of the insurgent architect, who designs and lives in their own home, thus offers a paragon for architects to make the personal political. In the words of Harvey: 'Through changing our world, we change ourselves.'[12] The insurgent architect can thus address the longstanding tension that has existed in architecture between the designers and the users of architecture.

However, architects often not only subject themselves to their own activist actions, but also their families, or a wider community – as shown in the Black Road example. When architects experiment through their own homes this raises questions about the personal, familial, and communal costs of domestic architecture that seeks to enact broader (social, political, economic, cultural) change through design. When, for example, Patty and Michael Hopkins built their own home in a comfortable historical London suburb in the shape of a glass box sporting a flat roof and industrial look, they not only evoked, aesthetically and materially, a new 'wave' in architecture (also coined 'high tech'), but they also broke with the conventional organisation of the home. The open-plan organisation separating spaces not by walls but by venetian blinds **(Fig. 4)** proved a simple and ingenious solution that would eventually meet some domestic resistance, particularly from the children. As Patty Hopkins reminisced, 'After a bit [the children] said they wanted walls, so you know, fair enough.'[13]

Themes

Through the dozens of examples submitted for the symposia that were held in Brisbane and Manchester, several themes have come to the fore that informed the organisation of this book into six different sections: (1) Paving the Way; (2) Between Theory and Praxis; (3) Domesticity and Public Life; (4) Communal Living and Collective Action; (5) Resisting Socioeconomic Norms and Regulations; and (6) Nature, Naturism, and Lived Resistance.

Some of the sections in this book focus predominantly on ways of resisting (e.g. communal living), others are organised around a particular wrong that is resisted (e.g. socioeconomic inequities),

10
Interview with Rod Hackney, 12 January 2018, Manchester, UK, via telephone, as part of the Research Methods elective course within the MArch program at the Manchester School of Architecture. Interview by Alexander Bradley, Sahibajot Kaur, and Isabelle Doucet.

11
Harvey, *Spaces of Hope*, 234.

12
Harvey, *Spaces of Hope*, 234.

13
Interview with Patty Hopkins, 10 January 2018, London, UK, as part of the Research Methods elective course within the MArch program at the Manchester School of Architecture. Interview by Victoria Adegoke, Hussain Jamalullail, Abigail Patel, Jake Vogtländer, and Isabelle Doucet.

Fig. 1 FAT, Blue House, London, UK. (Photograph by © Adrian Taylor)

Fig. 2 Jon Broome, Tree House, London, UK. (Photograph by Nigel Corrie. © Jon Broome)

Fig. 3 Rod Hackney with residents of Black Road in Macclesfield, UK, 2013. (Photograph by Dominic Harris. © Dominic Harris / RIBA Collections)

Fig. 4 Patty and Michael Hopkins, Hopkins House, London, UK. (Photograph by © Tim Sreet Porter)

while still others highlight the struggles that those who endeavoured to undertake activism at home encountered (e.g. paving the way). A division of chapters into such prescribed themes is, of course, limiting. Many chapters address several of the themes that have been identified. Furthermore, as this is an edited volume, some of the chapters relate more explicitly to the aforementioned fields of tension than others. Even so, all contributions – which are listed only summarily below, but are introduced in greater detail in the introductions at the start of each new section – describe different pathways towards activism at home, and through their analyses highlight the problems and opportunities that architects who have used their own dwelling as a site for resistance have encountered.

Section: 1
Paving the Way

When architects use their own home as a site for experimentation and for testing new ideas, it can become a vehicle for paving the way. Architecture indeed has a long tradition of such houses that paved the way, notably case study houses, which gives the architect's own home that air of progressiveness. But any act of 'paving' is, contrary to what glossy tabletop books about architecture might suggest, always messy and full of struggles. It is important to bring that struggle into the discussion of architects' experiments with their own houses.

The five chapters included in this first section of the book highlight some of the trials and tribulations that architects experienced as they endeavoured to implement their progressive social and political ideas in the designs of their own homes. The cases discussed in this section are the Walter Gropius house in Dessau (1923), Lina Bo Bardi's home in São Paulo (1951), the private residences of Victor Bourgeois, Adrien Blomme, and Paul-Amaury Michel in interwar Brussels, the houses by architecture partners Edwin Hayes (1947) and Campbell Scott (1949) in Brisbane, Australia, and the own homes of Kiyoshi Seike (1954) and Atelier Bow-Wow (2005) in Japan. These cases show the various ways in which the own house can become a vehicle for practical implementation of radical ideas, and also introduce many other factors that are at work in such adventure. Paving the way, these examples demonstrate, does not just challenge the architect to find recognition in their local community of peers and the wider public. Architects have also struggled to find ways to promote radical ideas imported from elsewhere through resituating these ideas in often substantially distinct local social, economic, and political circumstances. This section also demonstrates that paving the way does not always mean a radical break with all things in the past. Patty Hopkins explained how the structural steel and glass choice for their house in London, leading to its radical industrial look, was in fact inspired by earlier work they had done with a timber-framed structure in a holiday home when they were still students: 'We were sort of patching up this house [during our holidays] and we got very interested in timber frames [...] Then Michael went on and worked with Norman Foster for a bit and [...] started on steel frames, so when we came to this [in 1976], it was what we were obviously going to do.'[14]

14 Interview with Patty Hopkins.

15
Interview with Sean Griffiths.

16
Anderson, 'Alice in Wonderland's Hidden Messages'.

Section: 2
Between Theory and Praxis

Another theme that emerged during the various events and initiatives that informed this book is how architects rationalise and prepare their domestic activism through theoretical texts and treatises. In architecture, it is often said that those who can't design, write (or teach), and vice versa. However, numerous architects can be listed who productively use this dialectic between writing and designing; they sharpen their design practice through the act of writing while they simultaneously hone their thinking on architecture by engaging in design and building construction. These architects often use their own home, a place that can be perpetually redesigned, refined, rethought, or simply sold/demolished and rebuilt, as a vehicle to imagine alternative realities and formulate pathways towards positive change. For instance, Sean Griffiths from FAT pointed out how, contrary to the more paced work for clients, the own home allows the architect to experiment over long periods of time, which is 'quite important because it allows you to develop something in an awful lot of depth'.[15]

Architects' own homes that have come about through such a (prolonged) dialectic process between theory and praxis can be likened to Lewis Carroll's classic tale *Alice in Wonderland*.[16] They present alternative lifeworlds that – part built, part theoretical – allow architects to formulate social, cultural, or political critiques and test alternative modes of designing and dwelling.

The second section of the book examines this dialectic through five case studies. The first two chapters focus on the homes of architects who were also critics and educators; Charles W. Moore and Lars Lerup, who each built homes for themselves in North America in the latter half of the twentieth century. Charles W. Moore built eight homes for himself, of which three (built between 1960 and 1980) are discussed in this book; and Lars Lerup built his own home in Berkeley in the 1980s. Both chapters demonstrate how through a dialectic between writing and designing these two men not only questioned prevailing orthodoxies in architecture, but also challenged the commodification of the single family home. Ralph Erskine's home in Sweden, known as The Box, is the subject of the third chapter. Constructed in 1941–42, this modest building became one of the *Architectural Review's* posterchildren for what they called New Empiricism. The final two chapters in this section focus on the homes of Günther Domenig in Austria (realised between 1986 and 2008) and Bruno Taut in Turkey (built in 1938). More than an expression of an intensive exchange between theory and praxis, these two homes were shaped by personal experiences – trials and tribulations – that caused shifts to take place in the architect's thinking on architecture, and novel architectural idioms to emerge.

Section: 3
Domesticity and Public Life

The five architects' homes discussed in the third section of *Activism at Home* highlight the tensions that can occur between domesticity and public life when architects use their own dwellings to promote their practice and persona. Architects may benefit from the publicity and promotion surrounding their own homes, and the publication of architects' houses in professional journals and popular press can lead to future commissions. At the same time, these 'flagship' creations are, before anything else, also homes for architects and (often) also their families. In connection to the Blue House, for example, Sean Griffiths observed that while the project was hailed as a showcase of postmodernism, the many lived-in aspects of the house should also be highlighted: 'Actually all of these little battles and compromises and accommodations [informed by living requirements and constraints] are all going on within [the design of the architect house] and actually directly affect the architecture.'[17] The architect's house thus contains intrinsic tensions between the requirements of living well and the architect's striving for recognition. As Griffiths puts it, the architect may well be unable to escape considerations such as 'this house is my career' and 'how is this going to look when they take the picture?'[18] This tension between personal need and public promotion plays in most, if not all, architects' own houses, and the projects in this section help us to understand different ways in which this struggle can manifest itself. Case studies in this section include Arthur Erickson's 'garage home' in Vancouver (1957–2009), Alvin Boyarsky's London house (1964–today), Constantin Doxiadis' 1950s apartment overlooking the Acropolis in Greece, Flora Ruchat-Roncati's semi-communal, live-work experiment in Ticino, Switzerland (started in 1967), and Eileen Gray's E-1027 house in the south of France (1929).[19] This attentiveness to how specific circumstances determine how architects choose to self-identify seems to be a key issue in architects' own homes, where architects are forced to decide how much, or how little, of their private lives, including aspects of gender, class, and sexual orientation, can be permitted to enter the public domain.

Section: 4
Communal Living and Collective Action

Another theme that emerged was that of architects designing their own homes as part of larger experiments in communal living and collective action. Different acts of resistance can underpin such initiatives, including the desire to subvert societal constructs and cultural conventions, such as the concept of the nuclear family. This concept became commonplace in Europe and North America following the end of the Second World War, when it was increasingly upheld as an ideal to which to aspire. When designing their home as part of a larger collective, architects can question the values that underpin such societal constructs as well as the gender roles that they represent and perpetuate.

17 Interview with Sean Griffiths.

18 Interview with Sean Griffiths.

19 These two very different houses by women architects also offer an important warning against any categorisation of houses 'by women', and instead call for attention to be paid to the 'individual stories from women in architecture'. Burns, 'The Woman/Architect Distinction', 52.

20 Interview with Rod Hackney.

Architects have also used experiments in communal living and collective action as a way of questioning the economic and political systems that seek to perpetuate the supremacy of the single-family home, and to increase the value of land and real estate. Accordingly, such experiments often reject the privatisation of land and even of dwellings and question the relationships that exist not only between the individual and the collective, but also between the collective and the political and economic systems that govern society. A resulting desire for greater autarky – for freedom from both economic and political systems – has, in turn, often informed the testing of more sustainable modes of building and dwelling as part of these experiments in communal living and collective action.

Nevertheless, such experiments are not without their drawbacks. For instance, the blurring of the boundaries between private and collective life can place a high tax on those who participate in such actions, as Rod Hackney, the architect who was involved in the Black Road preservation project, attests to. After having been part of the community effort to save and refurbish these homes, Hackney and his wife moved away from the area, to a private farmhouse in the countryside. In a recent interview, Hackney observed, with some nostalgia: 'I was fed up with people ringing the doorbell at three a.m. in the morning, when the pubs had closed. Residents wanted to speak to the architect.'[20]

This fourth section of the book comprises five chapters that all show examples of architects experimenting with modes of communal living and collective action in the design of their own living environments. While the first two chapters examine the radical architect-led countercultural communes that emerged in 1970s Australia and Chile – Bodhi Farm and the Ciudad Abierta, respectively – the following two contributions focus on more mainstream, though no less subversive, architect-led experiments in communal living: first, the home of Suzana and Dimitris Antonakakis in 1970s Athens; and second, the R50 project by ifau and Heide & von Beckerath in early 2000s Berlin. The fifth and final chapter in the section focusses on the Taiwanese architect Hsieh Ying-Chun, who through his work with his practice Atelier-3 demonstrates how collective action and architectural practice and profiling can engage in a mutually beneficial relationship.

Section: 5
Resisting Socioeconomic Norms and Regulations

Houses designed and inhabited by architects can explicitly resist conventional social norms regarding what constitutes a good dwelling and a proper way of living, norms that are often closely intertwined with the ideas and ideals of the ruling social, economic, or cultural classes, for example, bourgeois society or suburban lifestyles. In response to such norms, architects, who have historically often but not always been themselves part of bourgeois society, have nevertheless used their own homes as a way to resist such ideals. In a sense architects were therefore resisting from within. They have done so through experiments with new construction and building manufacturing methods striving for greater affordability, through challenging restrictive planning regulations, and through radically rethinking the social and spatial programming of their homes in order to welcome and also try unconventional ways of living. Think, for instance, of the aforementioned example of Patty and Michael Hopkins, who chose to remove the interior walls from their home, to the (eventual) disquiet of their children.[21]

21 Interview with Patty Hopkins.

22 Interview with Jon Broome.

The houses discussed in this section originate from distinct geographical, societal, and political settings and from different time periods. Cases in this section include the C.E.C.A. House designed by Willy Van Der Meeren and Léon Palm in Belgium in the mid 1950s; the Pliable Praxis House and other experiments by Houston-based architectural practice Interloop (2000s); Paulo Mendes da Rocha's Casa Butantã in São Paulo, Brazil (1964–66); and Kirsty Volz's own, current house in Brisbane, Australia. Together, these projects give us a sense of how architects challenged social norms in their own homes and how resistance-from-within occurred. Importantly, they also show us the varying degrees to which architects (had to) embrace the dominant systems they were intending to subvert in order to develop effective and convincing alternatives. We learn that resistance from within the profession requires a complex and patient understanding not just of architectural design, but also of the construction, fabrication, legal, and economic mechanisms that underpin the production of the built environment.

Section: 6
Nature, Naturism, and Lived Resistance

A final theme that is dealt with in this book is the relationship between architects' own homes and nature, naturism, and lived resistance. When designing their own dwelling, architects often pay close attention to the way in which it relates to nature and the environment more broadly. Jon Broome, for instance, tested his ecological ideas on his own house, the Tree House: 'I don't know how possible I thought it was having tree trunks or anything else really, but it worked.'[22] The detrimental effects of building construction on our environment are of course well known. Not only does the production of construction materials and building components require vast amounts of minerals and other types of natural resources, but urban sprawl and haphazard planning also place a high tax on natural open space. For this reason, many architects eschew suburban housing estates. Some (those who subscribe to the mantra of urban densification) retreat within the confines of established urban centres; others refuse to build a home altogether, opting instead to reuse and inhabit found spaces; while still others seek out remote natural sites to construct their homes in close connection with nature. The environmental resistance of this latter group is based on the belief that it is possible to design and live in harmony with nature – both ecologically and phenomenologically.

Apart from challenging commonplace building practices that are detrimental to the environment, the quest to live in harmony with nature – the search for a closer connection between body, spirit, and nature – is sometimes also informed by a desire to challenge accepted norms of how bodies behave in, use, or relate to the space. The own home (the private sphere) is an ideal stage for such lived forms of resistance given that it is less governed by societal norms of decency and propriety. Such embodied experiments often also seek to resist consumerist dwelling practices.

This final section discusses these topics through five chapters. The first three chapters focus on three alternative holiday homes that were constructed (in close connection with nature) during the 1960s: by Belgian architect Jul De Roover in the south of France, by Bruno Mathsson in Frösakull in southern Sweden, and by Bernard Rudofsky in Frigiliana near Malaga in Spain. The fourth chapter discusses the home that Weizhong Ren, a Chinese self-taught architect, designed and built for himself with natural materials in the early 2000s; and the final chapter, by and about Australian architect Robert Riddel, narrates the story of his secret life in a second-hand, milk-delivery van in 1970s London.

Takeaways

With its rich selection of examples of resistant architecture, *Activism at Home* can be positioned within the growing scholarship on the radical and activist pedigrees of architecture. We think, for example, of the recent focus in architectural history on the countercultural moment and radical movements of the 1960s and 1970s, and the wealth of conceptual and practice-based studies on the critical, social, and political agency of architectural and urban design. Having developed this project for over four years, first in our capacity as conference organisers, and subsequently as editors of this volume, we hope that *Activism at Home* will contribute to this growing body of works through its focus on one particular resistant type: the architect's own home. We deem the architect's own home particularly suited to the study of resistance in architecture, not only because it is situated at the crossroads of ideology and heightened aesthetic performance, but also because a focus on the architect's own home – works that architects not only design, but also inhabit – offers a 'lived-in' or 'embodied' history of resistance.

With this compendium we explore the capacity of singular projects to question the social, political, economic, and cultural status quo and bring a broad historical and geographical scope. *Activism at Home* offers a collection of in-depth case studies taken from around the globe that shed light on different manifestations of resistance during key periods in architecture: from the Modern Movement, over the post-war welfare state and countercultural moment of the 1960s and 1970s, up to the more contemporary climate of austerity. The collection brings refreshing appraisals of canonical buildings that are already firmly located within the discipline's intellectual and geographical boundaries, and also sheds light on lesser-known projects that have thus far dwelled in the canon's peripheries.

We hope that the historical study of insurgent, embodied practices offered in this book will appeal to historians, theorists, and designers of the built environment alike. We feel that such critical appraisals of alternative living solutions are needed not just from a historical point of view, but also in response to ongoing challenges that the architectural profession faces, including rising real estate prices, mounting economic and social inequalities, and intensified environmental and cultural pressures. We thus see the scholarship presented and compiled in this book as a form of activism in its own right[23] and hope that *Activism at Home* will function as a manifesto: an appeal to architects to use the tools of the discipline and the profession to their full (insurgent) potential, and a plea to scholars and critics to continue to bring into focus architecture's activist practices – at home, or elsewhere.

23
Andrea Jeanne Merret aptly speaks of 'scholarship as activism' in connection to the historiography of women in architecture. Merret, 'Scholarship as Activism', 79–88.

Bibliography

Anderson, Hephzibah. 'Alice in Wonderland's Hidden Messages'. *BBC Culture*, 31 May 2016, https://www.bbc.com/culture/article/201 60527-alice-in-wonderlands-hidden-messages.

'An Architect's Own House: New House, Crockham Hill, Kent, Designed by H.G.C. Spencely'. *Country Life*, 7 November 1936, xliv.

Burns, Karen. 'The Woman/Architect Distinction'. In *Women, Practice, Architecture: 'Resigned Accommodation' and 'Usurpatory Practice'*, edited by Naomi Stead. Abingdon and New York: Routledge, 2014, 45–55.

Crafti, Stephen. *Architects' Houses: Twenty Australian Homes*. Crows Nest and London: Murdoch Books, an imprint of Allen & Unwin, 2015.

Gonzáles de Canales, Francisco. *Experiments with Life Itself: Radical Domestic Architectures between 1937 and 1959*. Barcelona: Actar, 2012.

Harvey, David. *Spaces of Hope*. Edinburgh: Edinburgh University Press, 2000.

Krier, Léon. 'Vertus Privées et Vices Publics'. *Bulletin des Archives d'Architecture Moderne* 18 (1980): 7–11.

Merret, Andrea Jeanne. 'Scholarship as Activism: Doris Cole's and Susana Torre's Pioneering Feminism in Architectural History', *Field Journal* 7, no. 1 (2017): 79–88.

Newton, Miranda H. *Architects' London Houses: The Homes of Thirty Architects since the 1930s*. Oxford: Butterworth Architecture, an imprint of Butterworth-Heinemann Ltd., 1992.

Olsen, Richard, with Kodiak Greenwood (photographer), and Lucy Goodhart (photographer). *Handmade Houses: A Century of Earth-Friendly Home Design*. New York and London: Rizzoli, 2012.

Patch, Bethany, ed. *Architects' Homes*. Mulgrave, Victoria: Images Publishing, 2017.

Pople, Nicolas. *Experimental Houses*. London: Laurence King Publishing, 2003, originally published in 2000.

Postiglione, Gennaro, ed. *One Hundred Houses for One Hundred European Architects of the Twentieth Century*. Cologne: Taschen, 2004.

Wagner, Walter F., and Karin Schlegel, eds. *Houses Architects Design for Themselves*. New York: McGraw-Hill, 1974.

Webb, Michael. *Architects House Themselves*. Washington DC: The Preservation Press, 1994.

Webb, Michael. *Architects' Houses*. Hudson: Princeton Architectural Press, 2018.

Zabalbeascoa, Anatxu. *The House of the Architect*. Barcelona: Editorial Gustavo Gili, 1995.

Paving the Way

This section taps into architecture's long history of houses that 'paved the way', that innovated and pushed the boundaries of the profession and discipline. Well-known progressive houses that play an instrumental role in advancing architects' new ideas do not, however, escape their share of contradictions between architects' radical intentions and inconsistencies that often occur when at the forefront of something new. The houses in this section also say something about the messy and conflicted ways in which new ideas travel globally. Through their own homes, architects reveal their struggle to both promote imported ideas that are recognised by a wider international community of peers and implement these ideas in specific local circumstances. By the same token, they also show that their own homes have the capacity to resist newly imported ideas that affect societal norms related to family life and domesticity.

In her chapter 'Those Who Live in Glass Houses Shouldn't Throw Stones', Isabel Rousset demonstrates how the house Walter Gropius built for himself in Dessau in 1923 as a promotional vehicle for a modern way of living that departs from bourgeois domestic norms did not entirely escape contradictions regarding the house's democratic claims on behalf of the Neue Sachlichkeit. Rousset demonstrates how the architect's own house, when presented as a showcase for design and even an entire lifestyle, became a target for criticism and ridicule by not only conservative commentators, as is often the case, but also by more open-minded architects, social critics, and the wider popular press. Rousset shows how the caricaturing of the Gropius House undermined its efforts to promote the aesthetic promises of mass prefabrication, and in doing so relocated it to the class pretensions it had intended to escape.

Also, when progressive ideas embark on transnational journeys, a newfound setting can offer a fertile ground for experimentation. Nevertheless, this landing in new social, economic, and cultural environments can also be bumpy. This is revealed in the chapter 'The House of a Modern Woman in São Paolo' by Silvana Rubino, which focusses on Lina Bo Bardi's efforts to incorporate modern ideas regarding housework efficiency developed in Germany, such as the Frankfurt Kitchen, into Brazilian society. Bo Bardi's iconic residence in São Paulo, completed in 1951, showcases an unmistakable asymmetry between, on the one hand, a woman architect carefully crafting a 'model' modern life for herself, which she hoped would inspire others, and the household's bourgeois reliance on domestic servants on the other.

That paving-the-way sometimes requires more than the lone activism offered by an architect's own house, relying instead on a broader, collective effort, becomes apparent in the case of the advancement, and acceptance, of the Modern Movement in Brussels, as discussed in the chapter 'Shaping Modernism in Brussels' by Linsy Raaffels, Inge Bertels, Stephanie Van de Voorde, and Barbara Van der Wee. In this chapter, the authors show how a significant number of architects' houses constructed in the interwar period in Brussels were inspired by the Modern Movement, and how this collective effort proved instrumental in creating a platform for modernism and the gradual acceptance of modern architecture among the general public. Through three prominent examples of such houses – namely, the private residences of Victor Bourgeois, Adrien Blomme, and Paul-Amaury Michel – paving the way here takes the shape of a gradual yet broad and collective effort.

By contrast, as Andrew Wilson shows in his chapter 'After War', which focusses on two architects' homes that were built in the late 1940s in St Lucia, a suburb of Brisbane, Australia, very different statements can emerge even within the same architectural partnership. The two houses realised by architectural partners Edwin Hayes and Campbell Scott demonstrated a shared interest in modern architecture which was also instrumental in the promotion of their joint architectural firm. However, in his chapter, Wilson demonstrates how these two houses also exposed significant differences in these architects' respective views on the agency of architecture. While Hayes's house offered a confident promotion of post-war modernity and was widely noted and published, the Scott residence was markedly more modest, hidden from view, scarcely published, and focussed more on affordability than on the advancement of architectural statements.

Paving the way takes on a different meaning in Cathelijne Nuijsink's chapter 'A House for Everyone', which describes how in Japan the detached family house has been a subject of debate and innovation ever since the Second World War. In this chapter we learn that architects were instrumental not just in pushing for new designs but also in critically examining newly imposed typologies and ideologies such as the two-bedroom-with-dining-kitchen floorplan (2DK). Through two architects' houses built fifty years apart, by Kiyoshi Seike (1954) and Atelier Bow-Wow (2005), Nuijsink highlights the capacity of the architect's house to resist the effects of social reforms that affected traditional Japanese arrangements of domesticity as well as the mainstreaming of such models in housing production. The two houses show how architects and their homes were instrumental in the long emancipation process from a newly imposed, Western family ideology based on privacy and a focus on the individual.

Those Who Live in Glass Houses Shouldn't Throw Stones

Isabel Rousset

The client's fondness for luxury and ostentation was a common source of complaint amongst modern architects of the early twentieth century, especially when such inclinations hindered these architects' higher aesthetic and/or lifestyle ideals. Hermann Muthesius and Adolf Loos spent their careers writing tirades against the decadence that characterised the domestic lifestyles of the bourgeois elite. When Bauhaus director Walter Gropius moved his design school from Weimar to Dessau in 1925, the house he built for himself served as a manifesto for a new, modern way of living that broke with the outmoded bourgeois dwelling habits of the past. However, Gropius's own house failed to materialise as a site of social activism as its own apparent ostentation was noted by both architectural peers and by the popular press.

Gropius's own brand of activism, exercised through his writings and Bauhaus pedagogy, was an ethical one. It was one posed against the traditional status of architects as the producers of singular and exclusive architectural objects and styles. In the Bauhaus manifesto of 1919, Gropius urged architects to shed their demiurge-like professional status and to work more like anonymous craftsmen.[1] In his book *The New Architecture and the Bauhaus*, Gropius envisioned the architect not as an artist, but as a researcher and 'a co-ordinator – whose business is to unify the various formal, technical, social, and economic problems that arise in connection with building'.[2] With this new type of architect came a new type of inhabitant. Having long railed against the 'drab, hollow, and meaningless fakeries in which we live', Gropius aimed to cast the inhabitant of the modern functional dwelling not as a connoisseur of Bauhaus style, modern style, or functionalist style, but as a citizen of a newly democratised society, liberated from the constraints of bourgeois taste.[3]

The reconfigured role of the dwelling imagined by Gropius signalled a preparation for what Walter Benjamin predicted as the coming of a new and liberating age of cultural poverty, which would arise following the liquidation of the bourgeois domestic interior that had taken place in the work of the Jugendstil artists.[4] In his own house, Gropius cast himself as this new kind of inhabitant who, freed from the inhibitions associated with occupying an artistic object, would define a new pattern of living liberated from outmoded dwelling habits and attitudes. Gropius built his own house as an experiment in transforming German society at the level of everyday practice. His contemporaries nonetheless perceived the building as a failure. The house came to represent not a new and liberating cultural poverty, but rather, the shallowness and decadence of the Neue Sachlichkeit (New Objectivity), a visual style that characterised bourgeois taste during the interwar period in Germany.

1 See Gropius, 'Programme of the Staatliches Bauhaus'.

2 Gropius, *The New Architecture*, 98.

3 Quoted in Fitch, *Walter Gropius*, 15.

4 See Benjamin, *The Arcades Project*. See also Benjamin, 'Experience and Poverty'.

The Gropius House

Gropius conceptualised his house, along with the three double houses for the other Bauhaus masters, as a series of intersecting blocks, in the formal vocabulary of the *Baukasten* (construction kit) diagram from 1921 produced by Gropius, Georg Muche, and Fréd Forbát **(Fig. 1)**. The diagram presented a building scheme for mass-produced housing units composed of a kit of six different building blocks of varying sizes that could be adjusted to accommodate different numbers of inhabitants. Like Le Corbusier's Dom-ino model, this scheme was conceived as a system of construction containing the raw material for the production of standardised housing types.

The building blocks that materialised on a physical site that sought to accommodate only Gropius plus the six other Bauhaus masters, however, resembled luxury villas more than they did experiments in mass-housing manufacture. The block of four houses was situated half a kilometre from the newly built Bauhaus building in Dessau. Paul Klee and Wassily Kandinsky occupied the first double house; Oskar Schlemmer and Georg Muche, the second; and Lyonel Feininger and László Moholy-Nagy, the third. The masters' houses conformed to bourgeois living standards; these double houses were composed of two stories, each with a living room, kitchen, and accommodation for service staff on the ground floor, and three bedrooms, studio space, and a spacious balcony on the second floor.

The fourth house was occupied entirely by Gropius and his wife Ise Gropius. From a large glazed terrace on the north side, one entered a large living and dining space. The ground floor had two bedrooms, a bathroom, and kitchen. Rather than studio space, the L-shaped upper floor contained two storage rooms, a laundry, the maid's room, a large guesthouse, and a roof terrace that almost matched the second-floor interior space in square footage. This house was the only one to have a garage (Gropius hired his own chauffeur).[5]

The photographs of the house, taken by Moholy-Nagy's wife Lucia Moholy, formed an important part of documenting the Bauhaus legacy. Circulated heavily within the school's publications, Moholy's sharply focussed depictions of cantilevering white blocks and expanses of glass behind the mature pines became iconic as examples of a new tradition in objective photography **(Fig. 2)**. In the interior, Moholy's depictions of the heavy doorframes of exposed steel and built-in furniture gave the impression of functionality and efficiency. The photographs portrayed the house as a display home for design objects by the masters, which were produced in the Bauhaus workshop on the basis of commissions from an elite clientele.[6] The living room contained Marcel Breuer's tubular steel chairs and tables, as well as Marianne Brandt's signature ashtray, tea set, and lighting fixtures **(Fig. 3)**. In Moholy's photographs, the shiny and reflective surfaces of the exclusive Bauhaus objects became lit up in the staged and stylised context of the Gropius family's living room, blending in seamlessly with the more functional aspects such as the exposed ventilators and radiators. Some of

5
Schuldenfrei, 'The Irreproducibility of the Bauhaus Object', 47.

6
See Schuldenfrei, 'The Irreproducibility of the Bauhaus Object'.

7
Gropius, *Bauhausbauten Dessau*, 92.

8
Gropius, *Bauhausbauten Dessau*, 101.

9
Gropius, *Bauhausbauten Dessau*, 112.

10
Gropius, *Bauhausbauten Dessau*, 99–131.

11
Teige, *The Minimum Dwelling*, 166.

the more conspicuously luxurious features included the elaborately styled guesthouse, the black reflective glaze of the concrete supports on the terrace, and the marble bathroom sinks.

Moholy's photographs of the house were reproduced in a Bauhaus pamphlet on the masters' houses. Alongside these images, Gropius discussed his house as a machine that enables a choreography of dwelling, facilitating efficient movement in the practice of leisure, hygiene, and domestic work. He remarked thus: 'Building is the shaping of life processes. The organism of a house results from the sequences of events that are played out within it. The residential house functions in the service of dwelling, sleeping, bathing, cooking, eating'.[7] This choreography of dwelling, Gropius explained, articulated a new ethical programme:

> The frictionless, sensible functioning of daily life is not a final goal but is only a prerequisite to achieving maximum personal freedom and independence. The standardization of practical life-processes here signifies no new enslavement and mechanization of the individual, but frees life from unnecessary burdens, which allows it to become richer and more uninhibited.[8]

Feeling it necessary to justify the more luxurious elements of his house, Gropius remarked alongside Moholy's photographs: '[W]hat today appears luxurious, tomorrow becomes the norm!'[9]

The rationalisation of the household had long been promoted in Germany through the work of architect Bruno Taut, who aimed to forge new links between the expertise of architects and the work of housewives. A short film produced in 1925 on the Gropius House, entitled *How We Can Live Efficiently and Healthily*, visually captured the precise choreography of dwelling efficiently. The film, however, showed the majority of these movements being conducted by Gropius's housemaid. Film stills were reproduced in the Bauhaus journal which displayed the maid operating the time-saving equipment in the kitchen and laundry. Gropius's wife was shown demonstrating the utility of the built-in furniture and storage systems before relaxing on the roof terrace.[10]

Among avant-garde architectural circles, Gropius's house was met with criticism. In his 1932 book *The Minimum Dwelling*, the Czech Marxist critic Karel Teige argued that, for all its technological capability, Gropius's house served as nothing more than a palace for new financial aristocracy:

> Ornaments have disappeared completely, and simple, geometric forms have triumphed. Unchanged, however, are all the fundamental characteristics of a bourgeois dwelling: the house remains a special, isolated object, posing as a work of art [...] in place of the luxurious ornaments of expensive drapery, vases, and so on, we experience the luxury of superfluous space, with its huge terraces, great halls, and sumptuous boudoirs, where comfort is now treated as a new species of supreme ornament.[11]

Fig. 1 Walter Gropius, Georg Muche, and Fréd Forbát, *Bauhaus Housing Development 'Am Horn,' Weimar, 1920–1922*, drawing. (Bauhaus-Archiv Berlin. © Walter Gropius / VG Bild-Kunst. Copyright Agency, 2020)

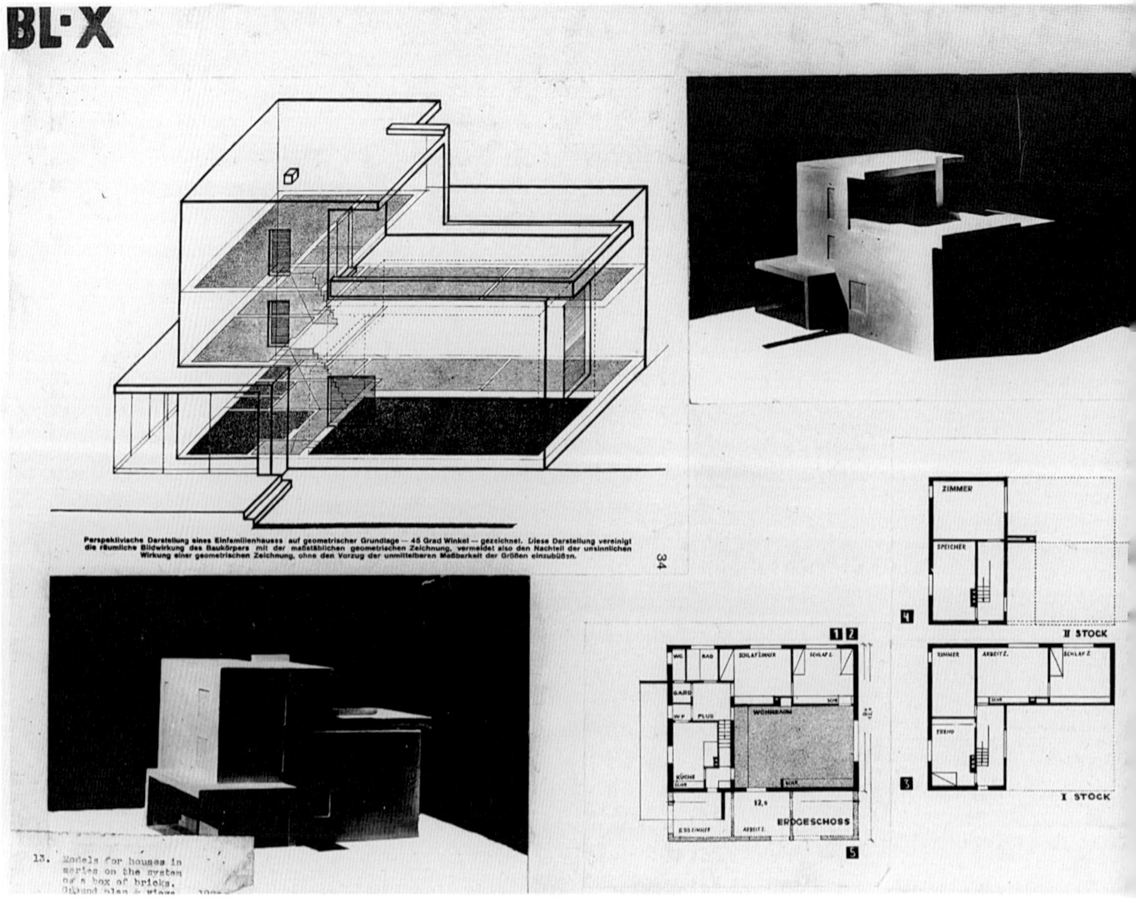

Fig. 2 Lucia Moholy, *The Gropius House by Walter Gropius (architect)*, gelatin silver print, 1925–26. (Bauhaus-Archiv Berlin. © Lucia Moholy / VG Bild-Kunst. Copyright Agency, 2020)

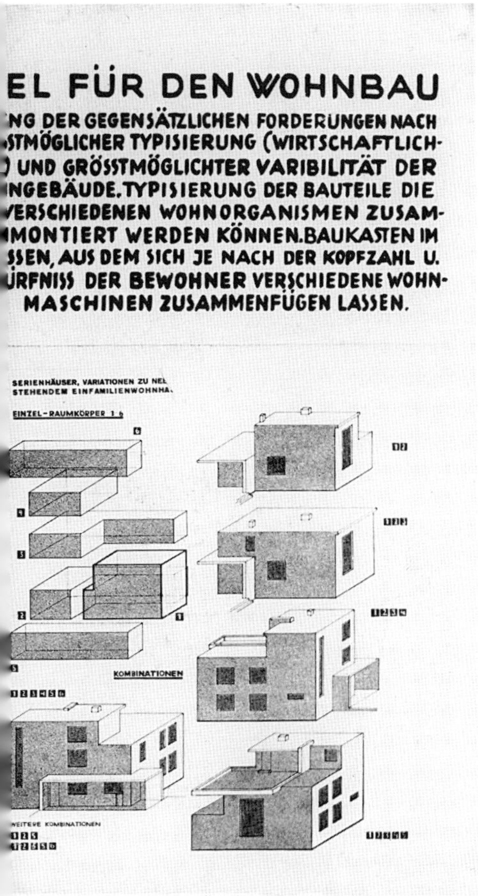

Fig. 3 Lucia Moholy, *The Gropius House. Ise and Walter Gropius in the Living Room*, gelatin silver print, 1925–26. (Bauhaus-Archiv Berlin. © Lucia Moholy / VG Bild-Kunst. Copyright Agency, 2020)

It was largely within the popular press, however, that the house received the greatest amount of critical attention. The Bauhaus had long been held in suspicion in the popular press for its left-leaning politics, especially after Gropius had finished construction of a workers housing estate in Törten-Dessau shortly after finishing the masters' houses. Like the Weissenhof Estate in Stuttgart (which was mockingly described as an 'Arab village'), the white walls and flat roofs of the Törten-Dessau estate likewise provoked fears over the loss of a German 'Heimat' style. Its foreignness was read by the conservative public as a sign of cosmopolitanism, cultural bolshevism, Jewishness, and the proletarianisation of workers.[12]

In the midst of the controversy over the housing estate, a newspaper article noted the hypocrisy of Gropius's house, describing it as a 'technical marvel' compared to the relative poverty of the nearby housing estate. Titled 'The Problematic Glass House' (perhaps in reference to a well-known proverb, 'those who live in glass houses shouldn't throw stones'), the article claimed that Gropius's house embodied all the class pretensions and fakeries that he had once criticised in the so-called style-architecture. The article noted that while the Bauhaus masters could decorate their houses according to their personal style, it was unfair to push such a style onto workers who would not have the time to personalise their homes. The author noted that, 'with its Russian furniture Kandinsky has decorated his house entirely differently from Gropius, whose house is a technical marvel. But is the spiritual system of building and the teaching system that it embodies all that suitable for the building of estates?'[13]

For conservative commentators and progressive social critics alike, the Gropius House thus remained a contradiction. For conservative critics, the house represented a loss of national tradition. For progressive critics, the house symbolised bourgeois decadence.

Gropius and the Neue Sachlichkeit

Teige's criticisms, in particular, fitted comfortably in a general atmosphere of class critique regarding the consumer culture of the new white-collar masses (of the kind who aspired to own Bauhaus kettles). This critique crystalised in the works of the Frankfurt School, particularly through Siegfried Kracauer's 1927 essay, *Ornament der Masse*. Criticisms over the conformity of avant-garde art to the logic of mass efficiency in the aftermath of the world's first mechanised war closely resembled pre-war criticisms over the tyranny of the artistic *Gesamtkunstwerk*. The bourgeois client's enslavement to the higher ideals of the architect was famously mocked in Adolf Loos's 1900 short story of the 'poor little rich man', who, in hiring a Secessionist architect to design his home, was prevented from decorating it with anything not designed by the architect himself (and was even prevented from wearing his own slippers, perhaps in mockery of Henry van de Velde and Richard Riemerschmidt, who were known to impose sartorial restrictions on their wives).[14] For Loos, the cladding of the domestic interior according to one's own idiosyncrasies ought to

12
See Miller Lane, *Architecture and Politics in Germany*.

13
Natonek, 'Das problematische Glashaus', 1.

14
Loos, 'Poor Little Rich Man'.

15
Scheerbart, *The Gray Cloth*.

16
Scheerbart, *The Gray Cloth*, 107.

17
Ward, *Weimar Surfaces*, 9.

18
Rousset, 'Satirical Representations'.

serve as respite from the constraints that public society imposes on the sensibilities of the individual in the name of cultural progress.

Architectural critic Paul Scheerbart's 1914 satirical novella *Das Graue Tuch* covered similar themes in telling the futuristic story of a world-famous 'coloured-glass architect', who travels around in a luxurious airship with his wife to various projects commissioned from the world's most elite clientele. So as to not compete with her husband's careful formal experimentation in colour, displayed on the dematerialised surfaces of semitransparent glass, she is forced, by marriage contract, to wear only grey clothing, ten per cent of which was trimmed in white. The arrogant contractual obligation sparks a media storm. The fictional architect's own house in Sicily, however, is sensuously clad, with walls covered with thick monochromatic cloth, dark linoleum, embroidered silk, fur, and colourful hummingbird feathers.[15] 'It is remarkable', notes one of the novel's characters, 'that our architect has only sealed walls in his own house. It is very healthy when one sits completely enclosed by walls and is not aware of the outside world through the exceedingly close glass windows'.[16] Scheerbart's description of the decadent lifestyles of a travelling bourgeoisie, in which the sartorial publicity stunt plays out as a scandal to a receptive mass audience (from which the four walls of their Sicilian home serves as a retreat) resembles little in its (rather ambivalent) ethical programme to the concessions that Loos believed ought to be given to the domestic interior for the common benefit of society. Neither does it especially anticipate the new era of cultural poverty that Benjamin would describe. Instead, it anticipates a media-saturated world, identified by the likes of Kracauer and Theodor W. Adorno, where architecture exists purely within the flows of mass entertainment.

It was within this world that the Gropius House largely circulated as a site of contention. For the remainder of the 1920s, it was frequently represented within satirical media seeking to expose the inner decadence of lifestyles behind the ostensible sobriety of Weimar mass culture. Soon after the construction of the masters' houses, the Bauhaus Style was already becoming synonymous with the popular visual culture of the Neue Sachlichkeit, a term describing a kind of visual pragmatism suitable for the sobering psychological effects of the First World War. As Janet Ward states, the movement replaced expressionism's rough, religious warmth with a smooth, logical coolness.[17]

The *sachlich* (the sober, the objective) described not just a visual quality but also a range of social codes that represented common lifestyles, tastes, and dispositions (or, what sociologist Pierre Bourdieu described as a common habitus). A person described as *sachlich* not only conformed to dress and grooming codes, such as bobbed hair for *sachlich* women, but also lived in an apartment with Bauhaus furniture.[18] The assimilation of the Bauhaus object into a fashionable visual vocabulary that defined the habitus of a left-wing elite was observed by the editor of the Bauhaus magazine, Ernst Kállai, who lamented: 'The snob would like something new. Very well. There are enough architects making the Bauhaus style into a new decorative attraction'.[19]

In a 1928 edition of the popular satirical magazine *Simplicissimus*, the Gropius House was ridiculed in a satirical piece entitled 'Neue Sachlichkeit'. The short piece told the story of a journalist who visits the house of the fictional architect Benno Schwartz, the 'pioneer of the modern apartment', whose own house is 'a symphony of steel, glass, light, functionality, and hygiene that one usually finds in the pictures in the illustrated magazines'.[20] The journalist and the architects sit down and converse on elastic steel chairs, before Benno Schwartz becomes restless and excuses himself. After an hour, the journalist goes in search of the architect and encounters the following scene:

> There was another room. A proper room from yesteryear: windows with curtains and drapery, a red plush sofa with curved armrests, a vertiko which housed an unbelievable amount of knickknacks, an armchair, an embroidered doily, cushions, carpets, hide rugs, goldfish bowl – in short, a perfectly fine room. And in the chair – Benno Schwartz.
>
> 'Oh', I said, 'I see that the master gets inspiration from constructing a museum of counterexample, so that there will be contrast.'
>
> 'Blah!', said Benno, 'this is my living room. Everyone has to have a room in their house where they can feel comfortable'.[21]

While the extensive recording of Gropius's house through film and photography initially served to illustrate how old dwelling habits could be liberated through the scientific reorganisation of the dwelling, the house soon became a tool for detractors to expose precisely a new kind of social enslavement behind the cool facade of the Neue Sachlichkeit. In 1928, a cartoon by satirist Thomas Theodor Heine (who had been a proponent of Jugendstil) again evoked Gropius's house in order to ridicule the hypocrisy of the Neue Sachlichkeit **(Fig. 4)**. It featured a husband and wife standing outside their new house (which strongly resembled Gropius's own house) both with stiff postures and aloof expressions which embodied typically *sachlich* demeanours. The caption read: 'My husband employed the first architect of modern nests to design a concrete nest for our songbirds, but the stupid animals prefer to hatch in their self-built kitsch.'[22]

A cartoon from 1928, titled 'Sachlichkeit!', once again mocked Gropius, depicting a Dessau architect in his home who, 'consistent with the struggle against ornament', had 'cut off his ears and the ears of his family', as the caption read **(Fig. 5)**.[23] Far from promising individual liberation, the domestic setting depicted in the cartoon resembles a cold drafting room and suggests a new enslavement of the family under the tyranny of the architect's stylistic doctrine. The cool and detached expressions that characterise the Neue Sachlichkeit sensibility are replaced, in this cartoon, with traumatised faces, as the family's ears are carried off on a plate by the maid.

19 Kállai, 'Ten Years of Bauhaus', 162.

20 H.S., 'Neue Sachlichkeit', 102.

21 H.S., 'Neue Sachlichkeit', 102.

22 Heine, 'Kleine Bilder', 103.

23 Heine, 'Sachlichkeit!', 303.

Fig. 4 Thomas Theodor Heine, 'Kleine Bilder', *Simplicissimus*, 21 May 1928: 103.

Fig. 5 Thomas Theodor Heine, 'Sachlichkeit!', *Simplicissimus*, 10 September 1928: 303.

Variations of this theme continued in the cartoons of satirist Marcel Frischmann. In a 1929 cartoon entitled 'The Architect', Frischmann reproduced Gropius's iconic cantilevering white cubes as the setting for a conversation between an architect and his client. The caption read; 'Just don't plant anything around the house, Mr Meyer – nature lags behind, it has not yet grasped my style.' Frischmann's 1931 cartoon, entitled 'Sense of Style', also featured a house that reproduced Lucia Moholy's iconic photographs of the masters' houses behind the mature pines. The architect, in a bowtie and spotted jacket similar to the apparel often sported by Gropius, stands with his client, a woman with typically *sachlich* dress and demeanour. The caption read, 'Say, Mr Architect, where should my husband sleep?' to which the architect replied: 'If the shadow distribution of the bed does not blend organically within the room – in a hammock beside the window'.

Conclusion

After the rise of Nazism in Germany, the city of Dessau closed the Bauhaus in 1931. Gropius left Nazi Germany in 1934 and, after living in London for a short period, moved to the US where he taught at the Harvard Graduate School of Design. Gropius's house in Dessau was well known (but not much better received) on the other side of the Atlantic. In the catalogue accompanying the exhibition of International Style architecture at the Museum of Modern Art in 1932, Henry-Russell Hitchcock described the Bauhaus masters' houses in Dessau as undisciplined, and suggested that the 'arbitrary piling of the blocks and the strong contrasts in window shapes' continued in the experimental mode of De Stijl, failing to encapsulate the formal sophistication of the International Style.[24] Citing the Dessau-Törten estate that Gropius had constructed nearby in the same year, Hitchcock suggested that the architect's expertise was better suited to 'problems of general sociological significance' and the design of workers' housing, rather than the 'building of bourgeois houses'.[25]

The tensions that exist in an architect's ethical programme (and how such tensions play out before a mass public keen to identify signs of hypocrisy) become illuminated when analysed in the context of the houses architects design for themselves – especially when the architect's oeuvre is built on championing not just a design aesthetic, but a complete lifestyle. While many modern architects designed their own houses in order to express the feasibility of their utopian ideals, frequently the architect's own house became a site whereby detractors sought to locate contradiction in their aesthetic and ethical programme. In the case of Gropius's house in Dessau, its initial conceptualisation within the construction kit diagram proposed possibilities for housing to meet the needs of a future democratic society. However, as its iconic blocky white cubes and cantilevering platforms were photographed, filmed, and subsequently caricatured, the house soon came to (very publicly) represent the decadence of the Neue Sachlichkeit. Far from expressing a new freedom and cultural poverty, the house became overburdened with symbolic content synonymous with the bourgeois lifestyle that it initially sought to reject.

24
Hitchcock, 'Walter Gropius', 58.

25
Hitchcock, 'Walter Gropius', 58–9.

Bibliography

Benjamin, Walter. *The Arcades Project*, edited by Rolf Tiedemann, translated by Howard Eiland and Kevin Mclaughlin. Cambridge, MA: Belknap Press of Harvard University Press, 1999.

Benjamin, Walter. 'Experience and Poverty'. In *Selected Writings, Volume 2: Part 2: 1931–1934*, edited by Michael W. Jennings, Howard Eiland, and Gary Smith, 731–6. Cambridge, MA: Belknap Press of Harvard University Press, 2005.

Fitch, James Marston. *Walter Gropius*. New York: George Braziller, 1964.

Gropius, Walter. *Bauhausbauten Dessau*. Munich: Albert Langen, 1930.

Gropius, Walter. *The New Architecture and the Bauhaus*, translated by P. Morton Shand. London: Faber and Faber, 1935.

Gropius, Walter. 'Programme of the Staatliches Bauhaus in Weimar'. In *Programs and Manifestoes on 20th-century Architecture*, edited by Ulrich Conrads, 49–53. Cambridge, MA: The MIT Press, 1971.

H.S., 'Neue Sachlichkeit'. *Simplicissimus*, 21 May 1928, 102.

Heine, Thomas Theodor. 'Kleine Bilder'. *Simplicissimus*, 21 May 1928, 103.

Heine, Thomas Theodor. 'Sachlichkeit!'. *Simplicissimus*, 10 September 1928, 303.

Hitchcock, Henry-Russell. 'Walter Gropius'. In *Modern Architecture: International Exhibition*, edited by Philip Johnson and Henry-Russell Hitchcock, 57–70. New York: Museum of Modern Art, 1932.

Kállai, Ernst. 'Ten Years of Bauhaus'. In *Bauhaus: Weimar, Dessau, Berlin, Chicago*, edited by Hans M. Wingler, 162. Cambridge, MA: The MIT Press, 1969.

Loos, Adolf. 'Poor Little Rich Man'. In *Spoken into the Void: Collected Essays, 1897–1900*, translated by Jane O. Newman and John H. Smith, 124–7. Cambridge, MA: MIT Press, 1987.

Miller Lane, Barbara. *Architecture and Politics in Germany, 1918–1945*. Cambridge, MA: Harvard University Press, 1968.

Natonek, Hans. 'Das problematische Glashaus'. *Hamburger Anzeiger*, 6 December 1926.

Rousset, Isabel. 'Satirical Representations of the Bauhaus Architect in *Simplicissimus* Magazine'. In *Fashioning Professionals: Identity and Representation at Work in the Creative Industries*, edited by Leah Armstrong and Felice McDowell, 103–20. London: Bloomsbury, 2018.

Scheerbart, Paul. *The Gray Cloth: A Novel on Glass Architecture*, translated by John A. Stuart. Cambridge, MA: The MIT Press, 2003.

Schuldenfrei, Robin. 'The Irreproducibility of the Bauhaus Object'. In *Bauhaus Construct: Fashioning Identity, Discourse and Modernism*, edited by Jeffrey Saletnik and Robin Schuldenfrei, 37–60. Oxon: Routledge, 2009.

Teige, Karel. *The Minimum Dwelling*, translated by Eric Dluhosch. Cambridge, MA: The MIT Press, 2002.

Ward, Janet. *Weimar Surfaces: Urban Visual Culture in 1920s Germany*. Berkeley: University of California Press, 2001.

Fig. 1 Lina Bo Bardi, sketch of Casa de Vidro (Glass House), no date. (© Instituto Lina Bo e P. M. Bardi, São Paulo)

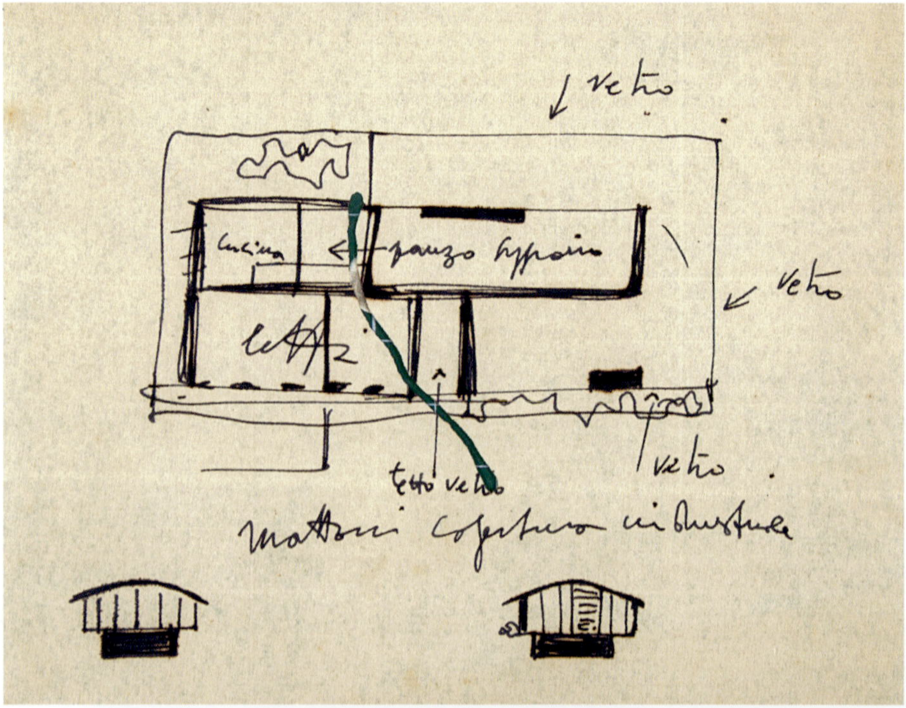

Fig. 2 Casa de Vidro (Glass House), unidentified photographer, circa 1953. (© Instituto Lina Bo e P. M. Bardi, São Paulo)

The House of a Modern Woman in São Paulo

Silvana Rubino

Introduction

The couple formed by architect Lina Bo (1914–1992) and art dealer and journalist Pietro Maria Bardi (1900–1999) left Italy for Brazil in 1946 and settled down in São Paulo.[1] Only five years after their arrival, they built a new house – Casa de Vidro (Glass House) – on a two-and-a-half-acre plot in Jardim Morumbi, a new garden-city neighbourhood in the remote south of the city. The house is still there, marvellous and undaunted in its materiality. However, if a visitor should not grasp the tense desire for resistance that the house expresses, the designer's writings express them. In the form, there is an architectural and urban resistance; a proposal for a lifestyle that questions the condition of women; and an ambiguous desire for class resistance, as if it were possible to both be part of São Paulo's upper classes and break up with them. To examine these contradictions is the challenge of this chapter.

The Bardi couple and their Glass House

The couple were highly active directors of the São Paulo Art Museum (MASP), created by the businessman and journalist Assis Chateaubriand in 1946, where they edited the journal *Habitat*, a periodical of arts, architecture, and culture. *Habitat* published the Glass House in detail with magnificent images, and in most of them, Lina is present, as a model, by the enormous windows or the impressive staircase. In an article published in *Habitat* in 1950, Lina[2] stated:

> This house is, in a sense, controversial as, indeed, all buildings of responsible architects should be, especially if there are no commitments with the commissioner. Almost all contemporary architecture, even when executed by architects of responsibility, denounces 'ideas' and 'tastes' of the owners who, in most cases, lack basic knowledge. If a new generation architect makes a mistake, it is almost always due to the interference of the client. In this case, the situation was different: the client was the architect herself. [3]

The client was not only the architect herself, as she lived there the rest of her life with her partner Pietro Maria Bardi. As such, the large dwelling is the home of a modern couple. One could use for them the notion of *Künstlerehepaar*, a term used during 1920 in Germany to invoke a self-conscious idea of the artist-couple, a manifestation of modern marriage, a kind of partnership between equals.

It is important to underline that the house was her first built design, expressing this strong autonomy that was secured by herself and her husband; therefore, it acquires the aspect of a built manifesto. It could be understood to be a manifesto pro modern architecture; a claim of inclusion in the potent narrative of the modern Brazilian

1
For some aspects of the couple's trajectory, especially Lina, see Rubino, 'Introduction'.

2
The use of her first name instead of the surname Bo Bardi is intentional for two reasons. Firstly, people and scholars in Brazil refer to her as only Lina; and secondly, and mainly, the family name can hide the dimension of gender.

3
Bardi, 'Residência no Morumbi', 38.

architecture, which was compelling at that moment; a manifesto opposed to the conventional bourgeoisie – most of them Italians – whom the couple met in São Paulo; a manifesto for a new modern neighbourhood. Pietro Maria Bardi longed for the Morumbi neighbourhood to be an experiment like that of the Case Study Houses, and his residence was the first to be built there.[4]

While the house was an architectural and urbanist manifesto, it was also, perhaps, a business card. Many scholars have written about the formal aspects of the house, the very thin pilotis, the Miesian references. Lina might have been the first to underline the technical qualities of the project: 'Mannesmann steel tubes support an ultra-light, reinforced-concrete platform constructed using "lost-formwork", where the timber shuttering is absorbed into the slab. Glass walls enclose the house on three sides.'[5] The fourth side of the house is important here, and Lina mentioned it in the same article:

> The rear of the house, which rests directly upon the terrain, is a standard stone-and-cement construction; a long courtyard, sealed on one side, *separates* the front of the house from the service area to the rear, though both volumes are connected via the kitchen.[6]

Lina thus admits the Glass House may be, in fact, two houses. The former is glassy and floats over the thin pilotis over an idealised forest;[7] the latter is grounded on the terrain and used traditional techniques and materials. These contradictory aspects of the house are evident, and they allow us to pose some questions about the compatibility (or lack thereof) of a contemporary project in an ambiguous and non-egalitarian town, and society as Brazil was then, and still is now.

At the beginning of the 1950s, São Paulo had a population of almost four million inhabitants, including many immigrants from Europe, especially Italy, and from Japan, as well as from other states of Brazil. Unlike the capital Rio de Janeiro, it counted on less presence of the state and, therefore, constituted an open place for risky business adventures, as in any liberal economic environment.[8] In the new garden-city borough Morumbi, Pietro Maria Bardi imagined an open-air panorama of modern and good (for him the two words were almost interchangeable) architecture for the 'good taste' bourgeoisie of the town. The isolated area already had a new modern house by architect Oswaldo Bratke and the remodelling of an ancient church by Gregori Warchavchik, recognised as the first modern architect of Brazil.[9] Therefore, the Glass House was intended to present a good example of modern architecture for the whole neighbourhood and town, contrasting with the other garden-city boroughs of São Paulo, full of houses in different historical styles.

The secret house, *il segretto*

Although the choices of the architectural concept are clearly rationalistic, the Glass House also expresses the limitations imposed by Lina's class and her time. She longed to promote a kind of modern life, somehow distant from

4
The well-known garden-city developments, idealised by Ebenezer Howard (1850–1928) became garden neighbourhoods when they were proposed for Brazilian cities, like São Paulo and others. The City of Sao Paulo Improvements and Freehold Land Company, known as Cia City, was created to urbanise new neighbourhoods, in a kind of garden-city manner, that is, houses on large plots integrated in nature. The British urbanists Barry Parker and Raymond Unwin collaborated with Cia City to develop Jardim America, a wealthy garden-city neighbourhood. Although not part of Cia City developments, Jardim Morumby (now Morumbi), an urban development on the terrain of a former tea farmer, shared the same principles.

5
Bardi, 'Residência no Morumbi', 43.

6
Bardi, 'Residência no Morumbi', 43. Emphasis added.

7
Rubino, 'Lina and Nature'.

8
The couple probably enjoyed this aspect of São Paulo. Such a distinction between São Paulo and Rio can be compared with a declaration by the young Lina about the difference between Rome and Milan.

9
The Ukrainian Gregori Warchavchik started his studies of architecture in Odessa and moved to Rome in 1918. In Rome, he studied and worked with Marcello Piacentini (who was professor of the young Lina Bo). He moved to Brazil in 1923, where he is considered the author of the first modernist house, in São Paulo. Oswaldo Bratke (1906–1997) was an important Brazilian architect, inspired by the work of Frank Lloyd Wright and Richard Neutra.

Fig. 3 Lina showing how to fold the table of the kitchen. Illustration of *Enciclopédia da Mulher*, 1958. (Photograph by Jack Pires. © Instituto Lina Bo e P. M. Bardi, São Paulo)

Fig. 4 Lina's hands cleaning the dishes, with a watch and manicure. Illustration of *Enciclopédia da Mulher*, 1958. (Photograph by Jack Pires. © Instituto Lina Bo e P. M. Bardi, São Paulo)

Fig. 5 Garbage incinerator in the kitchen. Illustration of *Enciclopédia da Mulher*, 1958. (Photograph by Jack Pires. © Instituto Lina Bo e P. M. Bardi, São Paulo) the São Paulo bourgeoisie of the 1950s, as a form of cultural resistance; however, it seems she stumbled into the limits of her social inscription. To examine that further, the aforementioned text of Lina, published in *Habitat*, can be compared with another one, a few years later, included in a book of feminine advice. In 1958, Lina published a shadowed, secret text, free of most of the analysis of her work, entitled 'A casa, sua organização e arranjo' (The house, its organisation and planning). It is a long article written for a woman's encyclopaedia, in a language that uses both the conventions and vocabulary of the advice books for women and the lexicon of modern architecture.[10] The year 1958 was an incredibly special time for Lina, as it was when she designed the prior versions of the new headquarters of MASP and was beginning her crucial relationship with the State of Bahia, in northeastern Brazil.[11]

The advice that Lina offered to her female readers includes some of the concerns she had already expressed in Italy, especially in her work as a publisher (*Grazia*, *Stile* and other popular journals): how to deal with the house. The 330-page encyclopaedia contains, with the exception of Lina's chapter, articles all translated from French about fashion, textiles, fur, handcrafts, cooking, children, social life, leisure, among others. Contrasting with this conservative feminine outlook, Lina defined the house in its biological, environmental dimension: it is in the house that people acquire habits and form their personality. The house, for her, could not be a sanctuary; otherwise, the housewife could become a slave. This idea of a housewife's alienated and lonely work was the main focus of generations of women aiming to reduce the burden of the home, especially the works of Christine Frederick, Erna Mayer, and Paulette Bernège. It has echoes of old concerns of Lina's as well. Before leaving Italy, she had edited with Bruno Zevi a journal that lasted less than one year. *A—Cultura della vitta* was aimed at the common housewife, and in the first issue, there are a couple of interesting articles. The first, quoting a poem by Percy Bysshe Shelley, asked in the title 'Can a man be free if the woman is a slave'?[12] The second article brought the answer: the planned American kitchen. However, in this manuscript in the woman's encyclopaedia, Lina addressed the Brazilian middle-class housewives, advising them to get rid of old furniture and memorabilia and proposing:

> [t]he evolution of taste, the continuous simplification of things, the constant reference to the origins, or rather to authentic things, in which copies are eliminated and things redone, [to] help in the formation of an open mentality, free of prejudices and limitations.[13]

The text of the encyclopaedia advocated a whole group of interdictions rather than pedagogically instructing this (supposedly) 'naive', unaware housewife: no mirrors, no bar, and no *copa*.[14] Two houses illustrated the chapter: one was a house designed by the architect Vilanova Artigas and the other her own Glass House.[15] Lina wrote about Vilanova Artigas in *Habitat*:

> Every Artigas house breaks all the rules of the bourgeois halls. In the Artigas homes that one gets to see, inside all is open, with

10
The encyclopaedia was entitled *Enciclopédia da Mulher*.

11
Lina Bo Bardi's articles 'Theory and Philosophy of Architecture', 'Culture and Non-Culture', 'Architecture or Culture', 'Houses or Museums', 'The invasion', 'The Moon', 'Industrial Art', 'Technology and Art', and 'The Northeast', all included in the collection *Stones against Diamonds*, were written during the Bahia period (1958–64), which she would describe as 'five years among white people'. For more about Lina and Bahia, see Rubino, 'Lina Bo Bardi en Salvador de Bahia'.

12
'Come può esse il uomo libero si la donna è schiava'.

13
Enciclopédia da Mulher, 76. Emphasis added.

14
In Brazilian homes of middle and upper classes, the *copa* is a second, small dining room where the family have the daily meals, or where the children eat, as do the maids, drivers, and other household employees. As I could not find an exact translation – because this is a cultural practice, and it does not occur elsewhere – instead of using pantry, kitchen dining space, or breakfast room, I kept the term in Portuguese.

15
She discusses the Dr. Bittencourt House by João Batista Vilanova Artigas (1915–1985). This house was designed in 1948 for the architect's close friend, communist doctor Mario Taques Bittencourt. Artigas designed his own house the next year and both designs are much alike. Artigas was also an important member of the Brazilian Communist Party and the majority of his clients shared the same political orientation.

16
'Casas de Vilanova Artigas', 2. For the English translation, see *Vilanova Artigas*, 11.

17
I explored this aspect of hiding the face in the images in Rubino, 'Bodies, Chairs, Necklaces'.

18
Enciclopédia da Mulher, 86.

> plenty of glass and often low ceilings; the kitchen is not separate and the bourgeois who might be attracted by the novelty and requisition in an Artigas home would be shocked with 'so little privacy', blinded by so much light, would hurry to close the windows with heavy curtains, grow hedges and reinforce the doors to continue well-defended, his carefree life among his 'Chippendale' furniture and hand-painted *abat-jours* [...] The Artigas houses are spaces sheltered from the weather, wind, and rain, but not from man, rendering them as far as possible from the castle house, the sealed house, with an indoors and outdoors, a remnant of the days of mortal hates. The Artigas house, which one superficial observer defined as being absurd, is the patient and courageous message of he who sees the first light of a new era: the era of human comradeship.[16]

It seems that for Lina, the association of glass with transparency would be enough to break the bonds of bourgeois life. It makes some sense since we know most of Artigas's clientele to be active members of the Brazilian Communist Party, despite belonging to the upper-middle class.

The second house was the Glass House, the residence of the Bardi couple. So, she presented to female readers two unusual, exceptional modernist houses, two uncommon ways of dwelling.
As in the *Habitat* article, Lina is present in the images, as a model and an example of her statements. Even though she does not face the camera, we can recognise her silhouette.[17] They photographed her as the modern housewife herself, as a statement: in this modern glassy house, the textiles and walls should not be printed, to avoid bad patterns. The same should be said for carpets, except for Persian and Gobelins, authentic ones, of course:

> If you do not have the means to buy a Picasso pottery, use an earthenware pot where people keep fat milk. As to the aesthetic value, they will be in the same plane as the first one, whereas this will not happen with a dog or elephant made of German or Czechoslovakian porcelain whose price will reach almost that of the pottery by Picasso.[18]

The principle for room organisation should be clarity, and in that she specified that eating should be reserved for the dining room, and the dining room only – there is a whole section for 'kitchen and *copa*'. In Lina's words:

> The *copa* is a useful but not indispensable element; there the serving dishes are washed; the cabinets are placed for the table service and the dishes are prepared. It is usual to have a table in the *copa* to have meals at your leisure, in pyjamas or sleepwear. *We are against these habits*; whoever has the dining room must use it always and at any time, or else abolish it using the *copa* to eat. This use has a bourgeois touch and recalls the habit of closing the living room [...] For those who do not have the dining room, the *copa* is no longer a *copa*, but it automatically becomes the dining room which, in this case, is attached to the kitchen, a very modern criterion and facilitates meals, especially for

> those who do not have *copeiras*. The *copa* can also be used for the employees' meals, but if the house is large and if it has resources, it is good to make a separate room for the household workers, where they can rest and have their meals.[19]

Lina offered advice for the bedroom and dressing room as well, but perhaps most notable was the section on the kitchen, which she argued should be considered a scientific laboratory, distant from the hard work of ancient times. At this point of the article, a cluster of gender and class tensions is activated, and the presence or absence of servants was an indirectly named subject, but it is there, especially when she praised the electric appliances. On one hand, she proposed hot water and electricity in the kitchen, which every middle-class house had in São Paulo at that time. On the other hand, she showcased a food waste disposer in the sink; no one had one then, nor even are they common today in Brazil. Rubbish was a crucial theme, as she considered the habits of bins in the sidewalk, a common practice by then, to be unhygienic.

The modernity of the household appliances still not very affordable in Brazil and an assembly-line kitchen were informed by the Frankfurt Kitchen and other Taylorist ones. Still, Lina's modern kitchen had some items that referred to quite artisanal work, such as a table to make pasta (well, she was Italian) or cakes. Moreover, she promoted a division of spheres, with the *copa* being used by the domestic employees.

Francesco Tentori, a biographer of Pietro Maria Bardi, recalls with irony his astonishment when he saw the servants' rooms in the Glass House.[20] He assumed that it was an appropriation, by the architect, of the memory of colonial Brazil, by incorporating a scheme of 'casa grande e senzala'.[21] In the Glass House, the service area is strictly separated from the body of the house by a courtyard and a door. The kitchen, located between the service area and the block where the couple lived, is a transitional space, a scheme that is not that different from any bourgeois house or apartment built in that decade, or even today in Brazil. The spatial distance is a reflection of the social and cultural distance, as the employees had separate (and minimal) housing, independent of the rest of the residence.

The architect (and close friend to the couple) Giò Ponti noticed the situation of the workspace of the servants, denominating this part as the *viscere* (guts) of the dwelling, arguing that the house had two different sectors: one transparent for the visitors, and another opaque, sheltered and secret – *segretto* – for the house servants. As we mentioned before, Lina was aware of the coexistence of these two houses: the glassy one and the hidden one. However, this is not frequently addressed in the analysis of the house, maybe because this kind of social division inside the home is quite naturalised in Brazil.

By designing this independent accommodation, this minimal space for dwelling, Lina translated in a quite bourgeois manner the

19
A *copeira* is a maid who cooks, serves the meals, and works in the *copa*; it is a type of specialisation in a residence that has more than one servant. *Enciclopédia da Mulher*, 101–2. Emphasis added.

20
Tentori, *P.M. Bardi*.

21
Casa Grande & Senzala (1935) was written by the Brazilian sociologist Gilberto Freyre, translated into English as *Master and Slaves*. The main idea concerns the opposition between the manor (*casa grande*) and the slaves' quarters. The English translation of the title did not capture the dimension of this opposition. Even nowadays, when one sees a very unequal situation, one can say, 'so casa grande and senzala', to underline the incompatibility of those two worlds so close and at the same time so apart. So, when Tentori pointed out that she incorporated this as a scheme, it was quite an accusation.

22
Although Morumbi was a neighbourhood in the middle of nowhere, it should not be compared to the tradition, after Levittown, of suburban housing in North America.

achievements of the CIAM in 1929, in Frankfurt, which was dedicated to discussing the housing of workers, the so-called minimal housing. At that moment, the Frankfurt Kitchen became known as a functional and Taylorist space for the modern woman who worked and took care of the house. As we know, Margarete Schütte-Lihotzky designed this kitchen for social housing, *Siedlungen*, for the German working class. These two points of debate in 1929 re-emerged in the modern house of the Bardi couple: there was the the functional, spacious kitchen, used by maids; and a small apartment for the working class, even though it was part of the employer's house. One could argue that the service apartment had spatial qualities that placed it well above not only the colonial slave quarters but also the employee rooms in other residences. However, this scheme somehow mirrors the unequal urban structure: the bourgeois housing in a privileged neighbourhood and the housing of the worker in a peripheral or suburban area of the city, two places not only separate but apart as well.

Lina wrote: 'The house is spacious, especially as far as service facilities are concerned', and in the chapter, these apartments are the type of 'minimal apartments, species of cells – for one or two girls at most'. It is the secret that amazed the Italian fellows Tentori and Ponti, and evidence of the blind faith of modernism about its gains, no matter the context, and the bet on a universal man. Aiming to be progressive and democratic in a neighbourhood in Frankfurt in the Weimar Republic, the tiniest apartments of social housing were, instead, a hidden and secret room in a modern house in Morumbi in São Paulo of the 1950s.

The kitchen in the Glass House may have been inspired by the Frankfurt Kitchen, designed by the Austrian architect Schütte-Lihotsky, shown in *Die neue Wohnung und ihr Innenausbau* in 1925, and immediately included in various housing projects constructed in the city by Ernst May. The unit in question was a *Kochküche*, a kitchen made for cooking, small with an aura of modernity that came from the use of electricity. The novelty crossed back over the Atlantic and in 1934 the book *Modern Housing*, written by Catherine Bauer and published in New York, lauded Schütte-Lihotsky's kitchen as one of the major achievements of the new architecture. Nevertheless, the modern kitchen was meant for countries that had dealt with the so-called servant problem.

The images of the chapter of the encyclopedia show a 'modern' woman who avoids the iconographic stereotypes of the period, that is, the woman in a Dior New Look dress. In the shots, Lina appears wearing long trousers; she uses a watch on the wrist and does not wear a dress or an apron. The Glass House kitchen could be compared to the functional American kitchen, a more spacious and more equipped version of the Frankfurt Kitchen. It was, after all, a bourgeois house, while the latter was intended for housing complexes. But Lina did not introduce herself as the suburban housewife of the Kitchen Debate that entertained North America during the Cold War.[22] The kitchen of Glass House was both

German and American, far from the tradition of household space in Brazil.

However, the captions are revealing. In one image, Lina reminds us that domestic work is greatly facilitated by the mechanisation of the home, and adds: 'The dishwasher eliminates everything *humiliating* in this type of work: the fat and waste is not touched by the hands, as a special rubber spatula helps to remove the latter to the crusher, which eliminates them.'[23] This passage denotes us to all notions of impurity, danger, filth, pollution, and the social taboos related to them, as treated by Mary Douglas in the classic *Purity and Danger*. The kitchen is the place of the debris of the house. However, the dirt is also in the eyes of the beholder: 'When we honestly reflect on our brushings and cleanings', wrote the British anthropologist, 'we realise that we are not mainly seeking to avoid diseases and rather (we are) separating, demarcating boundaries, making visible statements about the home that we intend to create from the material home.'[24]

In the 1950s, the middle class of São Paulo relied on the domestic worker; liberating the housewife from hard tasks was not an issue for Lina and her article. Nevertheless, the result of the use of this new technology, from the delicate relationship between the owner of the house and her housekeeper, was the lack of prestige of the latter's traditional knowledge, which seemed to resist innovation. At that moment in Brazil, the household appliances began to appear in the market while the servants remained in the houses; the enlightened bourgeoisie thus enjoyed the best of both worlds. This became quite clear when, on a visit to the Glass House in 2010, I asked to examine the household appliances. They were intact, untouched. When I commented so with the housekeepers, the response came promptly: 'The employees did not know how to use them, as they were imported from the United States and the instructions were in English.' If such an observation does not underrate this proposal of a kitchen far from the traditional one and close to the doctor's office – clean, hygienic – it is certainly revealing of the gender, generational, and class constraints that perhaps, notwithstanding Lina's efforts and intentions, end up being revealed in the text.

The Glass House was not designed for a show or an exhibition, but there are clues that it could have been thought of as a studio or even residence for artists invited by the São Paulo Museum of Art. To conclude, whether it was conceived as an annex to MASP or not, the house was a kind of museum. A modern museum for the couple to exhibit their modernity as materialised in their house; or, perhaps the museum of a modern and fallible dwelling proposal in a wealthy neighbourhood of a divided town, in divided mid-century Brazil.

23
Enciclopédia da Mulher, 94. Emphasis added.

24
Douglas, *Purity and Danger*, 85.

Bibliography

Bardi, Lina Bo. 'Residência no Morumbi'. *Habitat*, no. 10 (1953): 31–40.

Bardi, Lina Bo. *Stones against Diamonds*. Architecture Words 12. London: Architectural Association Publications, 2013.

'Casas de Vilanova Artigas'. *Habitat*, no. 1 (October–December 1950): 2. Translated to English in Instituto Lina Bo e P.M. Bardi and Fundação Vilanova Artigas. *Vilanova Artigas*. São Paulo, 1997, 11.

'Come può esse il uomo libero si la donna è schiava'. *A—Cultura della vita*, no. 1. Milano, 1945.

Douglas, Mary. *Purity and Danger: An Analysis of Concepts of Pollution and Taboo*. London: Routledge, 2003.

Enciclopédia da Mulher. Porto Alegre: Editora Globo, 1958.

Rubino, Silvana. 'Bodies, Chairs, Necklaces: Charlotte Perriand and Lina Bo Bardi'. *Cad. Pagu* 2 (2010). http://socialsciences.scielo.org/scielo.php?pid=S0104-83332010000100003&script=sci_abstract. Accessed 2 June 2021.

Rubino, Silvana. 'Introduction'. In *Stones against Diamonds*, by Lina Bo Bardi, 3–16. Architecture Words 12. London: Architectural Association Publications, 2013.

Rubino, Silvana. 'Lina and Nature'. In *Lina Bo Bardi: Material Ideologies*, edited by Monica Ponce de León. Princeton, NJ, Princeton School of Architecture, forthcoming.

Rubino, Silvana. 'Lina Bo Bardi en Salvador de Bahia: tanto en cinco años'. In *Lina Bo Bardi Tupí or not tupí. Brasil 1946–1992*, edited by Llorens et al., 117–28. Madrid: Fundación Juan March, 2018.

Tentori, Francesco. *P.M. Bardi*. Milan: Nuove Edizioni Gabriele Mazzotta, 1990.

Shaping Modernism in Brussels: Through the lens of Victor Bourgeois, Adrien Blomme, and Paul-Amaury Michel and their personal residences[1]

Linsy Raaffels, Inge Bertels, Stephanie Van de Voorde, and Barbara Van der Wee

The slow rise of modernism in Belgium

In Belgium, the first modernist ideas were shaped in response to discontent with the eclectic and historicising architecture of the 1800s. By the end of the nineteenth century, influenced by international debates, Belgian architects started to defend theories that architectural ornamentation should either solely originate from natural geometries or should even be rejected completely.[2] In response, the heydays of art nouveau coincided with the turn of the century, yet the later modern philosophy did not get off the ground before the First World War. Although the first visionary, theoretical principles of modernism were already taking shape, no single example of Belgian modernist architecture was shown during the World Fairs of 1910 and 1913, held in Brussels and Ghent, respectively.[3]

The main incentive for modernists came two years later in reaction to the large-scale destruction in Belgium early in the war. In 1915, the International Garden Cities and Town Planning Association hosted a reconstruction conference on the Belgian reconstruction issue in London, in which no less than three hundred Belgian architects participated. For young modernist-inspired architects, such as Jean-Jules Eggericx (1884–1963), the conference offered an excellent opportunity to discuss their modern thoughts with international colleagues and to nourish their own ideas to rebuild Belgium with innovative, modernist principles. These principles related to an unambiguous form of design – often a cubical volume without ornamentation – for which the used materials were limited and implemented according to contemporary technology.[4]

Yet, upon their return to Belgium, neither the public at large, nor the rather traditional Belgian government and influential architectural circles were open to the ideas of participants such as Eggericx, Raphaël Verwilghen (1885–1963), and Louis Van der Swaelmen (1883–1929). As such, without any political support, the opportunities to realise modern principles in practice remained scarce. Nevertheless, strengthened in their philosophy, an intense architectural debate between modernists and traditionalists followed.[5] In the early 1920s, the tide seemed to turn in favour of the modernists with the emergence of a new architectural concept: social housing. By virtue of its novelty, this concept proved rather receptive to the innovative modern design principles.[6] This modern concept was especially well received in the Brussels-Capital Region since it faced a very high shortage of dwellings for the most disad-

1
Research funded by Innoviris.

2
Culot and Pirlot, 'l'Art Déco', 21–2.

3
Demey, 'Het Modernisme', 28–31.

4
Celis, 'De Wederopbouw', 140; Demey, 'Het Modernisme', 32.

5
Celis, 'De Wederopbouw', 143; Van Loo, *Repertorium*, 420.

6
Demey, 'Het Modernisme', 32; Poulain, 'Woord Vooraf', 3.

7
Hennaut, 'Het Interbellum in Brussel', 167–9.

8
Culot and Pirlot, 'l'Art Déco', 23; Hennaut, 'Het Interbellum in Brussel', 171.

9
Raaffels, 'Architects' Houses in Brussels'.

10
Culot and Pirlot, 'l'Art Déco', 24; Demey, 'Het Modernisme', 34.

vantaged, compounded by a steady population growth. In response, from 1921 onwards, dozens of garden city projects were launched in the region, often designed after the English examples shown during the reconstruction conference of 1915.[7] However, in 1925, the financing for these social projects was mainly cut off when the government launched low premium offers for the acquisition of private land ownership instead, resulting in the stagnation of the building programme for social housing. As such, modernist architects were once again forced to refocus their actions, especially since most private landowners and bourgeois clients were not in favour of an architecture identified with social housing. As a result, many modernists turned to polemic activities to diffuse their ideas and aspirations: more than ever, the modernist debate was held in architectural periodicals, within specialised associations, and at international conferences, such as the Congrès Internationaux d'Architecture Moderne (CIAM).[8] Moreover, to illustrate their stance more powerfully, many modernists started to colour their portfolio with their own houses.

The catalysing role of architects' houses for Brussels

Recent research on architects' houses in the Brussels-Capital Region showed that architects often deployed their private homes as a tool to formulate a new architectural vocabulary, experiment with a new construction method, or even turn it into a sort of physical business card.[9] As over one hundred architects' houses were constructed in the Brussels-Capital Region during the interwar years, it can likewise be questioned whether modernist-inspired architects also used their own homes to invigorate concepts of modernism in practice, or even aspired to generate a positive turnaround in Brussels' policy by means of such personal statements.

Although half of all architects' houses built at the time still demonstrated the stylistic features of art deco, Beaux-Arts, or an eclectic version thereof, over one-third of all architects' houses constructed in the interwar period were unmistakably inspired by the Modern Movement, with an additional seven per cent displaying a rather modern approach to art deco. Remarkable is the fact that over one-third of those modernist architects' houses were built in Ukkel. One of the first architects to do so was Louis Herman De Koninck (1896–1984, Ukkel, 1924). After him, between 1924 and 1970, at least thirty other architects followed, such as Pierre Verbruggen (1886–1940, Sint-Gillis, 1924), Victor Bourgeois (1897–1962, Koekelberg, 1925), Adrien Blomme (1878–1940, Brussels, 1928), Robert Puttemans (1902–1978, Ukkel, 1929), and Paul-Amaury Michel (1912–1988, Ukkel, 1935). Their personal realisations often represented their manifestos, and consequently inspired contemporary influential artists to share their mindset. For example, after the completion of his own residence, De Koninck received commissions for the personal houses of painter Jacques Lenglet (Ukkel, 1926) and art collector Philippe Dotremont (Ukkel, 1931), among others.[10] Yet the public at large retained their reservations towards his modern architectural expression: passers-by referred to his house as the creation of a madman.[11] Nonetheless, a wider platform for modernism was slowly created. Therefore, this article unravels to what extent interwar architects' houses indeed aided to clear the path for modernism in Brussels, which is examined through the lens of three prominent cases, namely the private residences of Victor Bourgeois, Adrien Blomme, and Paul-Amaury Michel.

Victor Bourgeois's headquarters of modernism

Victor Bourgeois studied architecture at the Brussels Fine Arts Academy but in protest to the historicising teaching practices, he refused to hand in his graduation project in 1919.[12] Thereby, he became an advocate of the Modern Movement and in 1922 he was commissioned for the design of Cité Moderne, a modernist garden city in Sint-Agatha-Berchem.[13] Yet, shortly after, Bourgeois's opportunity for work was affected by the low premium offers for private land acquisition. In response, with the revenue of Cité Moderne, Bourgeois redirected his plea for modernism to the private housing sector with the construction of his personal residence in Koekelberg **(Fig. 1)**.[14] The house resembled his statement of what private modern architecture should be, and Bourgeois even intended it to house the Brussels headquarters of modernism. Thereby, regardless of public opinion, Bourgeois aspired to generate a broader support for the theoretical development of modernism in Brussels.[15]

The strength of the house in Koekelberg was that it showcased a synopsis of the modernist idiom; it was a pure concrete cubical volume with a smooth, white-plastered facade and meticulously positioned apertures.[16] Furthermore, each floor was characterised by its function, as is was heralded by the 'machine à habiter' of Le Corbusier (1887–1965) published in 1923 in *Vers une Architecture*. The house, situated on an inclined site, was two storeys high on the street side and three storeys facing the garden. The middle floor, which was accessible from the street, comprised the working area of the architect at the back, while the garage was located near the front. The living spaces were on the bottom floor giving on to the garden to let in light and air, while the sanitary and cellar spaces were situated near the retaining wall at the opposite side. Lastly, the upper floor was designed for guests and was conceived as one large dining and living room with large-glazed surfaces to ensure an intensive illumination throughout the day. As early as 1928, Bourgeois had transformed the house by adding two additional storeys. The original plans remained virtually the same, and the modern facade was extended. The newly added volume incorporated additional bedrooms, an extension of the architectural workspace, and a partially covered solarium **(Fig. 2)** in accordance with Le Corbusier's 'Cinq Points d'une Architecture Moderne', also published in *Vers une Architecture*.[17]

Although the house never truly became the central office of the Modern Movement, Bourgeois's intentions were successful; he was able to convince several contemporaries of the artistry of modernism, and was commissioned by many artists for their personal resi-

11
De Koninck, 'Confidences of an Architect', 49.

12
Culot, Hennaut, and Liessens, 'Victor Bourgeois', 100; Van Loo, *Repertorium*, 168.

13
Meganck, 'Volkshuisvesting', 41; Dubois and Poulain, 'Interbellumarchitectuur in Vlaanderen', 129.

14
Demey, 'Het Modernisme', 35.

15
Directie Monumenten & Landschappen and Pirlot, *Koekelberg à la Carte.*

16
Demey, 'Het Modernisme', 35.

17
Koekelberg, *Avenue Seghers* 103, Archief Stedenbouw; 'Fonds Bourgeois', Brussels, CIVA.

18
Dubois and Poulain, 'Interbellumarchitectuur in Vlaanderen', 135; Culot, Hennaut, and Liessens, 'Victor Bourgeois', 100.

19
Goldfinger, 'Hommages de E. Goldfinger', 386.

20
Culot, Hennaut, and Liessens, 'Adrien Blomme', 92.

21
'Auparavant j'avais été souvent séduit par l'équilibre de l'architecture du 18ième siècle, ... mais je me suis rendu compte que les exigences nouvelles de la vie d'aujourd'hui ne pouvaient plus être sincèrement satisfaites par les enseignements des réalisations du passé.' Blomme, 'Au lecteur'.

22
Brusselse Hoofdstedelijke Regering, 'Besluit Tot Bescherming: Franklin Rooseveltlaan 52–Antoine Depagelaan 1'.

23
Blomme, '1928–1994: l'Histoire Peut-Elle Se Répéter?', 1; Blomme, 'Avenue Des Nations 1928', 97.

24
Eggericx, 'l'architecture d'Adrien Blomme', 29.

25
Immeuble A. Blomme, 2043-0779-0, Brussels, Documentation Centre urban.brussels; Blomme, 'Avenue Des Nations 1928', 100; Brusselse Hoofdstedelijke Regering, 'Besluit Tot Bescherming: Franklin Rooseveltlaan 52–Antoine Depagelaan 1'.

26
Blomme, 'Avenue Des Nations 1928', 97.

27
Avenue Des Nations et Antoine Depage, TP354.54, Letters, Brussels, Stadsarchief Brussel; Blomme, '1928–1994: l'Histoire Peut-Elle Se Répéter?', 1.

dences, including painters Georges Latinis (Sint-Agatha-Berchem, 1926) and Albert Lamblot (Ukkel, 1929), sculptor Oscar Jespers (Sint-Lambrechts-Woluwe, 1928), and cellist Jean Mondalt (Sint-Agatha-Berchem, 1927). He was appointed the first vice-president of CIAM and inspired architects abroad.[18] According to Ernö Goldfinger, 'In the early twenties, Victor Bourgeois was to us a legendary figure, [. . .] one of the pioneers of modern architecture.'[19]

Adrien Blomme's residence as an urban and political hinge

By virtue of the growing theoretical support of modernism, even rather traditional architects such as Adrien Blomme – whose early realisations were characterised by a blend of traditionalism and art nouveau – became inspired by the modern principles.[20] He wrote: 'I often used to be seduced by the balance of eighteenth-century architecture, [. . .] but I realised that the new demands of today's life could no longer be satisfied solely by the lessons of past achievements.'[21]

Consequently, his architecture was subject to a constant evolution, and by the age of fifty he designed his third personal residence as a modern statement on the corner of the newly paved Avenue des Nations and Avenue Antoine Depage **(Fig. 3)** in the Brussels South-Extension.[22] The Brussels authorities desired to develop the area of the Avenue des Nations as a prestigious, new traffic artery leading into Brussels. Therefore, the prospective architectural style of the avenue was heavily debated among traditionalists and modernists. As this private residence was situated on the corner of one of the largest intersections, the design of the building would become a defining feature for the iconic status of the avenue, not least because of its scale. The building did not only include the private dwelling of the architect, his wife, and their six children, but also integrated his architectural office and several rental apartments.[23]

The design was an unmistakably modern building because of the volumetric and spatial organisation and the choice for a concrete, plastered facade complemented with finely profiled, steel window frames. But, although Blomme embraced modern design principles, he was not a modernist of *la premiere heure*.[24] Consequently, some architectural features, especially regarding the interior decoration, still referred to art deco. Nevertheless, the design resembled one of the first modern-inspired apartments in Brussels.[25] It was exactly because of this modern aesthetics that the city council rejected the building permit in January 1928; they were convinced that it would not fit, and even violate, the envisioned iconic streetscape. Struck by the refusal of the authorities, Blomme invited his prominent contemporaries to critique his design.[26] He thereupon received letters from Jules Berckmann (art historian), Alfred Nyst (1877–1972, president of the Belgian Society of Modern Urbanists and Architects), and contemporary architects Jules Ghobert (1881–1971), Adolphe Puissant (1878–1950), Jean Fernand Petit (1885–1955), Alexis Dumont (1877–1962), Georges Hobé (1854–1936), and Victor Horta (1861–1947). It is remarkable how they all took a unanimous modernist position and defended the project.[27] Overall, it

Fig. 1 Private residence of Victor Bourgeois in 1925. (© CIVA, Brussels, 'Fonds Bourgeois')

Fig. 2 Partially covered solarium. (© CIVA, Brussels, 'Fonds Bourgeois')

Fig. 3 Modernist composition of the private residence of Adrien Blomme, represented on the cover of *Bâtir*, 1933. (© CIVA, Brussels)

was especially praised for the reflection of the taste and spirit of the modern time through the well-articulated simplicity, clarity, and logic of the design aimed solely at a balance of masses.[28]

Thereby, these letters reflected the broadmindedness of their authors and endorsed the growing modernist platform among vanguard architects, regardless of their own favoured architectural style. Reassured by the opinions of his colleagues, Blomme resubmitted the original project on 26 March without any alteration. He requested his building permit – complemented by the letters and a personal outline on modernism – to be unconditionally accepted. As such, by joining forces with high-profile architects, Blomme raised the debate invigorated by Bourgeois among contemporaries to the level of policymakers. Yet, this initiative to directly question the city council represents an act made much more likely with the design of an architect's own dwelling. Such processes can entail a tremendous amount of time, effort, delays, and subsequent financial uncertainties; risks a client might not be willing to take just for the sake of architecture. But in this case, on 30 March – only four days later – the project was approved without reservations.[29] The urban planning policy of the Brussels South-Extension also seemed

28
Letters of Jules Ghobert (19 March 1928) and Jules Berckmann (20 March 1928), TP354.54, Stadsarchief Brussel.

29
Building permit 26 March 1928, Stadsarchief Brussel; Text by Françoise Blomme (15 September 1991), 2043-0779-0, Documentation Centre urban.brussels.

to be officially revaluated from that moment forward; the Inventory of Built Heritage includes no example of modernism for the Brussels South-Extension before 1928, while sixty-two modern buildings of the period 1928–40 are included.[30]

La Maison de Verre of Paul-Amaury Michel

The conservative mindset of policymakers was less apparent in newly emerging municipalities, such as Ukkel where the first official urban development regulations were not fully enacted until 1949, attracting interwar modernists to the commune.[31] Among them was Paul-Amaury Michel, one of the first modern architects trained in Brussels. Michel graduated in 1934 from the modern-inspired Institut Supérieur des Arts Décoratifs de La Cambre, founded in 1927. During his studies, he was taught by the modernist avant-garde, including Bourgeois for the *forme pure* and Eggericx for the architectural studio.[32] After his studies, Michel visited several internationally renowned examples of modernism, such as the Maison de Verre (Paris, 1932) by Pierre Chareau (1883–1950). In 1935, at the age of twenty-three, Michel harmonised the modern principles he was taught with those he had observed into his own architectural language in his first building: his own Maison de Verre (Glass House) **(Fig. 4)**.[33] Thereby, he deployed his own residence as a business card to show himself as a modernist. He consequently aspired to persuade potential clients – and the still rather conservative wider public – of the modern design principles.

Michel designed his house as a terrace on a compact site of six by twenty metres. Despite the short distance from the house to the adjacent plot at the back, Michel designed a fully glazed rear facade composed of glass bricks, following the example of Chareau in Paris.[34] The design included over 3,000 half crystal tiles from the glasswork firm Val-Saint-Lambert in Liège **(Fig. 5)**.[35] These glass bricks were chosen for their translucent properties; they ensured privacy while maximising the incidence of light.[36] Furthermore, the main advantage of the site was that the adjacent one-storey building was constructed away from the edge of the plot. Michel convinced both his neighbour and the urban planning department to grant him an exception on the general policy of blind separation walls.[37] As a result, Michel had the opportunity to showcase Le Corbusier's Five Points of Architecture: he opened one side of the ground floor to show the structural *pilotis* (1) at the corner, which was also visible on the corner of the roof terrace (2), while new construction techniques enabled him to realise a free floor plan (3) and free facades (4) with large strip or horizontal windows (5) that stretched from one edge of the facade to the other.[38] Almost immediately after the house's completion, it was recognised in various architectural journals such as *Bâtir* (1936) and *L'Émulation* (1937) and also attracted a modern clientele from all around Brussels.[39]

In time, however, Michel was able to translate his modernist ideas more effectively through the design of various five- to six-storey-high apartment buildings, which stood out for their austerity and

30
Directie Monumenten en Landschappen, 'Inventaris'.

31
Municipal Administration of Ukkel, 'Concordantietabel Nummering BBP's'.

32
Van Loo, Delevoy, and Culot, *La Cambre 1928–1978*, appended list.

33
Fontaine, *Het Glazen Huis*, 7–8.

34
Fontaine, *Het Glazen Huis*, 14–8.

35
Denonne, *Maison de Verre*; Bart De Beir, Guided tour: Residence Paul-Amaury Michel, interview by Linsy Raaffels, 26 November 2017.

36
Van Loo, *Repertorium*, 418.

37
Brusselse Hoofdstedelijke Regering, 'Besluit Tot Bescherming: Jules Lejeunestraat 69'; Fontaine, *Het Glazen Huis*, 14–8.

38
Avenue Jules Lejeune 69, Ukkel, Archief Stedenbouw; '*Maison de Verre*', 2311-115-0, Brussels, Documentation Centre urban.brussels.

39
Fontaine, *Het Glazen Huis*, 7, 37–39.

Fig. 4 Front facade of the Glass House of P.-A. Michel in *Bâtir*, 1936. (© CIVA, Brussels)

Fig. 5 Construction of rear facade.
(© CIVA, Brussels, 'Fonds Michel')

efficient floor plans, rather than through individual houses.[40] But, regardless of his success, it would still take the public at large several more years before they would recognise how modern the ideas of the vanguard actually were, and how well they were suited to contemporary life.[41]

40
Archives d'Architecture Moderne, 'Paul-Amaury Michel', 288.

41
Demey, 'Het Modernisme', 37; Baucher, Architects' houses in Brussels, interview by Linsy Raaffels, 19 October 2017.

Conclusion

The assessed cases represent three exemplary architects' houses that helped lay the path for modernism in Brussels, though in very different ways. First, Victor Bourgeois deployed his personal home in 1925 to encourage the architectural debate on modernism. He even aspired his manifesto-residence to become the headquarters of the Modern Movement in Brussels. He was successful in drawing in an increasing number of affluential artists to join the avant-garde. A couple of years later, even classically trained architects started to see the perks of modernism. For instance, Adrien Blomme finetuned his architectural language into a mixture of art deco and modernism, and by the time the building permit for his modernist residence was declined, he rebelled against the city council with the support of influential contemporaries such as Victor Horta. In only four days' time, they persuaded policymakers of the qualities of modern architectural style and convinced them to set their traditionalist convictions aside, which helped bend public policy towards modernism. Half a decade later, when the modernist mindset had spread among architects and policymakers had embraced the design principles, Paul-Amaury Michel sought to also win over the public at large with his own Glass House, displaying a personal interpretation of modernism that was appreciated by various potential clients. And even though the broader conservative society might have retained their reservations, it was by virtue of the combination of these three different approaches that the path for modernism was paved for the next generation.

Bibliography

Archives d'Architecture Moderne. 'Paul-Amaury Michel'. In *Catalogue Des Collections Des Archives d'Architecture Moderne Tome I*, 288–92. Brussels: AAM éditions, 1986.

Blomme, Adrien. *Travaux d'architecture / Par Adrien Blomme, Architecte, Bruxelles*. Strasbourg: Edari, 1934.

Blomme, Françoise. '1928–1994: l'Histoire Peut-Elle Se Répéter?' S.*C.A.B. Bulletin Mensuel*, no. 2 (1994).

Blomme, Françoise. 'Avenue Des Nations 1928'. In *A La Rencontre d'Adrien Blomme 1878–1940: Sa Vie, Son Oeuvre Racontées Par Françoise Blomme*, 97–107. Brussels: CIVA, 2004.

Brussels, CIVA. 'Fonds Bourgeois', Plans and Photographs.

Brussels, Stadsarchief Brussel. *Propriété de Monsieur Blomme, Angle Avenue Des Nations et Antoine Depage*, TP354.54.

Brusselse Hoofdstedelijke Regering. 'Besluit van de Brusselse Hoofdstedelijke Regering Tot Bescherming Als Monument van Bepaalde Delen van Het Appartementsgebouw Gelegen Franklin Rooseveltlaan 52 En Antoine Depagelaan 1 Te Brussel'. Brussels Hoofdstedelijk Gewest, 27 September 2007.

Brusselse Hoofdstedelijke Regering. 'Besluit van de Brusselse Hoofdstedelijke Regering Tot Bescherming Als Monument van de Totaliteit van Het "Glazen Huis" Gelegen Jules Lejeunestraat 69 Te Ukkel'. Brussels Hoofdstedelijk Gewest, 5 March 1998.

Celis, Jo. 'De Wederopbouw'. *Openbaar Kunstbezit in Vlaanderen*, no. 4 (1987): 139–43.

Culot, Maurice, Eric Hennaut, and Liliane Liessens. 'Adrien Blomme (1878–1940)'. In *Catalogue Des Collections Des Archives d'Architecture Moderne Tome II*, 92–93. Brussels: AAM éditions, 1999.

Culot, Maurice, Eric Hennaut, and Liliane Liessens. 'Victor Bourgeois (1897–1962)'. In *Catalogue Des Collections Des Archives d'Architecture Moderne Tome II*, 100–9. Brussels: AAM éditions, 1999.

Culot, Maurice, and Anne-Marie Pirlot. 'l'Art Déco et l'esprit Moderne'. In *Modernisme Art Deco*, by Directie Monumenten en Landschappen, 9–34. Sprimont: Mardaga, 2004.

De Koninck, Louis Herman. 'Confidences of an Architect of Our Time or How in the "Good Old Days" a "Modern" Architect Matured'. In *L.H. De Koninck, Architecte*, edited by Robert L. Delevoy, 39–50. Brussels: Archives d'Architecture Moderne, 1980.

Demey, Anthony. 'Het Modernisme'. *Openbaar Kunstbezit in Vlaanderen*, no. 2 (1998): 28–38.

Denonne, Xavier-Pierre. *Maison de Verre-Court-Métrage En Images de Synthèse*, 2009, http://www.alicelab.be/tfe/Maison_de_Verre_-_Court-metrage_en_images_de_synthese/203/. Accessed 20 November 2018.

Directie Monumenten & Landschappen, and Anne-Marie Pirlot, eds. *Koekelberg à la Carte*. Brussels: A. Verkruyssen, 2010.

Directie Monumenten en Landschappen. 'Inventaris (Homepage)'. Inventaris van het bouwkundig erfgoed - Brussel, 2019, https://monument.heritage.brussels/. Accessed 16 October 2019.

Documentation Centre of urban.brussels. *Immeuble Personnelle de A. Blomme*, 2043-0779-0.

Documentation Centre of urban.brussels. *'Maison de Verre' P.A. Michel*, 2311-115-0.

Dubois, Marc, and Norbert Poulain. 'Interbellumarchitectuur in Vlaanderen en Brussel: Een Historische Schets'. *Openbaar Kunstbezit in Vlaanderen*, no. 4 (1987): 129–38.

Eggericx, Laure. 'L'Architecture d'Adrien Blomme: Modernisme et Tradition', edited by l'Association des Amis de l'Unesco. *Les Nouvelles Du Patrimoine*, no. 59 (1994): 28–9.

Fontaine, Julien. *Het Glazen Huis: Paul-Amaury Michel*, edited by Maurice Culot. Les Carrés d'architecture 12. Brussels: Archives d'Architecture Moderne, 2004.

Goldfinger, Ernö. 'Hommages de E. Goldfinger'. *La Maison*, no. 12-Victor Bourgeois, 5 ans après (1967): 386.

Hennaut, Eric. 'Het Interbellum in Brussel'. *Erfgoed Brussel*, Additional Issue 2013 (2013): 167–85.

Koekelberg, Archief Stedenbouw. *Avenue Seghers 103*.

Meganck, Leen. 'Volkshuisvesting in Het Interbellum: Van Beluik Tot Tuinwijk Tot Flatgebouw'. *Openbaar Kunstbezit in Vlaanderen*, no. 2 (1998): 39–43.

Municipal Administration of Ukkel. 'Concordantietabel Nummering BBP's'. Stedenbouw Ukkel, http://www.ukkel.be/nl/bestuur/stedenbouw/bbp/concordantietabel-nummering-bbps. Accessed 30 October 2019.

Poulain, Norbert. 'Woord Vooraf'. *Openbaar Kunstbezit in Vlaanderen*, no. 2 (1998): 3.

Raaffels, Linsy. 'Architects' Houses in Brussels. Strategies for Valorisation'. PhD dissertation, Vrije Universiteit Brussel, 2021.

Ukkel, Archief Stedenbouw. *Avenue Jules Lejeune 69*.

Van Loo, Anne. *Repertorium van de Architectuur in België: Van 1830 Tot Heden*. Antwerp: Mercatorfonds, 2003.

Van Loo, Anne, Robert Delevoy, and Maurice Culot. *La Cambre 1929–1978*. Brussels: Archives d'Architecture Moderne, 1979.

After War: The St Lucia homes of Edwin Hayes and Campbell Scott

Andrew Wilson

St Lucia, an inner western suburb in Brisbane bounded on three sides by the Brisbane River, witnessed a proliferation of houses designed by architects immediately after the Second World War due to the area's proximity to the city, ready availability of land, and river views. Many of these houses were designed by architects for themselves. Two of these were designed by Edwin Hayes (1918–1984) and Campbell Scott (1921–2007), partners in Hayes and Scott (1946–1984), one of the first partnerships formed between architects educated locally. The houses declared the shared interest in modern architecture fundamental to the newly formed partnership and brought into sharp focus differences in each partner's architectural ethos.

Housing shortage

The economy of Queensland, the north-eastern state of Australia of which Brisbane is the capital, did not recover from the Great Depression until 1935, a consequence of the drought conditions that prevailed between 1927 and 1930. The population at this time numbered less than a million, with the capital, Brisbane, hitting 305,000 that year.[1] The population of Brisbane increased during the Second World War, due to people moving to the capital to work in essential war industries and the influx of Allied forces, from 330,000 in December 1939 to 393,580 in December 1945, an increase of nearly twenty per cent over the course of the war, double the rate of growth in the five years prior.[2]

In the years after the war, there was an acute housing shortage in Australia. Housing was identified as a priority area during the war, and often discussed in the popular press.[3] Like other architects, Hayes and Scott had to contend with the lack of skills and material shortages in the building industry. 'Manpower provisions' that had been put in place for the war effort meant that building-materials manufacturers found it difficult to find required labour.[4] House designs were subject to plan restrictions imposed in capital cities that allowed a maximum plan area of 1,050 square feet (97.5 square metres) without a permit.[5]

Housing revolution

The proliferation of houses designed by architects in St Lucia was first given coverage in Australia by Nora Cooper – Melbourne journalist and long-time advocate of architect-designed houses – for the journal *Australian Home Beautiful*, in an article 'Queensland Architects Crusade for Better Subtropical Living' **(Fig. 1)**. It announced a 'revolution in domestic housing design' in St Lucia and featured a photograph taken from the interior of a house designed by architect Peter Newell for himself, framed to look out through venetian blinds towards a sunlit terrace,

1 'Population of Brisbane', 41.

2 'Brisbane's Population', 1; 'Population Figures', 2.

3 'Acute Housing Need Demands Action', 2; 'Greater Housing Construction', 4.

4 'Acute Housing Need Demands Action', 2; 'Greater Housing Construction', 4.

5 'Government Homes Restrictions', 3.

Fig. 1 'Better Subtropical Living' by Nora Cooper. (*Australian Home Beautiful*, November 1948)

Wide sliding glass doors open into a cool secluded entrance court. This is how the modern architect sees Queensland's new front door.

Queensland architects crusade for

Better sub-tropical living

by Nora Cooper

IN Brisbane a revolution has started in domestic building design. The well-worn formula of a bungalow on stilts, with rooms darkened by a shuttered verandah, which has done duty for nearly a hundred years, is being blown sky-high by a group of young architects in the suburb of St. Lucia. They are using a vigorous modern technique in their attack on sub-tropical living problems.

St. Lucia lies on the Brisbane River and it is growing up around the new University buildings, now nearly

November, 1948 The Australian HOME BEAUTIFUL 19

capturing the atmosphere of these houses. The 'housing revolution', as Melbourne architect and critic Robin Boyd also described it in a follow-up article written with Newell, singled the high-set EJ Hayes House (1947) out for praise.[6] It was promoted as a subtropical modernist exemplar in the campaign for modern architecture in popular journals and the local press **(Fig. 2)**.[7] Like Newell's house, it featured a 'sun trap' terrace, an American house idea advocated by Sydney architect Walter Bunning (1912–1977) in *Homes in the Sun* (1945), from work undertaken for the Commonwealth Housing Commission formed in 1943. By contrast, the CR Scott House (1949) was never published, but tested ideas for affordable houses built on the ground (traditionally houses in Brisbane were built off the ground on wooden posts, or stumps), house-gardens, and outdoor living, ideas advanced in the publication *Subtropical Housing* (1944) by Austrian architect and town planner Karl Langer (1903–1969), who had arrived in Brisbane in 1939 with his wife and collaborator Gertrude Langer (1908–1984), having fled the *Anschluss*.

6
Cooper, 'Better Sub-Tropical Living'; Boyd and Newell, 'St Lucia', 106, 108.

7
'Modern Line'.

Fig. 2 View towards the terrace of the Hayes House. (Photographer unknown; © Hayes and Scott Collection, Fryer Library, UQFL278, Box 1)

8
'State Advances Corporation', 11.

9
'A Linray Home', 4.

10
'Young Draftsman Helped'; Hitch, 'Meritorious Architecture Award', 113.

11
Langer, *Subtropical Housing*, 4.

12
'Tropical House Designs'; 'Report on Tropical Housing', Sir Raphael Cilento Collection, Fryer Library, University of Queensland, UQFL44, Box 29, item 219.

13
'Modern Architecture in Australia', 35.

Architect-designed houses

The first campaigns for architect-designed houses in local newspapers argued for or against the 'Queensland House', the regional detached 'timber and tin' idiom, constructed in large numbers as worker's cottages in inner-city Brisbane after the First World War, financed by the State Advances Corporation.[8] It was a distinctive type that featured timber construction, platforms elevated off the ground with verandas and corrugated iron roofs. Through the 1930s, architects in Brisbane worked in various styles, with brick promoted as an alternative to timber for house designs. In 1933, one advocate, architect Arthur Bligh (1905–1998), was commissioned by the company Linray Homes, to design brick houses for a speculative suburban estate in the inner-city suburb Newmarket, a precursor to post-war project home developments.[9]

Architectural training and influence

The 1940s were a productive time for architectural culture in Brisbane due in part to the war economy and Brisbane's strategic role in the Pacific. The Lucas House, Hamilton (1941), was a two-storey timber house on a brick plinth with a terracotta tile roof designed by architect and teacher Frederick Bruce Lucas (1898–1973) for himself, which established a new benchmark for house construction in Brisbane.[10] From the mid 1930's, Hayes was articled with the partnership Chambers and Ford, and was credited with the design of the firm's Player's Building (1940), arguably the first commercial or institutional commission in Brisbane to attempt a move beyond style. During the war, Scott assisted Karl Langer with the production of *Subtropical Housing*, a publication that advocated affordable housing, consideration of climate, building on the ground, and treatment of the site as a unified living area.[11] Scott also made a contribution to Tropical House prototypes for the north of the state while working with the State Department of Public Works, which employed architectural principles established by Robert Cummings (1900–1989). Cummings contributed to a 'Report on Tropical Housing' commissioned by the state's Bureau of Industry in 1942.[12] Langer had significant influence on Scott's architectural ethos and designed Jimbour Cottage, Surfers Paradise (1941), a coastal family retreat published in *Architectural Review* in the United Kingdom in 1948 as part of a feature on Australian architecture.[13]

With two other students, Scott contributed to a model prepared for the Town and Home Planning exhibition held at Brisbane City Hall in 1944. It used the suburb St Lucia as the site for a speculative layout of a 'Model Suburb to House 9,000–10,000 People', working in collaboration with Karl Langer and Robert Cummings under the auspices of the Brisbane City Council Community Centres Advisory Committee, which was established to develop planning strategies to deal with projected post-war housing shortages and anticipated problems associated with expected growth. The committee championed the 'Neighbourhood Unit Scheme for Metropolitan Areas', advanced by Clarence Perry (1872–1944) for the New York Regional

Fig. 3 Campbell Scott, 'Your Post-War Home' competition entry. (John Oxley Library, State Library of Queensland)

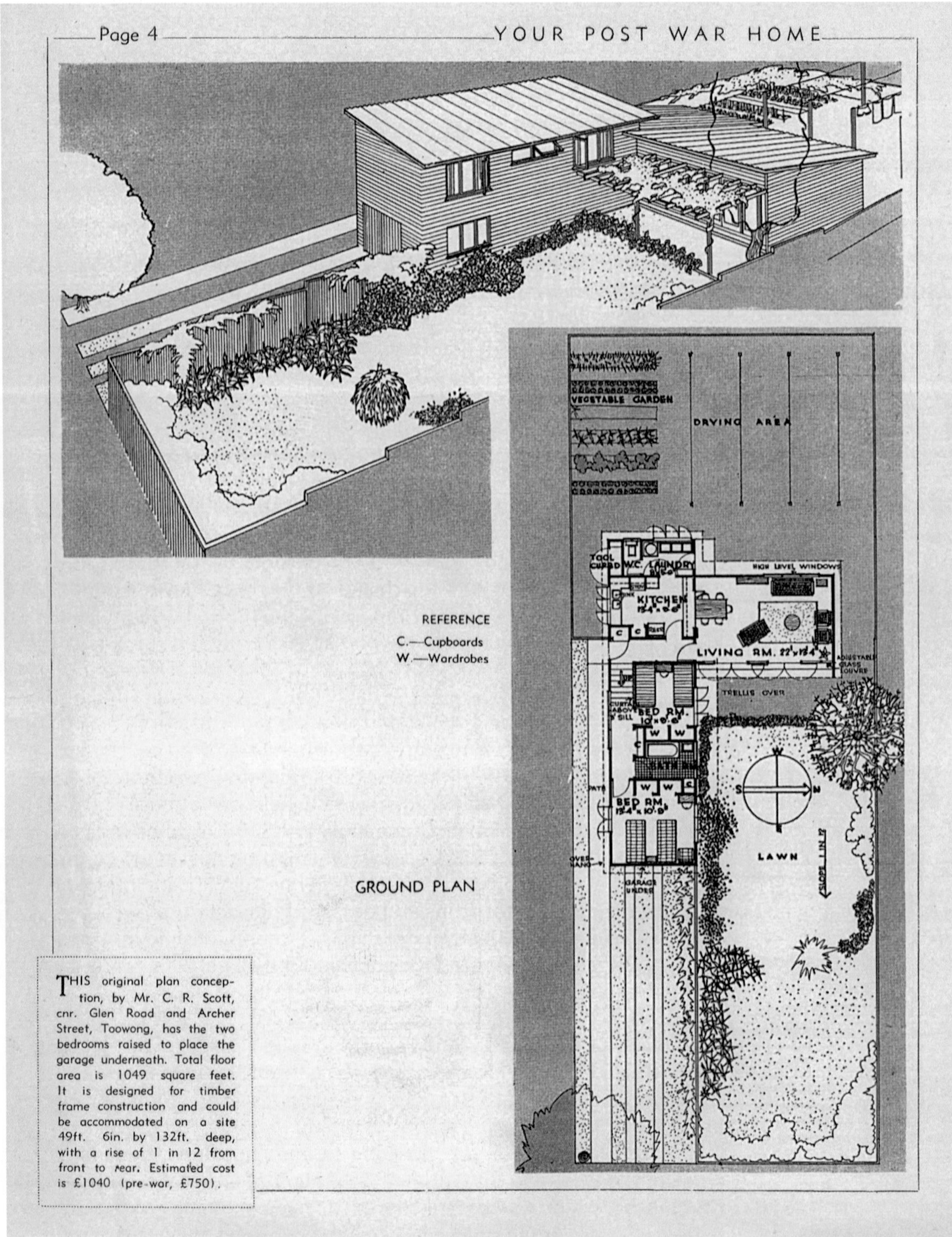

Page 4 YOUR POST WAR HOME

REFERENCE
C.—Cupboards
W.—Wardrobes

GROUND PLAN

THIS original plan conception, by Mr. C. R. Scott, cnr. Glen Road and Archer Street, Toowong, has the two bedrooms raised to place the garage underneath. Total floor area is 1049 square feet. It is designed for timber frame construction and could be accommodated on a site 49ft. 6in. by 132ft. deep, with a rise of 1 in 12 from front to rear. Estimated cost is £1040 (pre-war, £750).

14
'State University. Lecturers Appointed'.

15
'The Courier-Mail Presents Your Post War Home', 4.

16
'Model Design Competition', 4.

17
Kapfinger, 'The Art of Urban Architecture', 91. The Viennese Settlement Movement (öVSK, Austrian Association for Settlements and Small Gardens), which had its origins as a self-help initiative, advocated small affordable houses with productive gardens in settlements, or *Siedlungen*, in Vienna in the early 1920s.

18
Bunning, *Homes in the Sun*, 67; 'Prefabricated, Temporary, Mobile Houses'.

Plan (1929), which had become a popular planning model on the east coast of Australia.

Both Edwin Hayes and Campbell Scott were trained locally, but their three-year age difference resulted in divergent educational experiences. Hayes attended the Brisbane Central Technical College (CTC) and was one of the last students to be articled to an architect. He was taught by Cummings, who had been appointed as part-time instructor in architecture at the CTC from the start of 1934 and then took a position as lecturer at the University of Queensland in 1937.[14] Scott transferred to the University of Queensland after completing three years at the CTC, where he first came into contact with Karl Langer. The partners met working in the office of Chambers and Ford, and collaborated on houses and flats in various styles, such as the English-style Falls Residence, Hamilton (1936), completed when Edwin Hayes was eighteen and in his second year of study. Hayes also worked for Sydney architect Emil Sodersteen (1899–1961) just prior to the outbreak of war. Although both partners were taught by Robert Cummings, who had attended the Architectural Association (AA) in London, Scott's education continued through the course of the war. This allowed productive interactions with his lecturer Karl Langer and art critic Gertrude Langer (1908–1984).

In 1945, Scott's entry to the *Courier-Mail* and *Sunday Mail* Home Design competition was selected for publication in 'The Courier-Mail Presents Your Post-War Home' booklet, one of two affordable two-bedroom timber house proposals chosen for publication **(Fig. 3)**.[15] His contribution, entered in the 950–1,050-square-feet category, was sited on a gently sloping, narrow site in Toowong and brought into play two intersecting skillion roof forms that separated sleeping and living areas, with a garage situated under the bedrooms.[16] It included a productive garden – recalling the agenda of the Viennese Settlement Movement – and a drying area in the back yard; a pergola and enclosed lawn stretching from the living area to the street facilitated outdoor living, ideas that were indebted to Karl Langer's plan concepts in *Subtropical Housing*.[17]

Hayes House

The Hayes House was central to the campaign for the advancement of modern architecture locally. Like the Lucas House, it was set on a plinth with the incorporation of white pilotis along the front, in reference to Le Corbusier (1887–1965). These supported the darker timber-clad upper-storey form of the house proper, inspired by a two-storey prefabricated house with open undercroft and upper level balcony by Swedish architect Erik Friberger (1889–1968), reproduced in Bunning's *Homes in the Sun* (1945) from an article in the *Architects' Journal*.[18] Hovering over the street, the house was oriented to take advantage of oblique views down the St Lucia reach of the Brisbane River.

Colour was an important compositional component of the design. The colours of the house were influenced by Karl Langer's advocacy for the use of colour, demonstrated in his own projects during the war, and adopted by both partners. The exterior was painted 'cocoa brown with white trim and a front door of primrose yellow', and internally, the main bedroom was painted cream with a rose-coloured feature wall.[19] The external face of the fireplace was painted white for dramatic effect. The interior design also featured 'curtains of white nylon'. As journalist Arthur Richards noted, 'One set of them may be drawn around a semicircle to veil the dining-table from the rest of the lounge.'[20]

The brick plinth supported the outdoor sun-trap terrace at the rear, benched into the site. The plan used for publication purposes delimited a site within the plot. Despite the adherence to an L-figure in plan – the dominant plan form at this time – the influence of Marcel Breuer is evident in the sharp separation of sleeping and living areas, provision for outdoor living made possible by the outdoor terrace, and play area for the children adjacent to the nursery.[21] The site was organised into distinct bands, and the plan itself separated living and sleeping spaces on either side of a wet area spine. The clothesline was positioned at one end of a thin lawn terrace at the rear of the site, in close proximity to the laundry. A separate garage, not shown in plan, was built into the retaining wall at street level, a common approach in Brisbane at this time, given the hilly terrain. The house made use of hopper windows, with a fixed picture window adjacent to the dining area, and white painted sliding doors. Plate glass, which had only recently become available locally, allowed full-height glass doors and windows to maximise views down the river.

In April 1948 it was reported in the *Truth* newspaper that the house had been 'much admired by Sunday motorists around St Lucia', and in May it was featured in the *Sunday Mail* as one of two houses that represented a modern approach to houses under the headline 'Twentieth Century Subtropical'.[22] As already noted, it then featured in Nora Cooper's article on Queensland architecture for *Australian Home Beautiful*, 'Queensland Architect's Crusade for Better Sub-tropical Living'. The Hayes House received a mention as a commended house in an article in the *Courier-Mail* on the Royal Australian Institute of Architects (RAIA) Meritorious Architecture Award in January 1949, awarded to the Fulton House, Indooroopilly (1941), from a selection of nominations accepted from the previous decade as a consequence of the war.[23] This was followed in October by an overview of the award process compiled by John Hitch for *Architecture*, the quarterly journal of the RAIA, that compared the winner and the four commended houses, and described the Hayes House as a 'free plan governed by the desire to give the rooms most used [. . .] a good view over the river below the house.'[24] The Hayes House was also used as a precedent by Hayes and Scott for a 'Small Suburban Home' prototype that featured in the *Courier-Mail* in 1950, to represent 'The "New Look" in Queensland Homes'.[25] The brick proposal was modelled on the Hayes House and represented an early attempt to develop a repeatable modern-house type suitable for steep sloping sites in Brisbane. The promotional

19
Cooper, 'Better Sub-Tropical Living'.

20
Richards, 'The New Look'.

21
Breuer, 'Design for Postwar Living'.

22
'The Jottings of a Lady'; 'Modern Line'.

23
'"Dream" Home Wins Award.'

24
Hitch, 'Meritorious Architecture Award'.

25
Richards, 'The New Look'.

Fig. 4 Hayes House, 'Planned for Views'. (*Home Builders Annual*. Brisbane: Penrod Press, 1950)

PLANNED FOR VIEWS

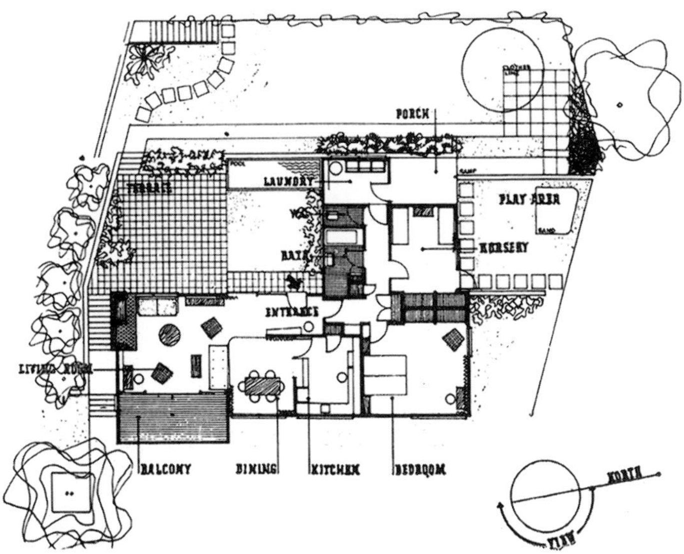

THIS home of Brisbane architect, E. J. Hayes, received favourable mention in the Queensland Architects' Institute award.

The house is built on a sloping site overlooking the Brisbane River, and the plan shows how the main rooms have been given full benefit of the view to the front.

Worthy of note is the grouping of the nursery and play area together with the ramp leading to the house.

The terraced area allows for the enjoyment of outdoor living.

Architects: Hayes and Scott, Brisbane.

Page 75

Fig. 5 Plan, CR Scott House, St Lucia, 1949. (© Hayes and Scott Collection, Fryer Library, UQFL278, Box 1)

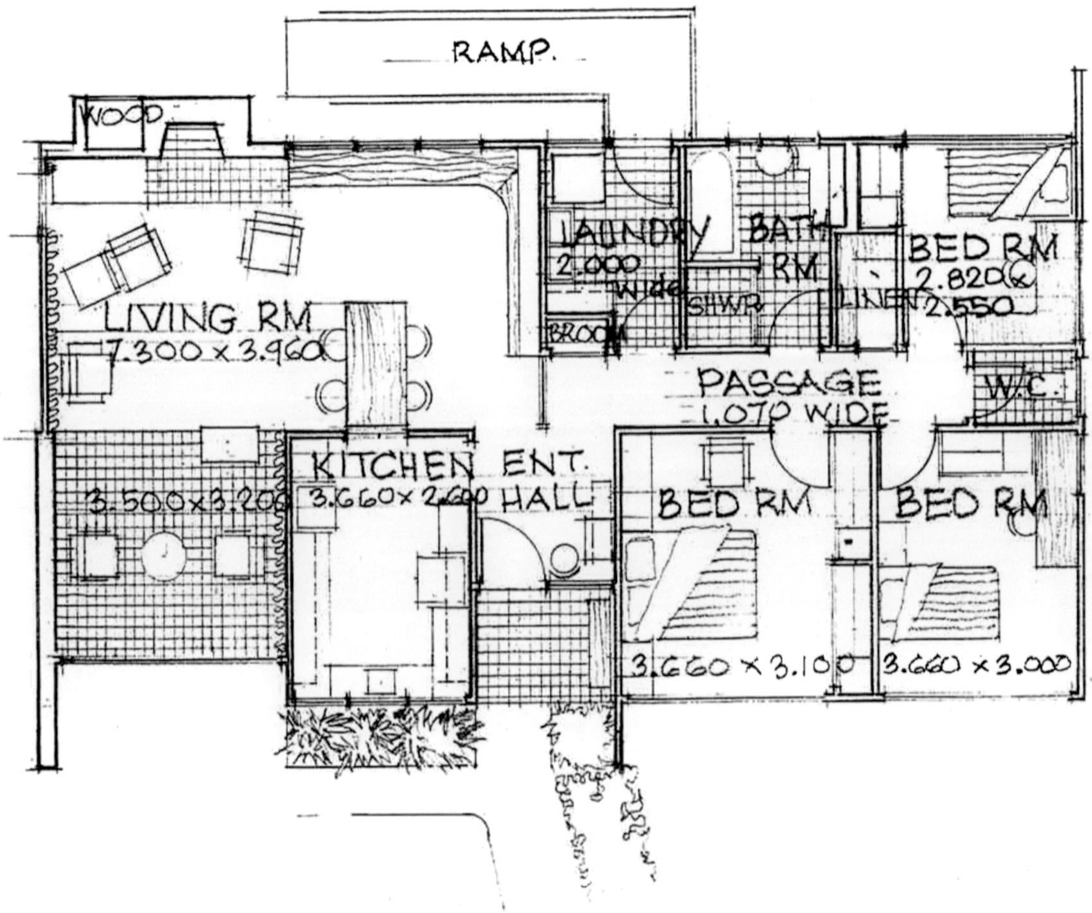

26
Boyd and Newell, 'St Lucia', 114.

27
Boyd and Newell, 'St Lucia', 114.

28
'Pleasant Vistas'; 'Planned for Views'.

29
'House Costs Still Rising'.

30
'House Costs Still Rising'.

31
'In Queensland'.

32
'In Queensland'.

black-and-white render included a substantial fireplace chimney with distinctive cap – like the Hayes House – and a flat roof, with a prominent eave projecting over a balcony hovering over the street.

That same year, a photograph of the Hayes House headed the article published in *Architecture* by Robin Boyd and Peter Newell entitled 'St Lucia, A Housing Revolution', which claimed that the Hayes House, by 'developing the traditional form with concrete piers and partially enclosed ground floor utility sections' recognised characteristics common to the local idiom, the Queensland House, and the influence of Le Corbusier. The article noted, 'With its brise-soleil veranda devices and floating floor, it seemed naturally to point to a Corbu-style development in popular house design', or, put another way, a productive modernist updating of the local idiom.[26]

The Hayes House again featured in a photographic catalogue of fourteen houses compiled as a centrefold of the article, houses that Boyd and Newell argued were 'seeking answers to Brisbane's special building problems without reference to stylistic precedent'.[27] As a means of extending the campaign's reach to a broad audience, the Hayes House was also featured twice in the *Home Builder's Annual*, a publication for architects, builders, and the broader public: first in a piece on contemporary window types, and then for the innovative character displayed in plan **(Fig. 4)**.[28] The terrace of the house was eventually landscaped and extended, and a pergola added to provide shade. In 1966 the house was renovated with an extended living area and a bar and entertainment spaces added below, to meet the needs of a growing family.

CR Scott House

From 1947, housing costs in Brisbane rose sharply, climbing fifteen per cent each year for three years.[29] In May 1948, the average cost of a house in Brisbane was £1,165; in May 1949, the year the CR Scott House was completed, the average cost of a house was £1,404.[30] Unlike the Hayes House, it was not used to promote the practice, and was only referred to once in a publication, in *Architect*, in 1951, as part of a report on recent projects of note in Queensland.[31] In fact the house was hidden from view, set back on a narrow (cheaper) lot in the middle of the St Lucia peninsula that gently fell away from the street. It was a single-storey house benched into its site in a manner that served to accentuate the roof. It was further screened from the street behind a garden trellis positioned at the front boundary. Scott designed the house out of his long-held commitment to the idea of the affordable house, formed out of experiences working with his uncle and local builder Ron Scott, his personal interactions with Karl and Gertrude Langer, and exemplars collected from journals and magazines over the course of his education before, during, and after the war.

The house was precisely calibrated to meet plan area restrictions at 1,025 square feet (95.2 square metres). As noted earlier, no permit was required to build a house in Brisbane under 1,050 square feet (97.5 square metres) at this time.[32] Scott left the area adjacent to the living room as an unenclosed outdoor room. It was built in later as a 120 square foot (11.2 square metre) dining room addition adjacent to the kitchen **(Fig. 5)**.

Like the Hayes House, Scott's house was a timber frame construction with a terracotta tile roof, supported by circular concrete footings. The rectilinear plan relied on a central corridor and was organised around a separation of living and sleeping areas at the entry. A stub wall was extended on the bedroom side, to serve as a privacy screen for the bedrooms. The brick end wall was extended to screen the living area from the morning sun. A timber screen was positioned diagonally opposite in the back garden to screen a child's bedroom from the western sun. The house was raised off the ground at the back due to the slope of the site, and as a consequence a concrete ramp was provided to give access to the clothesline from the laundry. The fireplace chimney was kept economically low, and a timber garage (not shown in plan) was located in the backyard adjacent to the house.

Benching into the site allowed for the establishment of a landscaped outdoor area facing the street, hidden by a low retaining wall. This area immediately in front of the house was paved with bricks pressed into the ground as a terrace and screened with a breeze-block privacy screen on the boundary. The house, again following precedents designed by Karl Langer during the war, was painted a restrained olive green, with a recessed entry and a vermillion red front door. The interior was remarkable for the range of bespoke, built-in blackbean furniture, including a retractable cabinet designed to house a record player.

Conclusion

Both the Hayes House and the CR Scott House stake a claim for the architect's role in the design of houses post-war and reveal modernist precedents encountered over the course of both partners' educations. Compared to the Hayes House, Scott's house was self-effacing, and while both houses demonstrate a negotiated agreement with respect to a palette of elements and materials, and similar approaches to colour elaborated in subsequent house projects, one can detect the importance of Hayes's experience working in Sydney, the design skill developed in projects he contributed to prior to the partnership, and a broader ambition and facility in bringing different modernist precedents together. Scott, on the other hand, reveals his fundamental commitment to house affordability and the important role of collaborations on the publication *Subtropical Housing*, the Town and Home Planning exhibition, and discussions at the home of his teacher Karl Langer and his wife Gertrude during the Second World War. These differences set the trajectory of ideas tested in the work, as productive tensions revealed in prototypes for mass housing, designed alongside larger houses for wealthier clients, in over one hundred houses designed by the partnership Hayes and Scott.

Bibliography

'Acute Housing Need Demands Action'. *Telegraph* (Brisbane), 7 January 1943, 2.

Boyd, Robin, and Peter Newell. 'St Lucia: A Housing Revolution is Taking Place in Brisbane'. *Architecture* 38, no. 3 (July 1950): 106–9, 114.

Breuer, Marcel. 'Design for Postwar Living. Project for a Worker's House'. *California Arts and Architecture,* no. 60 (December 1943): 24–5.

'Brisbane's Population'. *Worker* (Brisbane), 4 October 1943, 1.

Bunning, Walter. *Homes in the Sun: The Past Present and Future of Australian Housing*. Sydney: W.J. Nesbit, 1945.

Cooper, Nora. 'Queensland Architects Crusade for Better Subtropical Living'. *Australian Home Beautiful* 27, no. 11 (November 1948): 19–21, 80.

'The Courier Mail Presents Your Post War Home'. Brisbane: *Courier-Mail* (Brisbane), 1945.

'Disporting in Florida Sunshine, Scheme for a Florida Seaside House: Marcel Breuer, Architect'. *Architectural Record* 99, no. 4 (April 1946): 82–5.

'"Dream" Home Wins Award: Brisbane's Best'. *Courier-Mail* (Brisbane), 26 January 1949, 5.

'Greater Housing Construction'. *Townsville Daily Bulletin*, 13 July 1945, 4.

'Government Homes Restrictions Not Meant to Irritate'. *Telegraph* (Brisbane), 2 November 1945, 3.

Hitch, John. 'Meritorious Architecture Award Queensland Chapter RAIA: House by C.W.T. Fulton'. *Architecture* 37, no. 4 (October 1949): 113.

'House Costs Still Rising'. *Courier-Mail* (Brisbane), 4 August 1949, 5.

'In Queensland'. *Architecture* 39, no. 4 (October 1951): 102–3.

Kapfinger, Otto. 'The Art of Urban Architecture from Below'. In *Josef Frank Against Design The Architect's Anti-Formalist Oeuvre*, edited by Christian Thun-Hohenstein, Hermann Czech, and Sebastian Hackenschmidt, 91. Basel: Birkhäuser, 2016.

Langer, Karl. *Subtropical Housing*. St Lucia, Qld: University of Queensland, 1944.

'A Linray Home'. *Courier-Mail* (Brisbane), Building and Real Estate, 26 January 1934, 4.

'Model Design Competition'. *Courier-Mail* (Brisbane), 16 February 1945, 4.

'Modern Architecture in Australia: A Pictorial Review'. *Architectural Review* 104, no. 619 (July 1948): 20–39.

'The Jottings of a Lady about Town'. *Truth* (Brisbane), 18 April 1948, 22.

Macarthur, John, Deborah Van der Plaat, Janina Gosseye, and Andrew Wilson, eds. *Hot Modernism: Queensland Architecture, 1945–1975*. London: Artifice, 2015.

'Modern Line Taken in These City Homes. It's Called "Twentieth Century Subtropical"'. *Sunday Mail* (Brisbane), 9 May 1948, 5.

'Planned for Views'. *Home Builders Annual*. Brisbane: Penrod Press, 1950, 75.

'Pleasant Vistas with Ample Windows'. *Home Builders Annual*. Brisbane: Penrod Press, 1949, 31–2.

'Population of Brisbane'. *Queenslander* (Brisbane), 28 February 1935.

'Population Figures'. *Queensland Times* (Ipswich), 15 November 1946, 2.

'Prefabricated, Temporary, Mobile Houses'. *Architects' Journal,* no. 13 (July 1944): 22–6, 33–6.

Richards, Arthur. 'The New Look in Queensland Homes'. *Courier-Mail* (Brisbane), 9 June 1950, 2.

'State Advances Corporation'. *Courier-Mail* (Brisbane), 29 September 1934.

'State University. Lecturers Appointed. Education and Architecture'. *Cairns Post*, 9 February 1937, 10.

Thun-Hohenstein, Christian, Hermann Czech, and Sebastian Hackenschmidt, eds. *Josef Frank Against Design The Architect's Anti-Formalist Oeuvre*, Basel: Birkhäuser 2016.

'Tropical House Designs'. *Townsville Daily Bulletin*, 30 September 1944.

Weller, Edward J. A., ed. *Buildings of Queensland*. Brisbane: Jacaranda Press and Royal Australian Institute of Architects, 1959.

Watson, Donald, and Judith McKay. *A Directory of Queensland Architects to 1940*. St Lucia, Qld.: University of Queensland Library, Fryer Memorial Library Occasional Publication no. 5, 1984.

'Young Draftsman Helped Win 1941 Architecture Award'. *Courier-Mail* (Brisbane), 7 October 1941, 4.

A House for Everyone: Architects challenging the post-war myth of 'the house for the nuclear family' in Japan, 1954–2005

Cathelijne Nuijsink

The design of the detached house has been the focus of architectural developments in post-Second World War Japan. An acute housing shortage caused by war damage, a rapid economic recovery, a fast-growing middle class, and a government push for home-ownership created new design opportunities for architects, which (in turn) propelled a lively debate – largely played out in architectural magazines – as to what makes a good house. Focussed on how architects used the design of their own houses to experiment with new images of 'house' and 'family', this text explores two chapters in this decades-long housing debate. It explains how the introduction of a new constitution prompted a critical examination of Japanese lifestyles and the promotion of reforms based on Western ideologies. These reforms resulted in the introduction of a prototypical two-bedroom-with-dining-kitchen floorplan (2DK) in public housing with two divergent effects. While the housing industry extracted from this floorplan the Western ideology of privacy and individuality and made a private room for each family member the rule (*n*LDK), individual architects favoured the observations of real domestic life that lay at the basis of this floorplan. Two architects' own houses will serve as case studies to illustrate architects' continuous efforts to propose houses for alternative lifestyles and families beyond this new, post-war *n*LDK ideal: Kiyoshi Seike's My Home (1954) and Atelier Bow-Wow's House & Atelier Bow-Wow (2005).

Post-war family and the nLDK floor plan

One of the social changes that profoundly affected the design of houses in post-war Japan was the breakdown of the traditional family system. After the country's defeat in the Second World War, the Allied Forces occupied Japan with the goal of transforming it into a peaceful and democratic country. One of their measures was the introduction of a new Japanese constitution which came into effect on 3 May 1947. Contrary to the old constitution that highlighted a patriarchal society, the new constitution promulgated egalitarianism, respect for the individual, and marriage based on the mutual consent of both sexes and the equal rights of husband and wife. By introducing a shift in family ideals and cultural beliefs, the new constitution advocated a Western family ideology based on a couple or nuclear family living separately from the rest of the family as opposed to the pre-war notion of the extended family living under one roof.

A key person in the push for reforms in the domestic setting was architect and Kyoto University professor Uzō Nishiyama (1911–1994).

1
Nishiyama, 'Jūkyokukan no yōtokōsei'.

2
Suzuki, *'51C' kazoku o ireru hako*.

3
Yatsuka, 'Jūtaku kenchiku', 156.

Convinced that scientific study was crucial to defining a prototype for a standardised floorplan, he started researching the houses and daily lives of people in Osaka, Kyoto, and Nagoya. Already during the war, Nishiyama in his treatise 'The Theory of Separate Eating and Sleeping for a Functional Composition of Living Spaces' laid the ground for a new prototype of a standardised floorplan for 'all people'.[1] By observing the lives of ordinary people, Nishiyama concluded that what Japanese houses needed was a better sleeping arrangement in order to create a clear, separate space for eating. At the time, people ate in the tatami-clad room located closest to the kitchen and did not bother to transform this dining room into a sleeping room. After dinner, they collectively moved into the second tatami-clad room where they slept together. A small house could only have comfort if it had order, Nishiyama argued, and this was to be achieved by separating the eating-related area from that of the sleeping quarters. In response to this custom, Nishiyama proposed the revolutionary idea of a hard-floored, eat-in kitchen (Dining-Kitchen, or DK) suitable for Western-style furniture so that each house would have two proper tatami-clad, Japanese-style bedrooms, one for the parents and one for the children.

The rational planning ideas drafted by Nishiyama were applied in the design of public housing after the Second World War. One of the members of a broader committee consisting of architects, scholars, and bureaucrats in charge of the design of a new type of public housing was Tokyo University professor Yasumi Yoshitake. Together with his student Shigebumi Suzuki, Yoshitake drafted a floorplan that, in line with Western standards of 'hygiene, sexual morality, and personal privacy', advocated for parents and children to sleep separately.[2] Introducing two proper bedrooms, one for the couple and one for the children, it aimed at eliminating the Japanese habit of co-sleeping. Yoshitake and Suzuki met these requirements by combining the cooking and eating spaces into an eat-in kitchen. The resulting prototypical floor plan '51C' – first realised in public housing in 1951 – was revolutionary for introducing a new lifestyle for the post-war nuclear family. It not only rearranged Japanese co-sleeping habits to promote the nuclear family ideal through the separation of eating and sleeping spaces but also rationalised the kitchen to streamline housework. Devoid of any hierarchical features related to non-family aspects, such as the entrance space (*genkan*), reception room, and formal guest room (*zashiki*), as well as adding the idea that a couple now slept together in one room rather than a couple co-sleeping with their children, the 51C model demonstrated a new, more egalitarian role for men and women. Simultaneously, it introduced a chair-based way of living on a hard kitchen floor for the standard family — rather than only for the elite — while realising for the first time in Japanese apartments a one-to-one functional division of rooms in the modernist sense.[3]

With increasing wealth and changing domestic needs, the housing industry increasingly emphasised the Western 'qualities' of individuality and privacy within the 2DK model. At first, they added a central living room (2LDK), which separated family gatherings from individual activities in the private rooms. Following new demands, they catered to the wish that each family member obtained their own private room. As a result of this focus on privacy and individuality, the *n*LDK model was born; a national quotation system in which *n* came to indicate the number of rooms, besides the Living and Dining-Kitchen. Although originally designed for collective housing, the *n*LDK model effortlessly found its way into the design of single-family houses. Starting from the 1960s, newly established house manufacturers eagerly catered to the sweeping transition from pre-war renting to post-war home ownership in Japan with the design and construction of prototypical models for prefabricated single-family houses. What was initially introduced as a hygienic and practical solution for a limited floorplan (2DK), the separation of functions came in the years of high economic growth to be exploited as an ideal of privacy and individuality akin to the modern family.

The prefab housing industry took off in the 1960s as a result of the middle-class desire for home ownership, making 'the house for the nuclear family' a reality for many.[4] The prefab housing industry offered varieties of the *n*LDK model, which came to embody a national ideal. Alongside homogeneity in the housing types, the prototypical house layout also promoted one type of family.[5] In the following decades, house-making companies continued to make average models for the average family, despite an ever-growing discrepancy between the ideology of 'the post-war nuclear family' and alternative forms. Awareness of this gap and a growing demand for alternative spatial models led individual architects to resist the tendency to standardise the image of 'house' and 'family'. Initially, these initiatives took the nuclear family as a starting point but did not adhere to the notion of strict privacy between individual members in the family, as visible in Kiyoshi Seike's My Home. Once architects recognised the nuclear family as a failed logic, they started to cater to a diversity of lifestyles beyond the nuclear family, like Atelier Bow-Wow's House & Atelier.

My Home (Seike House) by Kiyoshi Seike (Tokyo, 1954)

An architect who actively questioned 'house' and 'home' right after the Second World War was Kiyoshi Seike (1918–2005). Seike studied under architect Yoshirō Taniguchi (1904–1979) at Tokyo Institute of Technology and, three years after his graduation (in 1943), became a professor-architect at the same institute. During the 1950s, Seike, together with architects like Kiyoshi Ikebe, Makoto Masazawa, and Kenji Hirose, contributed to a golden age of small house designs that embraced the new family ideology of a nuclear family. What made Seike's small houses different from most others was his pioneering efforts to find comfort within a limited floorplan, instead of a focus on new construction methods.

With six single-family houses in his portfolio, Seike in 1954 was given the opportunity to build his own house using a loan from the

4
Both government and businesses supported home ownership. While the government provided housing loans, corporations granted company men lifetime employment and the prospect of climbing the housing ladder with a gradually rising income. Hirayama, 'Reshaping the Housing System', 20–2.

5
Architect Kengo Kuma has argued that the desire to own a house in Japan is paired with the illusion of a house based on *n*LDK. Kuma, '*n*LDK igo', 30.

6
Fujioka, *Architect Kiyoshi Seike: 1918-2005.* In this publication, architecture historian Hiroyasu Fujioka makes an insightful analysis of the work of Kiyoshi Seike, which was also translated into English.

Government Housing and Loan Corporation. First introduced in 1950, the loan was a government incentive to support home ownership through the introduction of long-term, fixed, low-interest mortgages on standard lending conditions. Accelerated by the rapid influx of young people into the cities, the loan contributed significantly to the demographic change from living in an extended family to living in nuclear families. Commonly, the loan gave children the opportunity to leave their parents' houses in search for life in the city. However, Seike and his family used the loan somewhat differently. Because Seike's parents already owned a large site in Tokyo, they were able to assign their son a building plot on their land, allowing the parents to live close to Seike's newly established nuclear family.

Seike took this commission as an opportunity to offset the house's smallness and experiment with the idea of extending the living space into the garden. As the loan restricted the house to a mere fifty square meters, he looked for a way to integrate the interior space with exterior life. Instead of a rationalist focus on how to fit functions in a limited space, he designed a one-story, reinforced-concrete structure measuring ten by five metres, placed it on the northern corner of the twelve-by-thirty-five-metre plot, and created a 'living-garden' on the southern side. A randomly shaped stone pavement covering the twelve-square-meter garden space extended into the interior of the house which, apart from a fifteen-centimetre height difference, seamlessly connected the interior with the exterior. The glazed south side of the building could be opened completely to facilitate contact with the outside spaces. Moveable furniture items, such as a specially designed tatami bench on wheels enhanced the idea that living could seamlessly continue outdoors.

An even more radical design decision was that this house did not adhere to a strict functional division. Convinced that certain aspects of Japanese culture should be preserved in the modern house, Seike refrained from assigning clear functions to rooms as advocated by the 2DK model. Instead, he explored to what extent one can live without any doors at all. Arguing that the Japanese managed 'privacy' through behaviour and did not need solid walls, Seike used only shoji screens, curtains, and moveable furniture items to loosely define his one-room interior space.[6] Much like his earlier house experiments in wood, My Home avoided a traditional understanding of the house as a combination of 'rooms' and was instead planned according to the concept of 'free space'. Other than a single curtain between the kitchen/toilet/living area and the work/sleeping area, My Home was a one-room space inclusive of the outdoors. The decision to not provide husband and wife with a private room contested the need for individuality in private (bed)rooms that was being actively pushed in public housing models at that time.

Modernisation for Seike, however, did not imply a total negation of Western living styles. As much as he experimented with a Japanese mode of living emphasising a relationship with the outdoors,

My Home also tested the Western habit of 'living indoors with shoes on'.[7] During his time in the navy (from 1943 to 1946), Seike had become accustomed to the 'American' habit of not taking off one's shoes inside the house. The idea of living with shoes nicely aligned with his overall concept of 'a house where one can spend time in the outdoors like one is doing indoors'. For a Japanese perception of space, where shoes are habitually taken off upon entry and architectural devices such as a veranda (engawa) protrude from the interior to the exterior, Seike's materialisation of the interior of the house with outdoor materials was highly unusual.

7
Seike, 'The Architect's Home', 9.

8
The original Japanese title of Tsukamoto's doctoral dissertation is 'Gendai nihon no jūtaku sakuhin ni okeru kōsei no jyūji ni kansuru kenkyu'. Conferred on 26 March 1996 at the Faculty of Engineering, Tokyo Institute of Technology.

This proposed new lifestyle, however, failed to live up to its promise. Although Seike's wife and children grew accustomed to the shoes-on way, their visitors ruined the experiment. For some reason, Japanese guests could not behave appropriately when they were still wearing shoes inside the house. After three years of finding cigarette ash on the floor and butts on the carpet, Seike changed direction and treated the house as a continuation with the exterior barefoot. Also, following orders from his wife, he installed a door in front of the toilet. Nevertheless, in spite of the failure of its radical intentions, My Home went down in history as a 'house without doors' that not only solved the problems of a small house in an original way, but also introduced a new paradigm for a family in post-war Japan.

House & Atelier Bow-Wow
by Atelier Bow-Wow (Tokyo, 2005)

Five decades after Seike built My Home, architects in Japan still hesitated to follow the complete Westernisation of the house according to the one-room-for-each principle. House & Atelier Bow-Wow by Atelier Bow-Wow (2005) is an emblematic example of a house that challenges the ongoing individualisation of Japanese society. Recognising that the nuclear family is mere fiction, and that society is made of a diversity of families and lifestyles, Atelier Bow-Wow returns to the idea of using a single space for multiple purposes.

Trained under the supervision of architect Kazunari Sakamoto, Atelier Bow-Wow's partners Yoshihara Tsukamoto (b. 1965) and Momoyo Kaijima (b. 1969) both earned master's degrees in architecture from the Tokyo Institute of Technology and were very much influenced by the theoretical foundation of this department, that is, the compositional studies of the professor-architects and public intellectuals Kiyoshi Seike, Kazuo Shinohara, and Kazunari Sakamoto. In his doctoral thesis, 'Study of the Compositional Rhetoric in Contemporary Japanese Houses', Tsukamoto examined grammatical rules such as composition and division and the articulation of indoor and outdoor spaces of building elements.[8] Over the years, he developed doubts about the classification system of compositional elements, including the standardised floorplan of Japanese housing in the *n*LDK system. In a search for differentiation, he developed a view that the character of a place is not the result

Fig. 1 Situated on a typical flagpole site, the house-cum-atelier explores rather than ignores the banal urban issues of a city like Tokyo. (© Atelier Bow-Wow)

of normative activities but rather a synthesis of multiple explanatory variables.[9]

Following the realisation of the Ani House (1996) and Mini House (1997), Atelier Bow-Wow quickly became affiliated with the production of houses that gave smallness, which commonly had a negative connotation, a positive meaning. Tsukamoto responded to the challenges of the urban fabric with a clever and original use of small urban plots. Atelier Bow-Wow also used the design of the detached house to shape social change. Tsukamoto developed within clients a personal notion of a dwelling, which commercial houses failed to produce. As he explained in an interview:

> My criticism about the quotidian house is that the housing industry treats people as unknowledgeable about living and about houses and what is the appropriate typology for their towns and streets. Perhaps people do know little about it, but it is very hard for people to step out of this system. Atelier Bow-Wow wants to teach people again about housing typologies, what is good and bad about the appearance of houses on the street.[10]

With a dozen small houses realised on banal urban sites, Tsukamoto and Kaijima found the resources to design and build their own inner-city house-cum-office in Tokyo. The site of House & Atelier Bow-Wow is a typical flagpole site; it is surrounded on all sides by other buildings and only connected to the street by a narrow path **(Fig. 1)**. The limited access made it hard to construct, but also relatively cheap to buy. Acknowledging the constraints imposed by the city's urban regulations, the architect couple took the design of their house-cum-office as an opportunity to formulate an alternative to previous generations of post-war houses which they saw as introverted and 'isolated from the reality of life'.[11] According to Atelier Bow-Wow, the house in Japan has become too much of a cloister for the nuclear family in which not only communication among family members but also with neighbours has all but disappeared. House & Atelier Bow-Wow attempts to break this 'spiral of intolerance' that causes domestic violence or elderly people dying alone in their houses by introducing non-family members into the house.

In their proposal, the architects return to a Japanese lifestyle in which office and house are intertwined. Through including the additional function of office space, the staff of their architecture firm inhabit the two lower parts of the five-storey structure. The architects' own house sits, on paper, on the top two levels. The two functions are connected by means of an open staircase. Since the landings vary between three and ten square meters, the structure is not a collection of rooms but conceived as a seven-storey split-level house. Inclining columns and walls devise a 'unique spatial composition' that, according to the architects 'inspires our imagination of use'.[12] Most importantly, the boundary between office spaces and private living spaces is not fixed. Variously sized landings and floors overlap the semi-public space of the office with the privacy of the couple's own house, allowing for a continual shift in the division between the two functions **(Fig. 2)**.

9
Stalder, Atelier Bow-Wow et al. *Atelier Bow-Wow*, 7.

10
Interview with Yoshiharu Tsukamoto, March 2016, Delft, The Netherlands.

11
Tsukamoto, 'hikanyō no supairaru kara mekedasu tameni "boido metabolizumu ni okeru daiyon sedai jūtaku"' (Escaping the Spiral of Intolerance: Fourth-Generation Houses and Void Metabolism), 28.

12
Tsukamoto, Kaijima, and Atelier Bow-Wow, *Bow-Wow from Post Bubble City*, 277.

Fig. 2 Variously sized landings and floors overlap the semi-public space of the office with the privacy of the couple's own private house. (© Atelier Bow-Wow)

Fig. 3 The house-cum-atelier contains large windows that project onto the gap spaces and thereby extend the living area visually into the facade of the neighbours. (© Atelier Bow-Wow)

Fig. 4 The balcony and rooftop space push its residents beyond the confines of a standard nuclear family box. (© Atelier Bow-Wow)

Fig. 5 With the design of a rooftop space and balcony, Atelier Bow-Wow aims to make the house part of a larger network of urban activities. (© Atelier Bow-Wow)

Like My Home, House & Atelier Bow-Wow disapproves of a rationalist division of functions in favour of designing a container for a tangible lifestyle. It also considers the neighbourhood beyond the house's own plot. House, as Kaijima and Tsukamoto envisage it, is not a stand-alone object designed according to the interests of the architect but an animate hub within an entire ecosystem.[13] Objects and people, neighbouring houses, the site, and weather conditions constantly influence the design of this interactive nucleus and, as such, make the house part of a larger network of urban activities. In order to invite people and activities from outside into a way of living that is part of the wider order of the urban environment, the architects took several measures. First, the house invites exterior life to become part of the interior activities. Emblematic of this stance is the design of the large windows in the second-floor living room that, facing the blank wall of the neighbouring building, accept the tightness of the site and consider the wall as an attractive wallpaper for its own space **(Fig. 3)**. Second, the design of a balcony and rooftop space push the living space outside the house's building envelope and, with that, pushes its residents beyond the confines of a standard nuclear family box **(Figs. 4 and 5)**.

13
Atelier Bow-Wow compares the design of a house with a study of an animal's behaviour in its natural habitat and its relationship to other animals in a larger network. Tsukamoto, 'Architectural Behaviorology', 8.

Conclusions

The two case studies discussed in this chapter are representative of architects' attempts to propose a diversity of images of 'house' that do not adhere to the post-war myth of 'a standard house for the standard Japanese family'. Instead, architects introduce a new way of living that, in the case of Seike, countered the aspirations for individuality embedded in the 2LDK nuclear model and, in the case of Atelier Bow-Wow, challenges the straightforward adaptation of a Western model, while proposing a return to a more traditional Japanese lifestyle based on community, but without ignoring contemporary urban conditions. Although My Home and House & Atelier are emblematic in their willingness to break with social and architectural conventions in Japan regarding layout, materialisation, and notions of enclosure, they are merely two examples of architects' efforts to cater to a growing demand for alternative housing options. Seike's and Atelier Bow-Wow's experiments are part of a broader and ongoing discussion among Japanese architects on how the house can be used as a tool to critique 'house' and 'family'. As socioeconomic conditions today have made the newly built single-family home unaffordable, such experiments now take place on the level of collective living.

Acknowledgements: This book chapter developed from the author's PhD dissertation 'What Is A House?: Architects Redesigning The Domestic Sphere In Contemporary Japan, 1995–2011'. University of Pennsylvania, August 2017.

Bibliography

Fujioka, Hiroyasu. *Architect Kiyoshi Seike: 1918–2005*. Tokyo: Shin Kenchikusha, 2006.

Hirayama, Yosuke. 'Reshaping the Housing System: Home Ownership as a Catalyst for Social Transformation'. In *Housing and Social Transition in Japan*, edited by Yosuke Hirayama and Richard Ronald, 20–2. London: Routledge, 2007.

Hirayama, Yosuke and Richard Ronald, eds. *Housing and Social Transition in Japan*. New York, London: Routledge, 2007.

Kitayama, Koh, Yoshiharu Tsukamoto, and Ryue Nishizawa. *Tokyo Metabolizing*. Tokyo: Toto, 2010.

Miyawaki, Mayumi, Riken Yamamoto, Kengo Kuma et al. 'nLDK igo'. *Kenchiku Zasshi*, no. 1371 (April 1995): 24–33.

Nishiyama, Uzō. 'Jūkyō kūkan no yōto kōsei ni okeru shokushin bunriron'. In *Kenchiku gakkairon bunshu* (1942): 149–55.

Seike, Kiyoshi. 'The Architect's Home'. *The Japan Architect* (March 1957): 2–9.

Stalder, Laurent, Atelier Bow-Wow and Eidgenössische Technische Hochschule Zürich. *Atelier Bow-Wow: A Primer*. Cologne: Walther König, 2013.

Suzuki, Shigebumi. *"51C" kazoku o ireru hako no sengo to genzai*. Tokyo: Heibonsha, 2004.

Tsukamoto, Yoshiharu. 'Architectural Behaviorology'. In *Behaviorology* by Yoshiharu Tsukamoto, Momoyo Kaijima, and Atelier Bow-Wow, 8. New York: Rizzoli, 2010.

Tsukamoto, Yoshiharu. 'hikanyo no supairaru kara mekedasu tameni "boido metabolizumu ni okeru daiyon sedai jutaku"'. (Escaping the Spiral of Intolerance: Fourth-Generation Houses and Void Metabolism). In *Tōkyō metaboraijingu* (Tokyo Metabolizing), 28. Tokyo: Toto, 2010.

Tsukamoto, Yoshiharu, Momoyo Kaijima, and Atelier Bow-Wow. *Behaviorology*. New York: Rizzoli, 2010.

Tsukamoto, Yoshiharu, Momoyo Kaijima, and Atelier Bow-Wow. *Bow-Wow from Post Bubble City*. Tokyo: INAX Publishing, 2006.

Yatsuka, Hajime. '"Jūtaku kenchiku" no kigen in XKnowledge'. In *Jūtaku to wa nanika*, 156–9. Tokyo: X-Knowledge, 2013.

Between Theory and Praxis

One aspect that the five chapters gathered in this second section of the book have in common is how they shed light on the productive exchange that can take place between theory and praxis when architects design their own homes. The section also highlights the struggle that architects face when they endeavour to design a home that is an expression of the self *and* a reflection on prevailing architectural idiom *and* a statement regarding current social, political, cultural, and economic conditions.

The first two chapters focus on two architects who are perhaps better known for their work as writers and educators than practitioners. In 'A Self-Portrait in Three Houses', Richard W. Hayes discusses three of the eight homes that Charles W. Moore built for himself in North America between the mid 1960s and the mid 1980s, and in 'Conflicting Imaginaries', Luke Tipene examines Lars Lerup's interventions to the 1920s bungalow that he bought in the early 1980s in Berkeley.

Both Hayes and Tipene's chapters demonstrate how the homes of these architect-educators questioned prevailing orthodoxies in architecture. As one of the leading proponents of postmodernism, Moore embraced colour, ornament, and narrative in the homes that he designed for himself, thus opposing what he considered the self-importance of establishment architectural culture. Tipene explains how Lerup productively used the interventions to his bungalow as a way of challenging the doctrine of 'essentialism', the presupposition in architecture that the meaning of a design is predetermined by its author and translates from the drawing to the building without loss or external contribution.

In both cases, the critique formulated through these domestic designs also extended beyond the bounds of the discipline. In his chapter, Hayes describes how Moore's quirky homes evince his interest in the sensing body and the role of memory in architecture. Moore made his homes into highly personalised spaces charged with meaning; an approach that is diametrically opposed to common practice in real estate, in which all too personal architectural touches are eschewed to ensure the future saleability of the house. Lerup also challenged the commodification of the single-family home, but in an entirely different manner. He was particularly interested in the liminal space that opens up between the drawing and the building, which allows for polemics to take shape. Lerup believed that in this gap between imaginary and physical realities the meaning of architecture remains in flux; it resists ossification into built form, and in doing so, challenges the commodification of the single-family house, as well as its propensity to structure and define social relationships.

On the opposite side of the spectrum from Moore and Lerup when it comes to exchange between theory and praxis in architectural design is British-born Swedish architect Ralph Erskine. Contrary to Moore and Lerup, Erskine was not particularly enamoured with architectural theory or the productive exchange between writing and designing architecture. As Eva Storgaard describes in her chapter 'The Box and the search for a loyal architecture', Erskine lamented the categorisations of architecture following predefined 'isms', and provocatively suggested that academic, theoretical discussions about architecture should be eliminated as these only create distance between the architect and the user. It is then ironic that his own house, a simple box built in Lissma outside Stockholm in the winter of 1941–42 as an experiment in autarkic living, became representative of what *The Architectural Review* called New Empiricism. But perhaps even more ironic is that in denouncing the categorisation of his work under this term – a result of his wariness for architectural 'isms' – Erskine put forward an architectural theory of his own, 'the loyal architecture'.

The two final chapters in this section demonstrate how, in the architect's own home, thinking through architecture and architectural idiom can become entwined with personal narratives and struggles, and result in very singular architectural statements. Rather than building a new house over and over again, as Charles W. Moore did whenever he moved to a different part of the country in connection with a new academic appointment, Günther Domenig chose to refine, revise, and revisit the design for his own house, the Steinhaus, which is situated in the Austrian region of Carinthia, continually for more than two decades, between 1986 and 2008. In his chapter 'Günther Domenig's Rational Centre', Giacomo Pala argues that for Domenig, this house was never meant as just a home, but rather as a venue for hosting events, as well as a didactic space for his students, and a workplace for himself and his office. Nevertheless, even if the house was in this respect a business card in built form, it did not dissuade Domenig from also making it a highly self-reflexive and personal statement – an autobiography of sorts. In examining the different meanings, theories, and interpretations that have been ascribed to Domenig's Steinhaus, Pala's chapter stakes a claim for an architecture that is activist for the way in which it rejects worldly concerns and creates a highly personal universe – architecture through the looking glass.

In comparable fashion, Paola Ardizzola's contribution, which focusses on the house that Bruno Taut built for himself in the late 1930s, demonstrates how personal tribulations can affect architectural belief, and lead to novel architectural expressions. In such cases, the own home offers a very fertile testing ground. After having fled Germany in 1933, Taut first moved to Japan and then Turkey, where he built a house for himself in Istanbul in 1938. Taut's thinking on architecture was affected by this journey, as well as by the sociopolitical shifts that necessitated it – he was persecuted by the Nazis. In her chapter, 'Our Homeland is Where We Build', Ardizzola demonstrates how, as a result of this journey, Taut's architectural thinking and design, which was initially closely associated with functionalism, became infused with tradition and an appreciation of place (the *Heimat*).

Charles W. Moore: A self-portrait in three houses

Richard W. Hayes

Introduction

Charles W. Moore, one of the leading architects of the late twentieth century, explored to an unparalleled degree the architect's own house as a design challenge. Moore acknowledged this when he stated, 'My own houses have given me opportunities, spread over forty years and stretching between the coasts, to test theories about establishing my presence without threatening the comfort or sensibilities of anyone but myself.'[1] In fact, Moore designed a total of eight houses for himself.[2] Viewed as a group, they show both shared themes and changes in the architect's thinking over the course of four decades. In 1954, before entering graduate school at Princeton, Moore designed a spare and simple, wood-framed house in Pebble Beach, California, that was inspired by Japanese and Korean architecture.[3] The pavilion-like home contrasts markedly with the last house Moore designed for himself – his house and studio of 1985 in Austin, Texas, a project that manifests the full flowering of his embrace of vivid colour, complex ornament, decorative clutter, and symbolic narrative.[4] This chapter seeks to clarify how Moore got from the house in Pebble Beach to the house in Austin, from reserved late modernism to exuberant postmodernism **(Fig. 1)**.

Consequently, of Moore's eight houses, I selected three that exemplify important phases of his hybrid career as practitioner and educator. Each of these houses was designed and built when he was a faculty member at one of America's prominent research universities: Yale, the University of California at Los Angeles, and the University of Texas at Austin. Moore taught for a decade at each school and upon moving to each different university town he designed a distinctive house for himself. As experimental works, the houses evince Moore's interest in the sensing body, the role of memory, and contrasts between high art and mass culture. These formal themes embody acts of resistance to prevailing architectural orthodoxies. In particular, the humour and ludic aspects of Moore's designs were intentional strategies to oppose what he considered to be the dour pretentions and self-important bombast of establishment architectural culture.[5] Finally, each residence manifests how Moore conceived of the architect's house as an opportunity to explore in built form the theoretical and historical research he was simultaneously pursuing as a teacher. For Moore, the act of building and the act of writing commingled in a career that was an ongoing process of exploration, experiment, and clarification. To elucidate this interrelationship between buildings and books, I will associate each house with one of the eight books Moore published.

1 Quoted in Keim, *An Architectural Life*, 168.

2 The eight houses are as follows: Pebble Beach, CA, 1954–55; Orinda, CA, 1962; Moore's own unit in Condominium One at the Sea Ranch, Sonoma County, CA, 1965; Elm Street House, New Haven, CT, 1966; a renovated former factory in Essex, CT, 1971; the Moore-Rogger-Hofflander Condominium, Los Angeles, 1975–78; a cabin in Pine Mountain, CA, 1983; and the Moore-Andersson compound in Austin, TX, 1985.

3 Keim, *An Architectural Life*, 165.

4 Keim, *An Architectural Life*, 174–81.

5 Moore, 'The Establishment Invites You', 71–9.

Fig. 1 Overleaf: Interior, Moore-Andersson Compound, Austin, Texas. (Photograph by © Timothy Hursley)

New Haven, Connecticut

In 1965 Moore was named chairman of Yale's Department of Architecture, succeeding Paul Rudolph, and beginning in 1966, he radically transformed an existing Victorian cottage in downtown New Haven as his home.[6] Located on Elm Street just a few blocks from the campus, the wood-sheathed house was originally built in the 1860s.[7] Although a prominent academic, Moore was not wealthy and so when contractors' price proposals exceeded his initial budget of $4,000, Moore took on the role of general contractor himself, assisted by two graduate students, Edward C. Johnson and William Grover.[8] The final cost of the renovation was a little over $11,000.[9] Part of the design challenge Moore set himself was to achieve a strong architectural statement using inexpensive materials such as painted plywood instead of the travertine and pig skin that an establishment architect like Philip Johnson was using at that time.[10]

In addition to building with inexpensive materials, Moore explored the degree to which domestic interiors can sustain a variety of symbolic and historical references. Notable for its visual humour, the design conflated bold spatial cut-outs with pop accoutrements including neon lighting, vivid graphics, and saturated colours **(Fig. 2)**. Such unexpected, if not jarring, combinations were intended to provoke responses from students and faculty who were invited to dinners and social functions.[11]

Moore's intention was to explode the interior so that the inside would contrast radically with the staid and proper outside. As he put it, the house 'needed some kind of inner explosion' so that 'my California-based sense of ample space' would not feel claustrophobic.[12] He inserted three tubes or open vertical volumes, two of which opened the basement to the ground floor and were two stories in height, and the third of which, running from the ground floor up to the attic, was almost three stories tall **(Fig. 3)**. Moore conceived of these light-filled shafts as Brobdingnagian furniture, as 'giant cabinets filled only with space'.[13]

Moore exaggerated both the spatial radicalism of these insertions and amplified the whimsy. He gave the tubes ironic names – Howard, Berengaria, and Ethel – thus incarnating them as campy tutelary deities who guarded his domestic realm.[14] It is relevant to note that during these years, Yale art historian George Hersey, a renaissance scholar, investigated Pythagorean ideas of 'the monster in the building'.[15] Moore's internal monsters – Howard, Berengaria, and Ethel – were imaginary companions for the house's bachelor owner, who created a disorienting yet upbeat ambience through concatenations of complex geometry, intense colours, light introduced from unexpected sources, and witty juxtapositions of pop artifacts. Moore was inspired by Giovanni Battista Piranesi's etchings of imaginary prisons to suggest expansive space from within tight confines. 'It is a latter-day manifestation of a Piranesi complex', he stated, explaining how 'the 18th Century got its kicks by drawing the people too small, and I thought I could get mine

6
Littlejohn, *Architect*, 77.

7
Brown, *New Haven*, 73.

8
Box E21, Project Records, The Charles W. Moore Archives, Alexander Architectural Archives, University of Texas Libraries, University of Texas at Austin.

9
Box E21, Project Records, The Charles W. Moore Archives, Alexander Architectural Archives, University of Texas Libraries, University of Texas at Austin.

10
Littlejohn, *Architect*, 80.

11
Littlejohn, *Architect*, 77.

12
Moore, Allen, and Lyndon, *The Place of Houses*, 61–6.

13
Moore, Allen, and Lyndon, *The Place of Houses*, 62.

14
Moore, Allen, and Lyndon, *The Place of Houses*, 62.

15
Hersey, *Pythagorean Palaces*, 117–21.

Fig. 2 Interior, Charles W. Moore House, New Haven, Connecticut. (© Charles Moore Foundation, Austin, Texas)

Fig. 3 Volumetric diagram, Charles W. Moore House, New Haven, Connecticut as published in *Architecture and Urbanism* 5 (1978). (© Avery Architectural and Fine Arts Library, Columbia University, New York City)

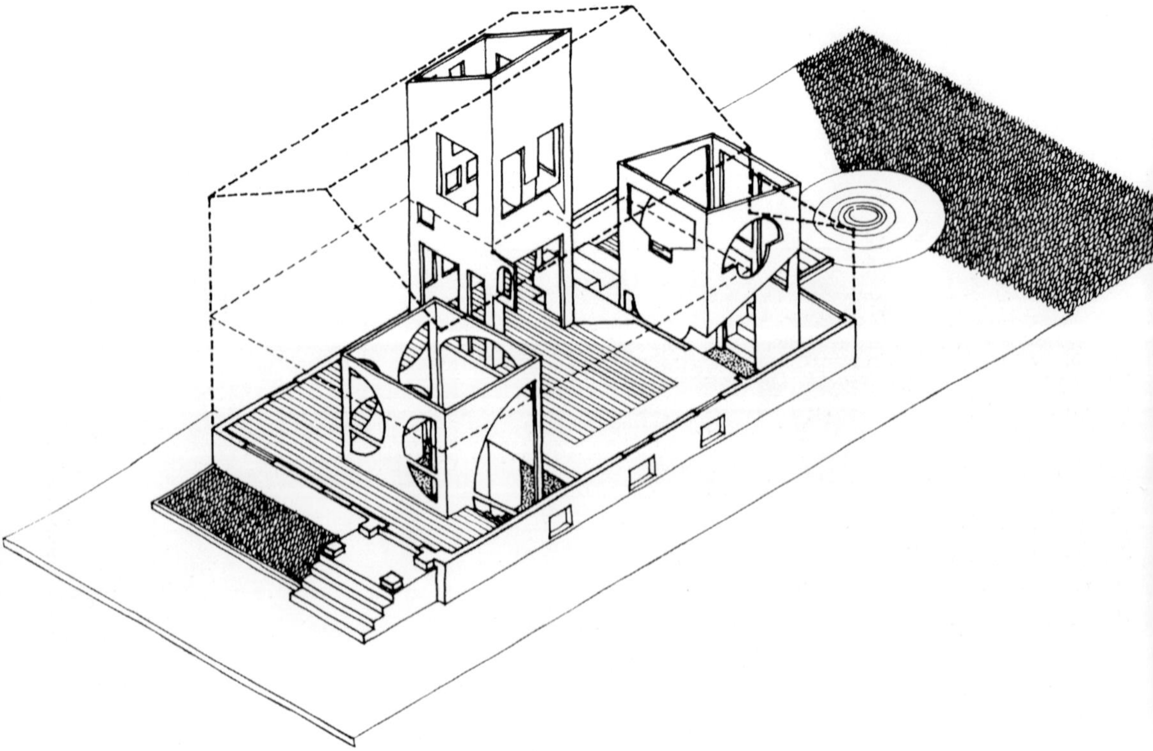

by making the graphics twice too big.'[16] Such an irreverent attitude to history was shared by fellow postmodernists Robert Venturi and Denise Scott Brown, who sought to fuse unlikely combinations of high art and mass culture, such as Lutyens and Route 66, Michelangelo and Las Vegas.[17] Moore, however, would never have agreed with Venturi and Scott Brown's injunction 'Piranesi is too easy', their catchy shorthand for preferring communication and signage, often in big, low spaces, instead of volumetric elaboration.[18] Moore remained interested in complex interior spaces. This is apparent in the following passage on the New Haven house, which shows how he thought simultaneously of the physical and associational facets in architectural design:

> Each of these towers is made of double-layered plywood walls with large geometric cut-outs that play against each other, emphasizing what depth they have and suggesting much more. The shapes of the cut-outs, especially in Howard, are meant to set the mind going to complete the geometric patterns they start, letting it, for instance, extend an arc to a full circle too large to fit in the tiny house. These shafts [. . .] serve to expose and enliven the house, to lead the mind beyond it and thus loose its claustro-

16
'In His Own House', 110–15.

17
Hayes, 'Las Vegas By Way of Rome', 171–2.

18
Venturi, Adams, and Scott Brown, 'Mass Communication on the People Freeway: or, Piranesi is Too Easy', 49–56.

Fig. 4 Interior, Charles W. Moore House, New Haven. (Photograph by © John Hill)

phobic grip. They lead your eyes down into its depths, up into the attic, or along a path of associations towards Rome. Stairs beside each shaft allow the body to follow the mind's eye [. . .] plunging directly from the entry to the lower floor, twisting around Berengaria to the second-floor bedroom, bath, and sauna, or easing down broad steps toward the garden at the rear with its panoramic vista of the adjacent Holiday Inn, then doubling swiftly back beside Ethel to protection of the kitchen.[19]

Moore's passage echoes ideas from Gaston Bachelard's seminal text, *The Poetics of Space*, which he had read at Princeton.[20] But Moore treated Bachelardian concepts with the same explosive force he used in tearing out the interiors of the existing building: he updated Bachelardian phenomenology to make it relevant to the free-wheeling context of the 1960s.

For historian Eve Blau, this house exemplifies Moore's 'own spatial and phenomenological line of investigation' and she notes how the interior was almost entirely given over to circulation and communication. Consequently, the primary effect of the architecture was to 'create the setting for action'.[21] Moore himself observed that the three towers served no practical function and so could not be designated by traditional terms such as loggia, sitting room, or conservatory.[22]

Furthermore, the house had a sybaritic aspect which was in tune with its era. It was featured as a cynosure of the swinging 1960s in an article in *Playboy* Magazine entitled 'New Haven Haven'. The unnamed author gushed, 'Amid Connecticut's early Americana, a bachelor architect fashions a flipped-out domain', and clearly staged photographs featured comely partygoers inside 'Charles Moore's far-out fun house'.[23]

Opposed to the bacchanal spirit of the *Playboy* article, however, is one black-and-white photograph that has survived from the years Moore was in residence – it shows him reading at a table at the lower level of the tower named Howard **(Fig. 4)**. This image reminds us that this is the home of a scholar, the chairman of Yale's Department of Architecture, a prolific author, and one of the few architects of his generation to have earned a doctoral degree. The photograph of Moore calmly reading in the lower level of his residence is a clear statement by the architect on how he wished to be portrayed – and one with resonances in architectural history. The idea of a scholarly figure in the lower depths of an architect's house suggests Sir John Soane's comedic conceit of an imaginary monk, Padre Giovanni, residing in the basement of his house in London.[24] Beginning in around 1824, Soane created a 'monk's suite' in his house in Lincoln's Inn Fields to satirize Gothic antiquarianism.[25] Despite the *Playboy* article, Moore was in fact discreet about his sexual preference; a lifelong bachelor, he was most likely gay and most definitely a scholar-practitioner.[26] In this regard, Soane's figure of the monk as an ironic alter-ego is a pertinent historical reference to the singular figure Moore remained. Indeed, Moore's friend

19
Moore, Allen, and Lyndon, *The Place of Houses*, 62.

20
Keim, *An Architectural Life*, 64. See also Otero-Pailos, *Architecture's Historical Turn*, 105–7.

21
Blau, *Architecture or Revolution*.

22
Littlejohn, *Architect*, 79.

23
'A Playboy Pad', 186. See also Eversole, 'The Chairman's Pad', 8–9.

24
Stroud, *Sir John Soane Architect*, 182.

25
Stroud, *Sir John Soane Architect*, 182.

26
Robert A.M. Stern stated that Playboy models 'were not [Moore's] taste' in '100 Years of Architectural Education at Yale', https://www.youtube.com/watch?v=Bi-U3Hc1dZ4. Accessed 10 March 2020.

27
Quoted in Keim, *An Architectural Life*, 244.

28
Watkin, 'Introduction', 10.

29
Moore, Allen, and Lyndon, *The Place of Houses*, 229–35.

30
Littlejohn, *Architect*, 77–80.

31
'In His Own House', 114.

32
Middleton, 'Soane's Spaces', 26–37.

33
Middleton, 'Soane's Spaces', 62–4.

34
Bloomer and Moore, *Body, Memory and Architecture*.

35
Kent Bloomer. Interview with Richard W. Hayes, 3 October 2020.

36
Littlejohn, *Architect*, 159.

and colleague, landscape architect Lawrence Halprin, once described Moore as 'a hermit straight out of Capability Brown' – an allusion to the fashion for ornamental hermits in British landscape gardens of the eighteenth century.[27]

Devising a Monk's Parlour and Monk's Cell inside the subterranean reaches of his home, Soane was lampooning these ornamental hermits while alluding to his own penchant for tenacious study.[28] Moore was an enthusiast for Soane's unique house-museum well before it became celebrated in postmodern architectural culture.[29] The three vertical light shafts Moore created in his New Haven house bear similarities to Soane's introduction of daylight into his residence, and Moore's conception of walls as thin layers finds a precedent in Soane's spatial layering. Like Soane, Moore tinkered with his house during the years he lived there, making changes over time in so that the house became an ongoing design project.[30] In contrast to Soane, however, Moore occasionally collaborated with his students, allowing them to design some of the light fixtures and graphics.[31] Finally, an important point of connection between the late Georgian architect and the postmodern designer was their use of objects as bearers of architectural meaning. Soane assiduously assembled antiques, sculptures, and architectural fragments – including, as Robin Middleton has noted, 'flotsam and jetsam' – in ingenious, three-dimensional compositions.[32] In a similar vein, Moore placed Mexican curios, folk art baskets, and toys throughout his house as a decorating strategy intended to critique orthodox modernist interiors with their severe prohibitions of clutter. Moore learned from Soane's use of the fragment in architectural space at the same time he undercut the solemnity of the historical allusion by his emphasis on toys and folk objects. Moore wrote:

> Surrounded on all sides by alien turf, the house develops vistas and dimensions internally. Photographs, drawings, statues, favored objects, and especially toys inhabit the recesses of its layered and interweaving walls at every available scale, peopling the house with recollection and fantasy to enlarge the illusion of place.[33]

The themes alluded to in this passage were later developed in the book *Body, Memory and Architecture* by Moore and Yale colleague Kent Bloomer.[34] Although largely written in 1974, the book reflects discussions between Bloomer and Moore that began in the mid-1960s at Yale.[35] Ideas that Bloomer and Moore introduced to their students were concurrent with the themes Moore explored in his house located just a few blocks from the university. In this way, the house stands as witness and emblem of Moore's years at Yale, a wellspring of ideas, locus for collaboration, and *chantier* for experimentation.

Los Angeles, California

Moore left Yale in 1975 and returned to California to accept a teaching position at UCLA.[36] Once again seeking to design a house for himself, he found an available lot on Selby Avenue in West Los Angeles where he constructed a new house as a condominium shared with two other academics. Richard Chylinski was the associate architect.[37] The Los Angeles design expanded on two of the central ideas in *Body, Memory and Architecture*: the first is the moving body as a form of haptic experience, with buildings conceived of as stimuli to movement.[38] The second is the role of domestic collectibles as initiators of memory since they could intimate larger worlds and thus expand the referential power of the interior realm.[39] Writing *Body, Memory and Architecture* may have helped clarify Moore's ideas, and a greater focus characterises the Los Angeles project. Moore's unit in the condominium was effectively a continuous interior staircase, as he described:

> The idea [. . .] was a giant stairway that cascaded through three levels like a waterfall and had several landings. Entering at the lowest level, one caught a long diagonal view up through the entire house [. . .] Movement up the stairs was animated by places to be and put things in, and at the top a nineteenth-century pediment framed the final ascent up the stairway along a great wall of books.[40]

The spatially complex staircase accentuated Moore's interest in haptic experience and the role of the active body **(Fig. 5)**. When architect Robert A. M. Stern first visited the residence, he exclaimed, 'You're trying to squeeze the Spanish Steps into 1,200 square feet!'[41] Stern's reference was apposite: Moore and Bloomer had illustrated the Spanish Steps in *Body, Memory and Architecture*, and Moore had analysed the fountain at the foot of the steps, La Barcaccia, in his Princeton dissertation.[42] Moore's version of the Roman staircase was, however, intensely personal, since it featured a variety of counters and niches holding the architect's collection of toys, Kachina dolls, ceramic tchotchkes, and Mexican curios. Even more than the New Haven house, this domestic interior was a mash-up of Soane and Toys-R-Us; Moore countermanded distinctions between high and low, popular and elite, serious and whimsical, space and object in a manner inspired by Soane but exaggerated for a twentieth-century context. For Moore, 'Soane's poignant exaltation of the almost trivial is peerless, beyond any hope of emulation. For most of the rest of us, a more relaxed assemblage will have to suffice.'[43] Displaying such personal objects was in Moore's view essential to the act of inhabiting, part of his effort to recuperate a humanistic understanding of buildings as places charged with personal meanings for their owners or residents. Moore explained this when he wrote:

> By surrounding yourself with things that have special meaning for you [. . .] you can add dimension to the place you inhabit and to its capacity to nurture your imagination. Whether they are collections of chairs, rocks, engravings, toys or [. . .] books, they gain their power from the act of discrimination and commitment that they represent and from the investment of care and knowledge that attends them.[44]

The upward ascent through the Los Angeles apartment reaches a final wall of books, reminding us that once again this is the dwelling

37 Los Angeles Conservancy, 'Moore-Rogger-Hofflander Condominium Building'.

38 Bloomer and Moore, *Body, Memory and Architecture*, 34–7.

39 Bloomer and Moore, *Body, Memory and Architecture*, 49–52.

40 Quoted in Keim, *An Architectural Life*, 173.

41 Quoted in Kevin Keim, 'Ascending Interest', 99.

42 Moore, *Water and Architecture*, 78.

43 Moore, Allen, and Lyndon, *The Place of Houses*, 233.

44 Moore, Allen, and Lyndon, *The Place of Houses*, 226–9.

Fig. 5 Staircase, Charles W. Moore's Unit in the Moore-Rogger-Hofflander Condominium, Los Angeles, California. (Photograph by © Tim Street-Porter)

Fig. 6 Bookcase, Charles W. Moore's Unit in the Moore-Rogger-Hofflander Condominium, Los Angeles, California. (Photograph by © Tim Street-Porter)

Fig. 7 Exterior, Moore-Andersson Compound, Austin, Texas. (Photograph by © Timothy Hursley)

of a writer and educator **(Fig. 6)**. But in contrast to New Haven, where descent to the basement was emphasised, the Los Angeles apartment is an elevated eyrie that maximises Californian sunlight and features views out across the city. In this regard, it is fitting that is where Moore composed a book about Los Angeles, his 1984 volume *The City Observed*.[45] In his forward to the book, critic Paul Goldberger stated, 'There is no one who understands Los Angeles better than Charles Moore.'[46] Los Angeles is home to several important examples of architects' own houses, including two Moore discusses in his book: Charles and Ray Eames's house of 1947–49 in Pacific Palisades (also known as Case Study House No. 8) and Frank Gehry's house of 1978 in Santa Monica.[47] Moore's house stands as a median between these two. From the Eames's, Moore learned how modern interiors could be humanised by eclectic arrangements of decorative objects.[48] As Kathryn B. Hiesinger observed, the Eames's use of plants, Mexican masks, paper flowers, and toys 'expressed a mood of wit and informality then largely unknown in modern interiors.'[49] Evincing influence on a younger architect, Moore's artful ability to introduce daylight from unexpected sources inspired Gehry, a detail Reyner Banham pointed out in 1971.[50]

45
Moore, Becker, and Campbell, *The City Observed: Los Angeles*.

46
Moore, Becker, and Campbell, *The City Observed: Los Angeles*, xi.

47
Moore, Becker, and Campbell, *The City Observed: Los Angeles*, 118–9 (Eames); 161–2 (Gehry).

48
Keim, 'Ascending Interest,' 103.

49
Hiesinger, 'Decorative Art and Interiors', 188.

50
Banham, *Los Angeles*, 198.

51
Quoted in Keim, *An Architectural Life*, 174–5.

Austin, Texas

The last project I will consider is the house and studio Moore designed in 1985 in Austin, Texas. He accepted a chaired professorship at the University of Texas at Austin and with Arthur Andersson, a young architect educated in Kansas and London, transformed a nondescript existing structure, located about two and a half miles southwest of the university, into a compound consisting of a generous-sized house for Moore, a smaller house for Andersson, and two design studios. Moore took advantage of the region's temperate climate by centring the compound around an outdoor stairway leading to a pool, placing the sensing body at the centre of domestic design **(Fig. 7)**. Besides privileging sensory experience, Moore combined vernacular sheds with references to Italian baroque architecture to demonstrate how the everyday landscape and high-art architecture could be synthesised. In plan, a large ellipse differentiates public rooms from private spaces in each of the two houses. The ellipse also helped to fashion a geode inside what appears from the outside to be ordinary, shed-roofed structures appropriate to Texas's Hill Country.

In 1985 Moore turned sixty, so, apart from the entry steps, the residence does not have the dramatic changes in level of his earlier houses. Moore was aware of his aging body and need for creature comforts; he ruefully described how 'a notion that often got left behind in most of [my earlier houses] was comfort; either I left out the heat or had too little space or made places too vertical. So, when I moved to Austin, I took it upon myself to make a place considerably more comfortable and inhabitable than its predecessors.'[51]

More than in any of his previous designs, this house features objects collected over a lifetime spent travelling, researching, and

52
Keim, *An Architectural Life*, 168.

53
Keim, *An Architectural Life*, 181.

54
Pettit and Pettit, *Mexican Folk Toys*, 128–31.

55
Pettit and Pettit, *Mexican Folk Toys*, 132.

56
Wagner, 'Capas de México', unpublished paper presented at the Charles Moore Foundation, 9 November 2018.

57
Lyndon and Moore, *Chambers for a Memory Palace*.

58
Lyndon and Moore, *Chambers for a Memory Palace*, xii.

visiting buildings **(Fig. 1)**. As Kevin Keim wrote, this house is 'the fullest expression of his quest to completely integrate his spatial motives and his now overflowing collections.'[52] Moore stated:

> [E]verywhere are shelves jammed with books and objects – awash with objects – and that is its most notable characteristic. All of these things, souvenirs of places I have visited, miniature cities and scenes with staggering leaps of scale, all of these things contribute by default to the ornament of my house. It's important to note that ornamentation, far from being frivolous, is one of the very serious and urgent needs of an architecture that people can have any connection to.[53]

Exemplifying Moore's efforts to connect people and buildings, the Austin compound attests to the architect's own house as a bulwark of personal memory and heightened physical experience. The Austin house displays a greater number of Mexican folk-art pieces than the New Haven house and fewer emblems of American pop culture. The interiors thus reveal Moore's deepening fascination with the combined Amerindian and Spanish traditions in Mexican culture. Moore regularly took his Texas students on field trips to Mexico, scheduled to coincide with the Day of the Dead festival – a religious and social holiday that lasts from the first to the second of November.[54] Conjoining pagan and Christian beliefs, the Día de los Muertos is celebrated by the creation of temporary altars decorated with flowers and candles, piled up with the favourite food of the deceased. Craftsmen make special toys, masks, and miniature representations of skulls and skeletons for children.[55] The festival held a particular resonance for Moore, whose own birthday was 31 October.[56] The many examples of Mexican folk art in Moore's Austin house suggest intimations of mortality underneath the humour.

Consequently, the house may be associated with Moore's final book, *Chambers for a Memory Palace*, cowritten with Donlyn Lyndon and published after Moore's death in 1993.[57] The authors state that their interest is in the 'mental intermingling of people, places, and ideas'. No better example exists than the house in Austin for the authors' challenge that buildings become places that foster memory. They wrote:

> Places are spaces that you can remember, that you can care about and make a part of your life. Much of what is built now is too tepid to be remembered. The spaces with which we are surrounded are so seldom memorable that they mean little to us. We think it should be otherwise, that the world should be filled with places so vivid and distinct that they carry significance.[58]

In creating vivid and distinctive houses for himself, Moore left a lasting self-portrait of an incisive architectural mind at work – and at play. Erudite yet jesting, Moore conceived of the architect's house as stronghold for the mind and springboard for action.

Bibliography

Banham, Reyner. *Los Angeles: The Architecture of Four Ecologies*. London: Allen Lane The Penguin Press, 1971.

Blau, Eve. *Architecture or Revolution: Charles Moore and Yale in the Late 1960s*. New Haven: Yale School of Architecture, 2001.

Bloomer, Kent, and Charles W. Moore. *Body, Memory and Architecture*. New Haven: Yale University Press, 1977.

Brown, Elizabeth Mills. *New Haven: A Guide to Architecture and Urban Design*. New Haven: Yale University Press, 1976.

Eversole, Britt. 'The Chairman's Pad, or the Problem of the Playboy Architect'. *Archis* 33 (2012): 8–9.

Hayes, Richard W. 'Las Vegas By Way of Rome: The Eternal City and American Postmodernism'. In *Rome, Postmodern Narratives of a Cityscape*, edited by Dom Holdaway and Filippo Trentin, 171–2. London: Pickering & Chatto, 2013.

Hersey, George. *Pythagorean Palaces: Magic and Architecture in the Italian Renaissance*. Ithaca: Cornell University Press, 1976.

Hiesinger, Kathryn B. 'Decorative Art and Interiors'. In *Out of the Ordinary: Robert Venturi, Denise Scott Brown and Associates*, edited by David B. Brownlee, David G. Delong, and Kathryn B. Hiesinger, 182–243. Philadelphia: Philadelphia Museum of Art, 2001.

'In His Own House, a Noted Architect Plays Games'. *House & Garden* 133 (January 1968): 110–15.

Keim, Kevin. *An Architectural Life: Memoirs & Memories of Charles W. Moore*. Boston: Little, Brown and Company, 1996.

Keim, Kevin. 'Ascending Interest'. *Modern Magazine* (30 January 2018): 99–103.

Littlejohn, David. *Architect: The Life and Work of Charles W. Moore*. New York: Holt, Rinehart and Winston, 1984.

Los Angeles Conservancy, 'Moore-Rogger-Hofflander Condominium Building'. https://www.laconservancy.org/locations/moore-rogger-hofflander-condominium-building. Accessed 27 September 2020.

Lyndon, Donlyn, and Charles Moore. *Chambers for a Memory Palace*. Cambridge, MA: MIT Press, 1994.

Middleton, Robin. 'Soane's Spaces and the Matter of Fragmentation'. In *Sir John Soane Architect: Master of Space and Light*, edited by Margaret Richardson and MaryAnne Stevens, 26–37. London: Royal Academy of Arts, 1999.

Moore, Charles, Gerald Allen, and Donlyn Lyndon, *The Place of Houses*. New York: Holt, Rinehart and Winston, 1974.

Moore, Charles, Peter Becker, and Regula Campbell. *The City Observed: Los Angeles. A Guide to its Architecture and Landscapes*. New York: Random House, 1984.

Moore, Charles W. 'The Establishment Invites You to Join in Hushed and Sumptuous Appreciation of the Several Arts, Lincoln Center, Most Evenings: Arrival Optional but Difficult', *Architectural Forum* 125 (September 1966): 71–9.

Moore, Charles W. 'Water and Architecture'. PhD dissertation, Princeton University, 1957.

Pettit, Florence H., and Robert M. Pettit. *Mexican Folk Toys: Festival Decorations and Ritual Objects*. New York: Hastings House, 1978.

'A Playboy Pad: Amid Connecticut's Early Americana, a Bachelor Architect Fashions a Flipped-out Domain', *Playboy* (October 1969): 126–9; 186.

Otero-Pailos, Jorge. *Architecture's Historical Turn: Phenomenology and the Rise of the Postmodern*. Minneapolis: University of Minnesota Press, 2010.

Stern, Robert. '100 Years of Architectural Education at Yale'. Lecture at J. Irwin Miller Symposium, 'Learning/Doing/Thinking: Educating Architects in the 21st Century', 15 April 2016. https://www.youtube.com/watch?v=Bi-U3Hc1dZ4. Accessed 10 March 2020.

Stroud, Dorothy. *Sir John Soane Architect*. London: de la mare, 1996.

The Charles W. Moore Archives, Alexander Architectural Archives, University of Texas Libraries, University of Texas at Austin.

Venturi, Robert, Bruce Adams, and Denise Scott Brown, 'Mass Communication on the People Freeway: or, Piranesi is Too Easy'. *Perspecta* 12 (1969): 49–56.

Wagner, Logan. 'Capas de México', unpublished paper presented at the Charles Moore Foundation, 9 November 2018.

Watkin, David. 'Introduction'. In *Sir John Soane: The Royal Academy Lectures*, 1–23. New York: Cambridge University Press, 1999.

Conflicting Imaginaries: Lars Lerup's aesthetic dissonance in the plan composition of his suburban bungalow

Luke Tipene

In December 1981, when he returned to the University of California, Berkeley after running the internship programme with Peter Eisenman at the Institute of Architecture and Urban Studies in New York, Lars Lerup purchased a small bungalow on Stannage Avenue in the suburban neighbourhood of Westbrae, Berkeley.[1] He sold the bungalow seven years later in August 1988;[2] during his brief stay, he completed a series of interventions that he summarised in a short essay for the design journal *Places* in 1987 **(Fig. 1)**.

Since being built in 1923, this Craftsman-style bungalow had undergone 'low-maintenance home improvement', which had obscured the clarity of its original design.[3] In the essay, Lerup outlines his interventions, designed to 'retrieve an aspect of the myth that may lie manifested in a certain architectonic specificity that mass production had covered up.'[4] He summarises these interventions in three thematic categories: the 'Erasure' of materials and architectural elements such as walls and rooms; the 'Overlay' of new structural and material elements; and the 'Addition' of what he describes as a 'new dimension to the house that would bring it into the here and now.'[5] In spite of the seemingly straightforward approach to renovating this common building type, Lerup's explanation of the project in drawings and text describes a highly idiosyncratic idea of resistance in design. By using his own home to challenge the role of the architectural drawing and its relationship to the building, Lerup's bungalow acts as an incubator for his theoretical opposition to the commodification of architecture via the consumption of lifestyle images of the American dream.

Lerup begins by describing the process of 'Erasure' as a dissection of the building, that, 'like an exploratory surgeon', removes architectonic features.[6] Continuing with emphatic language, he describes the creation of an unscaled 'avenue of "open" space' that 'lobotomized' the 'typical narrative' of the bungalow plan with 'unspecified use.'[7] Referring specifically to the disruption of social patterns embedded in bungalow planning, Lerup uses the additional terms of 'freeway' and 'void' to introduce his concept of the 'tripartite plan'.[8] This characteristic planning principle of Lerup's architectural projects refers to the production of an undefined open space between two zones of functional space. Lerup describes these two functional zones in the bungalow as 'cul-de-sacs' comprising 'sitting areas, an inglenook, a service nook, and a new kitchen', and a 'file of rooms', including bedrooms, bathroom, and studio **(Fig. 2)**.[9]

1
City of Berkeley, *Grant Deed* (Alameda, 1981), 81203378; Kutnicki, 'Appendix A. 27 Accounts: Lawrence Kutnicki', 254.

2
City of Berkeley, *Grant Deed* (Alameda, 1988), 88218437.

3
Lerup, 'Craftsman Bungalow', 56.

4
Lerup, 'Craftsman Bungalow', 56.

5
Lerup, 'Craftsman Bungalow', 60.

6
Lerup, 'Craftsman Bungalow', 56.

7
Lerup, 'Craftsman Bungalow', 56.

8
Lerup, 'Craftsman Bungalow', 56.

9
Lerup, 'Craftsman Bungalow', 56.

Fig. 1 Lars Lerup, *1234*, 1985. (© Lars Lerup)

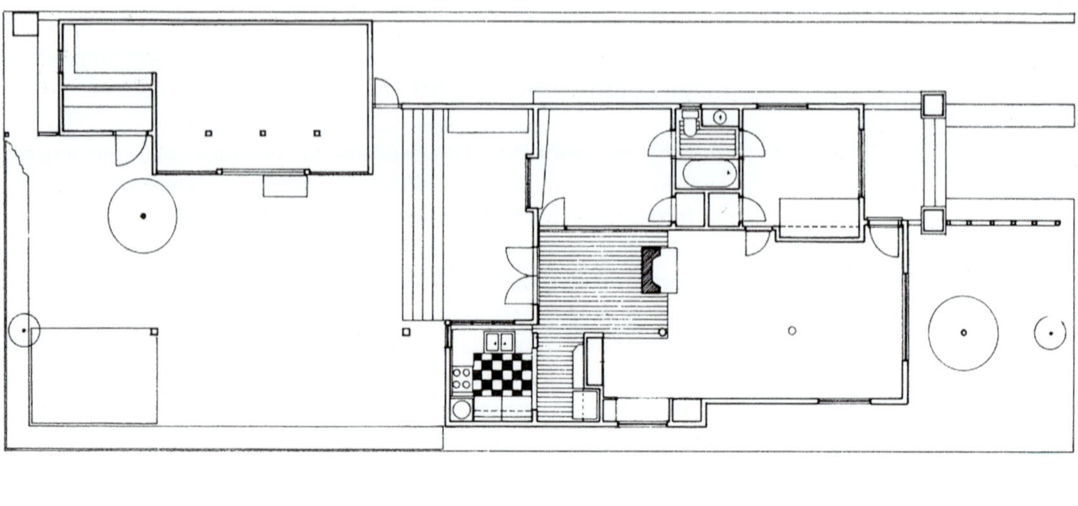

Fig. 2 Bungalow plan with interventions. From: Lars Lerup, 'In the Shadow of a Craftsman Bungalow: Erasure, Overlay, and Addition', *Places* 3, no. 4 (1987): 55. (© Lars Lerup and The MIT Press. The image creator has indicated the original is no longer available.)

10
Lerup, 'Craftsman Bungalow', 56.

11
Lerup, 'Craftsman Bungalow', 56–7. Additional (unlabelled) columns appear in the project documentation. Their placement is not in line with the columns discussed here and they do not contradict later findings regarding column alignment.

12
Evans, 'Translations', 181.

Moving on to the process of 'Overlay', Lerup drops his emphatic language and describes an excess of new eclectic elements with only a few common terms. Specifically, the terms 'column' and 'wall' are used to inclusively describe a range of new, irregular architectonic elements that demarcate the new 'avenue of "open" space' in the bungalow.[10] Lerup's columns extend the length of the property, with little reference to the bungalow's planning. Each is made from a different and unexpected material that challenges their common classification. They include a rosebush near the front fence, a 'red plum tree' in the front yard, a 'column footprint' from a column since removed in the middle of the new sitting area, a 'freshly cut trunk of red madrone' between the fireplace and the new inglenook, and a 'redwood pilaster' that frames the entrance to the new kitchen. This line of columns continues into the backyard of the property, with one black and one white freestanding column and a second rosebush near the rear fence.[11]

When considering the bungalow's new spatial experience represented in the published photographs, it is evident that without Lerup's written description, it is very difficult to identify these irregular column elements. Further, only when viewing these elements in a highly selective oblique projection drawing does their linear arrangement and, by extension, their parallel alignment to the wall elements of the design, become apparent. Lerup uses this parallel placement of the columns and walls to introduce his idea of the architectural promenade as the framing device for the open space of unspecified use that runs through the centre of the tripartite plan. However, the spatial experience of the tripartite plan – Lerup's characteristic planning principle – is only intelligible when viewed as an abstract graphic representation in the oblique drawing **(Fig. 3)**.

Whether using emphatic language or a few common terms, there is an incongruity between Lerup's description of the composition of the space and its physical reality. In his drawings, this incongruity manifests as misperception; highly relevant spatial knowledge of the columns and walls described in the oblique drawing is not immediately apparent in the inhabitants' experience of the building. This misperception demonstrates a gap between the spatial knowledge of the design accessible in the drawings compared to that in the building, and suggests a resistance in Lerup's design process to the commonly held idea of the 'doctrine of essentialism'.[12] This idea of essentialism was identified and criticised by the architectural historian Robin Evans in his seminal essay on drawing one year earlier in 1986. The term describes the presupposition in architectural design that the spatial knowledge of a design, and by extension its meaning, is predetermined by the designer and translates through the drawing to the building without loss or external contribution. Lerup, like Evans, appears to challenge the validity of this claim.

Phyllis Lambert, the founding director of the Canadian Centre for Architecture, recognises the opening of this gap between drawing and building as a key methodological driver to Lerup's work. In her foreword to Lerup's book of drawing projects, *Planned Assaults*,

Fig. 3 Comparison between photographs of the interventions and a highly selective oblique projection of the interior. From: Lars Lerup, 'In the Shadow of a Craftsman Bungalow: Erasure, Overlay, and Addition', *Places* 3, no. 4 (1987): 57–8. (© Lars Lerup, Fatimah Namdar and The MIT Press. The image creators have indicated the originals are no longer available.)

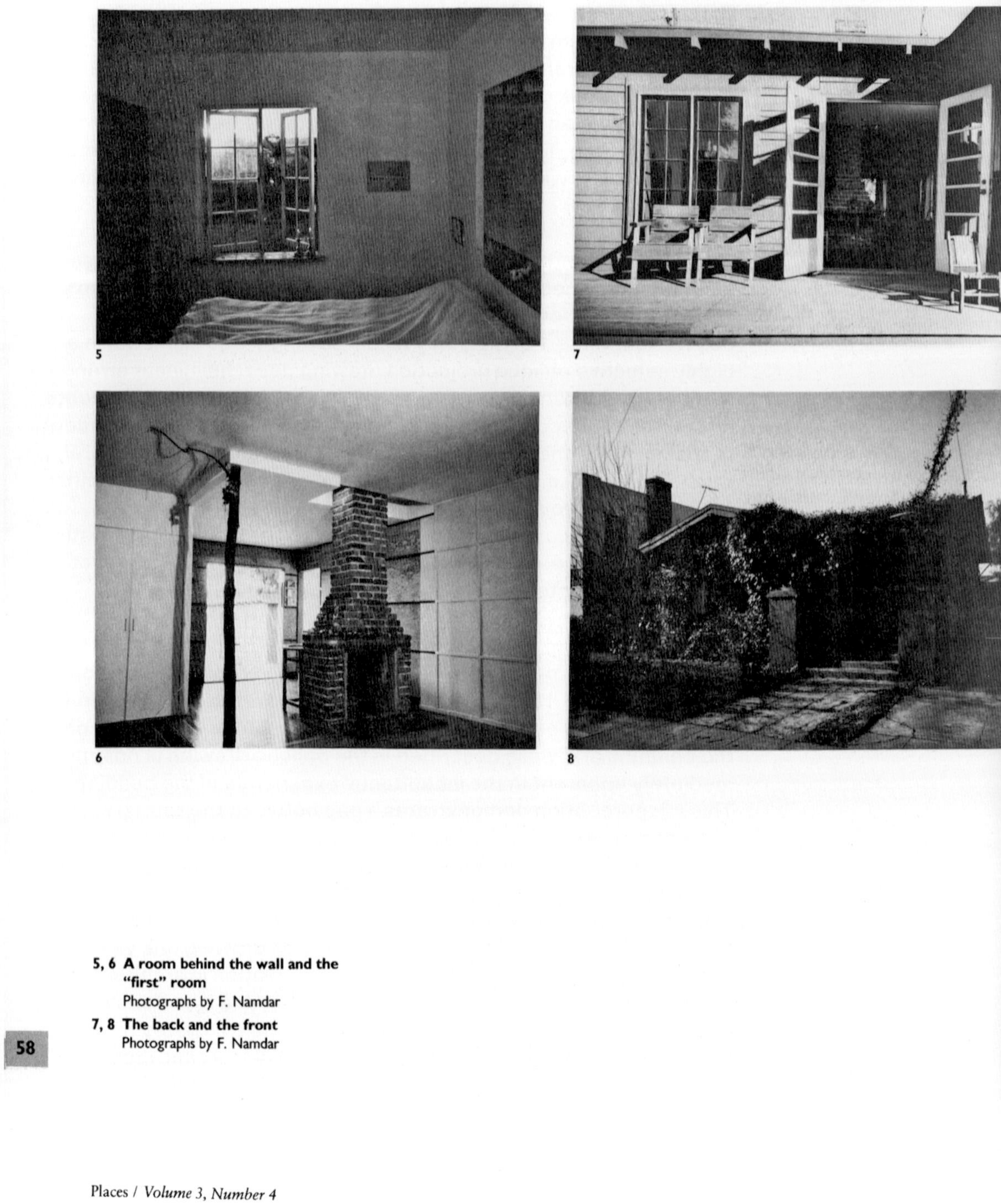

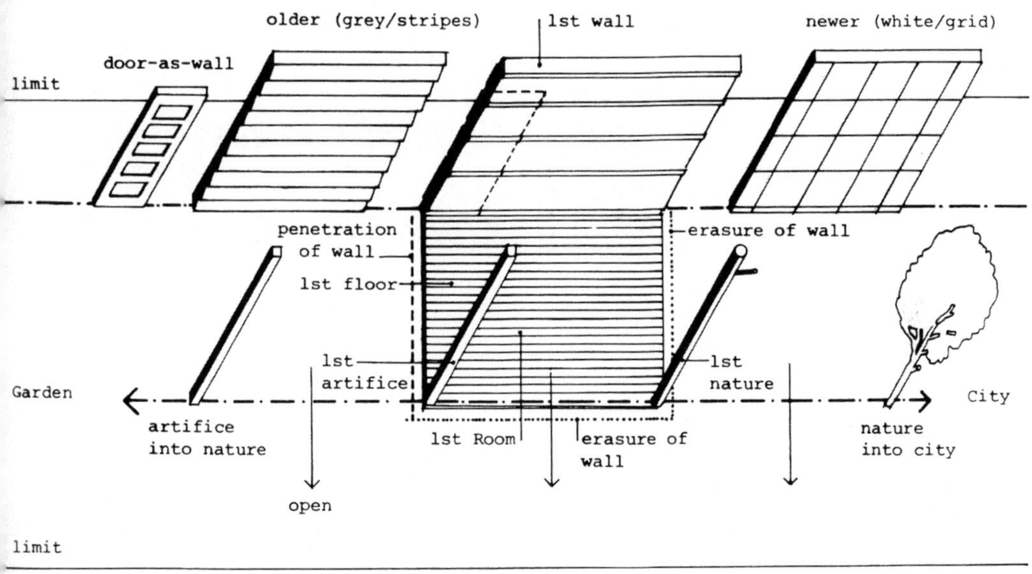

Array of Columns: rose, white column, three white columns, black column, redwood pilaster, madrone column, column footprint, red plum tree, rose.

Array of Walls/Doors: grey door-as-wall, grey siding with gridded door, wide white grid, grey grid, varnished plywood with redwood stripes, white grid, white built grid.

4 "Principles for making (instant) history"
Figure 4 by Lars Lerup.

also published in 1987, Lambert describes Lerup's architectural work as occupying a space between plausible design ideas and strictly imaginary propositions.[13] She states that the strength of work in this liminal zone is polemical, as it resists normative contributions of built work to 'social and economic structures which engender the single-family house.'[14] By occupying a space in-between the imaginative and the buildable, Lerup's work affords a 'critical view of society and demand for revision.'[15]

Lerup himself addresses this in-between state when discussing the tripartite plan, referred to as a 'tripartite figure' in *Planned Assaults*.[16] In the section entitled 'Transformation', Lerup describes the 'in-between' as a type of technology that 'transforms the elements of building into architecture.'[17] The term 'building' refers to the book's subject, the single-family house, which Lerup describes as a syntactic structure of hegemonic social relations that order and discipline the family via their consumption of lifestyle images of the American dream.[18] He defines architecture as a form of resistance to this hegemonic commodification of daily life – one that challenges static house images by animating them with a 'transformational principle'.[19] Lerup does not explain how this transformational principle of architecture animates the house, although he does describe the process spatially by again referring to the architectural promenade. Citing Le Corbusier's *promenade architecturale*, among other references, Lerup describes the transformational principle as a void introduced into an existing structure, framed 'between column and wall'.[20] This reflects the exact architectonic arrangement of the bungalow interventions and equates the void of the tripartite plan in the bungalow to the principle of transformation in these drawing projects.

In order to unpack how Lerup's transformational principle resists the commodification of the house through the tripartite plan, it is necessary to consider the relationship in the plan's composition between the open space of the architectural promenade and the house's hegemonic structuring of social relations. A historical example addressing the emergence of this relationship is discussed by Richard Etlin in his book on the origins of social symbolism in built form during the Enlightenment.

Citing the eighteenth-century French *hôtel* as the 'birth of the "modern dwelling"', Etlin describes its key characteristic – *la distribution* – as the arrangement of rooms based on specific use inseparable from new, clearly articulated social systems that defined those uses.[21] The major architectonic feature that organised these rooms was their arrangement *en enfilade*, the planning principle that he describes as the foundation for Le Corbusier's 'architectural promenade' two centuries later.[22] The enfilade was not a new feature of housing, although its relationship to the socially determined distribution of rooms was.[23] It was an open space that was required to 'pass through the length of the building, and it could not be interrupted.'[24]

13 Lambert, 'Foreword', 9.

14 Lambert, 'Foreword', 9.

15 Lambert, 'Foreword', 9.

16 Lerup, *Planned Assaults*, 17.

17 Lerup, *Planned Assaults*, 17.

18 Lerup, *Planned Assaults*, 15–6.

19 Lerup, *Planned Assaults*, 17.

20 Lerup, *Planned Assaults*, 17.

21 Etlin, *Symbolic Space*, 124, 127, 129–30.

22 Etlin, *Symbolic Space*, 126, 130–1.

23 Etlin, *Symbolic Space*, 129–31.

24 Etlin, *Symbolic Space*, 130–1.

25
Evans, 'Figures', 71, 75.

26
Evans, 'Figures', 73–4; Etlin, *Symbolic Space*, 131.

27
Evans, 'Figures', 73–4.

28
Evans, 'Figures', 74.

29
Evans, 'Figures', 74.

30
Lerup, *Planned Assaults*, 15.

31
Lerup, *Planned Assaults*, 15.

32
Lerup, *Planned Assaults*, 16.

33
Lerup, *Planned Assaults*, 16.

34
Lerup, *Planned Assaults*, 16–7.

An earlier example of a similar condition from seventeenth-century English housing was discussed by Evans in his 1978 essay, 'Figures, Doors and Passages'. Like Etlin, Evans argues that the same impulse towards privacy led to the detachment of common spaces for closed rooms and established the corridor – like the enfilade – as the ordering feature for compartmentalised houses.[25] In spite of the influence of both the enfilade and the corridor on orienting the social hegemony of rooms, neither directly contributed to these systems of classification. Rather, Etlin and Evans demonstrate that the motivation for the linear arrangement of these features was compositional and not social. Each was introduced in a manner that contradicted the social and functional planning principles of rooms, in order to maintain the aesthetic pleasure of their appearance as single-point perspectives when viewed along their length.[26] Evans suggests that this division of purpose between corridors and rooms fundamentally split the perception of the house into 'two quite separate realities': one that integrated spaces for 'the sake of beauty', and the other that separated spaces 'for convenience'.[27] He identifies this split as an 'unbridgeable gap dividing commodity from delight, utility from beauty, and function from form'.[28] The result was a diatomic conceptualisation of domestic architecture into two unrelated and conflicting imaginaries or 'standards of judgement' in plan composition: one of social symbolism and the other of compositional aesthetics.[29]

Returning to the bungalow, this conflict between imaginaries is comparable to Lerup's conflict between the open space of the architectural promenade and the house's hegemonic structuring of social relations. When describing the spaces of the single-family house, Lerup addresses the classification of rooms according to specified use. He states that the plan is an 'assembly of parts': 'rooms, doors, and windows are only stepping stones, objects of use'.[30] Referring to the arrangement of these functional elements in terms of social symbolism, Lerup states, '[t]he plan is the primary territory of the American Dream. Its syntax of spatial relationships is the master plan of the same dream.'[31] Lerup goes on to suggest that the authorship of social symbolism in the plan has passed on from the architect to the atomised inhabitants of late capitalism. He describes how inhabitants subjugate themselves by internalising 'the rhetoric of politics and law, ceremonial oratory, the language of everyday life, and various texts and image assemblies, from the codes of behaviour whose sources range from advice columns and advertising to television soap operas.'[32] For Lerup, modern social symbolism has ossified the bungalow plan as a commodity of static social images.

Lerup's resistance to these images is through a return to architecture, now in the role of emancipator rather than indoctrinator. Lerup states, '[i]n order to bring architecture back onto centre stage, the flow of the narrative must be stopped or delayed.'[33] Resonating with the aesthetic drivers of the enfilade and the corridor, Lerup suggests the 'insertion' of architecture into the plan is 'confined to the principles of architectural composition.'[34] The compositional element he refers to is the tripartite figure, which emulates the enfilade and corridor as a linear 'freeway', 'avenue', or 'promenade', articulating a 'void' of 'unspecified use' that interrupts the social symbolism of the plan.[35] It is unclear whether Lerup was aware of the historical precedent for his actions, although his insertion of a linear open space in the bungalow exhumed the 'unbridgeable gap' between the conflicting imaginaries in space planning discussed by Evans and Etlin.[36] By re-establishing the original architectonic condition that split our 'standards of judgement' for domestic space, Lerup's work enables an aesthetic feature of his design to participate in a conflict of values, by resisting the economic imperatives of social classification in functional planning.[37]

In order to understand how Lerup's aesthetic feature of the tripartite figure can resist social classification in functional planning, it is useful to consider its difference to the aesthetic principles of the enfilade. This is best exemplified by the differences implied in Lerup's and Etlin's references to Le Corbusier's *promenade architecturale*. As discussed, Etlin describes the 'architectural promenade' as resulting from the enfilade's principles.[38] He implies an authority of vision, as it is only through a highly choreographed instance of vision that the single-point perspective of the enfilade appears. In order to experience the aesthetic pleasure of the enfilade, one must stand still, with one eye closed, without visual interruption along its length; this process effectively reduces the spatial experience of the interior to a static image.

This reduction of the interior to images is exactly what Lerup attempts to resist in the bungalow. In spite of his inclusion of the promenade feature, Lerup denies the opportunity to experientially recognise the linear and parallel arrangements of columns and walls that define it.[39] Accordingly, this interrupts the suggestion of a single-point perspective, the dominance of views, and the authority of vision implied in Etlin's description of the enfilade. Instead, Lerup uses the term *promenade* to specifically refer to the irregular collection of architectonic elements, including his columns and walls, which frame the void at the centre of the tripartite plan. This interruption of perspectival dominance and emphasis on irregular elements suggests that the experience of his interior is a highly stimulating – although non-perspectival – visual field, described by Lerup as 'a kind of Sweets Catalog of architectural elements'.[40] Further, when referring specifically to Le Corbusier's *promenade architecturale* in *Planned Assaults*, Lerup describes it as a foundation for the 'transformational principle' of the tripartite figure, suggesting its principles 'animate' the static image of the single-family house.[41] This dynamic understanding of *promenade architecturale* grounds Lerup's description of '*mouvement architectural*, in which architecture itself rather than the pedestrian "moves" through a building.'[42] Unlike the enfilade's aesthetic based on maintaining static images, Lerup's aesthetic is based on maintaining dynamic movement in the tripartite plan through the deliberate agitation of irregular visual stimuli.

35
Lerup, 'Craftsman Bungalow', 56.

36
Evans, 'Figures', 74.

37
Evans, 'Figures', 74.

38
Etlin, *Symbolic Space*, 126.

39
Lerup, 'Craftsman Bungalow', 56.

40
Lerup, 'Craftsman Bungalow', 56.

41
Lerup, *Planned Assaults*, 17.

42
Lerup, *Planned Assaults*, 17.

43
Evans, 'Translations', 181–2.

44
Lerup, 'Craftsman Bungalow', 60–1.

45
Lerup, 'Craftsman Bungalow', 60–1.

46
Lerup, 'Craftsman Bungalow', 61.

47
Lerup, 'Craftsman Bungalow', 60–1.

48
Lerup, 'Craftsman Bungalow', 60–1.

Returning to the question of how Lerup's transformational principle resists the commodification of the house, we can now describe his interventions as disrupting the socially classified, static images of functional planning with unspecified open space that uses irregular visual stimuli to agitate dynamic movement. Importantly, this description does not explain what kind of movement is maintained by the open space of the tripartite plan. In his description of *mouvement architectural*, Lerup implies that architecture is the dynamic object that moves – a concept that is as impossible experientially as the graphic abstraction of single-point perspective. Movement, like perspective, is a compositional aesthetic device that exists as spatial knowledge in drawing. As such, it is necessary to consider what effect this feature of drawing composition has on the building when considering the type of movement Lerup's project maintains.

Returning momentarily to Evans's critique of the doctrine of essentialism, his key criticism is that there are major differences between architecture's two mediums of drawing and building, and like the perceptual irregularities of Lerup's columns discussed earlier, significant spatial knowledge of a design cannot translate without loss, or perhaps not at all, between these two mediums.[43] With this in mind, the question of how movement in Lerup's drawings affects the spatial experience of the building must be complexified by recognising the uncertainty of translation between the two. Lerup's third and final thematic category of intervention in the bungalow, 'Addition', appears to address this complexity by producing architectural ideas in drawing that are impossible to experience spatially in the building, although they maintain a unique effect on our understanding of the bungalow.[44]

Lerup describes the process of 'Addition' as creating an extra structure made from 'the mythical "shadow" cast by the bungalow', and abstract variations of three interior elements, including the 'madrone trunk' column, the fireplace, and one of the rooms.[45] In spite of his claim that this addition may later be constructed, it never was, and remained unbuilt until he sold the bungalow in 1988.[46] Importantly, beyond Lerup's claim, his descriptions of the addition suggest that he never intended for it to be buildable. He describes it as an immaterial other to the rest of the design, rather than a form, a 'dream-house' process of 'transformation' conceptualised from occupying the bungalow's 'fleshy shadow'.[47] The three abstracted interior elements are also referred to as transformations and not literal objects, conceptualised as 'platonic' object-types of architectonic elements.[48]

When describing this immaterial addition in drawing, it is not *what* is drawn, but *how* Lerup draws it that is most evident of his intention for it to remain imaginary. Unlike the other drawings of this project, which use architectural conventions to convey the design, the addition is depicted as highly unconventional spatial scenes. These scenes interrupt orthographic and perspectival logic by appropriating elements from both, use multiple scales, and depict interior/exterior features simultaneously. Furniture, wall, and

Fig. 4 Spatial 'scene' depicting the addition. From: Lars Lerup, 'In the Shadow of a Craftsman Bungalow: Erasure, Overlay, and Addition', *Places* 3, no. 4 (1987): 60. (© Lars Lerup and The MIT Press. The image creator has indicated the original is no longer available.)

Fig. 5 Lars Lerup, *1234 House – 3*, 1985. (© Lars Lerup)

shadow lines are used interchangeably, creating optical illusions. Rough rendering introduces Lerup's hand in the line work and produces contrasting shadows that obscure implied depth **(Fig. 4)**.

In the doctrine of essentialism, the illusion of equivalence between drawing and building is maintained by the idea of shared properties across both mediums. One foundational property discussed by Evans is orthographic dimensionality, which he suggests is accepted unequivocally across the real and imaginary paradigms of architecture, creating the illusion of 'preservation in which both meaning and likeness are transported from idea through drawing to building with minimum loss.'[49] Lerup's drawings of the addition contain several deliberate attempts to disrupt this logic of orthographic dimensionality, exacerbating the gap between plausible design ideas and strictly imaginary propositions. Lerup describes this as introducing a 'new dimension to the house that would bring it into the here and now', implying that his intention is to cultivate an autonomous 'presence' with the addition of non-orthographic spatial knowledge between drawing and building.[50] Beneath Evans's discussion of the illusion of universal orthographic dimensionality is a distrust of the idea of uniform space as a ubiquitous medium grounding architectural thought and action. He describes this unquestioned assumption of uniform space as architecture's great 'suspension of critical disbelief'.[51] Lerup's new dimension appears to resist this suspension by critically embracing disbelief.

If Lerup's drawings are not constructed on the belief in a systematic, measurable concept of uniform space, what spatial knowledge about movement do they offer the interventions in the bungalow? One conjecture can be made when we learn that Lerup's published drawings of the addition were reproduced from paintings he created during the bungalow renovation **(Fig. 5)**. In these paintings, Lerup's use of colour evokes a close comparison to the artwork of the metaphysical painter Giorgio De Chirico, whom Lerup cites as the direct influence on the addition to the bungalow and a key inspiration for *Planned Assaults*.[52] In his analysis of De Chirico's use of shadows, colonnades, and distorted perspectives in the painting *Mystery and Melancholy of a street* (1914), Victor Stoichiță writes poignantly of De Chirico's compositional effects: '[t]he unenlightened viewer is unable to differentiate between anticipation and impending danger. All he can do is picture himself crossing the empty space between the two agents.'[53] Stoichiță is specifically referring to the empty space created between the two figures in the painting, one which is visible, the other only implied by a shadow. The compositional arrangement of the empty space between these narrative agents establishes a tension of anticipation, which, Stoichiță suggests, compels the viewer to occupy the image with their own exploration of its meaning. This provocative use of empty space resonates with Lerup's spatial void in the bungalow and suggests his potential intention for its occupation.

Lerup's painterly exploration of his imaginary addition negates its ability to be measurable with the use of orthographic dimensional-

49
Evans, 'Translations', 181.

50
Lerup, 'Craftsman Bungalow', 60.

51
Evans, 'Translations', 154, 181–3.

52
Lerup, 'Craftsman Bungalow', 60; Lerup, *Planned Assaults*, 100.

53
Stoichiță, *Short History of the Shadow*, 145.

54
Evans, 'Translations', 160.

55
Stoichiță, *Short History of the Shadow*, 145.

ity, although this does not diminish the paintings' effect to a 'formulated experience' without relevance to the building.[54] Rather, like De Chirico's art, where '[t]he questions raised by the painting are more important than the facts', Lerup's works attempt to agitate questions of the space's meaning, irrespective of empirical proof.[55] The result are autonomous painterly and graphic artefacts that relate to the bungalow as generative devices, to extend the scope of the building's value beyond the limits of essentialism.

Viewing the paintings and photographs of the bungalow simultaneously infers the kind of movement Lerup intends his interventions to maintain. It is not the physical architecture that moves, but the meaning of the architecture in the gap between its imaginary and physical realities. This new dimension is the site of Lerup's own process of creative invention that resists the commodification of architecture by resisting the ossification of its meaning in built form. This finding would be unremarkable if Lerup did not aim to maintain this uncertainty as the purpose of his design. As a test site for constructing an architecture that remains unfinished, Lerup's bungalow resists the occupation of static, commodified social values in the plan's composition by literally intervening with empty space. Surrounded by columns and walls of irregular materials, the tension of this emptiness in the tripartite plan compels resistance through the continuous agitation of its unexplainable meaning.

Bibliography

City of Berkeley. Grant Deed. 81-203378. Alameda, CA: City of Berkeley, 1981.

City of Berkeley. Grant Deed. 88-218437. Alameda, CA: City of Berkeley, 1988.

Etlin, Richard. *Symbolic Space: French Enlightenment Architecture and its Legacy*. Chicago, IL: The University of Chicago Press, 1994.

Evans, Robin. 'Figures, Doors and Passages'. In *Translations from Drawing to Building and Other Essays*, by Robin Evans, 54–91. Cambridge, MA: The MIT Press, 1997.

Evans, Robin. 'Translations from Drawing to Building'. In *Translations from Drawing to Building and Other Essays*, by Robin Evans, 152–93. Cambridge, MA: The MIT Press, 1997.

Kutnicki, Lawrence. 'Appendix A. 27 Accounts: Lawrence Kutnicki'. In *IAUS: The Institute for Architecture and Urban Studies: An Insider's Memoir*, by Suzanne Frank, 253–6. Bloomington, IN: AuthorHouse, 2011.

Lambert, Phyllis. 'Foreword'. In *Planned Assaults: The Nofamily House, Love/House, Texas Zero*, by Lars Lerup, 9–12. Montréal: Centre Canadien d'Architecture/Canadian Centre for Architecture; Cambridge, MA: distributed by The MIT Press, 1987.

Lerup, Lars. *Planned Assaults: The Nofamily House, Love/House, Texas Zero*. Montréal: Centre Canadien d'Architecture/Canadian Centre for Architecture; Cambridge, MA: distributed by The MIT Press, 1987.

Lerup, Lars. 'In the Shadow of a Craftsman Bungalow: Erasure, Overlay, and Addition'. In *Places* 3, no. 4 (1987): 55–61.

Stoichiță, Victor. *A Short History of the Shadow*. London: Reaktion Books, 1997.

Ralph Erskine: The Box and the search for a loyal architecture

Eva Storgaard

In 1947, the English periodical *The Architectural Review* launched a new movement in architecture: New Empiricism. The characteristics of this movement, which was said to initially have been a Swedish phenomenon, were discussed in the article 'The New Empiricism: Sweden's Latest Style' and exemplified by means of a number of architectural projects.[1] One of these projects was designed by British immigrant Ralph Erskine (1914–2005). The young architect had caught the attention of *The Architectural Review* with his own dwelling, popularly known as The Box – or in Swedish, *Lådan*. According to the article, The Box represented the reorientation that post-war architectural culture needed and epitomised the notion of New Empiricism. It was one of the very first projects that Erskine realised in Sweden. The design, construction, and inhabitation of The Box informed Erskine's architectural thinking and his (later) attention to participatory design processes and contextual design. The Box explored how everyday activism in the domestic sphere, manifested in the innovative capacities of ordinary dwelling practices, could inform an alternative for a universalist design approach to housing. Erskine's attention to everyday activism offered him the opportunity to develop a modern architecture that was not rooted in abstract theoretical points of departure, but rather in the contingencies of everyday life.

Sweden: hotspot for an architecture of democracy and welfare

Ralph Erskine studied architecture and urban design in the mid 1930s in London. Stimulated by vivid discussions during his study at the Regent Street Polytechnic[2] – including those with his friend and fellow student Gordon Cullen[3] – Erskine cultivated a special interest in pacifism and socialism.[4] For Erskine, these lines of thinking seemed to correspond with developments in Sweden where the social, political, and economic conditions during the 1930s had nurtured a society that put peace, democracy, and welfare centre stage. Being strongly receptive to these qualities, Erskine developed an increasing interest in Sweden.[5]

An additional factor that might have caught Erskine's attention was that much of the social progress in Sweden was achieved by means of architecture. It was likely the progressive Stockholm Exhibition in 1930 that had introduced the basis for this ideological conception of modern architecture, by suggesting a firm relationship between architecture, human needs, and democratic concerns.[6] These ideas were subsequently generalised in Swedish society and became not only part of the discourse of architects and urban planners, but also of sociologists and politicians.

1
Richards, 'The New Empiricism'.

2
Now Westminster University.

3
Cullen, *Townscape*.

4
Egelius, *Ralph Erskine*.

5
This interest and first encounter with Sweden are described by Mats Egelius, former employee of Erskine and author of the monograph *Ralph Erskine, Architect*.

6
This reflection was explicitly articulated in the legendary manifesto *acceptera*, which was authored by architects Gunnar Asplund, Sven Markelius, Gregor Paulsson, Uno Åhrén, Wolter Gahn, and Eskild Sundahl. It was republished in Creagh, Kåberg, and Miller Lane, *Modern Swedish Design*, 140–347.

Fig. 1 The Box was portrayed in *The Architectural Review* as an example of New Empiricism. One of its main characteristics is the marriage of site and building. (Photograph by unknown. © ArkDes Collection)

In the period from 1930 to 1950, Sweden became known for its broadly shared belief in the connection between architectural quality and political ambition. This led, for instance, to joint projects among architects, politicians, and intellectuals. A telling example of such an interdisciplinary project is the collaboration between writer, feminist, and sociologist Alva Myrdal and architect Sven Markelius.[7] The introduction of social and political knowledge to the very centre of architectural reflection exemplifies what Erskine at the end of the 1970s would point to as a development towards 'a new architecture' that is not driven by any reference to a preconceived architectural theory, tendency, or style, but rather by insights derived from the sciences or any other knowledge-producing field.[8] Markelius and Myrdal discussed new visions on family housing in which social emancipation – particularly for women – played a chief role, both as a base for architectural innovation and as a political concern. This shared interest led to the development of the concept of the 'collective house', in which the role of the woman in the house was redefined by collectivising and outsourcing tasks such as cooking, cleaning, and childcare. The Kollektivhus John Ericssonsgatan by Markelius and Myrdal would become a model that would lead to multiple other collective houses across the country.[9]

The Swedish welfare state coupled far-reaching programmes in the fields of social security, social equality, and human rights to architecture. The People's Home (Folkhemmet) state programme, initiated by the Social Democratic Party in 1928 and geared towards stimulating the production of healthier modern housing accessible to the every Swede, is a case in point.[10] But also other actors, such as the Swedish Cooperative Union KF (Kooperativa Förbundet) and its architecture office KFAI (Kooperativa Förbundets Arkitekt- och Ingenjörsbyrå) made an explicit connection between the good architecture of its shops and factories and the wellbeing of its members. It was also an important actor in the development of collective housing as well as of new urban neighbourhoods.[11] A similar attitude can be discovered in the endeavours of the HSB Riksforbünd (Hyresgästernas sparkasse- och bostadsförening), the Tenants, Savings, and Building Society. This national cooperative established its own architecture department, HSB Arkitektkontor, that aimed to produce cheap, but good-quality, well-equipped flats through standardisation and rationalisation. The HSB Arkitektkontor would also become Erskine's first entry point to Sweden. Eager to join the Swedish welfare state enterprise, Erskine applied for a job at HSB's architecture department at the very beginning of his stay in Stockholm, although without success.[12]

A Briton falls in love with Sweden

At the age of twenty-five, freshly graduated and highly attracted to this advanced sociopolitical and architectural culture, Ralph Erskine decided to go to Sweden. The narrative of Erskine travelling by bike from the UK, across Denmark to Stockholm in Sweden, often accompanies introductions to Erskine's architecture and his approach to architecture. Erskine had

7
Sven Markelius was one of the architects behind the manifesto *acceptera*.

8
Erskine, 'Den Lojala Arkitekturen', 5–6.

9
Kollektivhus John Ericssonsgatan and other collective house projects are discussed in Storgaard, 'Curating the Collective House', 50–81.

10
For more information about the architecture of the People's Home, see Rudberg, *Folkhemmets byggande: under mellan- och efterkrigstiden*.

11
An in-depth description of KFAI is offered in Brunnström, *Det svenska folkhemsbygget*.

12
Egelius, *Ralph Erskine*, 8.

13
Egelius, *Ralph Erskine*, 8.

14
Egelius, *Ralph Erskine*, 8.

15
See Faber, 'Stockholm som Nordens Mekka'.

16
Faber, 'Stockholm som Nordens Mekka'.

no detailed plan for his journey and stayed overnight where possible – a circumstance that enabled spontaneous meetings with locals.[13] The fact that he made the journey by bike, travelling thousands of kilometres on his own, somehow typified Erskine. It seemed rather natural for him to undergo things physically, being someone who quite literally explored certain conditions and situations first-hand.

Shortly after Erskine's arrival in Stockholm he found a job as an architect, after which he soon decided to emigrate and settle down in Sweden with his British fiancée Ruth Francis. The couple married immediately upon her arrival. Unfortunately, things did not work out as they had expected. When the newlyweds returned from their honeymoon, Erskine was fired – and the Second World War broke out.

Although Sweden remained neutral, the uncertainty of the war also reduced building activity and led to scarcity of building materials. According to an anecdote, however, it was not the drop in commissions that caused Erskine's dismissal, but his habit of talking more than working.[14] Despite this unexpected adversity, Stockholm remained an attractive place for the Erskines. The capital, which – due to the success of the Stockholm Exhibition 1930 – had become known as the modern architectural 'Mecca of the North', had turned into a favoured destination for young architects from all over Europe.[15] When the war broke out, the already-existing international environment in Stockholm extended significantly.

However, while the exile in Sweden offered an interesting architectural culture, the start of a family life and a steady income remained troublesome for Erskine. When a friend offered him the free use of a nature site in Lissma, outside Stockholm, Erskine decided to build a house of his own there. The site was hilly, forested, and rocky. The absence of access to public utilities such as tap water, gas, or electricity encouraged Erskine to think about an autarkic way of living, in which his family would become self-sufficient and have a certain financial independency. In the middle of the winter of 1941–42, probably unaware that he was about to make an important contribution to architectural history, Erskine started to build his house, which would become known as The Box.

Laboratory of everyday practices

The concept of The Box was based on employing the absolute minimum in terms of construction method, materials, and programme. Due to a tight budget and because of material shortages caused by the war, Erskine constructed the cabin mainly out of timber, which in wooded Sweden was abundantly available. For the choice of other construction materials Erskine also relied primarily on what was 'at hand', including bricks from an abandoned brick factory in the vicinity and iron recovered from an old bedstead, used as reinforcing material.[16] These found materials were probably used to construct the centrally positioned fireplace and its chimney, the only elements that are not made of timber.

Basically, The Box was erected according to the simple contours of a box, consisting of a floor, four walls, and a slightly sloping roof. Although this point of departure seems rather straightforward, both the exterior as well as the interior illustrate Erskine's elaborate architectural approach, which at this point in time was strongly influenced by traditional Swedish construction methods and materials.[17] The architecture and orientation of The Box are determined in the first place by the Swedish climate, which is characterised by very cold, harsh winters and warm summers. Consequently, Erskine opens the cabin towards the sunny south, providing it with large glass partitions; and encloses it towards the cold north, where the stacked firewood gives it an extra layer of insulation. Situated at the top of the site, The Box moreover offered a wide view of the undulating, descending landscape. The original site plan reveals that Erskine intended to grow his own vegetables around the cabin as part of his desire to become self-sufficient – an aspiration likely propelled by the fact that The Box was remotely situated and the straightforward need for food in times of war. A meticulously detailed drawing of the layout of the plant beds with different vegetables, flanked by a row of beehives and softly following the existing topography, illustrates that the design of the immediate surroundings is afforded just as much attention as that of the cabin's floor plan. It illuminates how Erskine conceives of dwelling as strongly entwined with specific local conditions such as the topographical, spatial, and climatological features of the site – a perspective that in Erskine's subsequent work continued to be of key importance. In 1960 he further explained this approach, stating: 'Each situation makes its own rules: the shape of the ground, the kinds of weather and the sorts of people who live there will all vary so much that they make a new design problem of every case.'[18] This stance is legible in the design of the interior of the cabin itself, which as a consequence of its very limited floor plan size of 6 by 3.6 metres, demanded accurate and inventive design solutions. The bathroom and toilet were situated outside the cabin, which simplified the design of the dense programme inside the cabin. Erskine separated the kitchen from the remaining part of the interior and positioned the fireplace centrally in the cabin. Besides its functional purpose, with heat distributed through sixteen shafts, the fireplace is characterised by a distinctive, plastic design.

The kitchen is organised both conventionally and at the same time peculiarly, as it has no visual relationship with the outside, and therefore is only indirectly lit.[19] The remaining dwelling space displays how knowledge about everyday life is coupled with a highly ingenious, multifunctional, and space-saving interior design. Within this space Erskine arranged his architecture office, dining room, living room, and bedroom. Erskine used the closed northern wall for cupboards and custom-made shelves for the storage of plans and other items for his architecture practice. The working table could be folded up against this wall when work was done and other domestic activities required the space. A similar space-changing element was a combined double bed/sofa that could be winched up to the ceiling when it wasn't in use. Every piece of furniture, its alter-

17
Erskine worked for a while for a commissioner who specialised in traditional Swedish wooden houses (*stuga*), Faber, 'Stockholm som Nordens Mekka', 8.

18
Erskine, 'Town Planning in The Swedish Subarctic', 2.

19
This aspect is also critically noted by a former colleague of Erskine, Vernon Gracie, in the documentary *Erskine*, available online at https://www.youtube.com/watch?v= ipax8ZR_v0k&t=6s. Accessed 9 March 2020.

Fig. 2 Ruth Erskine in front of the naked timber structure of The Box. According to Swedish craft tradition, a wreath made of spruce twigs was hung at the edge of the rafter structure to celebrate the completion of the basic structure of the house. (Photograph by unknown. © ArkDes Collection)

600
600
300
900
1200
2
3
4

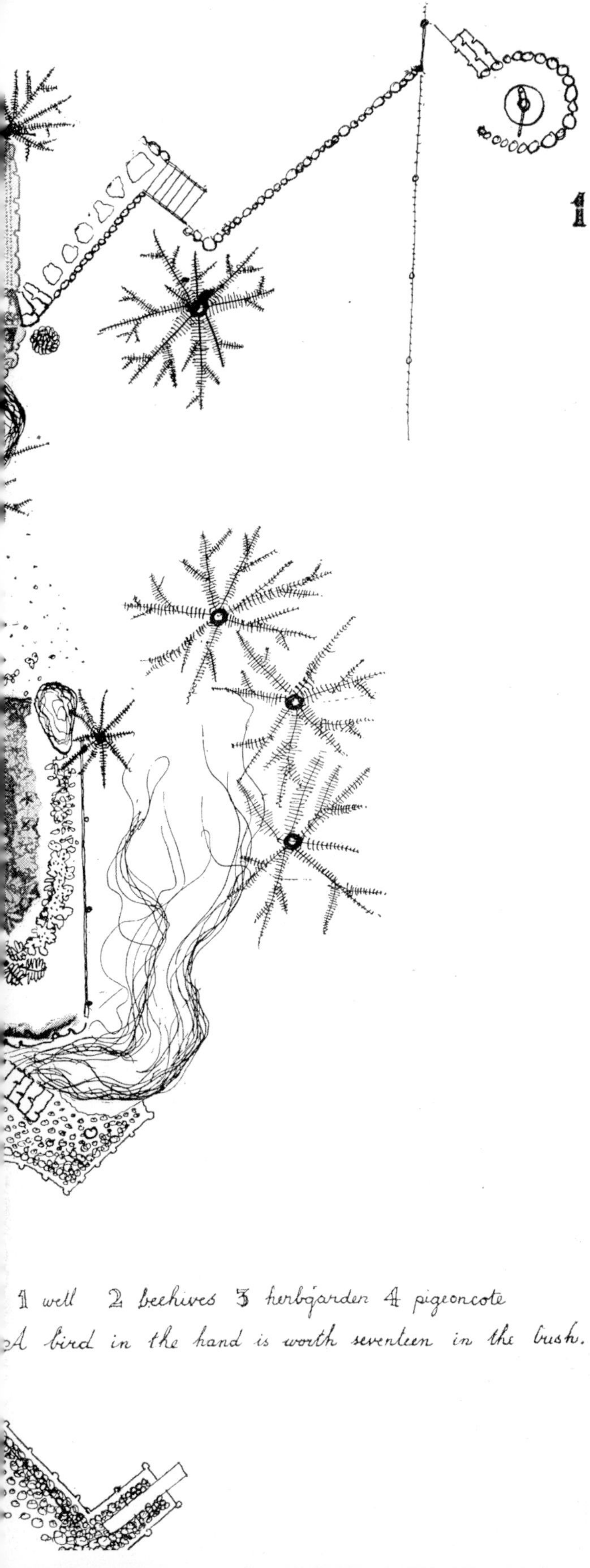

Fig. 3 Site plan with the proverb 'A bird in the hand is worth seventeen in the bush'. Erskine paid great attention to the site, which served as an extension of The Box. Apart from a meticulously arranged herb garden, the site also accommodated a well, beehives, a pigeon cote, an exterior bathroom, and a toilet. (© ArkDes Collection)

ability and precise position in the space, as well as its relation to other elements can be seen as the result of a continual negotiation between function, actions, users, and objects as every act – eating, sleeping, relaxing, and working – demanded a refurbishment.

The Box became a laboratory for knowledge on the interrelation between architecture and everyday practices. The architecture of The Box engaged with the life world of the Erskine family for four years, before they moved back to Stockholm. At this moment the family consisted of Ruth, Ralph, and their first daughter, staging and accommodating their daily routines. One could argue that the minimal tenets of The Box look like an interpretation of the idea of 'Die Wohnung für das Existenzminimum', as propagated by the CIAM (Congrès Internationaux d'Architecture Moderne) in 1930.[20] However, contrary to the modernist conception, Erskine did not aspire to conceive a general type of dwelling that could serve everybody, or at least 'the largest number'. Instead of this universalist idea, he rather aspired to create a modern dwelling that was specific to a site and to a family. The minimal dwelling of The Box was for Erskine a continuous negotiation between the various practices of its inhabitants, as well as their furniture and spaces. In Erskine's view, dwelling was a matter of everyday activism.

Home of architects: site for new expressions

That Erskine looked upon his own home as a laboratory for a radical architectural experiment, less constrained by conventions, was not an exception. Other architects who stayed in Stockholm during the war would also become known for their 'radical' homes. The private homes of the Swede Sven Markelius (Kevinge, Sweden, 1945), the Danes Arne Jacobsen (Klampenborg, Denmark, 1951) and Jørn Utzon (Hellebæk, Denmark, 1952), and the Norwegian Arne Korsmo (Oslo, Norway, 1955), in particular, have become important milestones in post-war architecture history. With the exception of Korsmo, who developed a completely new vision on dwelling, expounded through the so-called 'Home-Meccano' (Hjemmets Mekano Methode),[21] none of these architects, Erskine included, explicitly theorised the architectural concepts and visions in relation to their own houses. Compared with the theoretical production in French, English, Dutch, and German architectural culture, for instance, the role and manifestation of theoretical reflection in the north of Europe seem less prominent. Instead of focussing on metatheoretical discussions, architects like Erskine – who in that sense seemed to have been assimilated into the Swedish architectural culture – were more geared towards pragmatic issues related to human needs, everyday problems, and practices.[22] Even though he later articulated his ideas more theoretically, Erskine always remained rather down-to-earth in his approach and ways of communicating. In an interview from 1991 about his view on Team 10, and his role as a member of its inner circle, he noted that he always felt a bit on the outside during the meetings, stating: 'Too much philosophy, too much theory is quite alien to my way of thinking.'[23]

20
In English: The Dwelling for Minimal Existence. *Existenzminimum* had become a term often used in modern housing projects; it was the central theme of the second CIAM meeting in Zurich in 1929.

21
This method can be described as a flexible system of building and furniture that could be adapted to different needs. Korsmo defined it as a 'working method and analysis of man, the home and the house – the aim of which is to give the individual, the family and the environment a chance to free themselves from passivity and become consciously active in dwelling and building'. See Norberg-Schulz, *Arne Korsmo*, 72.

22
The attention paid to pragmatic issues, human needs, and everyday problems above the development of theoretical reflection was especially present in Denmark, it can be argued. This phenomenon is discussed, for instance, in Bjerregaard, 'Naturvidenskab og "det andet"'.

23
Tuscano, 'At the Heart of the Matter Is Life'.

Figs. 4–6 The interior of The Box was a result of Erskine's study of the interrelation between architecture and the everyday practices of his own family. Except the room-dividing fireplace, every piece of furniture could be adapted to different needs and functions. (Photographs by unknown. © ArkDes Collection)

Although today The Box has become one of the best-known radical architectural statements from the early 1940s, it was probably not Erskine's intention to make an architectural statement. The primary aim of The Box was to live autarkically and to support his young family. He was, however, very aware of its architectural significance and, accordingly, produced and played the main role in a photographic narrative of his family's life in The Box. Through well-orchestrated, lived-in photographs showing Erskine working at the fold-out table, Erskine at the entrance door with his hands full of firewood, Erskine keeping the fire in the fireplace, and Erskine with his wife and child in and around the sofa/bed, The Box reached the attention of the editorial board of *The Architectural Review*.

In search of a loyal architecture

When from the mid 1940s, *The Architectural Review* launched a quest for a new direction of architectural culture, they showed a particular interest in rethinking architectural modernity in a national context.[24] Sweden's New Empiricism, which adjusted modern architecture to regional needs, climatological conditions, traditional construction methods, and indigenous materials, appealed to the editorial board of the magazine, and raised their interest in Erkine's The Box. For *The Architectural Review*, New Empiricism also stood for an architecture that was based on a very precise knowledge of users and their practices, departing from empirical evidence. The periodical's definition of New Empiricism thus matched the architecture of The Box quite

24
The role of *The Architectural Review* in the debates on modern architecture is mentioned in Jacobus, *Twentieth-Century Architecture*, 36–7; see also Pevsner, *Pioneers of the Modern Movement* and Richards, *An Introduction to Modern Architecture*.

25
Erskine, 'Den Lojala Arkitekturen'.

26
Erskine, 'Den Lojala Arkitekturen', 5–6.

27
Erskine, 'Byker'; Gilroy, Pendlebury, and Townshend, 'Making Better Places'; Vall, 'Social Engineering and Participation'; Erskine, 'Den Lojala Arkitekturen'; Erskine, 'Architecture and Town Planning in the North'.

closely. Carefully married to its site, built with local construction materials and methods and – above all – based on empirical observations regarding everyday practices and needs, The Box became an illustrative example of New Empiricism.

Nonetheless, Erskine never associated himself with New Empiricism. In an article that he wrote in 1979, 'Den Lojala Arkitekturen' ('The Loyal Architecture'), he laments categorisations of architecture as well as definitions of architectural 'isms'.[25] Provocatively, he suggests eliminating the academic, theoretical discussions about architecture that he claims only create a distance between architect and user. In the article, Erskine pleads for a new method in architecture, one that could generate 'genuine' modern architecture and lead to a change in architectural expression. For Erskine, the idea of democratic participation processes, in which future users and their voices are centre stage and influence both the definition of the programme of a building and the architectural design, is central to this new conception of architecture. Such a 'loyal architecture' implied for Erskine a responsibility towards natural and energetic resources, as well as to citizens. He maintained that the need and rights of all citizens, including the least vocal people in society, had to be taken into account during the design process.[26]

The participative approach that he promoted in this article was not coincidental, but rather the continuation of a trajectory that had started with The Box in the early 1940s. During the process of constructing and designing The Box, Erskine and his family acted as the ultimate knowledge source concerning needs and everyday practices. After The Box was finished, its inhabitation by Erskine and his family continued to provide important knowledge about the relationship between architecture and dwelling practices. Put simply, it was during the making of The Box that Erskine developed his future sensitivity towards the importance of empirically based architectural knowledge. The use of participative processes in his later projects such as the Byker Housing Estate and the Arctic town of Svappavaara can be understood as a further development of this empirical method, based on observations and experience rather than theory.[27] Not abstract architectural theories, but the voices of (future) users provide the empirical basis that inform design decisions in such an approach. Out of such a perspective, the role of modern architecture was redefined from a universal and autonomous matter to a 'loyal architecture', devoted to the active engagement of the users.

Coda

Erskine and his family lived in The Box for four years. As a home, The Box might not have been ideal for long-term habitation, but it still offered an instructive site for learning about how architecture can accommodate everyday life practices. Everyday sanitary activities, for instance, demanded time and effort. Another problem occurred in relation to the large glazed facade that faced south – it let in a lot of heat in the summer and too much cold during winter. This disadvantage taught Erskine to avoid large glazed partitions in future projects, it has been suggested.[28] After having served as the family's holiday home, The Box gradually decayed and fell into disrepair. Due to the status of The Box as an important architectural statement in Swedish architectural history, it was reconstructed on the Swedish island of Lovön under the supervision of Erskine himself in 1989.[29] The Box has now become a museum, run by Sweden's National Centre for Architecture and Design.

28
Egelius, *Ralph Erskine*, 9.

29
The reconstruction was initiated by journalist Olle Bengtzon, who was known for his writings about societal questions and architecture.

Bibliography

Bedoire, Frederic. *Den Svenska arkitekturens historia 1800–2000*. Livonia: Norstedts, 2015.

Bjerregaard, Lotte Marianne. 'Naturvidenskab og "det andet": Historigrafiske vinkler på dansk glasarkitektur', *Nordic Journal of Architectural Research* 19, no. 1 (2006): 45–53.

Brunnström, Lisa. *Det svenska folkhemsbygget: Om Kooperativa Förbundets arkitektkontor*. Stockholm: Arkitektur Förlag AB, 2004.

Creagh, Lucy, Helena Kåberg, and Barbara Miller Lane, eds. *Modern Swedish Design: Three Founding Texts*. New York: The Museum of Modern Art, 2008.

Cullen, Gordon. *Townscape*. London: Architectural Press, 1968.

De Maré, Eric. 'The Antecedents and Origins of Sweden's Latest Style'. *The Architectural Review* 613 (1948): 9–22.

Egelius, Mats. *Ralph Erskine, Architect*. Stockholm: Byggförlaget, 1990.

Erskine, Ralph. 'Byker'. *The Architectural Review* 934 (1974): 346–62.

Erskine, Ralph. 'Den Lojala Arkitekturen'. *Arkitektur* 5 (June 1979): 4–9.

Erskine, Ralph. 'Architecture and Town Planning in the North'. *Polar Record* 14, no. 89 (1968): 165–71.

Erskine, Ralph. 'Town Planning in the Swedish Subarctic'. *Habitat* (November-December 1960): 5.

Faber, Tobias. 'Stockholm som Nordens Mekka'. In *Tiden i Stockholm*, edited by Finn Monies and Karen Zahle, 8–23. Skive: Arkitektens Forlag, 1999.

Gilroy, Rose, John Pendlebury, and Tim Townshend. 'Making Better Places Through Heritage Designation? The Byker Estate, Newcastle upon Tyne'. *Docomomo* 39 (September 2008): 59–63.

Jacobus, John. *Twentieth-Century Architecture: The Middle Years 1940–65*. New York: Frederick A. Praeger Publisher, 1966.

Norberg-Schulz, Christian. *Arne Korsmo*. Oslo: Universitetsforlaget, 2000.

Pevsner, Nikolaus. *Pioneers of the Modern Movement: From William Morris to Walter Gropius*. London: Faber and Faber, 1936.

Richards, J. M. 'The New Empiricism: Sweden's Latest Style'. *The Architectural Review* 606 (1947): 199–204.

Richards, J. M. *An Introduction to Modern Architecture* Harmondsworth: Penguin, 1940.

Rudberg, Eva, Paul Britten Austin, and Frances Lucas. *The Stockholm Exhibition 1930: Modernism's Breakthrough in Swedish Architecture*. Stockholm: Stockholmia, 1999.

Rudberg, Eva. *Folkhemmets byggande: Under mellan- och efterkrigstiden*. Stockholm: Svenska Turistföreningen, 1992.

Storgaard, Eva. 'Curating the Collective House: The Popularisation of a New Housing Model in 1930s Sweden'. In *The Housing Project: Discourses, Ideals, Models and Politics in 20th-Century Exhibitions*, edited by Gaia Caramellino and Stéphanie Dadour, 50–81. Leuven: Leuven University Press, 2020.

'The New Empiricism in Denmark'. *The Architectural Review* 618 (1948): 236–40.

Tuscano, Clelia, 'At the Heart of the Matter Is Life: Two Days with Ralph Erskine, Strolling from Rome to L'Aquila'. In *Team 10: 1953–81: In Search of a Utopia of the Present*, by Max Risselada and Dirk van den Heuvel, 323–5. Rotterdam: NAi Publishers, 2005.

Vall, Natasha. 'Social Engineering and Participation in Anglo-Swedish Housing 1945–1976: Ralph Erskine's Vernacular Plan'. *Planning Perspectives* 28, no. 2 (2013): 223–45.

Günther Domenig's Rational Centre: A reading of the Steinhaus

Giacomo Pala

On the shore of Lake Ossiach, in the Austrian region of Carinthia, stands a mountain of fragmented concrete structures and distorted cubes covered in brushed steel. This is Steinhaus (Stone House), the house Günther Domenig (1934–2012) built for himself: a manifesto built over a time span of twenty years.[1] Construction started in 1986 and the house was declared completed only on 5 October 2008, when it was baptised by some of Domenig's friends (including Peter Noever, Wolf D. Prix, Thom Mayne, Hans Hollein, and Raimund Abraham) during an opening event including a live set by the avant-garde jazz saxophonist Evan Parker.[2] The house was never meant to be just a house, but rather a space for hosting events for artists, his students, and his office. Inside the house, at first, one can see a wide opening towards the lake; now enclosed by an inclined glass cube. It is a space for events, workshops, lectures, and conferences. On the left, following one of the many staircases, one can enter the resident artists' and guests' spaces. On the right, by following a second set of stairs partially running outside the house, one can get in a smaller space to which Domenig's practice was meant to relocate for some time during the summer. From there, up yet another staircase, it is possible to visit Domenig's own room. The building's narrative is as clear as it is explicit: it is the labyrinthine incubator of its creator's life: Domenig's genius, his work, his students, and his privacy come together, all at once, under one roof.

Domenig worked on the design of the Steinhaus for more than twenty years, experimenting with different structural, formal, and technical solutions. The result is an incoherent agglomeration of differences; a mountain of expressive forms in concrete and steel; a swirl of cuts and joints. The vulgate: the house is the outcome of Domenig's personal obsessions and fantasies.[3] Therefore, the building is usually described as a sort of irrational, chaotic, and fragmentary fantasy. For example, for Peter Noever, this house's meaning would be 'invisible [...] to a perception which is not trained to look through the barbarism of triviality'.[4]

Indeed, it is possible to discuss this house in many other terms. We might say that this building is – quite simply – an example of expressionism. Or, following Matthias Boeckl, we might look at this house as one of those unique buildings that elude historical meta-categories, not unlike Vicino Orsini's Sacred Forest in Bomarzo, or *facteur* Cheval's Palais Idéal in Hauterives, France.[5] The house could be defined as surreal due to some of the objects one can find in it: three concrete structures designed by Domenig while thinking about when he broke his fingers when he was a child; or the lamp Nix-Nuz-Nix, resembling a bird flying in the house's main hall. Maybe, the house could be read by following Bruno Zevi's definition of Domenig's architecture (among others): 'Smash the idols directly'.[6]

1
The process of building this house was particularly painful, to the point that a former collaborator of Domenig, whom I have tried to speak to about the project, prefers not to even talk about this period, having been somehow traumatic.

2
The names are mentioned by Lebbeus Woods. See Woods 'Stonehouse', https://lebbeuswoods.wordpress.com/2008/10/02/stonehouse/. The event is reported by Peter Noever. See Noever, *Günther Domenig*, 21.

3
For example, this is how Domenig describes the house in *Daidalos* in 1995: 'The evolution of an architectural design and the result representing a correlation of my person and the experience, the living conditions and the landscape, my personal existence, my memories, and their subjective expression. "The natural and the artificial", "Nature and mind", "Interior and exterior", "the twilight of the future"'. See Domenig, 'Stone House as Steindorf', 66.

4
Noever, *Günther Domenig*, 22.

5
Boeckl, *Günther Domenig*, 254–7.

6
Zevi, 'The Seven Myths of Architecture', 420.

Fig. 1 The Steinhaus in its context.
(© Giacomo Pala)

7
For a short introduction, see Dezzi Bardeschi, 'Organic Manic Mannerism'.

8
I refer to what professor Peter Trummer – my PhD advisor, former student of Domenig at the University of Graz, and professor of urban design at the University of Innsbruck – has said during a public lecture at the University of Innsbruck.

9
Boyarsky et al., 'Drawing on Dreams'.

Or we could contextualise the house by looking at where and when it was designed; then, this house could be understood as the expression of what has been called the Grazer Schule: a school – a group of architects – sharing a similar aesthetic, expressive, subjective, and personal attitude towards architectural design, all working in Graz in the same period, among whom Domenig was the most internationally recognised.[7]

However we might like to frame it, because of its mysterious nature, this house is defined variably as barbarian, trivial, or irrational. This chapter's objective is to unpack why the house has been interpreted this way. As will be discussed, it is quite obvious that Domenig projected his own personality on the construction of the house. Nonetheless, it is less clear why such a fact has to be considered irrational. So, in order to jump into the topic, allow me to first ask a preliminary question: why did Domenig design this house in such an extreme manner?

As already said, we know that this house is a figment of its author's imagination. So, in order to answer the question, we should start with Domenig's biography and look at his personality. Günther was the son of Herbert Domenig, a Nazi judge who was executed at the end of the Second World War. Such a traumatic event undoubtedly influenced Domenig's personality. But is this personal history represented by the house? According to his former students, the Austrian architect was obsessed with the need to emancipate himself from the role of his father in the history of Austria; and his architectural language was part of this process of emancipation.[8] Simply put, as the architecture of the Nazi was symmetrical, monumental, and hierarchical, Domenig's architecture was deliberately asymmetrical, organic, and contradictory. It can thus (at least partly) be read as the outcome of such an ideological opposition. To strengthen this hypothesis, it is worthwhile to briefly focus on another project by Domenig: the restoration of the Nazi Rally Grounds Documentation Centre in Nuremberg, Germany. The project was to convert Ludwig and Frank Ruff's Nazi convention hall into a centre for documentation on the Nazi period. Domenig's intervention engages in a direct and almost violent confrontation; it slices through the imposing brick torso of the original complex with a diagonal incision that cuts one wing of the immense hall. In doing so, it disturbs the building's symmetry and activates novel spatial hierarchies.

However, assuming that Domenig's house is solely the outcome of his desire to confront and challenge his past is only partly interesting. Let's consider, then, the nature and the characters of this house's formalism. A lot, it seems, depends on irrational considerations. For instance, in a conversation between Domenig, Alvin Boyarski, Peter Cook, and Noever that took place at the Architectural Association in London in 1986, words like 'individualistic', 'dream', 'anti-rational', 'surrealist', or even 'demonic' were used to describe the house.[9] These words are used to imply a personal design method based on imagination; an architecture that apparently goes against the grain of systematic thinking. But what is

Fig. 2 Internal space joining the different levels of the house. (© Giacomo Pala)

Fig. 3 Steinhaus' plan. (© Architekt Günther Domenig)

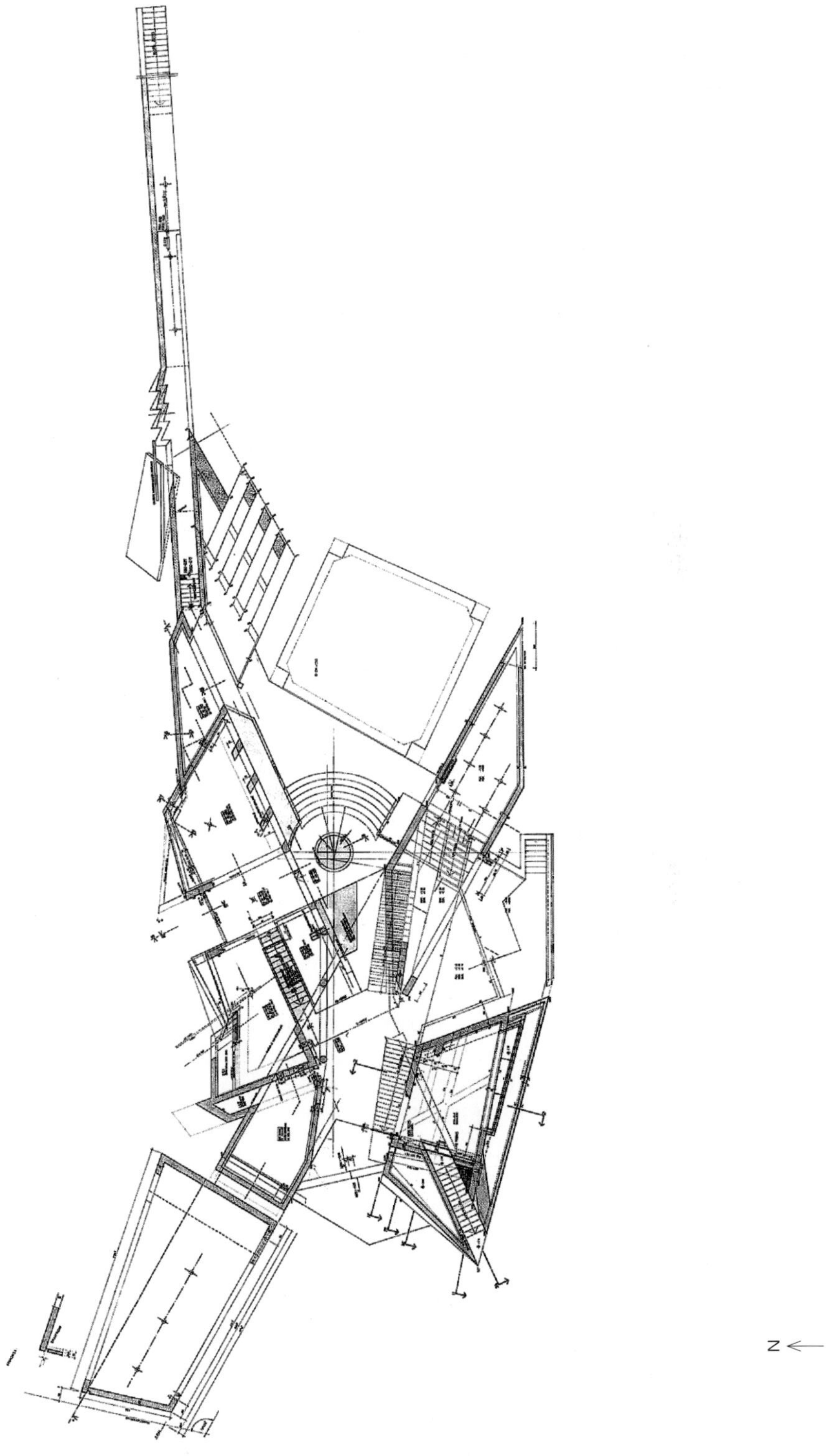

the difference between a rational and irrational design? Is apparent disorder necessarily illogical or irrational? Domenig told his peers, 'The most important part of my work is the attempt to develop out of the free sketches a controlled and geometric concept, to find a systematic order that retains the complexity of the sketches.'[10] This suggests that while his house looks surreal or irrational, it is the product of a rational (even linear) way of thinking.[11]

Reasonable irrationality

Domenig's house looks like a contradictory composition of parts, each unrelated to the other. Its plan clearly expresses such quality: several objects are asymmetrically arranged around a path and what seems to be a circular centre. What emerges are tensions between repetition and difference; centrifugal and centripetal; whole against parts. These tensions are amplified by the existence of one main directionality of the design (due to the site's shape) yet fragmented into multiple parts directed towards the outside of the building. The experience of the house, however, is far less irrational than its appearance in visual representations. Precise detailing joins this 'irrational' agglomeration of parts, straddling complex and sophisticated junctions between concrete, steel, and glass. One could hardly call this level of attention to detail irrational.

Even so, Domenig was obsessively devoted to the development of a sort of weird and personal architecture: 'the personal dimension of architecture', as he would say.[12] His house, then, could be said to be nothing more than the umpteenth excuse to experiment with such personal obsessions. After all, Domenig himself describes the house this way.[13] Nonetheless, as the author's declared intentions should not always be taken as fact, a different interpretation of the work can be proffered; one that may suggest the vagueness of words such as 'irrational', particularly after visiting the house. The house can appear as non-rational, but only if we decide to surrender to its official descriptions and to the meaning usually attributed to this word. Thom Mayne describes the house as a dream, and he does so by first quoting a poem by Rainer Maria Rilke: 'The house is dissolved and distributed within me.'[14] Such a sentence is an evocative reference, but why should the expression of an architect's subjectivity be a form of irrationalism?

Because we pretend to know what irrationality looks like: it is contradictory, irregular, and, above-all, fragmented. But still, why should we rely on this imaginary? Aldo Rossi's work, often defined as an example of rationalism, is a good example.[15] Rossi's projects – despite relying on pure volumes – are often designed as compositions of quotations and extremely illogical allusions to the architect's personal obsessions. In a sense, it is thus no less irrational than Domenig's house. Furthermore, both architects shared an obsession for personal memories to be symbolically embedded in their projects. Nonetheless, we describe Rossi's architecture as 'rational', and Domenig's as 'irrational'. We believe both these interpretations because we are used to them; they are obvious platitudes,

10
Boyarsky et al., 'Drawing on Dreams', 105.

11
The question of linearity is an interesting theoretical topic. In fact, Stone House has sometimes been related to the so-called complexity paradigm, particularly during the first phase of excitement for new digital tools in the 1990s. For instance, Charles Jencks has interpreted the house as a possible forerunner of a non-linear architecture, even though, I would argue, his interpretation relies on a metaphoric understanding, transforming the problem of non-linearity in a pure metaphor to be evoked by architecture's shapes. See Jencks, 'Nonlinear Architecture'.

12
Domenig, 'Stone House as Steindorf', 66.

13
'What the hand does / What the head does / It is the house', in Noever, *Günther Domenig*, 60.

14
Mayne, 'Emerging from Collapse', 6.

15
Rossi himself has often discussed the idea of rationalism in architecture as a form of realism. For instance, in 'Architettura e Città, Passato e Presente', he writes the following words: 'Le architetture utopiche, fantascientifiche hanno la loro debolezza [...] nell'allontanarsi dal reale. Un'architettura razionalista è necessariamente realista' (Utopian, science-fiction architectures have their weakness [...] in moving away from reality. A rationalist architecture is necessarily realist). Rossi, 'Architettura e Città, Passato e Presente', 480.

Fig. 4 Günther Domenig's room. (© Giacomo Pala)

Fig. 5 Steinhaus' main space. (© Giacomo Pala)

or – at best – they are shared 'critical' metanarratives. The real matter of dispute, as once brilliantly put by Robin Evans, resides in the problem of recognition: how we perceive and recognise values.[16] We perceive irrationality when we see it, as we perceive rationality when we see the shapes that have always been used to represent such 'meaning' (grids, pure volumes, regularity, axial symmetries). Irrationality, in this case, is nothing more – and nothing less – than an aesthetic effect since any design method is inherently rational. Why, then, keep on defining this house as irrational? Could Domenig's house be something other than that?

While it is undeniable that the Steinhaus is the outcome of a self-reflexive process mirroring Domenig's own construction of personality, it is less clear why such a fact has to be considered irrational, not to say demonic.

The house as a world

In order to find a new meaning, or to formulate a different interpretation of the house, it may be worth referring once again to Rilke's writing, only partially quoted by Mayne. Rilke's poem reads: '[T]he whole thing is scattered about inside me, the rooms, the stairs that descended with such ceremonious slowness, others, narrow cages that mounted in a spiral movement, in the darkness of which we advanced like the blood in our veins.'[17]

This poem describes a house as something similar to a body: a setting for a seemingly continuous and fragmented experience where we circulate like the blood inside our organs. In other words, the house defines a whole world in itself. And yet, the inner space of the house is in constant dialogue with its surroundings. The result is the visual fragmentation of the building in relation to its environment. In this sense, the possibly hidden meaning of this house resides in its ability to fragment the vastness of the outside space and recompose it in the security of an enclosed space by juxtaposing fragments and discrete pieces. In this respect, the building may be looked at as a cubist painting in which the different abstracted parts assume different configurations depending on the point of view from which we look at them. And yet, as the experience of a space can only be compared to that of a painting in a metaphorical sense, this house's interiority possesses much more interesting specificities. The intelligibility of Domenig's composed fragments is related to something different. What we see is a masterly alternation between masses in steel and concrete, next to cuts and openings allowing us to see what is outside of this house's spaces. Materials without any applied colour reveal properties that are both formal and material. Light has mass, but it is suspended in the alternation of cuts resembling wounds or loopholes and wide openings towards the landscape. Everything is lifted, cantilevered, suspended in the air, but everything has a mass and an extremely powerful visual weight. There is no sense of lightness, nor heaviness; we only see suspension. Some of the most striking properties of the house have to do with the perception of mass, figurative elements, symbols, and materials. That is one of the reasons why

16
In Robin Evans' words: 'The whole matter resides in recognition. I recognize plant life when I see it, and I recognize rationality in architecture when I see it, because I begin to understand, after much practice, what the word is applied to. I am then tempted to think that all things bearing the same name, whether or not they are architecture, must share an essential, but this is not necessary, nor, in this instance [Mies' Barcelona Pavilion], is it likely.' See Evans, 'Mies van der Rohe's Paradoxical Symmetries', 59.

17
Rilke, 'Notebooks of Malte Laurids Brigge', quoted in Bachelard, *The Poetics of Space*, 57.

the drawings and photographic reproductions of this house cannot help us to really understand what this house is like. This is also why, while visiting the house, it is particularly interesting to discover that the circle appearing in the building's plan, cuts through every floor and visually connects all the levels. A glass circle that, in the underground level, becomes a glass cylinder inside which water can run, entering a crypt-like room (Domenig used to call this the '*Spiralraum*' [spiral space]) coated in black marble, from where Domenig planned to have his urn shot with a missile towards his grandmother's village.[18] In spite of Domenig's odd intentions, it is interesting to find an element connecting all of the parts of the house vertically, thus reconstructing a unity of the space.

Usual descriptions of the problem of fragmentation – the ultimate shape of what we like to call 'irrational' – tell us that it insists upon individual notions, loose ends, and distrust in any defined system. As Julia Kristeva states: 'It [modern art] seizes this moment of fragmentation in a gesture that does not give it meaning but is, in its very formal existence, a gesture of fleeting sovereignty and of momentary enthusiasm.'[19] While it is easy to suggest that fragmentation is the outcome of an enthusiastic gesture, it is equally easy to claim that one may actually find meanings through fragmentation. The understanding of formal fragmentation as the 'meaningless' representation of a disembodied and corrupted world is one of the most spectacular and successful theoretical simplifications in art history and architecture critcism. Once we rid ourselves of such preconception, fragmentation may be recognised as a way to generate order, not chaos. Then, Domenig's centripetal centre may be finally seen as something defining some kind of order. It is a proper centre where forces collide; a centre of experience.[20] It is like inserting a point from where the house can be understood. It is like when, hiking through the mountains, one encounters a viewpoint from where the vastness of the environment is described by signs revealing the mountains' heights, and the peaks' names. It is a centripetal hole giving sense to the overall space. But then: what does Domenig want us to experience? There can be no definitive answer to this question. Yet, it is worthwhile to attempt a speculation. From the circle's centre, the space is continuous: there is no dichotomy between verticals and horizontals, nor between the inside and the outside. Maybe, in this case, Domenig wants us to simply experience space, asking us to forget our memories.

Surely, architecture may produce comments on society, culture, and history, reminding us of the world's unjust realities, in a more or less critical way. And yet, this house sheds a light on another option: architecture (with the arts) can also transcend commentary. By virtue of its spatial and material qualities, this house distances us from social reality, and builds a suspended world; a world where, as Raimund Abraham said, 'Expression and contents merge'.[21] In conclusion, this house may show a specific kind of activism – quite rational indeed – the attempt of both expressing and representing something other than the mundane.

18
Here I have to thank Raffaela Lackner for providing me with this information while I was visiting Steinhaus.

19
Kristeva, 'Interview with Catherine Francolin' (1986), 185.

20
In an interview with Paolo Vincenzo Genovese, Domenig gives us a clue about this issue, talking about the need of defining an 'essential' point to be found inside a project: 'Le opere che considero riuscite costituiscono un'unità, sia nel loro interno sia nel contesto nelle quali sono inserite e relativamente alla loro reciproca correlazione. il riferimento che personalmente ritengo più profondo è quello di riuscire a colpire un determinato punto essenziale che spesso si trova all'interno dell'edificio'. (The works that I consider successful constitute a unity in their interiority and in the context in which they are inserted as well as in relation to their mutual correlation. The reference that I personally believe to be the deepest is to be able to hit a certain essential point that is often found inside the building.) See Genovese, *Günther Domenig*, 37.

21
Noever, *Günther Domenig*, 57.

Bibliography

Bachelard, Gaston. *The Poetics of Space*, translated by Maria Jolas. Boston: Beacon Press, 1994. First published by Penguin Books (1964).

Boeckl, Matthias, ed. *Günther Domenig: Recent Works*, Vienna: Springer-Verlag, 2005.

Boyarsky, Alvin, Peter Cook, Günther Domenig, and Peter Noever, 'Drawing on Dreams: Günther Domenig: Steinhaus — Stonehouse', *AA Files*, no. 13 (1986): 100–5.

Dezzi Bardeschi, Marco. 'Organic Manic Mannerism'. *Domus*, no. 622 (1981): 12–37.

Domenig, Günther. 'Stone House as Steindorf: Workshop in Architecture'. *Daidalos*, no. 15 (December 1995): 64–6.

Evans, Robin. 'Mies van der Rohe's Paradoxical Symmetries'. *AA Files*, no. 19 (1990): 56–68.

Genovese, Paolo Vincenzo. *Günther Domenig*. Turin: Testo & Immagine, 1998.

Harrison, Charles, and Paul Wood, eds. *Art in Theory, 1900–1990: An Anthology of Changing Ideas*. Oxford: Backwell, 1992.

Jencks, Charles. 'Nonlinear Architecture: New Science = New Architecture?'. *Architectural Design* 67, no. 9/10 (1997): 6–7.

Kristeva, Julia. 'Interview with Catherine Francolin'. *Flash Art*, no. 126 (February–March 1986). Quoted in *Art in Theory, 1900–1990: An Anthology of Changing Ideas*, edited by Charles Harrison and Paul Wood. (Oxford: Backwell, 1992), 185.

Mayne, Thom. 'Emerging from Collapse'. In *Günther Domenig: Recent Works*, edited by Matthias Boeckl, 6–7. Vienna: Springer-Verlag, 2005.

Noever, Peter. *Günther Domenig, Steinhaus in Steindorf: Sketches, Drawings, Models, Objects*. Klagenfurt: Ritter Verlag, 2002.

Rossi, Aldo. *Scritti Scelti sull'Architettura e la Città*. Turin: Città Studi Edizioni, 1975.

Zevi, Bruno. 'The Seven Myths of Architecture'. *Myth in Contemporary Life*, special issue of *Social Research* 52, no. 2 (1985): 411–22.

‘Our Homeland is Where We Build’: Bruno Taut and his house on the Bosphorus

Paola Ardizzola

All nationalist architecture is bad, but all good architecture is national.
– Bruno Taut ‘Türk Evi, Sinan, Ankara’ (1938)

Bruno Taut (1880–1938) was an established architect in Berlin after designing a number of the innovative housing units, or *Siedlungen*, when he was forced to flee the Nazis in 1933. He first moved to Japan, where he devoted himself to understanding the local culture, which led him to write several texts on Japanese architecture and society. In 1936, he moved to Turkey, where he lived until his death.

Just two days after arriving in Japan, Taut visited the Katsura Imperial Villa, built in the seventeenth century. He marked in his notebook the clarity of the lines that made up the space articulation, considering the villa a timeless architecture with an empathic affinity to the Modern Movement. By emphasising the importance of traditional architecture as a stimulus for the architecture of the future in his book *Houses and People of Japan*, Taut warned against the uncritical imitation of Western life. In the design of his house in Istanbul, he reinterpreted old vernacular elements, such as the ribbon windows of the wooden residences along the Bosphorus and the eaves of the typical Turkish house.

Taut arrived in Turkey thanks to his former colleague Martin Wagner, who was already working in Istanbul. He was immediately appointed chief architect of the Ministry of Education’s construction office and head of the department of architecture at Istanbul Fine Arts Academy. After three years in Japan, a time which Taut himself defined as ‘my vacation from architecture’, the architect became strongly engaged in both academic life and designing in Turkey.[1] His twenty-four projects in the Middle East granted him a renewed activism in the process of *Baukunst*. During the 1920s, the central themes of Taut’s activism focussed on the effective engagement of the architect for the renewal of the society: ‘Activism arose out of a desire to reconcile the anarchic impulses of expressionism with the need for social reform.’[2] In Turkey, Taut reconfirmed this approach by trying to facilitate the dynamic between two impulses: the strong necessity of a modern Turkish cultural identity on one hand, and the strenuous attempt to achieve an inclusive language of architecture that referred to both tradition and modernity on the other.

In 1923 crucial changes took place in Turkey when a new republic was born from the ruins of the Ottoman Empire. The president Atatűrk introduced great innovations, bringing the state in line with to Western civilisation. He opened the doors to secular Western culture by welcoming intellectuals, especially from German-speaking

1
Although involved in the design of several buildings, Taut did not realise any architectural project in Japan. He did, however, redesign the interiors of Villa Hyuga and Villa Okura. He was also very active in the field of applied arts as an industrial designer.

2
Whyte, *Bruno Taut and the Architecture of Activism*, 16.

Fig. 1 South-east front towards the sea, House on the Bosphorus. Bruno Taut, Istanbul, 1938. (Photograph by © Haruhiko Fujita. Archive Paola Ardizzola)

3
Taut did not talk of form and function but of different lifestyle contents, from which new forms of architecture could arise. See Ardizzola, 'Architectural Practice and Theory'.

4
Zevi, 'Uno storico italiano in Turchia'.

countries, offering them prestigious positions in cultural and academic fields. The country was for the European exiles the ideal adopted homeland thanks to the open pro-Western attitude. Ankara was ready to receive the frankness and transparency of the Neues Bauen under the influence of German architects. In this promising environment, Taut decided to build his own house in Istanbul by integrating the principles of functionalism, which had guided the design of his former house in Berlin-Dahlewitz (1926), his personal interpretation of Neues Bauen.[3] In 1955, Bruno Zevi described Taut's house:

> Perhaps the most beautiful and undoubtedly the most human construction built by Taut is precisely the small villa erected to the north of Galata, in the midst of a park situated on a steep slope, set in a wonderful area along the Bosphorus. [...] This small villa raised up on four high columns evokes in the undulating play of the roofs the rhythms of Japanese domestic architecture. Its red walls stand out amidst the green of nature; the living room is connected by an inner staircase to the turret-studio wrapped by a continuous semi-hexagonal window that coagulates all the panoramic axes of the Bosphorus.[4]

Zevi argued that the house was perhaps intentionally ignored because of the difficulty interpreting its combination of features, inspired both by traditional architecture and functionalism. Indeed, the house requires a critical reading according to pluralistic aspects **(Fig. 1)**. Adherence to the criteria of the Modern Movement is legible only in plan; the functional distribution of the spaces dominates with the same strength conferred upon his previous house project in Berlin. But the mediation between tradition and modernity is the project's key architectural achievement. The house shows the synthesis of Taut's entire work, distinctly presenting aspects of German functionalism in the plan distribution and type of windows; of Japanese culture in the roof's profile and the sun-breaker, which he had used for the first time in Villa Okura; and Turkish features in the eaves, the projecting cornice, the offset roofs, and the ribbon windows. Together they accomplish an original synthesis. There can also be found aspects of Taut's previous work – the round shape of the studio and the sequence of the projecting line of the roofs in the verticality have a precedent in Taut's project for the pavilions of the Folkwang Schule in Hagen, designed in 1920. In the Hagen project, the geometrical form has its raison d'être in its strict relationship with the surrounding landscape to grant the utmost visual opening. Bülent Ozer, an architectural scholar who studied under Taut, wrote:

> The house built by Taut in Istanbul for himself is a perfect synthesis of his entire career, stirred by antithetical tendencies and nevertheless deeply soaked in humanism: hidden in a wood on the European shore of the Bosphorus, it is now very close to the gigantic pillars of a recently built bridge. Its plan – a main level and a lookout – is conformed to the essential features of Turkish and Japanese architecture, without giving way to a banal eclecticism. In other words, it is not the forms that have been borrowed, stylised or interpreted, but the abstract essences. Through the definition of new needs and new means, the profound principles

Fig. 2 Plan and west elevation, House on the Bosphorus. Bruno Taut, Istanbul, 1938. (Drawings by © Paola Ardizzola)

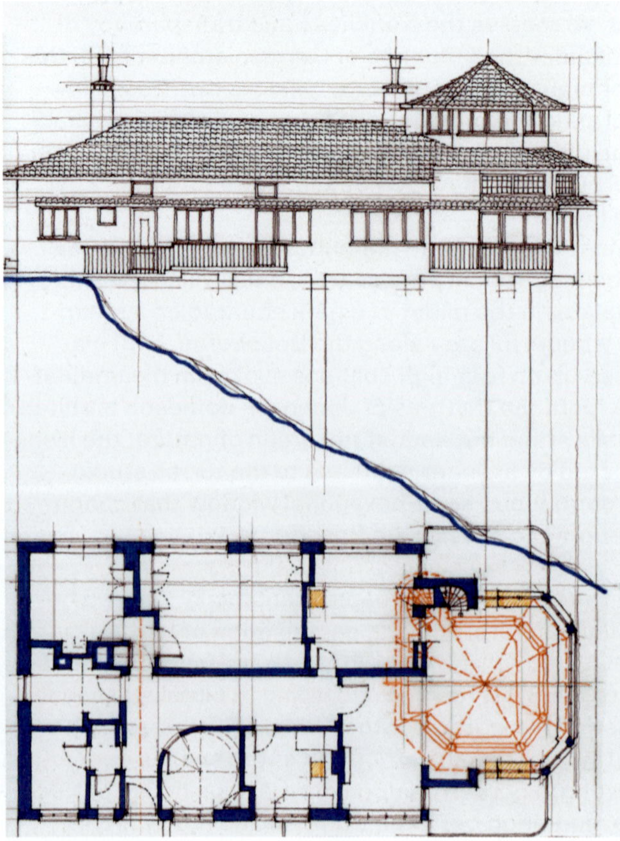

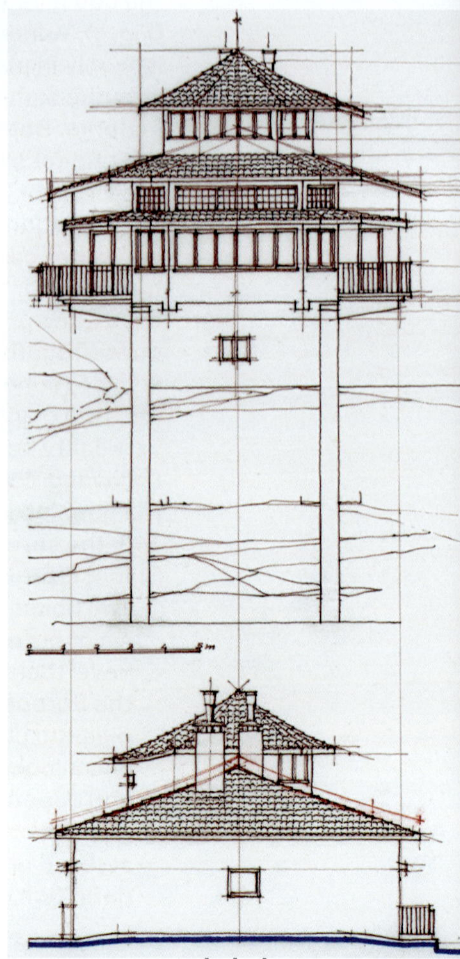

Fig. 3 South-east and north-west elevations, House on the Bosphorus. Bruno Taut, Istanbul, 1938. (Drawings by © Paola Ardizzola)

5
Őzer, 'La casa dell'anima/ A home for the soul', 28–9.

of two different civilisations converge and intertwine in a configuration that is completely modern and current.[5]

The building, realised in 1938, features a rectangular plan on one floor; it rests on a hill overlooking the Bosphorus with a daring cantilever **(Fig. 2)**. In fact, only a fifth of the house is anchored to the rock, while the remaining part is supported by two imposing reinforced concrete pillars. The living room, oriented to the south-east, looks over the water and supports the architect's octagonal studio, located in a turret similar to a captain's deck. To access the studio, Taut designed a very narrow, semi-spiral staircase, elegant in its sinuous curve and reminiscent of a ship's stairway. In the studio turret, Taut incorporated the concept of the crystal in a detail reminiscent of expressionist avant-garde: he placed a mirror on the back of the door; when the door is closed, the continuous walls become a surface of dialogue with the visual axes of the landscape.

The plan presents a rational distribution of the rooms in keeping with the flexibility of the different functions; the dining and living rooms feature comfortable built-in cupboards, and the access to the service zones is distinguished from the main entrance. The double-height living room refers to the architect's climatological theory: in Mediterranean areas, it is appropriate to filter the intense light. For this reason, the same room features different types of windows depending on whether they are positioned above or below the sun-breaker that runs the entire length of the building. The roofing echoes the traditional Turkish pavilion roof, with a Japanese flavour **(Fig. 3)**. Its external image refers to the morphology of Japanese dwellings in the roofline defined by Taut as 'reminiscent of a Samurai sword' while also referencing the traditional Turkish house.

An architect's own home represents a world in which they reveal aspects of their private needs; it can also, at the same time, be seen as a new architectural type. In few cases, the architect builds two different homes. Taut did so, in Berlin and Istanbul; the two projects have in common the will of creating functional and flexible spaces based on different requirements. The flexibility of spaces comes from the lesson of functionalism, but together with specific attention to the context, which includes climate and topography. Related to functionalism is the design of the kitchen, which is easily accessible from the living room to facilitate housework; the closets are mainly wall cabinets to ensure the least obstruction. There is a common trait, which has a precedent for both houses: it is the use of the circular shape. In the Berlin house, a quarter of a circle determines the general layout of the house's main body; in Istanbul, it is used for determining the living room and the studio. The use of circular plans dates back to 1921 when Taut designed several family houses for the Mitteldeutschen Ausstellung für Siedlung in Magdeburg **(Fig. 4)**; he justified the circular plan as follows:

> In a circular plan, the relationship between surface and perimeter is more advantageous, and this constitutes an essential factor for the economy of the external walls. [...] Even domestic life will be positively influenced and renewed by the new shape of the

Fig. 4 Bruno Taut, Family house-type project for a *Siedlung*, 1921. (Bruno Taut, *Frühlicht. 1920–1922*, Berlin: Ullstein, 1963)

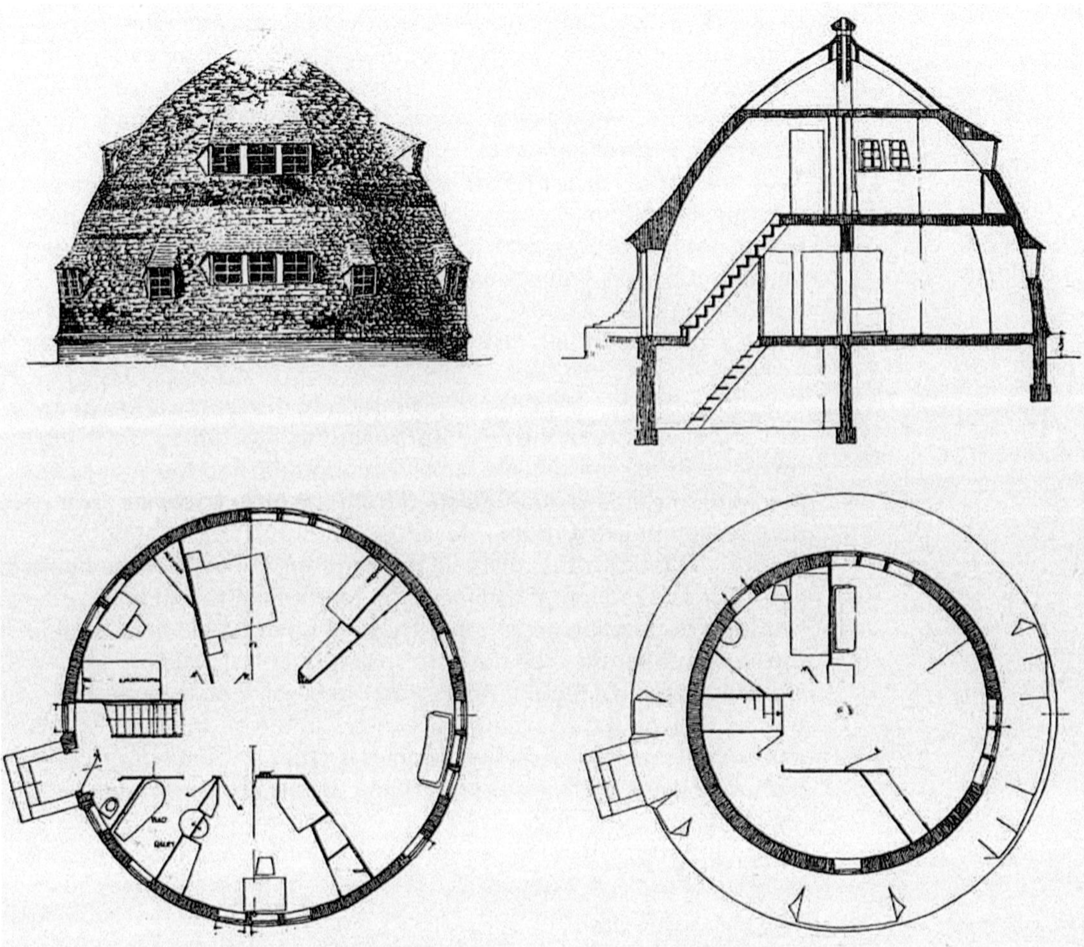

6
Taut, *1920–1922 Frühlicht. Gli anni dell'avanguardia architettonica in Germania*, 125–6.

7
Eldem, *Elli Yillik Meslek Jubilesi*, 19.

8
Taut, letter to Carl Krayl dated 6 May 1938, Akademie der Künste [AdK], Berlin, Bruno-Taut-Archiv- und Sammlung.

house. The cabinets become built-in wardrobes; only pieces of furniture and beds remain as real furniture; [...] the windows, conceived as a unit, are articulated in a different way, depending on whether they are used for lighting the rooms or to have a view from the outside.[6]

Subsequently, in his 1926 Berlin house and in his 1938 Instanbul house, he reiterated the same architectural assumption with great coherence.

The coeval Turkish architect Sedat Hakki Eldem highlighted the alienating impact of Western modernism, emphasising how the new architectural features of Turkish culture can neither be imported from the West nor be based only on the Ottoman culture. He suggested the search for an authentic expression of modern Turkish culture, cultivated exclusively on the basis of a passionate nationalist idealism. This is Eldem's limit, as epitomised in his writing *The Turkish House* (1948), with respect to Taut: in search for an idyllic style, the Turkish architect remained blind to the values of modernity, while for Taut the synthesis between cultural values and a new idea of architecture continued to be the primary objective to be pursued. The living room of Taut's house is the focal point of a functional plan, which daringly extends out over the Bosphorus thanks to new materials and technologies. The house also has a sense of warmth and intimacy through its interior space, which is that of the *diwan*, the Turkish living room, whose interior perimeter is surrounded by comfortable seats **(Figs. 5 and 5a)**. The rounded shape of the balcony slabs recover the typical corner solution of vernacular houses by means of wooden cornices. Even the continuous horizontal glazed surfaces do not derive from the ribbon windows claimed by the Modern Movement, but rather from the eighteenth-century Ottoman residence. Regarding the use of colour, Taut used a rusted red hue, referring to many houses along the Bosphorus, as well as to his earlier works – the family house at Weissenhof, the Hufeisen Siedlung *Rote Front*, and the interiors in Dahlewitz House.

With his house on the Bosphorus, the architect echoed Eldem's belief that the Turkish house could represent a criticism of modern architecture: 'The open plan, the emphasis on comfort over ostentation, honesty in the use of materials, a generous "supply" of rooms, open spaces and courtyards. Are these not perhaps the characteristics that we look for in the modern house? But we can find all them in the traditional Turkish house', stated Eldem, thereby expressing Taut's approach toward tradition in the light of modernity.[7]

In a letter written to Carl Krayl, a colleague while working in Magdeburg, Taut acknowledged the characteristics of modernism in his project: 'a new Dahlewitz is being born here', aware of the revolutionary impact the residential project in Berlin had.[8] Also communicating the modernism expressed by Taut's house is a drawing by Franz Hillinger – his partner in Turkey – realised in 1965 from memory in which the house looks like a spaceship just landed on the Bosphorus shore **(Fig. 6)**. In fact, Hillinger's recollection is the futuristic

Figs. 5 and 5a Typological comparison between the typical living room of the Turkish vernacular home, the *diwan*, and the living room of Taut's house. Taut's spatiality and search for brightness have a close correlation with the ancient Ottoman residence. (Drawings by © Paola Ardizzola)

approach of his colleague. It is relevant to recall the comparison with Dahlewitz outlined by Kurt Junghanns:

> Everything was modest there [in Dahlewitz], a Berlin suburb lacking artistic attractions and set in a uniform Brandenburg landscape with a relatively moderate climate; here a land rich in history, one of the most beautiful landscapes on earth and the Mediterranean climate. In Dahlewitz Taut had deepened the possible relationships between a building, the landscape and the sun, and had expressed through his house the principles he maintained even in the most trivial details; now he had disconnected his house from the constraints of the earth by presenting it, as a welcoming prism, in an environment of beauty and splendour in any direction one should happen to look.[9]

In the same letter to Carl Krayl, Taut wrote a few lines relevant to understanding the meaning he attributed to his stay in Turkey: 'With an absolutely different appearance there rises above the cobalt blue of the Bosphorus and on arboreal supports some 15 meters high the columbarium of a Noah soon nine hundred years old.'[10] Bernd Nicolai stated that the German architect lived with no pleasure in the land of Sinan: 'The situation of the exile is expressed by Taut with full knowledge. The isolated treehouse, which can be read as a wish for detachment from the foreign Eastern soil, stretches out towards the Bosphorus alluding to the deck of a ship.'[11] Yet the house is not a docked ship waiting to set sail, but a 'columbarium of a Noah soon nine hundred years old'. Not a ship, therefore, but its conceptual opposite: an ark, firmly placed on a promontory. Taut chose the site upon which to build his dwelling intelligently: on the European shore of the Bosphorus, only a few blocks from the Fine Arts Academy where he was working, at a point where the hill of the Ortaköy district folds and protects the entire area from the north winds.

From his octagonal turret studio, a geometry favoured in few other projects including the Stahlverband pavilion in Leipzig, Taut observed the East from the last outpost of the West. His home interiors are shaped by the daylight, which ranges from the dawn's rosy colour to the dusk's bright red. Far from mere functionalism, the house embeds the use of light as a spiritual element for stimulating the senses. This poetry is the *trait d'union* with Taut's early projects in Germany; this sensibility tinged with the romantic *Weltanschauung* guided the architect also in designing the Turkish buildings. Taut accepted the geographical, cultural, and environmental change not as a constraint but as a challenge for rephrasing his architectural ideas in a new context. Therefore, the house on the Bosphorus is the confirmation of the artistic will expressed in the early years of his career: 'Today more than ever we believe in our will, which creates for us the only life value. And this value is: everlasting change.'[12]

Thus, in spite of the confrontation with a different culture, Taut remained faithful to his motto – 'our homeland is where we build' – a chance he was not granted in Japan. On the basis of such a construct, Turkey was his adopted homeland.

9
Junghanns, *Bruno Taut 1880–1938*, 206.

10
Taut, letter to Carl Krayl dated 6 May 1938. The metaphor of the ark was already mentioned within the Gläserne Kette. Hermann Finsterlin wrote: 'My friends, isn't the ark our only symbol, the domestic house born from the cliff and the sea?' in Borsi, *Hermann Finsterlin*, 134.

11
Nicolai, 'L'esilio. L'architettura di Bruno Taut', 198.

12
Taut, 'Frühlicht (Daybreak)', 63.

Fig. 6 Franz Hillinger, Bruno Taut's house on the Bosphorus, 1965. (Kurt Junghanns, *Bruno Taut 1880–1938*, Berlin: Henschelverlag, 1970)

Fig. 7 Main front, Faculty of Letters, Geography, and History. Bruno Taut, Ankara, 1937–39. (Photograph by © Paola Ardizzola)

A month after his arrival in Turkey, Taut was engaged in designing the first Ankara University building **(Fig. 7)**. He worked on this project with passion and enthusiasm, as revealed in a letter written to Isaburo Ueno, a Japanese colleague:

> I have begun to build a great building for the Ankara University. As the new home of the Faculty of Letters and Geography, it will become a focal point of modern Turkish culture. For this reason, they have placed excellent stone and top-quality materials at my disposal for the building. But what makes me truly happy is that I enjoy complete artistic freedom.[13]

Perhaps it was the first time Taut could make this affirmation: free from the constraints of a tight budget, from the obligations imposed by the German *Baupolizei*, and from urban planning restrictions. Thus, the building is the result of a completely free design idea. Though it had to reify and celebrate the grandeur of Atatürk's vision, the university is a landmark in the architectural panorama and even Taut's Turkish schools become a typological prototype. But the final goal of Taut's architecture is represented in his house, a realm in which he evokes aspects of the Turkish culture combined with sound functionalism. Taut was a *Mitläufer*, an architect entitled to walk his architectural path in lands far from Germany; as long as he was able to build, he reified the concept of *gemütlich* as the most important aspect of a house to satisfy human needs.

At the end of his career, the process of generating new architecture was for Taut based on continuity, as a conjugation between tradition and modernity. According to this meaning, he seemed to be more of a romantic conservative than a modernist pioneer; in truth, he wanted to signify the impossibility for any culture of abandoning the link with its own milieu, in which the architectural process must be understood to generate new architecture. For Taut, to build in the best iteration of tradition was modernity, that is, searching for the relationship between the aspiration of a place and the inspiration of its tradition. This stimulated the architect's perception of a renewed activism, engaged in designing a house that is both modern and the repository of historical values that evolve by changing geographic, climatic, and urban scenarios. They epitomised the ultimate significance of a space designed in the light of humanism. The house on the Bosphorus adheres to these values that fluctuate between Taut's search for continuity and the paradigm of modernism. Considered in the light of Gaston Bachelard's concept of 'fundamental value',[14] Taut shows in his Turkish house, once more, the urgency of expressing spatial and emotional values: 'The house for living actually is the most immediate realm of human life, its first and last product.'[15] In the house on the Bosphorus, evidence that home is a privileged space for human experience becomes crystal clear.

13
Taut, letter to Isaburo Ueno dated 11 June 1937, in Technical University of Instanbul, *Thinking of Ataturk*, 63.

14
'The house, quite obviously, is a privileged entity for a phenomenological study of the intimate values of inside space, provided, of course, that we take it in both its unity and its complexity, and endeavor to integrate all the special values in one fundamental value'. Bachelard, *The Poetics of Space*, 3.

15
Taut, *Ein Wohnhaus*, 19.

Bibliography

Akademie der Künste [AdK], Berlin, Bruno-Taut-Archiv- und Sammlung.

Akcan, Esra, and Bernd Nicolai. *Building in Exile – Bruno Taut. Turkey 1936–1938*. Salenstein: Niggli, 2019.

Akcan, Esra. 'Towards a Cosmopolitan Ethics in Architecture: Bruno Taut's Translations out of Germany'. *New German Critique*, no. 3 (2006): 7–39.

Ardizzola, Paola. 'Architectural Practice and Theory: The Case of Bruno Taut's House in Berlin-Dahlewitz'. *Vitruvio*, no. 1 (2017): 44–56.

Bachelard, Gaston. *The Poetics of Space*. London: Beacon Press, 1994.

Borsi, Franco. *Hermann Finsterlin*. Florence: Libreria Editrice Fiorentina, 1968.

Eldem, Sedat Hakki. *Elli Yillik Meslek Jubilesi*. Istanbul: Mimar Sinan University, 1983.

Junghanns, Kurt. *Bruno Taut 1880–1938*. Milan: Franco Angeli, 1978. Original in German: Berlin: Henschelverlag Kunst und Gesellschaft, 1970.

Koenig, Giovanni Klaus. 'Bruno Taut: riflessioni e valutazioni sul destino dell'architettura'. In *Architettura del Novecento. Teoria, storia, pratica critica*. Venice: Marsilio, 1995.

Lejeune, Jean-François and Michelangelo Sabatino. *Modern Architecture and the Mediterranean: Vernacular Dialogues and Contested Identities*. London: Routledge, 2010.

Nicolai, Bernd. 'L'esilio. L'architettura di Bruno Taut e la Turchia kemalista del 1936-38'. In *Bruno Taut 1880–1938*, edited by Winfried Nerdinger, 192–207. Milan: Electa, 2001.

Nicolai, Bernd. *Moderne und Exil, Deutschsprachige Architekten in der Turkei 1925–1955*, Berlin: Verlag für Bauwesen, 1998.

Őzer, Bulent. 'La casa dell'anima/A home for the soul'. *Domus*, no. 611 (1980): 28–9.

Speidel, Manfred. *Bruno Taut, Natur und Phantasie*. Berlin: Ernst & Sohn, 1995.

Taut, Bruno. *1920-1922 Frühlicht. Eine Folge für die Verwirklichung des neuen Baugedankens*. Magdeburg: Kark Peters Verlag, 1921–1922. In Italian: *1920–1922 Frühlicht. Gli anni dell'avanguardia architettonica in Germania*. Milano: Mazzotta, 1974.

Taut, Bruno. *Frühlicht. 1920–1922.* Berlin: Ullstein, 1963.

Taut, Bruno. *Ein Wohnhaus*. Stuttgart: Franckh'sche Verlagshandlung W. Keller and Co, 1927. In Italian: *Una casa di abitazione*. Milan: Franco Angeli, 1986.

Taut, Bruno. 'Türk Evi, Sinan, Ankara'. *Her Ay*, no. 2 (1938): 93–8.

Taut, Bruno, 'Frühlicht" (Daybreak)'. In *Programs and Manifestoes on 20th-Century Architecture*, edited by Ulrich Conrads; translated by Michael Bullock. Cambridge, MA: The MIT Press, 1971.

Technical University of Istanbul. *Thinking of Ataturk: The Catafalque and Anitkabir. Two Architects: Bruno Taut and Emin Onat*. Istanbul: Technical University of Istanbul, 1998.

Whyte, Iain Boyd. *Bruno Taut and the Architecture of Activism*. Cambridge: Cambridge University Press, 1982.

Zevi, Bruno. 'Uno storico italiano in Turchia – Nel nome di Allah misura il tardo antico'. *L'espresso*, 25 January 1955; republished in *Cronache di Architettura*. Vol. 2. Rome-Bari: Laterza 1978.

Domesticity and Public Life

The five architect homes discussed in the third section highlight the synergy that can occur between domesticity and public life when architects use their own dwellings to promote their practice. They point to different ways in which the private lives of architects rub against their public stature and the nurturing of a public persona.

In two instances, the Boyarsky residency in central London and Arthur Erickson's home in Vancouver, architect houses played an explicit part in the public role of the architects. In her chapter 'A Non-Conformist Garage', Christina Gray tells the compelling story of how Canadian architect Arthur Erickson used his own house in Vancouver as a decades-long experiment (1957–2009) tailored at cultivating his flamboyant public persona and his qualities, as an architect, to challenge social conventions and planning regulations. Rather than using his own home as a showpiece to attract a suburban residential clientele, Erickson's house was just a small converted garage enlivened by lavish garden parties. The home – a mere pied-à-terre – here contributed to a narrative of the visionary, cosmopolitan architect whose real home was the world. A very different picture emerges in Nicholas Boyarsky's discussion of the physical and social transformations of a central London terraced house that has served as the Boyarsky family home – first Alvin then Nicholas – since 1972 and was before then the home of another architect and editor, Robert Middleton, and artist and poet Ruth Lakofski. Nicholas Boyarsky's chapter, 'House X', reveals how one private residence can reflect the changing architectural cultures of the time, and how it can transition from a private retreat rooted in the countercultural mood of the 1960s into a more outward looking home, connected to the Architectural Association and its network of global visitors cultivated under Alvin Boyarsky's chairmanship during the 1970s and 1980s. As its architect-occupants since the 1990s, Nicholas and his wife and partner Nicola substantially transformed the house into a private home, architectural office, and a living archive of the previous decades. Rather than using the private home to cultivate an architect's public image as Erickson did, the different generations of 'House X' used the house to facilitate productive exchanges with the outside world.

In two other houses discussed in this section – by women architects Flora Ruchat-Roncati and Eileen Gray – public life is closely intertwined with personal circumstances and gender. In their chapter 'A Collective Archipelago', Irina Davidovici and Eliana Perotti introduce the historical courtyard ensemble that Flora Ruchat-Roncati refurbished and extended for herself and others in Riva San Vitale, Ticino, Switzerland, beginning in 1967. They show how the collective living components of the residence reflect not just the resistant and convivial mood of 1968 but also, on a more pragmatic level, the needs of a young architect seeking to build a home for herself as a single parent while also finding recognition in a male-dominated profession. The project's resistant element offered by communal living must have arguably provoked the provincial setting of Ticino, but, so Davidovici and Perotti argue, this collective component also facilitated the architect's professional life in that it allowed her to be part of a community of intellectual peers while raising a family. Rather than boosting the architect's public image, as architect houses often set out to do, Flora Ruchat-Roncati's house shows the more embodied ways in which the own home can respond to the personal and professional needs of an architect, a capacity that seems especially important for women in the profession. Indeed, in their revisiting of Eileen Gray's iconic E-1027 house, built in 1929 in the south of France not far away from where Le Corbusier would later build his Le Cabanon, Thea Brejzek and Lawrence Wallen recount a very public stand-off between two architects and their holiday homes; a struggle, so Brejzek and Wallen argue, centred not just on Le Corbusier's resistance to Eileen Gray as an architect, but also as a woman. In their chapter 'Le Corbusier and Eileen Gray at Roquebrune', Gray's house becomes both the instigator and target of several 'performative acts of resistance' by Le Corbusier unfolding between 1929 and 1956. An architect's house (E-1027) is here mobilised not just to inform the public image of its creator, but is used, through acts of violation, domination, and appropriation, to mould the public image of *another* architect (Le Corbusier). The story of E-1027, as told in Brejzek and Wallen's chapter, expands our understanding of the own house as a site of resistance beyond the architect-creator and opens an uncomfortable space wherein resistance becomes directed towards another architect, in part to boost one's own public image.

In the final chapter in this section, 'Tomato, Acropolis, and the Power of Family', Farhan Karim discusses Constantinos Doxiadis's apartment built in 1957 in Athens, Greece. After a difficult stay in Australia this apartment building, which included his office and residence, signified Doxiadis's newfound success in Greece as an architect. Rather than radically departing from the dominant building practices of the time, Doxiadis's apartment tapped into the bottom-up entrepreneurial construction boom of Athens in the shape of multifamily, multistoreyed apartments known as *polykatoikia*. As an apartment located in such a development project, so Karim observes, Doxiadis challenged the understanding of an architect's own home as a consciously designed (single-family) 'house'. Instead, it embodied the Greek economic housing development model based on incremental growth and bottom-up entrepreneurial self-help, ideas that Doxiadis could connect back to his time in Australia where his struggles and frustrations had contributed to deepening his understandings of self-help and entrepreneurial aspects of family life.

House X

Nicholas Boyarsky

This is a story of a typical London terrace house that happens to have been in the hands of different generations of architects since the early 1960s. It has proved sufficiently robust and adaptable to accommodate different living conditions and has, in turn, expressed and shaped the owners' thoughts on architecture and the function of a house: as a safe haven (with submarine doors); as a place to shape global discourses on architectural education and culture; and as a site for architectural production and an archive.

The house is a five-storey terraced house in a mid-Victorian London square located north of Euston Road and sandwiched between rail infrastructure and the former rookeries of Somers Town. From 1963 to 1972 the architect, editor, and historian Robin Middleton and the architect, artist, and poet Ruth Lakofski lived in the house; and, since 1972, it has been the home to three generations of the Boyarsky family. The house has undergone many structural transformations in response to the changing needs and desires of its inhabitants, who have all been actively engaged in the architectural cultures of their times. Initially forming an experiment in domestic living based on the prevailing counterculture of drugs, sexual liberation, and a conscious withdrawal from everyday life, the house then became a highly personalised base for engagement with the radical architecture and education of the 1970s and 1980s that was closely linked to the Architectural Association (AA) in Bedford Square and to wider global networks. The house has since evolved into a site for architectural practice for formal and material experimentation, and into an archive of material from the preceding decades. Tracing the parallel histories of the house, both the alterations to its physical fabric and the emotional and intellectual lives of its inhabitants, reveals congruences and consistencies that represent both an active engagement in – and a resistance to – the outside world as framed and mediated by the particularities of interior experiences.

Hypodermic space to soul box: 1963–1972

Robin Middleton and Ruth Lakofski bought the house in the early 1960s and proceeded to transform it into their home from 1963. At some point shortly afterwards, Ruth met artist and transgender clothing designer Billy Walton on a park bench in St James's Park, London, and he joined their lives until his death in New York in 2004. Plans from October 1963 annotated by Middleton show that the existing house was to be stripped of existing services and subdivisions in order to form a home with two studios, two studies, three bedrooms, a kitchen, living room, three bathrooms, and a WC **(Fig. 1)**. The two bathrooms were designed to be capsule-like: they were painted white; all the corners were rounded and soft with recessed light fittings and white rubber flooring. Each bathroom had a central service core from which the white bath, toilet, basin, and bidet radiated. Porcelain urinal dividers were fixed horizontally into alcoves to form

Fig. 1 Second-floor plan with annotations by Robin Middleton, 1963. (© Alvin Boyarsky Archive)

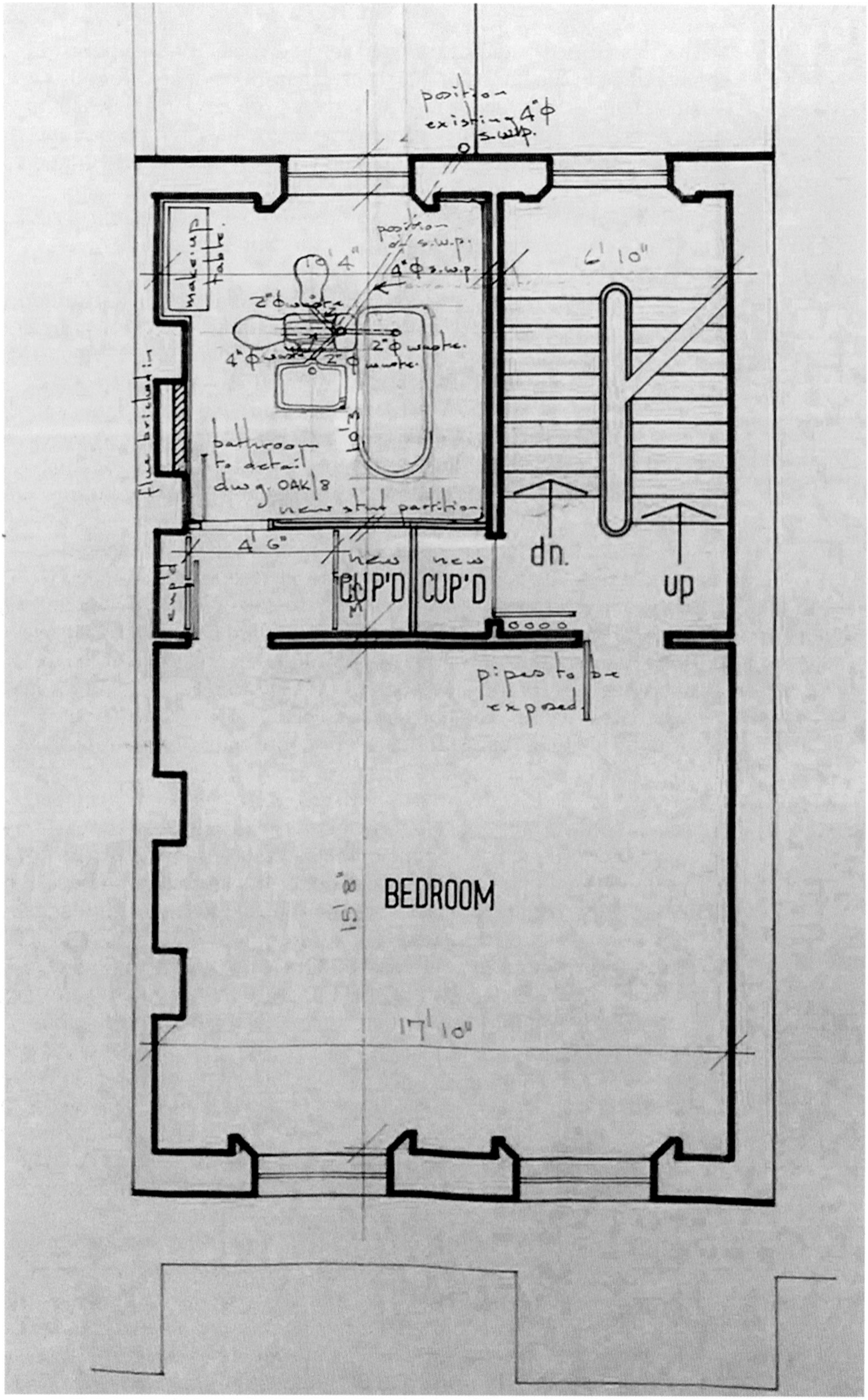

make-up tables, and the mirrors were silver mylar-coated, space-age ovals **(Fig. 2)**. Doors to the bathrooms and bedrooms were designed as submarine airlock doors, made from mirror-like polished aluminium with rounded corners and oval-shaped, aluminium-clad frames trimmed with black rubber gasket seals.[1]

Other key features included industrial bulkhead light fittings and rotating coloured siren lights at each landing. All vertical hot- and cold-water copper pipework was exposed. Walls to the basement study and bedroom were clad with floor-to-ceiling, galvanised zinc panels. The first-floor living room and kitchen were finished with mahogany floorboards and the space was heated by orange pipework that occupied most of the front room.

Work to the house took several years to complete and Robin enlisted the help and advice of Archigram members Ron Herron and Warren Chalk, whose influence can be seen in the capsule bathrooms. Robin was at the time working at the invitation of fellow South African Theo Crosby in his experimental Taylor Woodrow Design Group on an urban project for the redesign of Euston Station alongside several members of the Archigram group.

Robin became technical editor of *Architectural Design* magazine in 1964, then under the editorship of Monica Pidgeon, a position that Crosby had held from 1953 until 1962 when he was succeeded briefly by Kenneth Frampton. Robin's tenure, until 1972, saw *AD* become one of the key 'little magazines' of the period and 'probably the most international magazine at that time, as a network for underground, or half underground ideas'.[2]

While Middleton's career in London was very much at the forefront of radical avant-garde discourse, Lakofski was more introverted and reclusive. Trained as an architect at the AA, she became an artist and poet,[3] producing a body of work that is unfortunately barely known to the world.[4] Lakofski wrote for *AD* sporadically from the mid 1960s, and her critique of the social and political implications of the indeterminacy and often naive optimism in the future that she detected in the writings of Reyner Banham, the work of Archigram, and the projects of Cedric Price was mirrored by her increasing withdrawal from public life. In an article published in *AD*'s 'Cosmorama' section in July 1966, Lakofski takes issue with Banham's lecture at the Folkestone IDEA conference, where he foretold the end of architecture as 'enclosure business'.[5] She introduces a note of pessimism and uncertainty in the face of the celebration of the megastructural and technological vision of a liberated environmental architecture:

> I'm afraid the new romantic 'places' with their visual barriers – hoardings one year, neon the next – will fall quietly by the wayside as surely as have Cedric's queues for candles. Because just as surely as in our new hypodermic world we can have our 'shot' against the rain, so we can have our 'shot' against contact – all physical contact. For we have the picture-telephone, the closed circuit telly and the schools of the air. No need to get together

1
Hans Hollein designed a similar door for the Feigin Gallery in New York in 1969. *Architecture d'Aujourdhui*, no. 151 (1970): 75.

2
Robin Middleton quoted in Colomina and Buckley, *Clip Stamp Fold*, 28. 'Little magazines' refers to the 1960s term to describe radical independent architectural magazines.

3
Ruth's sister Denise Scott Brown, who also studied at the AA, later married Robert Venturi.

4
Middleton has curated the ground floor of their Manhattan home as an exhibition of Lakofski's work.

5
The International Dialogue of Experimental Architecture, Folkestone, June 1966 was organised by Archigram.

Fig. 2 Photograph of the second-floor bathroom, 1976. (© Alvin Boyarsky Archive)

for the no-food food. And when at last we have the no-sex sex – a 'shot' too perhaps in the dark – we will have cut the natal cord and we shall be free.[6]

In her article 'Going to Seed', published in 1970, Lakofski draws on the sexual and drug countercultures of the time, exemplified by the trio's own alternative and hermetic home lifestyle, to attack the puritanical and repressed life-denying qualities of modern architecture and to argue for withdrawal from everyday life in the pursuit of personal freedom: 'Freedom is obtained only by a sub-conscious confrontation of monsters; our own, our families and our spirit-damaging schools. We have all been victims of pre-programming, and the more active we are the more we ingrain our inhibitions.'[7] The layout of the house, whereby each member had distinct individual realms for withdrawal and creative work, set the pattern for their future homes and it also underlaid Lakofski's extremely critical take on the contemporary architectural scene. This position – together with her critique of the teleological view of the technological future – influenced the architectural writer Robin Evans, who acknowledged his debt to Lakofski in a dystopian *AD* article of 1971, suggesting that while information may be morally neutral 'it is certainly not inactive' and that it 'might just as easily discompose and confuse individuals and communities as enlighten them'.[8] Evans concludes darkly, noting, that the 'birth of a new technic of human failure' has led to a return of a collective 'desire for sanctuary'.[9]

Middleton, Lakofski, and Walton formed a series of homes after 1972 in London's Notting Hill; in Laight Street, Manhattan; in Willow, upstate New York; and, finally, in the East Village.[10] Each was characterised by an intense interiority and the desire to create a space, or 'soul box', that could be a daemonic 'container of the exploring soul' where, as Lakofski wrote in 1988, the fears and yearnings of individuals are subsumed into 'those forms of arts which manage to stay free of market pressures, as well as religious and even philosophical concepts'.[11] An indication of this interiority can be seen today in Lakofski's realm within her East Village home, which comprised the ground floor of the former tile factory where all walls, floors, ceilings, and windows are painted black and her artworks are displayed in various nooks and crannies.

X Square/Bedford Square: 1972–1990

I used to sit in my bathrobe at the kitchen table in Chicago and call Moscow, you know, and do things. – Alvin Boyarsky, interview with Bill Mount (1980)[12]

Alvin and Elizabeth Boyarsky purchased the house from Middleton and Lakofski in 1972 and moved in with their children, Victoria and me, shortly afterwards. They did little structural work to the property. They removed the kitchen from the first floor and made a new one on the ground floor; otherwise the house was painted, floors were clad with cork, and windows and doors were repaired where necessary. The layout of the house and the usage of different

6
Lakofski, 'Oh, Please, Mr Banham', 322.

7
Lakofski, 'Going to Seed', 325.

8
Evans, 'The Rights of Retreat and the Rites of Exclusion', 335–9.

9
Evans, 'The Rights of Retreat and the Rites of Exclusion', 335.

10
For the Laight Street home, see Perry Ogden's photographic essay in Bergdoll and Oechslin, *Fragments: Architecture and the Unfinished*; for the East Village home, see de Looz, 'Robin Middleton's Remarkable East Village Haven for Books'

11
Lakofski, 'Reflexions on the Soul Box', 101, 92–103.

12
Boyarsky, unpublished transcript of interview by Bill Mount, 1980, Alvin Boyarsky Archive, private collection.

rooms were adapted to their family's needs. The fourth-floor study became a bedroom, the two studios on the ground floor became the kitchen and dining room while the first floor became a living room and library. The studies lost their fixed locations: Elizabeth, a verbatim reporter, worked in a corner of the master bedroom; while Alvin worked at the long dining table in the first-floor living room overlooking the square. A garden was formed at the rear. Conceived as a sequence of outdoor rooms by Alvin and his friend and colleague Dale Benedict, who had joined him at the AA from the north-west of the United States, it was defined by plantings, recycled York stone and brick paving, Victorian chimney pots, and found statuary. North-facing and shaded, the garden became a significant social space for entertaining and for meetings in the summer months.

Despite relatively few alterations, the ethos of the house changed significantly from the Lakofski-Middleton model of the home as retreat and creative sanctuary, to become a central locus within a network of radical architectural and pedagogic discourse both in London and across the world. As a teenager I recall Alvin holding meetings and discussions each weekend, and that he and my mother would host dinners during the week. In fact, it would be fair to say that the majority of faculty and visitors to the AA during Alvin's tenure as chairman from 1971 to 1990 came to the house on numerous occasions. A guest list would include regulars such as Colin Rowe, Peter Eisenman, John Hejduk, Bernard Tschumi, Zaha Hadid, Dalibor Veseley, Daniel Libeskind, Sverre Fehn, and Peter Cook, alongside students, writers, and theorists. Architecture and politics were hotly debated as gossip and news were traded and exchanged.

X Square is a twenty-minute walk from the Architectural Association in Bedford Square, in the middle of Georgian London. Our house was triangulated with Bedford Square and Woburn Square, where Elizabeth had her offices. The AA occupied three Georgian houses at the time, which Alvin had refurbished with the architect Rick Mather. There were clear correlations between House X and the AA, which was infused with traces of domestic life. The Member's Room of the AA effectively became the school's living room; situated on the first floor, it overlooked the gardens of Bedford Square and led to the newly created bar. Alvin's office on the second floor had club sofas and comfortable Le Corbusier chairs, oriental rugs on the floor, and a fireplace which housed models and fragments of past exhibitions. There was a well-stocked drinks cabinet and the walls were lined with drawings and paintings from his collection. Alvin worked at a reproduction dining table designed by JJP Oud for the Weissenhof Siedlung in Stuttgart 1927. His conception of the living room as a club-like and creative space for education, debate, and events can be seen in the design of the AA125 exhibition of 1974. Celebrating the AA's one-hundred-and-twenty-fifth anniversary, the exhibition, which travelled the world, was focussed around a full-scale recreation, designed by Peter Cook, of the original Bedford Square Member's Room.[13] Also, at

13 **Architectural Association, *The AA 125 Exhibition*.**

14
Coop Himmelblau, *Just a House*.

home, the role of furniture within the public rooms of exchange and debate was central. The dining table, in particular, became a metaphor for discourse and social exchange. We have seen how the Oud table was central to Alvin's working methods in his living room/office at the AA; at home, life revolved around two dining tables: a circular table in the dining room and a long rectangular table in the living room. Family, guests, and visitors would gather around these tables, depending on the size of the event, for meals or meetings.

At home Alvin was an inveterate collector and bricoleur. The house was furnished with objects that were found, salvaged, or bought at street markets. These included vintage Baluchi rugs, Thonet chairs, Victorian chinaware, and a wide array of Victorian chests of drawers and sofas. A photograph from 1976 of the first-floor library reveals a constructed *mise en scene* of plants, a side table in front of the window, vintage furniture, books, and boxes of turn-of-the-century postcards of American cities **(Fig. 3)**. Books were a major subject for collection; they were mostly on architecture, but also included nineteenth-century travel books, art books, and photo books. The 1973 Coop Himmelblau workshop with AA students entitled 'The House with Flying Roof: Transformation of an Everyday Reality' initiated an expanded form of collecting and debate when a nearby terraced house was gutted and transformed into a sequence of constructed surreal spaces culminating in a roof garden with a large reflective hot air balloon.[14] Our house became a base camp for the project and, after the workshop, plants, and building elements migrated over to us to be added to the collection. Our home always had a public role which we took for granted, enjoying the house as a platform and vehicle for hosting and promoting exchange and debate around dinners and meetings. 'The house with flying roof' as a form of utopian squatting seemed a natural extension to this conviviality.

Domestic practices: 1992–present-day

Alvin Boyarsky died in August 1990 and his wife Elizabeth died in January 1991. Together with Nicola Murphy, I purchased my sister's share of the house in 1992 and we have lived here ever since. The house continues to evolve. It has become the site of our architectural practice, our family life, and of a growing archive of books, drawings, documents, and audio tapes. The transition from a private and deeply personal interior space for personal experimentation and alternative forms of living in the 1960s to a home linked into a global network of radical architectural discourse with intimate links to the AA in Bedford Square in the 1970s and 1980s became the site of spatial and material experimentation from the 1990s onwards. The house has also become an informal space for the curation of material from the previous decades of the house's occupation, which is open to researchers and students. In our digital age the lure of the analogue, of original printed material, ephemera, and hand drawings, is strong as it now represents a resistance to the increasing commodification of knowledge. Ironically Walter Benjamin's paradigm of 'the work

Fig. 3 Photograph of the first-floor library, 1976. (© Alvin Boyarsky Archive)

Fig. 4 Photograph of the first-floor library, 2016. (Photograph by © Anna Positano)

Fig. 5 *Left*: Photograph of the fireplace in Alvin Boyarsky's office at the AA, 1994; *right*: photograph of the fireplace at House X, 2019. (© Alvin Boyarsky Archive)

of art in the age of mechanical reproduction' has begun to give way to a new paradigm whereby the authentic and original, however incomplete or fragmentary, can seriously challenge the exponentially expanding data from the cloud.[15] This materialisation of dissent to the levelling of the digital age can be evidenced in ephemeral manifestations of new concepts and ideas that can be held and juxtaposed with others to stimulate and generate new thoughts. From this perspective, the struggles of Lakofski and Evans in 1971 to free of us from our demons and to question that our 'immersion in a milieu of indiscriminate emblems, images, messages and ideas might just as easily decompose and confuse individuals and communities as enlighten them' now seem eerily prescient.[16]

15
Benjamin, *Illuminations: Essays and Reflections*, 219–53.

16
Evans, 'The Rights of Retreat and the Rites of Exclusion', 335.

17
Sunwoo, 'Between the "Well-Laid Table" and the "Market Place"'; Marjanovic, 'Pedagogy into Practice'.

The work that we have undertaken to the house has been in different phases, starting with the separation of the basement from the main house by the removal of a flight of stairs in order to create a studio with its own separate entrance. Middleton's bathrooms had long ceased to work, and as the sanitaryware was encased in concrete, repair was impossible; therefore, we removed them. The submarine doors were kept and reinstalled as bedroom doors. A leaking pitched roof was replaced to become a roof garden and an additional outdoor room. We have experimented with materials such as leather, glass, resin, and wood to create furniture pieces, desks, and study areas. Our long-term work to the house has encouraged the development of an architecture of subtraction as slow demolition and the gradual exposure of fabric has led to the removal of elements such as walls, doors, and roofs and has stimulated dialogues between existing and new spatial conditions that have become central to our practice. This can be seen at the ground-floor level, where the constraints of a narrow corridor and a sequence of two rooms have been overturned by the creation a new dynamic of flow around two elements: the oval dining table, which is held by a curved wall, and a large, freestanding, rectangular marble kitchen island. The proximity of these two tabletops, one for the preparation of food and the other for eating at, and the tensions between them, provides for flexible and dynamic spaces of conviviality.

The relationship between home and work is similarly intertwined; and while the house is essentially a place for food and books, our studio is divided into two spaces – a room for drawing and a room for making models. New bookcases have been designed and built throughout the house to accommodate a growing library of architectural and photo books **(Fig. 4)**. Alvin never threw anything away so with the help and encouragement of Irene Sunwoo and Igor Marjanovic, who have both completed PhDs on Alvin Boyarsky,[17] we have been sorting through boxes and files of documents, audio tapes, and correspondence dating from the late 1950s until 1990 that help to trace the emergence of his ideas about architecture and education and the network of friends and colleagues that nurtured and stimulated his development. An example of this can be found in the International Institute of Design (IID) Summer Sessions that were held in London from 1970 to 1972. Alvin founded the IID in Chicago to develop a platform for a global network of architects,

18
Sunwoo, *In Progress: The IID Summer Sessions.*

19
Marjanovic and Howard, *Drawing Ambience: Alvin Boyarsky and the Architectural Association.*

students, theorists, and activists to gather and participate in a new radical form of architectural education and debate. Irene Sunwoo, in her recent book *In Progress*, captures how this strategy for cross-fertilisation was generated and spread by the reproduction, exchange, and interchange of photocopied correspondence between participants and also the extraordinary ephemera and publicity material in the form of stamps, postcards, and posters.[18] The book, based on original material from the archive in the house, records and brings to life the events and structuring of the Summer Session illustrated by these different forms of ephemera.

Shortly after Alvin's death, the contents of his office were removed from the AA and brought back to his home. Drawings were hung throughout the house, yet it took a period of over twenty years to be able to assess them critically and understand the relevance of pre-digital drawing to current architectural culture **(Fig. 5)**. Jan Howard and Igor Marjanovic curated the travelling show 'Drawing Ambience', which presented drawings, ephemera, sketchbooks, and publications from the 1970s and 1980s.[19] The show has drawn lively interest from students and architects and has contributed to a growing debate about the role of architectural representation in the digital age. We designed the travelling show around the notion of a room that references Alvin's rooms, encouraging visitors to sit in club chairs facing open windows while listening to interviews and looking at drawings.

Looking back over the years, since we moved into the house in 1972, the adaptability and resilience of the Victorian house has ensured that certain continuities persist whilst more temporal aspects have disappeared. The verticality of the terraced house continues to enable differentiation and spatial strategies for privacy, domesticity, and public life. While the internal form of the house has changed and its fabric has been altered and manipulated, the opportunity for interior experiences and conversations to mediate and frame the outside world through the lenses of its occupants and their furniture, artefacts, and collections continues to resonate.

Bibliography

Alvin Boyarsky Archive, private collection.

Architecture d'Aujourdhui, no. 151 (1970): 75.

Architectural Association. *The AA 125 Exhibition*. London: The Architectural Association, 1974.

Bergdoll, Barry and Werner Oechslin, eds. *Fragments, Architecture and the Unfinished: Essays Presented to Robin Middleton*. London: Thames and Hudson, 2006.

Colomina, Beatriz and Craig Buckley, eds. *Clip Stamp Fold: The Radical Architecture of Little Magazines 196x to 197x*. Barcelona: Actar, 2010.

Coop Himmelblau, *Just a House. Haus mit fliegende Dach*. Vienna: Coop Himmelblau, 1973.

de Looz, Pierre Alexandre. 'Robin Middleton's Remarkable East Village Haven for Books', *Pin-Up* (Fall/Winter 2016–17). https://pinup-magazine.org/articles/inside-architect-robin-middleton-east-village-home. Accessed 14 April 2020.

Evans, Robin. 'The Rights of Retreat and the Rites of Exclusion: Notes Towards the Definition of Wall'. *Architectural Design* (June 1971): 335–39.

Lakofski, Ruth. 'Oh, Please, Mr Banham: An Open Letter for Those Who Were There'. *Architectural Design* 36 (1966): 322.

Lakofski, Ruth. 'Going to Seed'. *Architectural Design* (July 1970): 325.

Lakofski, Ruth. 'Reflexions on the Soul Box'. *Daidalos* 28 (1988): 92–103.

Marjanovic, Igor. 'Pedagogy into Practice: Alvin Boyarsky's Collections and the Estrangement of Architecture'. PhD dissertation, The Bartlett School of Architecture, 2014.

Marjanovic, Igor and Jan Howard. *Drawing Ambience: Alvin Boyarsky and the Architectural Association*. St Louis, MO: Mildred Lane Kemper Art Museum, 2014.

Marjanovic, Igor. 'Lines and Words on Display: Alvin Boyarsky as a Collector, Curator, and Publisher.' *Architectural Research Quarterly* 14 (2010): 165–74.

Sunwoo, Irene. 'Between the "Well-Laid Table" and the "Market Place": Alvin Boyarsky's Experiments in Architectural Pedagogy'. PhD dissertation, Princeton University, 2013.

Sunwoo, Irene, ed. *In Progress: The IID Summer Sessions*. London: Architectural Association, Graham Foundation, 2016.

'A Non-Conformist Garage': Arthur Erickson at home in the world[1]

Christina Gray

In an instalment of her *New York Times* column in 1970, architectural critic Ada Louise Huxtable once quipped, 'What happens when architects build for themselves? All hell breaks loose.'[2] This riposte could have been aimed directly at Arthur Erickson, whose acclaimed architectural skills as Canada's pre-eminent modernist architect encountered numerous trials, many of his own making, when it came to the design of his own home. Much of this drama embellished his public persona. For the duration of his long and celebrated career, Erickson lived in a garage. In 1957 Erickson purchased a lot in the West Point Grey neighbourhood of Vancouver.[3] At that time, Erickson was a young and mostly untested architect with all of his high profile work still ahead of him. When he purchased the lot, the site contained only a ramshackle, forty-year old garage and a small, adjacent lean-to located at the edge of the rear lane.[4] Erickson moved temporarily into this garage. Fifty-two years later, he was still living in the garage when he died in 2009. In parallel with his career, this garage home, which he tinkered with for decades, developed into and remained a potent reference point for several narratives that fed Erickson's public persona.

The underlying commonality among these narratives was Erickson's cavalier attitude toward established norms. Repeatedly this garage home served to amplify for the public the numerous ways in which Erickson was willing to break both regulatory and social conventions. Furthermore, Erickson's persona as a rule-breaker reveals an underlying disquiet between his oft-stated beliefs that architecture should be generated in response to existing conditions and his similarly repeated demonstrations that architecture emerged as an exceptional phenomenon that remakes the rules around itself. Much of Erickson's provocative public persona, which propelled him to significant architectural achievements, was premised upon this nuanced conflict between respecting and flouting contextual expectations, an approach that he perfected and then promoted through his own experimental home.

Erickson often breezily dismissed the architectural merit of his home, for example, saying in 1965, 'It was a hideous little house.'[5] In other descriptions, he could also be evasive by rebuffing the building as merely provisional. The fact that the home was a renovated garage remained evident. One journalist described how 'his living room has the unmistakable rectangular dimensions of a narrow, one-car garage, and so does his bedroom-study'.[6] The tight interior space measured around fifty-five square metres.[7] Over time Erickson renovated some interior partition walls, but by and large he often referred to the place as 'a one-roomed house'.[8] Erickson's tiny bed was stuffed into 'a loft accessed via a childlike ladder'.[9] He gleefully described how he would 'dive into bed from the ladder'.[10]

1
An earlier version of this text appeared in the *Journal of the Society for the Study of Architecture in Canada/ Le Journal de la Société pour l'étude de l'architecture au Canada*. See: Gray, 'Domestic Boundaries'.

2
Huxtable, 'The Architects Design Their "Dream" Home', 88.

3
Erickson, 'The House at 4195 West 14th'.

4
Erickson, 'The House at 4195 West 14th'.

5
Reif, 'Home: 2 Garages and a Lean-To', 28.

6
Iglauer, *Seven Stones*, 28.

7
Whysall, 'Battle Blooms'.

8
Erickson, 'The House at 4195 West 14th'.

9
Ditmars, 'Former Home of Late Architect'.

10
Reif, 'Home: 2 Garages and a Lean-To'.

Fig. 1 Arthur Erickson in his living room, 1972. (Photograph by Selwyn Pullan. © Collection of West Vancouver Art Museum)

Fig. 2 Erickson Residence, garden and pond, 1959. (Photograph by Selwyn Pullan. © Collection of West Vancouver Art Museum)

Over time, he continued to tinker with this space, pushing the loft ceiling up into a skylight cut into the garage roof, allowing him to 'stand up to make the bed'.[11]

An eclectic mix of materials within the home reflected opportunistic curation and resourceful experimentation, often featuring remnants from a range of Erickson's projects. Marble slabs used in the interior had been salvaged by Erickson during a renovation from the urinals of the Vancouver Hotel.[12] Similarly, a City of Vancouver trolley car seat sat in the living room and, when covered with pillows, acted as a sofa.[13] At one point, the living room walls were covered in six-inch square beige suede fabric tiles, the result of an interior decorating experiment undertaken by Erickson's partner and interior design collaborator Francisco Kripacz.[14] At the end of the living room stood a repurposed turn-of-the-century column.[15] The narrative quality of this interior assemblage was emphasised in Erickson's dramatic retelling of this column's scavenged provenance: 'I set a destructive Irish sailor-handyman to taking down all the partitions, arriving only in time to save the collapse of the roof by propping it up with a wood-and-terracotta Ionian column I'd retrieved from the demolition of a former residence.'[16] The bathroom similarly featured an eclectic array of materials that reflected a range of Erickson's contemporaneous design commissions, including a fiberglass shower, mahogany cabinets, and glazed leather-clad walls.[17] The experimental application of many of the repurposed materials sometimes led to unintended consequences as when Erickson returned home to find his entire pond drained because he had chosen to line it with roofing paper.[18] This wide-ranging assembly of salvaged materials became compelling reference points for stories Erickson could delight his visitors with, each suggesting a cunning architect able to reappropriate materials in unexpected ways.

Erickson was prone to using his curious garage home as a narrative device that emphasised his visionary rule-breaking persona, unafraid of challenging municipal regulations. In numerous interviews with journalists, he relayed stories of how he had contravened local bylaws, frustrated neighbours, or otherwise disregarded norms. In doing this, Erickson often proclaimed his authority as a design professional to justify the breach. Soon after acquiring the property, Erickson described how '[he] could look out of [his] living-room windows across the road and see a neighbour's very ugly front door', a view which soon pushed him to dramatically regrade the site.[19] He hired a man with a bulldozer to shovel the garden into a hill at the end of the property until he could no longer 'see the ghastly door'.[20] Erickson described how this activity then attracted local attention: 'Everybody in the neighbourhood thought I was excavating to build a house, and chatted with me over the picket fence, very happy to believe that they were no longer going to have a nonconformist garage dweller among them.'[21] Erickson continued with his description, explaining how he then flouted their expectations, not only in not building a conventional house but also in replacing the existing low picket fence with a two metre solid cedar wall further hemming in the property. A neighbour complained to city officials that the

11 Erickson, 'The House at 4195 West 14th'.

12 Erickson, 'The House at 4195 West 14th'.

13 Reif, 'Home: 2 Garages and a Lean-To'.

14 Erickson, *Francisco Kripacz*, Erickson Estate, Vancouver, 2015, 4.

15 Reif, 'Home: 2 Garages and a Lean-To'.

16 Erickson, 'The House at 4195 West 14th'.

17 Ditmars, 'Former Home of Late Architect'.

18 Reif, 'Home: 2 Garages and a Lean-To'.

19 Fraser and Sabatino, *Arthur Erickson*, 13.

20 Fraser and Sabatino, *Arthur Erickson*, 13.

21 Iglauer, *Seven Stones*, 33.

Fig. 3 Living room, 1973. (Photograph by © Simon Scott)

22
Edmonds, 'The Architect Who Thinks', 44.

23
Iglauer, *Seven Stones*, 35.

24
Haden, 'Exotic Battle-ground'.

25
Iglauer, *Seven Stones*, 35.

26
Erickson, 'The House at 4195 West 14th'.

fence contravened the city-mandated maximum fence height. Erickson attempted to compromise by minimally decreasing the fence height before the city had to intervene.[22] At the subsequent City Council variance application meeting, Erickson recounted how he lost his temper when a councilman pressed him on the colour of the fence, erupting with, 'Surely with my background, I should be the judge of that!'[23] When compelled again by the city to paint the offending fence, Erickson threatened to hire a graffiti artist.[24] Eventually, he agreed to cut the unpainted fence down by a further ten centimetres, just as he encouraged his thick bushes and trees to grow ever taller.[25]

But such contraventions were all minor infractions compared to the larger issue that Erickson was unlawfully living in a garage with the domicile illegally abutting the edge of the lane. This unresolved issue was continually brushed aside by Erickson, who instead questioned the legitimacy of the underlying planning premise, saying: 'If I were making the laws, mine would be the only legal house in the city – it makes so much sense to build on the lane and keep all of your free land in one yard in front of you.'[26] This contention with planning regulations was symptomatic of Erickson's larger disregard for the role of urban planning in relation to architecture. While he had begun his career demonstrating an interest in how architecture sensitively responded to given planning regulations, over time he developed a far more antagonistic sense that architects should be given more authority to adapt planning to architecture.[27] This growing sense of architectural exceptionalism in the face of planning regulation was illustrated when Erickson declared in 1980: 'Social and economic theories? Bound to disaster. There's only one law. Call it Erickson's Law.'[28] Architect and long-time employee Bing Thom corroborated Erickson's growing antagonism toward regulatory compliance when he observed: 'He's always pushing governments to their limit. Regulatory authorities to their limit.'[29] Erickson prepared a text in 1988 in which he described how architecture naturally existed in a state of defiant conflict with its urban context. He argued that the challenge was to make the building appear as if the context had been shaped in response to the building, instead of the other way around: 'Since urban surroundings are usually given, the trick is to make them appear as if they were made for the building. Even though the building is a new intruder, it can appear as though it has orchestrated its own skyline, its own approaches and their unfolding spaces.'[30] This sleight of hand, in which architecture appeared to respond to its environment while instead it effectively recreated the environment in its own image, was a trick Erickson acknowledged was central to his architectural approach.[31]

In addition to flouting urban planning regulations, Erickson also used his home to project his crossing of social expectations. His professional success and public profile within Canada grew rapidly through the 1960s and 1970s, particularly with the well-publicised designs of Simon Fraser University in 1963, Vancouver's Museum of Anthropology in 1971, followed shortly by Vancouver's Provincial Law Courts in 1973. As his profile grew, his home increasingly became associated with bacchanalian parties among his vast acquaintances, his neighbours, and the public at large, creating a platform for his image as the intriguing man at the centre of an expansive and cultivated social sphere. The bon vivant Erickson was described in a local paper as someone who 'appears as predictably in the society columns as canapés at the soirees he frequents.'[32] The house parties grew legendary through retellings. Journalists detailed a party in 1967 for the London Royal Ballet where Rudolf Nureyev danced around Erickson's pond, which had been specially filled with black swans, before jumping into the water in the buff for some inspired skinny dipping.[33] Illuminated by Japanese paper lanterns, another party was described as having been choreographed around a climactic moment featuring two musicians playing traditional Japanese instruments, accompanying Erickson as he released a jar of fireflies that had been flown in from Eastern Canada earlier that day.[34] Erickson described using his home and garden as a malleable stage set for such elaborate events, describing: 'If I have a lavish party, I put musicians across the water, and it's as if they were playing from an island over the sea.'[35] The interest in Erickson's social

27
Vancouver City Council Archives, Meeting Minutes (May 22, 1963), 339, City of Vancouver Archives.

28
Freedman, 'In Erickson's Eden'.

29
Kines, 'Beautiful Things', D1

30
Erickson, *The Architecture of Arthur Erickson*, 19.

31
Erickson, *The Architecture of Arthur Erickson*, 19.

32
Hawthorn, 'High-Rolling World-Famous Architect', B2.

33
Ditmars, 'Former Home of Late Architect'.

34
Stouck, *Arthur Erickson*.

35
Iglauer, *Seven Stones*, 33.

Fig. 4 Arthur Erickson, 1984.
(Photograph by © Harry Palmer)

Fig. 5 Arthur Erickson at home, 1981.
(Photograph by © Roy Scully)

life was widespread. His biographer described how '[of] special interest to people in Vancouver were the elaborate themed parties he hosted in his bachelor's garden with sometimes as many as 200 guests looking for parking.'[36] For an intrigued public, the non-traditional approach embodied by Erickson's home seemed to match the vibrant social sphere contained behind those high hedges.

Erickson's makeshift home also reinforced narratives about the modern architect as an exceptional and globally peripatetic figure who, unlike others, did not require a home, merely a pied-à-terre where he could briefly touch base between world travels. In numerous interviews Erickson dismissed his home as merely 'a place to camp', as his 'real home [was] in the world'.[37] He explained how his frenetic professional schedule had created a strong sense of restlessness: 'I find that about every fourth day or so I become impatient and it's time to move along.'[38] He claimed that he had not stayed more than ten consecutive days in place since 1965.[39] One journalist stated, in 1985: 'It is possible, given his legendary jet-setting and near-compulsive travels, that Arthur Erickson has no home these days.'[40]

Erickson's restlessness became a selling point as he attracted a more international clientele. Erickson described hosting a reception at his home in 1976 for one hundred and fifty people that included a Saudi Arabian prince who happened to be in Vancouver. He described taking the incredulous prince on a tour of his tiny home, with the astonished prince laughing out loud when he saw the makeshift ladder leading to Erickson's bed tucked above a storage area. Two nights later, the prince invited Erickson to his own reception, whereupon he continued the running joke by inviting Erickson, should he feel tired during the party, to climb up into the canopy above the bar to have a rest.[41] Erickson had cemented his reputation as a cosmopolitan traveller among potential clientele. Soon after, he began several Middle Eastern design commissions, including the unbuilt Centre for Science and Technology in Saudi Arabia.

However, Erickson's home also conveniently reinforced his image as an architect still in touch with his modest background despite his ability to hobnob in elite circles.[42] Public intrigue around his social sphere had begun to sour in some quarters by the late 1970s and early 1980s, with some observers beginning to gripe about his 'King Arthur and His Court regal public image'.[43] As the impression of Erickson's profligate ways grew wider, he more frequently mentioned both his middle-class childhood and his home's modest origins in lectures and interviews.[44] The incongruity of this mixture was particularly striking during the 1970s when Erickson was beginning a number of large-scale projects in the Middle East. The architectural photographer Simon Scott recalled: 'Gulf sheikhs pulling up in big black limousines and being astounded at the simplicity of his home.'[45]

Ultimately, much of the rule-bending and -breaking surrounding the garage home and its proprietor became unsustainable. By

36
Stouck, *Arthur Erickson*.

37
Peck, 'Home Q & A', M32.

38
Peck, 'Home Q & A'.

39
Iglauer, *Seven Stones*, 20.

40
Godfrey, 'For Erickson', D13.

41
Peck, 'Home Q & A'.

42
Hawthorn, 'High-Rolling World-Famous Architect'.

43
Lamb, 'Erickson Home a Monument to Ingenuity', B1.

44
Sabatino, 'Arthur Erickson – Money', 73.

45
Ditmars, 'Former Home of Late Architect'.

46
Hawthorn, 'High-Rolling World-Famous Architect'.

47
Smith, 'Noted Architect Files for Personal Bankruptcy', D4.

48
Smith, 'Noted Architect Files for Personal Bankruptcy', D4.

49
Lamb, 'Erickson Home a Monument to Ingenuity'.

50
Lamb, 'Erickson Home a Monument to Ingenuity'.

51
Kines, 'Beautiful Things'.

52
Kines, 'Beautiful Things'.

53
Hawthorn, 'High-Rolling World-Famous Architect'.

54
Hawthorn, 'High-Rolling World-Famous Architect'.

the early 1990s it became clear that Erickson had overextended himself. Newspaper headlines screamed: 'Arthur Erickson, the High-Rolling World-Famous Architect from Vancouver is Broke'.[46] In 1992, Erickson declared bankruptcy with personal debts of $10.5 million with a list of three hundred creditors.[47] His home was listed as his only asset, but it too had been 'hopelessly over mortgaged' in the words of one of the officials handling the bankruptcy.[48] When the paperwork emerged, many were incredulous that Erickson had managed to carry $3.4 million in mortgages on a property that was only valued at four hundred and fifty thousand dollars.[49] One journalist offered that such audacious cunning at least deserved accolades for the 'work, thought and experimentation in the realm of financial ingenuity'.[50] Though partly obscured, the financial strain had been building for some time. In 1989 Erickson had closed his Toronto office leaving creditors and lawsuits in his wake.[51] In 1991 he had closed his Los Angeles office similarly under a cloud of debts.[52] Once the bankruptcy was underway, Erickson dismissed the financial troubles by calling himself an 'idiot savant', unable to square business with architecture.[53] Others suggested that it was Erickson's willingness to use company funds for his high-maintenance lifestyle that had been at the root of the problem. The more forgiving were willing to explain this financial problem as inherently linked to architecture, as in Bing Thom's explanation that 'you have to drink the fine wine your millionaire client drinks, even though you don't have those millions. That's a dilemma for architects of his stature.'[54] Disregarding financial conventions had been yet another component in how Erickson's garage home had contributed to burnishing his high-flying, visionary persona.

Back in 1957 Arthur Erickson had defied expectation by refusing to tear down a ramshackle garage and build a proper house as his neighbours expected. Instead he spent over fifty years tinkering with the little structure, pushing against a wide range of material, planning, social, and financial conventions. Through this process, Erickson was able to significantly amplify his public persona as a visionary architect not bound by standard limitations. In the process he also attempted his ultimate sleight of hand, trying to bend the world to make it look like his exceptional creation was simply the inevitable one.

Bibliography

Brewster, Hugh. 'Remembering Arthur Erickson'. *Xtra*, 3 June 2009.

Dafoe, Chris. 'Donors Come to Rescue of Erickson House'. *Globe and Mail*, 28 January 1997.

Ditmars, Hadani. 'The Former Home of Late Architect Arthur Erickson Faces an Uncertain Future'. *Wallpaper*, 1 March 2013.

Edmonds, Alan. 'The Architect Who Thinks People Matter More Than Buildings'. *Maclean's*, June 1970.

Erickson, Arthur. 'The House at 4195 West 14th Avenue, Vancouver, British Columbia'. 1978. In *Speeches by Arthur Erickson*. University of British Columbia Library, NA749.E75 A5.

Erickson, Arthur. *The Architecture of Arthur Erickson*. Vancouver: Douglas & McIntyre, 1998.

Fraser, Linda, and Michelangelo Sabatino. *Arthur Erickson: Layered Landscape*. Halifax: Dalhousie University Press, 2013.

Freedman, Adele. 'In Erickson's Eden, An Architect Can Improve on Nature'. *Globe and Mail*, 4 October 1980.

Ghanim, Zak. 'Interviews by Zak Ghanim with Arthur Erickson', 1994. https://www.youtube.com/watch?v=X0upz3gKndk. Accessed 25 May 2020.

Godfrey, Stephen. 'For Erickson, Home is Where the Work Is'. *Globe and Mail*, 19 October 1985.

Gray, Christina. 'Domestic Boundaries: Arthur Erickson at Home'. *Journal of the Society for the Study of Architecture in Canada/Le Journal de la Société pour l'étude de l'architecture au Canada* 43, no. 2 (2018): 3–14.

Haden, Bruce. 'Exotic Battleground: The Deceptive Tranquility of Arthur Erickson's Garden Belies a Three Decade-Long Struggle Against Pesky Bureaucrats and Roving Racoons'. *Canadian Architect* 40, no. 11 (November 1995).

Hawthorn, Tom. 'Arthur Erickson, the High-Rolling World-Famous Architect from Vancouver is Broke'. *Calgary Herald*, 15 March 1992.

Hume, Christopher. 'Is This A Ruined Man?' *Toronto Star*, 15 March 1992.

Huxtable, Ada Louise. 'The Architects Design Their "Dream" Home'. *New York Times*, 12 July 1970.

Iglauer, Edith. *Seven Stones – A Portrait of Arthur Erickson, Architect*. Seattle: University of Washington Press, 1981.

Kines, Lindsay. 'Beautiful Things, Beautiful Spaces'. *Vancouver Sun*, 27 July 1991.

Lamb, Jamie. 'Erickson Home a Monument to Ingenuity in Creative Financing'. *Vancouver Sun*, 25 June 1992.

Lazarus, Eve. 'Arthur Erickson's House and Garden Are on the Endangered List'. *Every Place Has A Strong Blog*. 10 January 2015. http://evelazarus.com/arthur-ericksons-house-and-garden-are-on-the-endangered-list/. Accessed 25 May 2020.

Liscombe, Rhodri. 'Critical Biography'. In *Arthur Erickson – Selected Projects 1971–1985*. New York: Center for Inter-American Relations, 1985.

Mulgrew, Ian. 'Erickson's Heritage Site Saved by Donors: "A Magical Poetic Spirit"'. *Vancouver Sun*, 24 January 1997.

Peck, Stacey. 'Home Q & A'. *Los Angeles Times*, 20 June 1982.

Reif, Rita. 'Home: 2 Garages and a Lean-To'. *New York Times*, 14 September 1965.

Sabatino, Michelangelo. 'Arthur Erickson – Money, Media and Canadian Architecture'. *Perspecta* 47 (August 2014): 68–76.

Smith, David. 'Noted Architect Files for Personal Bankruptcy: 300 Unsecured Creditors Listed'. *Vancouver Sun*, 26 February 1992.

Stouck, David. *Arthur Erickson: An Architect's Life*. Madeira Park: Douglas & McIntyre, 2013.

Vancouver City Council Archives, City of Vancouver Archives, Vancouver.

Walters, Donna. 'The Collapse of an Architectural Pillar Jolts LA'. *Los Angeles Times*, 15 July 1991.

Whysall, Steve. 'Battle Blooms Over Erickson's Abode: If You Think the Architect Was Great, You Probably Favor Preservation'. *Vancouver Sun*, 24 July 1993.

A Collective Archipelago: Flora Ruchat-Roncati's Cortile in Riva San Vitale, Switzerland

Irina Davidovici and Eliana Perotti

The catalogue cover of the Flora Ruchat-Roncati retrospective exhibition at ETH Zurich (1996) features the photograph of a facade detail **(Fig. 1)**. Partly concealed by abundant vegetation, a glazed curtain wall reflects the mountainous landscape, its modernist detailing gently undercut by the ivy-covered wall. The overall effect is of temporal uncertainty, the result of a trenchant yet sensitive architectural intervention in a historical setting. As the primary illustration for an architectural career, this image of Ruchat-Roncati's own house in Riva San Vitale acts as an encoded manifesto, offering a multilayered reading for her entwined life and work philosophies.

Flora Ruchat-Roncati (1937–2012) has entered the history of Swiss architecture as an important protagonist of the Ticinese production of the 1960s and 1970s. Alone and in a string of architectural partnerships, she was active in practice between the late 1950s and the 2000s, and became the first-ever woman professor at ETH, the Federal Institute of Technology in Zurich, where she taught between 1985 and 2002. In her working habitus she often assumed a conceptual, collaborative role, which resulted into the rather nebulous authorship of her heterogeneous built oeuvre. In this context, her house, one of few projects she designed on her own, appears as her most revealing. A discreet yet complex design reflecting a progressive societal vision, the homestead of Riva San Vitale breaks away from the stereotyped expectations of an architect's house, illustrating an approach calibrated between conservation and invention.

This chapter focusses on the residential compound restored and partly rebuilt by Ruchat-Roncati in Riva San Vitale, in her native Ticino, her primary residence until she died in 2012. Particularly important in this architect's home is not so much the question of an avant-garde formal resolution, but its social proposition as a hub for practices of collective living, all the more extraordinary when considered in the provincial context of the Ticino canton. The vision of communal life, embedded in the post-1968 intellectual climate, coincided in this case with a woman's search for balance between family life and professional career.

The background of a house

To understand the structure of the Ruchat-Roncati household, it is necessary to place her personal circumstances in the wider context of Ticinese architectural culture in the 1960s and 1970s. The granddaughter of a mason, Ruchat-Roncati was strongly supported in her career choice by her father, civil engineer Giuseppe Roncati, who introduced her to the trade and assigned to her some of his own contracts. Ruchat-Roncati studied architecture at ETH (1956–61) and completed her diploma

Fig. 1 Cover of *Flora Ruchat-Roncati* exhibition catalogue. (gta Verlag, Zurich 1998)

Fig. 2 Loggia of Flora Ruchat-Roncati's home, Riva San Vitale. Current state. (Photograph by © Irina Davidovici, October 2017)

1
See Fumagalli, 'Il Collettivo in Ticino'.

2
For more on this project, see Navone and Reichlin, *Il bagno di Bellinzona*.

3
Ruchat-Roncati, exhibition vernissage speech, 1997.

with Rino Tami, an important Ticinese modernist. During her studies, she married André Ruchat, a military pilot and student of civil engineering, and gave birth to their daughter Anna. Tragically, in 1960, Ruchat died in an aviation accident, and his widow threw herself into work as a way to internalise her grief. After finishing her diploma, she set up studio in Ticino, together with Aurelio Galfetti, a fellow ETH alumnus, and Ivo Trümpy. An early, perhaps most fruitful, period of her practice coincided with several years of bereavement, in which she worked long hours while living in virtual isolation with her daughter.

At this time, professional conditions were unusually favourable to a number of young Ticinese practices. While Ticino's socioeconomic setting customarily enabled private commissions such as single-family houses, in the 1960s the canton began pursuing an intensive school-building programme, as well as the restoration of historical sites.[1] This initiated a string of public architectural competitions, which assisted the emergence of a strong generation of local practitioners. Ruchat-Roncati designed several educational buildings and middle-class residences and brought a pedagogical progressiveness to the designs of Chiasso (1960–4) and Viganello kindergartens (1966–71), and to the educational complex (kindergarten, primary school, and gym) completed in collaboration with Galfetti and Trümpy in Riva San Vitale (1962–74). Their most significant project, the public baths in Bellinzona (1967–70), was partly public facility, partly territorial infrastructure.[2] While fascinated with the modernist heritage of Le Corbusier, Galfetti, Ruchat-Roncati, and Trümpy implemented a theoretical discourse imported from Italy, readily assimilated at this time in Ticino, focussing on issues of territory, typology, and the city.

For Ruchat-Roncati, this collaborative model not only helped consolidate her professional status, but also became a way to overcome her personal circumstances as a widowed mother. Throughout the 1960s, raising her daughter was integrated into her practice. Talking of her architectural partnership at this time, she mentioned 'Lio (Aurelio Galfetti), Ivo (Trümpy), and the growing Anna' in the same breath, her studio a surrogate for family life.[3] After the partnership dissolved in 1970, Ruchat-Roncati continued to work in formal and informal collaborations, mixing teaching and practice, friends and work colleagues. As her daughter, Anna Ruchat-Roncati, remarked: *Non ha separato le cose* (She didn't separate things). For this reason, it is important to perceive her designs, in particular her own house, as representing a conjunction of personal and professional horizons.

Design method: between ideology and pragmatism

In 1967, Ruchat-Roncati acquired the Cortile, a derelict ensemble of residential and agricultural buildings in the centre of Riva San Vitale. Adhering to the traditional features of a *cascina lombarda* (Lombardy farmhouse), the property comprised three wings of residential and agricultural

Fig. 3 Plans as built, Cortile. Flora Ruchat-Roncati, Riva San Vitale, ca. 1970. (Images produced by the FRR office and extracted from the FRR exhibition catalogue, 44)

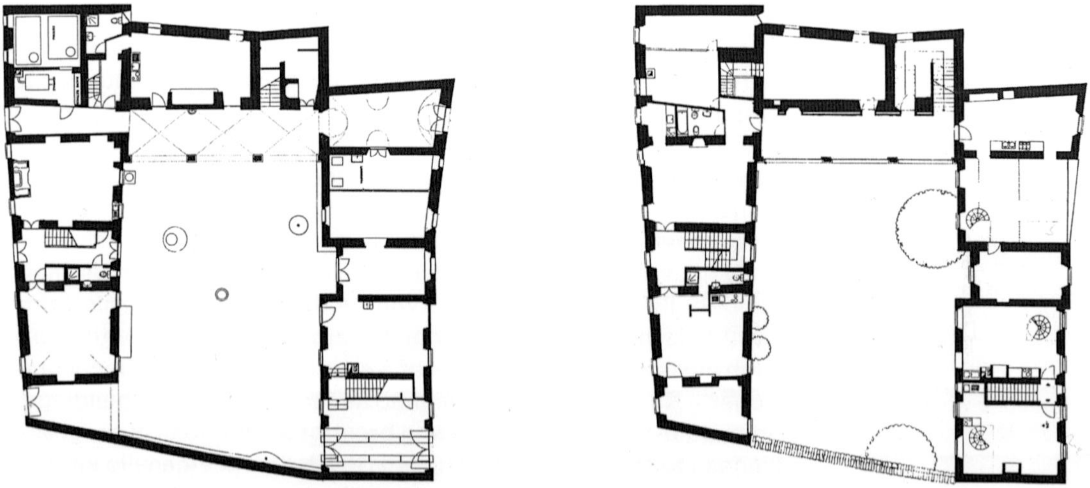

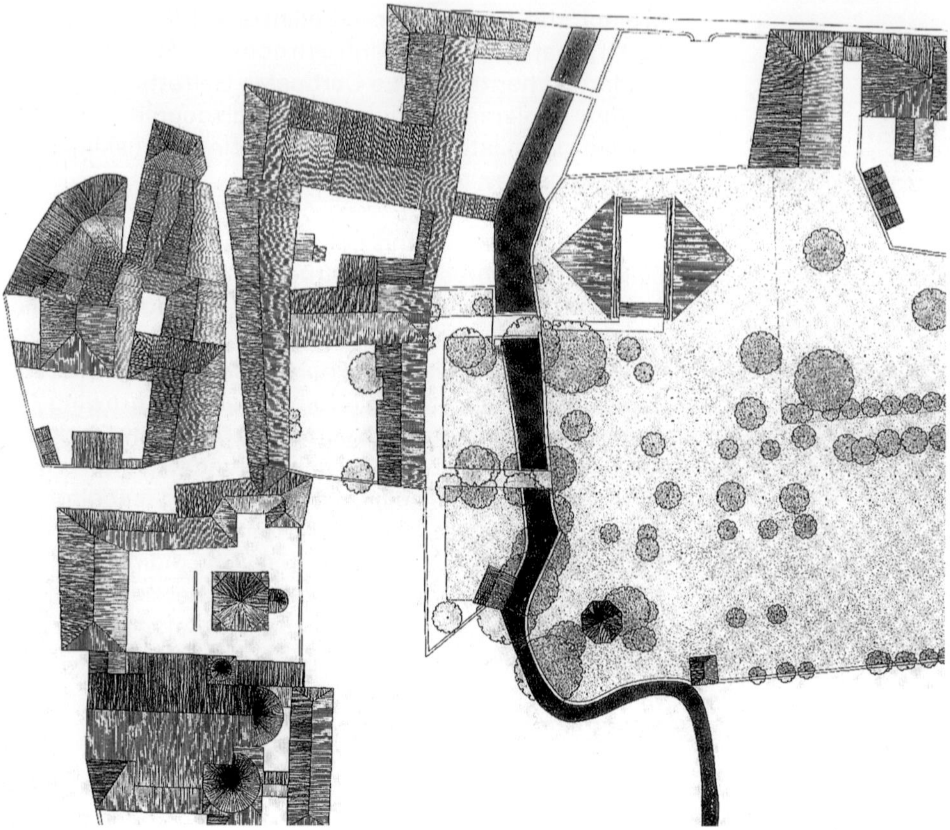

Fig. 4 Situation plan of Cortile with Stockli and Durisch House. Flora Ruchat-Roncati, Riva San Vitale. (Images produced by the FRR office and extracted from the FRR exhibition catalogue, 42)

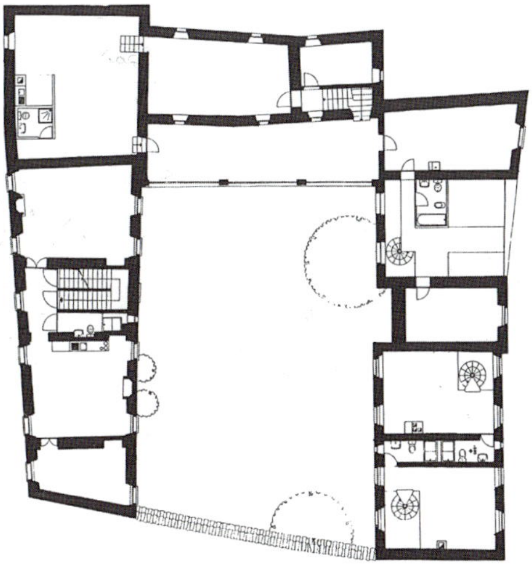

Fig. 5 Detail of Durisch House and Studio: relation to the Cortile. Giancarlo Durisch, Riva San Vitale, 1974–75. (Photograph by © Irina Davidovici, 2018)

structures, built between the fourteenth and eighteenth centuries, arranged around a paved courtyard with a seventeenth-century, south-facing loggia. The Cortile was annexed to a large walled garden, crossed by a small creek. This rural typology was incorporated into a dense urban setting in Riva's compact historical core, in close proximity to a listed sixth-century baptistery. At the time of purchase, the complex was ruined, its garden overgrown. Ruchat-Roncati restored the Cortile gradually and with minimal interventions, preserving its historical character: 'The determining parameters in the design were the landscape topography, the buildings' morphology, and the history of the site'.[4] The renovation took the form of discrete interventions, connecting the fragments of the past while declaring their own autonomy. The approach put into motion a continuous process of preservation and renewal, which continued for the next three decades.

At the time it could be occupied, in 1970, the property comprised nine apartments and an atelier-studio, which Ruchat-Roncati initially used together with Trümpy, one of her first tenants. Reflecting the original farmhouse's multifunctional spaces, the complex combined residential use with intersecting work and social activities. As architect-owner, Ruchat-Roncati determined the layout and design of the apartments, allowing the residents only minor determinations, such as the design of a kitchen or a fireplace.[5] Her own apartment occupies the oldest medieval structure, previously a storehouse overlooking the garden. Ruchat-Roncati's architectural interventions were here at their most radical, structuring the double-height space with a lightweight mezzanine, and introducing a new glazed wall overlooking Monte Generoso. Several flats open unto the central loggia, where large tables were used for al fresco dining **(Figs. 2 and 3)**. While the courtyard was preserved and enhanced through renovation, various hints signalled the modern character of the interiors: frameless, undivided glass panels in the windows facing the courtyard, and the glazed facade of Ruchat-Roncati's apartment towards the garden. These interventions preserved the inherited character of the Cortile, indicating a nuanced, critical attitude towards history.

The garden was integrated into this ensemble as a counterpart to the stony Cortile: an idyllic, protected setting in an implied state of natural innocence, over which the architect exercised a discreet control **(Fig. 4)**. A pergola was installed, followed in the early 1970s by the planting of a vine and rows of fruit trees: cherries, pears, apricots, and persimmon.[6] An expert in macrobiotics also laid out the first vegetable garden among the fruit trees.[7] Productive plants were supplemented by those for scent and atmosphere (wisteria, paulownia, woodbine, jasmine), suggesting a careful staging of the garden idyll.[8] The library and notebooks of Ruchat-Roncati corroborate that she invested both interest and ambition into botanical knowledge, employing a specialised vocabulary and their Latin nomenclature. At the same time, she left the garden open to rural uses, allowing a resident family to keep a pen for chickens, rabbits, and goats. Seen as a major asset, the garden was planned to be

4
Carrard and Ruchat-Roncati, *Flora Ruchat-Roncati*, 42–3. This and subsequent translations from texts in German and Italian provided by the authors.

5
Ivo Trümpy in email correspondence with Eliana Perotti, 18 June 2019.

6
Ivo Trümpy in email correspondence with Eliana Perotti, 18 June 2019.

7
Ruchat, 'La corte di Riva', 47–8.

8
Ruchat, 'La corte di Riva', 45–6.

shared and enjoyed by the inhabitants of the court. Ruchat-Roncati installed in places old slabs of Carrara, making it easier for the tenants to bring out tables and eat together under the trees.[9]

'Flora's kitchen'

What was the relationship between the architectural, landscaping, and collective aspects of this project? Was its commonality ideologically prescribed, or did it arise as an unintended, if positive, consequence of the design? Ruchat-Roncati seized upon the inherited communal setting as an opportunity to restructure the family life lost with the death of her husband. As property owner, she curated the social environment of her new home carefully yet generously, entering informal and, in some cases, symbolic lease agreements to attract the Cortile friends and creative professionals. The ensuing first period, from the 1970 to 1976, was consequently characterised by an unscripted, non-programmatic commonality. The Cortile and garden attracted a progressive and informal circle of artists and architects, both residents and visitors. The central figure was the poet Franco Beltrametti (1937–1995), a close school friend of Ruchat-Roncati, who lived in a two-room flat facing the street.[10] He provided 'a personal link between such disparate traditions as American beat – and New York school – poetry; the Fluxus group of artists; the European avant-garde; [...] the Italian revolutionary left; and Japanese Zen Buddhism'.[11] Beltrametti introduced an international dimension into the cultural activities of the Cortile, attracting a stream of visitors from Italy, the US, and Japan, and even founding a publishing house, Scorribande Productions. Communal dinners and art events, such as film projections and poetry festivals, created vivid social and cultural exchanges. In this context, the complex became a junction of social, cultural, political, and professional interests. The Cortile's inhabitants were politically engaged, mostly with socialist or anarchist inclinations. They attempted to engage the local community, and ironically rented out the local pornographic cinema to screen avant-garde films. The contrast with the tranquil, somewhat parochial setting inscribed the Cortile, unintentionally, into the historical tradition of utopian avant-garde communes that have dotted the Ticino since the early twentieth century.[12] Ruchat-Roncati meanwhile fulfilled the role of catalyst, hosting gatherings in her kitchen and combining hospitality, friendship, cooperative work, and communal interests. Together with Beltrametti, she initiated an interdisciplinary and open discourse around culture, creativity, and politics.

This communal period ended in 1975, around the time Ruchat-Roncati's second daughter, Elisa, was born. Together with her children and partner Leonardo (Leo) Zanier, a Friulian poet and labour unionist, Ruchat-Roncati moved to Rome in 1976, where she lived and practised until 1985. The cultural life of the Cortile, independently organised by Beltrametti, continued until his untimely death in 1995. Despite prolonged absences (during her time at ETH she split her time between Zurich, Friuli, and Ticino), Ruchat-Roncati used the Cortile as her primary residence. Following her retirement from teaching in 2002, she lived and worked there until her death

9
Ivo Trümpy in email correspondence with Eliana Perotti, 18 June 2019.

10
Trained as an architect at ETH, after graduating in 1963 Beltrametti dedicated himself exclusively to poetry and visual art, travelling extensively across the US and Asia during the 1960s. Beltrametti, 'Autobiografia'.

11
Raworth, 'Obituary: Franco Beltrametti'.

12
Ticino attracted a host of radical avant-garde figures from the early twentieth century. See Bollmann, *Monte Verità* 1900.

ten years later. Moreover, she viewed Riva San Vitale as a historical site requiring statutory protection and systematic improvement. Concerned by the threat of speculative and insensitive development, between 1986 and 1995 she conducted a collaborative master plan for the town's historical core.[13] The project carefully balanced interventions and proposed regulations, demonstrating professional responsibility, as well as her personal bond with the reality of local surroundings.[14]

Additions to the historical ensemble

The pattern of piecemeal growth of the Cortile was continued over two decades, with two new, highly distinct structures added to the garden. The first was the family home and studio of architect Giancarlo Durisch, to whom Ruchat-Roncati had leased a plot of the garden in the early 1970s. In contrast to the Cortile, the Durisch house and atelier (completed in 1974) provide one of the most radical illustrations of architectural autonomy in Ticinese architecture. The two functions were housed in two symmetrical triangular concrete prisms, divided by a small courtyard. This compound is ambiguously separated from the collective garden by a short wall, just tall enough to interrupt the visual continuity, leading the blank concrete walls of the two shells to appear as abstract volumes in the green depth of the orchard. Inscribed in the long tradition of architects' homes as demonstrative of the architect's skill, vision, and ambition, these sculptural volumes were a radical built manifesto, an explicit act of artistic emancipation. It is interesting therefore that Durisch's solitary and defensive gesture was integrated into the vision of the informal artistic commune generously orchestrated by Ruchat-Roncati. This counterpoint to the historical Cortile became, at the same time, an integral component of its communal life.

The second structure, the Stöckli, is a small cabin designed by Ruchat-Roncati in the late 1990s and intended as retirement workplace for her husband Leo **(Fig. 5)**. The cabin was built on top of an ancient utilitarian structure that for several years had served as a pen for chickens and goats. Ruchat-Roncati kept the old foundations and completed the walls with concrete and timber sections, adding a stone floor and a new, raised roof. The Stöckli was constructed by Laurie Hunziker and Giovanni Galfetti, two younger architects, friends, and collaborators of Ruchat-Roncati's who lived in the Cortile. Primarily, the word *Stöckli* denotes the rural typology of a small annex, close to the main house, with a residential or storage use. Although Flora gave its name playfully, referring to the retirement homes fitted into traditional Swiss farm housing, the essence of the building, in its reserved aesthetic expression and basic attitude, remains closer to an essentialist understanding of a study. This 'very private retreat' falls in the Renaissance tradition of the *studiolo*, a room set aside for solitary meditation and scholarly activity. Zanier, discussing the typological derivation of the Stöckli, insisted on its social value: for him, the Stöckli was an embodiment of the mental preparatory work necessary for the older age.[15] He used the Stöckli frequently, for as long as he was able.

13
Ruchat-Roncati worked on this project intermittently while in Riva San Vitale, together with her tenant Giovanni Galfetti, as well as Enca Mina and Edy Radaelli. Pasqualini, 'Gestaltungsplan für den Dorfkern von Riva San Vitale 1986–1995'.

14
Pasqualini, 'Gestaltungsplan für den Dorfkern von Riva San Vitale 1986–1995'; Geissbühler, 'Flora Ruchat Roncati (1937–2012)', 172.

15
Zanier, 'Stöckli'.

Fig. 6 Flora Ruchat-Roncati, Stöckli, Riva San Vitale, ca. 1996. (Photograph by © Detlef Leinweber)

16
Ruchat-Roncati's attitude towards the site was mainly influenced by the theoretical positions of Italian architectural debate in the 1950s, principally Saverio Muratori's typo-morphological studies, fed by the idealistic philosophy of Benedetto Croce and introducing a new understanding of city, territory, and history.

With reference to the site

It is safe to surmise that Ruchat-Roncati's approach to planning, as defined over decades of restorations and additions to the Cortile household, was situational rather than ideological. Her interest, principally driven by the contingencies of the individual task, tended towards the creation of a situated architecture. Significantly, in her teaching, she emphasised the connection between architecture and its locale (what she called '*Bezug zum Ort*', its 'relation to place').[16]

As a result of this attitude, Ruchat-Roncati paid scrupulous attention to the survey of the site, investigating it on a holistic scale, integrating all design and technical questions within a veritable humanist approach. Her conceptual procedure employed historical, literary, cultural, art historical, territorial, botanical, and other typologies of knowledge. While not shying away from formal resolution, it should therefore be interpreted as a counterpoint to the proposition of architectural autonomy. The acceptance and incorporation of an ultimate statement of autonomy, as embodied by the Durisch house, rather emphasised the character of the collective project as a profound reflection on the political function of architecture. Ruchat-Roncati's urban studies of Riva San Vitale, looking at possibilities of sensitive development that would not affect its original historical character, illustrate the progressive humanistic imprint of her entire oeuvre. They reflect a conviction in the social and political consequences of the built form, and therefore the social responsibility of the architect.

Long before the private retreat of the Stöckli became a conceptual counterpart to the communality of the Cortile, the Cortile itself became a refuge at several levels. As a politically active bohemia – a scene rooted in the post-1968 context – its inhabitants stood out from the local community, which was generally Catholic and politically conservative, just as the historical core of the town stands out from the indiscriminate suburban sprawl that surrounds it. Ruchat-Roncati's household adhered to an established narrative of progressive and radical settlements. Like the kindred enterprise of Monte Verità, here cultural figures were invited to experiment, reconnect with nature, and experience the freedom of an existential condition removed from the alienating modern metropolis. The Cortile's informal communality betrays an update of this ideological setting, under the influence of post-1968 culture. As Fabio Reinhart reflected:

> Flora not only grasped the spirit of the place, but also elaborated and applied a strategy to preserve, express, and amplify it. Part of this strategy, rather than its result, was the choice of tenants. This was a consequence of the attitude she brought indiscriminately to people and things alike, a behaviour which combined affability and benevolence, and that granted her the deep understanding that arises from mutual acceptance [...] All inhabitants of her framework-house, taken together, allow us to trace out the outlines of Flora's own personality, which perfectly matches the original rural character of the court: all close, next to each other, framing the protective maternal image of a seraphic mother-hen.[17]

The assemblage of individual interventions formed by the Cortile, garden, the ancillary Stöckli, and the Durisch house are tantamount to a collective project, an architectural archipelago, at the heart of Riva yet clearly distinct from it. The ensemble commands a characteristic atmosphere, at once peaceful and heterogeneous, intensely private and prone to interaction. The communitarian life setting, while grounded in Ruchat-Roncati's generosity, was realised through the collective input of many friends. The architecture of the Cortile thus embodies a lifelong interest in what Peter Linebaugh later called 'commoning'.[18] Partly rooted in post-1968 culture, this was the result of a highly personal and deliberate strategy on the part of Flora Ruchat-Roncati to create a familiar setting in which to live and work. As we showed elsewhere, her interest in *convivium* as a professional and social strategy reflected her lifelong interest in collaborative enterprises, in which authorship was indefinitely postponed, even deemed irrelevant.[19] The Cortile's preservation and the urban strategies at work represent the opposition to uncontrolled suburban and industrial sprawl. Ruchat-Roncati's Cortile thus represents a threefold resistance: cultural, political, and aesthetic.

17
Reinhart, 'I luoghi di Flora Ruchat-Roncati', 20–1.

18
Linebaugh, *The Magna Carta Manifesto: Liberties and Commons for All.*

19
This essay pertains to a comprehensive research project entitled 'Flora Ruchat-Roncati at ETH Zurich 1985–2002. Professor, Planner, Theoretician', founded by the Swiss National Science Foundation and conducted by Eliana Perotti at ETH. See http://www.flora-ruchat-roncati-snf.ch. Also see the monographic issue *Flora Ruchat-Roncati* of the journal *Werk, Bauen, Wohnen*; and Frey and Perotti, 'Flora Ruchat-Roncati'.

Bibliography

Beltrametti, Franco. 'Autobiografia'. In *Franco Beltrametti*, 19–52. Mendrisio: Museo d'arte Mendrisio, 1999. Exhibition catalogue.

Bollmann, Stefan. *Monte Verità 1900. Der Traum vom alternativen Leben beginnt*. Munich: Deutsche Verlags-Anstalt, 2017.

Carrard, Philippe and Flora Ruchat-Roncati, eds. *Flora Ruchat-Roncati*, Eidgenössische Technische Hochschule, Institut für Geschichte und Theorie der Architektur, Zurich: gta 1998. Exhibition catalogue.

Flora Ruchat-Roncati. Architektur im Netzwerk, special issue of *Werk, Bauen, Wohnen*, no. 12 (2017).

Frey, Katia and Eliana Perotti. 'Flora Ruchat-Roncati. First Woman Professor at ETH Zurich: Introducing Women's Standpoint in Architectural Pedagogy'. In *MoMoWo: Women's Creativity since the Modern Movement (1918–2018): Towards a New Perception and Reception*, edited by Helena Seražin, Caterina Franchini, and Emilia Gadda, 58–66. Ljubljana: ZRC SAZU, France Stele Institute of Art History, 2018.

Fumagalli, Paolo. 'Il Collettivo in Ticino'. *Archi: Rivista Svizzera Di Architettura, Ingegneria e Urbanistica = Swiss Review of Architecture, Engineering and Urban Planning*, no. 6 (2013): 65–71.

Linebaugh, Peter. *The Magna Carta Manifesto: Liberties and Commons for All*. Berkeley: University of California Press, 2008.

Navone, Nicola and Bruno Reichlin, eds. *Il bagno di Bellinzona di Aurelio Galfetti, Flora Ruchat-Roncati, Ivo Trümpy*. Mendrisio: Mendrisio Academy Press, 2010.

Pasqualini, Antonella. 'Zeichen der Abwesenheit'. In *Flora Ruchat-Roncati*, 34–59. Eidgenössische Technische Hochschule Zürich, Institut für Geschichte und Theorie der Architektur, Zurich: gta, 1998.

Raworth, Tom. 'Obituary: Franco Beltrametti'. *The Independent,* 3 September 1995, http://www.independent.co.uk/news/people/obituary-franco-beltrametti-1599393.html. Accessed 12 January 2017.

Reinhart, Fabio. 'I luoghi di Flora Ruchat-Roncati. Flora Ruchat-Roncatis Orte'. In *Flora Ruchat-Roncati*, 18–22. Eidgenössische Technische Hochschule Zürich, Institut für Geschichte und Theorie der Architektur, Zurich: gta, 1998. Exhibition catalogue.

Ruchat, Anna. 'La corte di Riva'. In *Negli immediati dintorni. Guida letteraria tra Lombardia e Canton Ticino*, edited by Matteo Terzaghi and Matteo Camagnoli, 43–9. Bellinzona: Casagrande, 2015.

Ruchat-Roncati, Flora. 'Zwischen Ort und Projekt' [audio]. Einführungsvorlesung von Flora Ruchat-Roncati, ETH Zürich. Abt. I, Abteilung für Architektur, Sommersemester 1986. Zurich: ETH-Bibliothek, 1986.

Ruchat-Roncati, Flora. Exhibition vernissage speech, 1997. Archive document gta 01-S-246-1-154-127.

Zanier, Leonardo. 'Stöckli'. In *Flora Ruchat-Roncati*, 23–30. Eidgenössische Technische Hochschule Zürich, ed. Institut für Geschichte und Theorie der Architektur, Zurich: gta, 1998. Exhibition catalogue.

Le Corbusier and Eileen Gray at Roquebrune-Cap-Martin: Some notes about resistance and performance

Thea Brejzek and Lawrence Wallen

In May 2018, the authors visited Cap Moderne, situated on the picturesque peninsula of Roquebrune-Cap-Martin on the French Cote d'Azur across from Monaco, to experience in person the built structures that have become intrinsic elements of the twentieth-century modernist architectural canon: Eileen Gray's iconic E-1027; Le Corbusier's monastic Le Cabanon; his multicoloured holiday units; and his workshop hut. Extant photographs, mostly grainy black-and-white images taken before the 2015 renovation, could not fully explain the unique topographic relationship of the buildings to each other. A relationship that to us, as we approached the steep site from above on foot, presented as an interlinked dramatic narrative. As theorists engaged with the nexus between architecture and performance, understanding culture not as text but as performance,[1] we read the site of Cap Moderne and its built history as the result of a series of performative acts undertaken by Le Corbusier over thirty years. These acts we understand to be subjective acts of resistance performed by one architect against another, with the final act comprising Le Corbusier's resistance against his own media image. In our performative reading, Cap Moderne emerges as a dynamic site of an architect's conflict between self-expression, competitiveness, and self-promotion when building his own house. Ultimately, this conflict is understood as a series of acts of resistance by Le Corbusier, as an architect and as a man, against Eileen Gray, as an architect and as a woman.

1
See Fischer-Lichte, 'Culture as Performance'.

Introduction

Our site opened to the public in 2015, concurrently rebranding itself as Cap Moderne following the complete restoration of Eileen Gray's 1929 modernist villa E-1027 and Le Corbusier's 1952 holiday house, Le Cabanon de Vacances. The opening was timed to coincide with the fiftieth anniversary of Le Corbusier's untimely death on the beach below. It comprises five structures – E-1027, Bar l'Etoile de Mer, Le Cabanon de Le Corbusier, Le Corbusier's workshop hut, and Unités de Camping – all built between 1929 and 1956. The site's history tracks Le Corbusier's biography, expressed through annual summer holidays, boating accidents, conceptual design work, and culminating with the construction of the austere Tombe de Le Corbusier in the Cimetière de Roquebrune on the hill above Cap Moderne where he and his wife Yvonne are inurned. The site has evolved as a 'built manifestation' of the well-documented, laden relationship Le Corbusier had with Eileen Gray and her holiday villa E-1027 in coalescence with his internal artistic incongruities.

This essay revisits the dramatic narrative that unfolded between 1929 and 1956 and reframes Le Corbusier's actions as three performative acts of resistance: the first was a pictorial intervention into Gray's modernist masterpiece E-1027; the second was a series of built interventions imposing on E-1027's secluded site; and the third was an act of resistance Le Corbusier performed against his public image. This essay, thus, shifts the focus from critiquing Le Corbusier's interventions (even though such critique is inevitable) or rehabilitating Gray's work in the history of modernist architecture.[2] Instead, we identify Le Corbusier's actions as three acts of resistance performed by the architect and link these to a set of the architect's subjective psychological motivations that he carried out stubbornly, violently, and creatively. Each act occurred at and was linked to the same site at Roquebrune. Each act originated from a different kind of resistance; each act constituted a performance in that it comprised the architect-protagonist, a chosen audience, and a site; and each act's performative character was revealed in its construction of reality. Each of Le Corbusier's three performative acts left a trace – first, an artefact; then, a set of built structures; and, finally, a new mediated self-image. In describing these acts (or actions) by the architect as performative, their capacity for the construction of reality is implied, be it temporary or permanent, that is, during or as a result of the performative act. Instrumental to what is termed in this essay as a 'dramatic narrative', the performative act also implies that the action is intended rather than arbitrary and that it is staged rather than improvised. At the centre, and acting as a catalyst for Le Corbusier, lies E-1027 and the architect-persona of Eileen Gray, both a constant provocation to the architect and one that drove him to overwrite E-1027's aesthetics, to dominate it visually through a built structure, and finally, posthumously, to erase the name of both building and creator.

2
For an examination of Gray's work, see Adam's biographies of Eileen Gray, published in 1987, 2000, and 2009; Constant, 'E.1027'; Colomina, 'Battle Lines'; and Rault, 'Occupying E.1027' and Rault, *Eileen Gray*.

Gray first toured the French Cote d'Azur in 1925 in search for a location to build a house for herself and her friend, Romanian architect Jean Badovici. After several visits, Gray settled on a steep piece of land between the coast and the train line that connected Ventimiglia and Marseille and designed the building that she named, enigmatically, E-1027. Le Corbusier first visited Roquebrune with the distinct purpose to look at E-1027. Le Corbusier, Gray, and Badovici had known each other for several years from Paris, Gray being one of the most prominent furniture designers of her time, and Badovici being the editor of the journal *l'Architecture Vivante* and a close friend of Le Corbusier's.

The formal language of the modernist and ship-like E-1027, which was completed in 1929, has direct tectonic, conceptual, and aesthetic similarities to Le Corbusier's houses of the time, including the Villa Stein-de-Monzie (1926), Villa Church (1927), and the Maisons de la Weissenhof-Siedlung, Stuttgart (1927). However, there is a heightened sense of metamorphosis in Gray's work that is arguably lacking in Le Corbusier's built work. E-1027, whose name is a numerical play on Badovici's and Gray's initials, has a fluidity and impermanence, allowing the space to respond to the movement

Fig. 1 View from outside Le Corbusier's Cabanon to Eileen Gray's 1929 villa E-1027, Roquebrune-Cap-Martin, France, May 2018. (Photograph by © Lawrence Wallen)

Fig. 2 Interior view of E-1027, Roquebrune-Cap-Martin, France, May 2018.
(Photograph by © Lawrence Wallen)

Fig. 3 An example of the Corbusian stencils scattered throughout E-1027, in this case, 'Défense de rire' (It is no laughing matter), May 2018.
(Photograph by © Lawrence Wallen)

3
Gray cited in Adam, *Eileen Gray*, 1987, 216.

4
Gray cited in Adam, *Eileen Gray*, 2009, 195.

5
Adam, *Eileen Gray*, 1987, 207.

6
Gray cited in Adam, *Eileen Gray*, 1987, 233.

7
Le Corbusier, *Towards a New Architecture*, 4.

8
Gray cited in Adam, *Eileen Gray*, 1987, 233.

9
Adam, *Eileen Gray*, 2009, 135.

10
From the Cap Moderne Association's website, capmoderne.com/en/qui_sommes_nous/. Accessed 4 July 2019.

of its inhabitants and combining architecture with furniture design in a seamless way **(Fig. 2)**. All is in flux; E-1027 is not a machine for living. Instead, as Gray writes in the 1940, 'A house is not a machine to live in. It is the shell of man, his extension, his release, his emanation.'[3] E-1027 developed as a 'living organism'.[4] Furthermore, Gray's casual yet carefully planned and designed seaside 'camping style' emphasised the flow of the interior.[5] She critiqued the modernist avant-garde movement as having privileged the exterior over the interior, and she actively articulated this critique in a special issue of *l'Architecture Vivante* dedicated to E-1027. She wrote: 'a house ought to be conceived more for the pleasure of the eyes than for the comfort of its inhabitants'.[6] The house has a detailed spatial choreography. A playful directorial note on the entrance walls in Corbusian stencils – 'Entrez lentement' (Enter slowly) – greets the visitor as one enters the house, and similar instructions continue throughout the house **(Fig. 3)**. In describing E-1027 as a creation that affirms but also challenges the central principles of Le Corbusier's architectural manifesto, the house becomes a prominent actor in our exposition of Le Corbusier's performative acts of resistance. In contrast to Le Corbusier's dictum of the house as a 'machine for living in'[7], Gray posits it as a '[dwelling] for people'.[8]

Gray and Badovici lived at E-1027 during the summer months until 1934 when Gray built her own house in nearby Castellar, leaving the house to Badovici. Between 1938 and 1939, Le Corbusier painted a series of eight explicit murals on the white walls of the house without consulting her. Gray, according to her biographer Peter Adam, responded by never staying in the house again.[9] Taking advantage of the fact that a friend of his, Thomas Rebutato, had opened a bar directly above E-1027, Le Corbusier acquired a small piece of land adjacent to it and in 1952 built a log cabin, in his own words, a *cabanon*. After Bodovici died in 1956, Le Corbusier, in exchange for the land beneath Le Cabanon, designed five holiday cabins for Rebutato, as a single-row two-storey structure. Their primary-coloured facades and location overlooking Gray's house from above visually conflict with E-1027 **(Fig. 6)**, striking the observer as an intentional and uncanny invasion into the territory so clearly defined by Gray's architecture. However, Le Corbusier's fixation with E-1027 did not stop there. His attempts to have the house turned into a museum for his murals failed, but Marie-Louise Schelbert, an architect and gallerist friend of Le Corbusier, bought it at auction on his suggestion. After the sale, he demanded payment from Schelbert for his wall paintings as well as their restoration, making it evident that his interest in her purchase of E-1027 was the preservation of his murals. Le Corbusier died in the sea beneath Gray's E-1027 on 27 August 1965. In 1999, the villa was bought by the not-for-profit organisation Conservatoire du Littoral to facilitate the restoration of the house, its internal fittings, and the garden. The organisation states that 'Le Corbusier's murals have been retained and restored as they embody a key phase in the history of the villa's occupation and are a reminder of the indelible imprint left by the architect.'[10] While overlooked and marginalised in the histories of modernist architecture for decades, a renewed interest in Gray's professional path from celebrated Parisian interior and furniture designer to an architect who proposed both in writing and as manifest in E-1027 a different kind of modernism has given rise to several publications. Caroline Constant's 1994 essay 'E-1027: The Nonheroic Modernism of Eileen Gray' offers a detailed reading of the building and its interior fittings through a feminist and gender lens, and Beatriz Colomina's 1996 essay 'Battle Lines: E. 1027' introduces a psychoanalytical and feminist reading of Le Corbusier's actions and interventions, focussing on the 'defacing act' of the murals.[11] Jasmine Rault's 2005 article, 'Occupying E-1027: Reconsidering Le Corbusier's "Gift" to Eileen Gray' convincingly posits Le Corbusier's murals as a 'covert, perhaps even unconscious (disciplinary) response to the aesthetic, philosophical and sexual threat that her work represented'.[12] Rault's subsequent 2011 monograph *Eileen Gray and the Design of Sapphic Modernity* reads as the psychogram of a society that must label women such as Eileen Gray, who did not conform to conventional gender roles, as 'Other', disregarding and marginalising them in disciplinary discourse and public attention. Our essay contributes to the existing body of research with the historical advantage of having visited and experienced the restored house and extends this body of research by offering a performative reading of the events at Roquebrune and beyond. This new reading allows for the entangled conflicts between Le Corbusier and Gray to be understood as scenes in the iconic architects' continuous strive for acceptance. It looks upon the persona of Le Corbusier as an architect-stage director who both directed and performed his play over thirty years, with Roquebrune as its single location and catalyst. In what we articulate as the first two performative acts of resistance, Le Corbusier performed resistance in the first act as an artist. In contrast, in the second act, he performed resistance as an architect against another architect and all she stood for. Le Corbusier recognised Gray as a fellow architect-persona who not only mastered but also consciously transgressed modernist practices and theories she denounced as sterile and devoid of 'instinct' with the highly sensual and subjective interiors of E-1027.[13]

While Le Corbusier's first two 'acts' carry elements of hubris and self-destruction, the third performative act of resistance, namely the public reinvention of himself from a controversial public urban persona to a nature-loving artist and collector, presents as a desperate and masterful show of force at a time when voices were decrying a dehumanised modernism that was increasingly connected with the names of the iconic architects of the time.

First act of resistance: an intervention into site

It takes time to paint a mural. Its site needs to be determined, and the size of the wall considered as well as the viewing axes from which it will be visible. The artist must decide on motif and colour scheme and possibly produce small-scale sketches and drawings before embarking on the final large-scale mural. Moreover, the act of painting a wall is decidedly physical, requiring the active involvement of

11
Colomina, 'Battle Lines', 101.

12
Rault, 'Occupying E.1027', 160.

13
'The poverty of modern architecture stems from the atrophy of sensuality. Everything is dominated by reason in order to create amazement without proper research. The art of the engineer is not enough if it is not guided by the primitive needs of men. Reason without instinct. We must mistrust pictorial elements if they are not assimilated by instinct'. Gray in Adam, *Eileen Gray*, 1987, 216.

Fig. 4 The wall of Le Corbusier's 1938 mural at E-1027 during restoration, May 2018. (Photograph by © Lawrence Wallen)

14
Constant, 'E.1027', 278.

15
Badovici cited in Constant, 'E.1027', 278.

the artist's full body. The tangible materiality of surface and paint, the necessary physical action combined with its emergence over time make the mural a creative act distinct from the production of other modes of representation.

The murals at E-1027 were not the first time Le Corbusier engaged with painting on large architectural surfaces. As Constant points out, Le Corbusier had painted his first mural in 1935 in Badovici's Vézelay house, possibly inspired by a courtyard mural Fernand Léger had painted there the year before.[14] Badovici emphatically embraced the genre of the mural as a spatial rather than decorative art and inscribed into its act a quality that indicates a future architecture: 'an idea occurred to us all: THAT OF THE DESTRUCTION OF WALLS BY PAINTING, crowning, above all, the architecture to come'.[15] To the delight of Badovici, Le Corbusier painted a series of eight murals on the interior walls of E-1027 between 1938 and 1939 when Gray had already left the house to live at Castellar. Le Corbusier had stayed at the house with his wife Yvonne earlier in 1938, and paradoxically expressed his appraisal and wonder at its originality in a letter to Gray: 'I am so happy to tell you how much those few days spent in your house have made me appreciate the rare spirit which dictates all the organisation inside and outside. A rare spirit which has given the modern furniture and installations such a dignified, charming, and witty shape.'[16] In the same year, Le Corbusier did not hesitate to inscribe his presence into the 'rare spirit of the house' through what Adam bluntly calls an act of 'rape'. He continued: 'A fellow architect, a man she admired, had, without her consent, defaced her design.'[17]

16
Le Corbusier in a letter to Gray from 1938 in Adam, *Eileen Gray*, 2000, 309–10.

17
Adam, *Eileen Gray*, 1978, 311.

18
Le Corbusier cited in Colomina, 'Battle Lines', 99.

The decision to inscribe his presence into the house that he called the Badovici House, thus erasing Gray's name, has been widely interpreted as an act of sexual violence. Actively contributing to this understanding is the murals' motif, depicting in a graphic style two nude female figures, intertwined and in their centre a small child-like figure. That the motif or explanation is, as Colomina claims, a 'theme for a psychiatrist' is doubtful as is her reading of the child as male.[18] More productive, the authors claim, is the fact that Le Corbusier was photographed nude in the act of painting the mural. The unnamed photographer's presence during Le Corbusier's act of overwriting Gray's work accentuates its performative quality in that there was an audience who witnessed (and did not hinder) the architect's victorious gesture. Thus, a performative space emerged in Le Corbusier's act in the interplay between him as an actor, the photographer as audience, and the architectural space. In this temporary and highly charged performative space, Le Corbusier's transgression was both validated and documented. Le Corbusier's performative act of resistance renders his intervention a mise-en-scène that actively resisted Gray's building and interiors and was constructing reality in its material manifestation. Furthermore, Le Corbusier proclaimed himself as the author publicly through the subsequent circulation of the photograph.

Second act of resistance: the domination of site

If Le Corbusier's first performative act of resistance occurred on a physical and pictorial level – namely, the portraits of himself painting murals onto the white walls of E-1027 – his second act of performative resistance manifested itself against the entire building with three structures that lay in stark contrast to the clean white lines of E-1027. What we call here the second act of performative resistance is one that posits building against building in a dramatic acceleration of the conflict between Le Corbusier and the apparent unbearable provocation of E-1027 played out in built form. This second act demonstrates Le Corbusier's desire to overwrite and dominate not only Gray's house but also its site and continues to establish his actions as an unfolding chain of acts of resistance.

In 1952, Le Corbusier designed the Cabanon de Vacances as his holiday house. Prefabricated and manufactured in Corsica, the log-cabin style Cabanon sits on a terrace above E-1027, directly adjacent to the Bar l'Etoile de Mer to which it had direct access through

Fig. 5 E-1027 with Le Corbusier's Unités de Camping in the background, May 2018. (Photograph by © Lawrence Wallen)

a door and a shared terrace with a view down to E-1027 **(Fig. 1)**. To the left and some distance away, Le Corbusier added a work shack whose single window looks out onto the Mediterranean Sea and diagonally down to E-1027.

At Cabanon, Le Corbusier employed his patented Le Modulor anthropometric-scaled proportions – previously applied to the Unité d'Habitation à Marseille – though at a significantly smaller scale to create a volume 2.66 metres high and 3.66 metres in length and width. Upon entering the Cabanon, one proceeds along a hallway along the western edge of the structure to access a wood-lined room with built-in furniture, small windows, and several murals. While the work shack is configured to look outwards, the Cabanon spirals inward and reads as a hermetic space, in contradiction to its watchtower-like position. With the Cabanon, Le Corbusier asserted himself as an architect with an ideal embodied in his own holiday home: it was designed not for pleasure like E-1027, but as a monastic cell for living and creative work.

The third structure, the Unité de Camping, was built in 1956 directly above E-1027 and on the same height line as the Cabanon. It comprised five holiday units that utilised the same anthropometric proportions that he had applied to the Cabanon and the Unité d'Habitation à Marseille. While the materiality of the wooden structure of the holiday units lies in stark contrast to the concrete construction of Le Corbusier's Unité d'Habitation à Marseille, the formal composition and the use of extensive primary colours link the projects in a common language.

Le Corbusier's decision to build the holiday units directly above Gray's villa is argued here as the fulfilment of his second performative act of resistance against the solitary spirit of E-1027. With the Cabanon, Le Corbusier had already asserted his bodily and spiritual presence onto the site. With the addition of the brightly coloured holiday cabins, he added an audience positioned directly above the building that visually encroached on its site. It is, however, the building processes of the Cabanon, hut, and holiday units that are identified here as performative. Their durational, intended, and staged quality is in direct interaction and confrontation with E-1027. As the buildings emerged from the site, a long-drawn, complex narrative of one architect observing and dominating another through the occupation of the territory began to be played out in a built form that culminated with Le Corbusier's pictorial violation of the walls of E-1027. This narrative, with no objective other than to demonstrate his power over woman, site, and building, is argued here as performative and therefore explicitly reality-constructing.

Third act of resistance: site as symbol

Le Corbusier built the Cabanon in 1952, the same year that his Unité d'Habitation à Marseille was completed, garnering hostile reactions from the population, who nicknamed it 'La Maison du Fada' (The House of the Fool). Even though Le Corbusier described his design for the Unité as wanting

Fig. 6 Internal view of Le Corbusier's restored work shack with bones and seashells arranged on the table as per the 1955 press photos of the same space, May 2018. (Photograph by © Lawrence Wallen)

to establish a close relationship between man and nature in that it provided 'silence and solitude, in the light of the sun and amid space and green a dwelling that would be the perfect receptacle for a family',[19] his public image remained very much as the brilliant but socially controlling architect of the design of the monumental, dense living machines that prescribed the behaviour of the inhabitants of the 337 near-identical apartments. In 1955, the year the Roman Catholic chapel Notre Dame du Haut at Ronchamp (that Le Corbusier claimed he had designed at Roquebrune) was completed, he invited journalists from the French science magazine *Science et Vie* to visit him in Roquebrune. It is argued here, following Maak, that Le Corbusier intended with this invitation to reinvent his public image away from the austere creator of living machines toward a man of nature who drew inspiration from the natural form. The journalists entered a mise-en-scène complete with the Cabanon and hut, surrounded by a wildly romantic setting of landscape, flora, and sea, with the protagonist-architect positioned in its very centre. This time, he did not have himself documented as the victorious artist in the very act of conquering and largely annihilating another architect's masterpiece but rather as the solitary creator who draws inspiration for a humane architecture from natural forms and objects. Consequently, Le Corbusier received the journalists not in the Cabanon, but rather in the work hut next to it (**Fig. 6**). There, he housed his collection of natural *objets trouvés* – pebbles, seashells, bones, a crab shell. *Science et Vie*'s press image shows Le Corbusier in a crumpled, short-sleeved casual shirt seated at his worktable before a background of drawings of organic shapes and forms and looking intently at a pebble he holds in his right hand. The published article reads:

> A wooden hut with three drawings on the wall, a project for a carpet and a few coloured sketches. Light from two windows falls on a large rectangular table covered with paper and on shelves full of variously coloured stones, pieces of bones eaten away by the sea and a lobster shell. A man in his shirt sleeves is sitting upright at the table: the architect of happiness, Le Corbusier. The wooden hut is his workshop.[20]

The purpose of the Parisian journalists' visit to Le Corbusier, as Maak writes, had not been to witness the architect in his holiday house but rather to inquire about his plans for post-Second World War housing reconstruction in France. Le Corbusier's presentation was an intentional staging of the architect of the biomorphic Notre Dame du Haut resisting the rational rectilinear forms of the Unité d'Habitation à Marseille for which he had become renowned.

Coda

The first act of resistance preceded Le Corbusier's Cabanon in the form of a violent pictorial intervention into E-1027, an act that still today inscribes his presence on the building. In the second act of resistance upon Gray's building and design philosophy of a 'humane modernism', Le Corbusier chose to site his hut directly overlooking the building he had already vandalised by adding the wooden, primary-coloured holiday cabins as an aesthetic and

19 Le Corbusier cited in Maak, 'Le Corbusier', 35.

20 *Science et Vie* cited in Maak, 'Le Corbusier', 44.

formal counterpoint aimed towards visual domination of E-1027. Finally, in the third act of resistance, Le Corbusier rewrote his public image toward that of the 'architect of happiness' surrounded by natural objects and landscape with press photographs of himself seated amongst his collection in the hut adjacent to the Cabanon. The resistance an architect offers concerning their house is, as we have shown, not necessarily directly linked to (their) building but can take many forms and originate from diverse motivations and desires. In what we have called here Le Corbusier's 'performative acts of resistance', resistance is directed towards another architect, Eileen Gray, towards this architect's building (E-1027), and finally, in a masterfully staged performance, towards their public persona. By naming these events performative acts, we identify that these were, in fact, reality-constructing interventions while their manifestation differed in each instance: from a two-dimensional pictorial intervention to several three-dimensional built structures to the rebranding of Le Corbusier's media image. It all started, however, with the cataclysmic reaction of one architect to another architect's holiday house.

Bibliography

Adam, Peter. *Eileen Gray: Architect Designer*. New York: Harry N. Abrams, Inc., 1987.

Adam, Peter. *Eileen Gray: Architect Designer: A Biography*. London: Thames & Hudson, 2000.

Adam, Peter. *Eileen Gray: Her Life and Work*. London: Thames & Hudson, 2009.

Colomina, Beatriz. 'Battle Lines: E.1027'. *Renaissance and Modern Studies* 39, no. 1 (1996): 95–105.

Constant, Caroline. 'E.1027: The Nonheroic Modernism of Eileen Gray'. *Journal of the Society of Architectural Historians* 53, no. 3 (1994): 265–79.

Fischer-Lichte, Erika. 'Culture as Performance'. Special issue *Performance: Modern Austrian Literature* 42, no. 3 (2009): 1–10.

Le Corbusier. *Towards a New Architecture*. Translated by Frederick Etchells. London: J. Rodker, 1931. Reprint New York: Dover Publications, Inc., 1986.

Maak, Niklas. *Le Corbusier: The Architect on the Beach*. Munich: Hirmer, 2011.

Rault, Jasmine. *Eileen Gray and the Design of Sapphic Modernity*. Farnham, Surrey: Ashgate, 2011.

Rault, Jasmine. 'Occupying E.1027. Reconsidering Le Corbusier's "Gift"'. *Space and Culture* 8, no. 2 (2005): 160–79.

Fig. 1 Front elevation of the Doxiadis residence. (© Constantinos and Emma Doxiadis Foundation, Photographs 30905)

Tomato, Acropolis, and the Power of Family

Farhan Karim

Constantinos Doxiadis's five-storey residential apartment building stands at the foot of Mount Lycabettus in Athens, overlooking the Parthenon in the distance **(Fig. 1)**. Doxiadis built this apartment building in 1957, four years after he returned from a self-exile in Australia.[1] Having a typical sleek, white, modernist facade with large glass windows, an open plan, an open facade, thin columns, and an unbroken balcony, the building continues the legacy of the 1920s and 1930s Greek modernists such as Nikolaos Mitsakis, Pratsika, and Georgios Kontoleon. However, underneath the familiar rhetoric of a modernist social utopia reminiscent of the Weissenhof Estate (1927), Doxiadis's residence makes a statement of resisting the nation-state centric view of history and upholds the power of anonymous *folk* and autonomous family as the central political agent of development.

In 1951, at the age of thirty-five, Doxiadis left Athens for Australia, jobless, moneyless, ill, and deemed a failure by his colleagues after having served in a series of high-ranked government positions in the Greek reconstruction programme.[2] In order to meet the costs of his family's migration, Doxiadis and his wife Emma sold the piece of land that they had purchased years before as a site for their future home and Doxiadis's office. Doxiadis struggled for three years to settle himself and his family in Queensland, working first as an architect and builder and then as a tomato farmer, before returning to Athens in 1953. Less than one decade after his return, Doxiadis founded one of the busiest architectural and planning practices in Greece, whose projects stretched from America to Pakistan. He repurchased the same piece of land that he once sold and built his office and his residence there. In a sense, the apartment building is a proud symbol of his resurrection from oblivion, as noted by his old friend and contemporary journalist Philipe Deane.[3]

In this chapter, I employ two analytical tools to discuss the role that the building played in Doxiadis's conceptual formation of architectural resistance. First, the house is a constant reminder of the entrepreneurial potential of a self-starting family and its power to animate 'development'. By expressing solidarity with the bottom-up entrepreneurial construction boom of Athens, Doxiadis's apartment building imagines a world that is free from any form of structural hegemony imposed either by the state or by the real estate industry. Secondly, Doxiadis presented his residence as the material embodiment of folk, the collective yet abstract will of 'common' people. Doxiadis held that the creativity and agency of architects lay in giving the folk – the true agents of history – a tangible expression in the contemporary world. The building embodied the concept of a 'natural', interconnected, and holistic world constituted of self-driven, entrepreneurial, and autonomous folk. These two concepts,

1
For a brief account of Doxiadis's life in Australia, see Kyrtsis, *Constantinos A. Doxiadis*, 355–8.

2
For a discussion of Doxiadis's involvement and subsequent departure from the Greek reconstruction programme, see Kakridis, 'Rebuilding the Future', 135–60.

3
Deane, *Constantinos Doxiadis*.

which Doxiadis believed would equip the architects and planners to empower the common folk, were later (quite paradoxically) appropriated by his clients – various developmental agencies and despotic states – to disempower the common people.[4]

Self-help as entrepreneurial force

Isabelle Doucet and Janina Gosseye explained in the introduction to the current volume that the architect's house (mostly a single-family house) is often perceived as a polemic and representative of the personality of the architect-owner. Doxiadis's multifamily apartment, instead of being a polemic in a conventional sense, effaced the idiosyncrasy of an architect and conformed to the sweeping 1950s construction boom of multifamily, multistoreyed apartments known as *polykatoikia* (πολυκατοικία, from πολυ-, meaning 'multiple,' and -κατοικία, meaning 'residence'),[5] which, ironically, resulted from Athens' long-standing housing shortage.[6] Athens faced a formidable housing crisis when a surge of refugees from the newly established Turkish Republic poured into Athens through the 'population exchange' in 1923.[7] In 1929, faced with a paucity of resources to deal with the population growth, the state approved the *antiparochi* law to incentivise small-scale, private development projects, which, in the following decades, became a determining factor for Athens' urban and social fabric.[8] According to this law, any landowner could turn over their land, regardless of its location in the city, to a general contractor, allowing them to build a multistorey apartment building. In exchange for the land, the contractor would give the landowner an agreed-upon number of apartments in the finished building; this was considered tax-free wealth for the landowner. In a sense, *antiparochi* was a kind of social welfare policy of a state with limited resources that could not offer any social housing programmes in Athens. *Antiparochi* and *polykatoikia* turned every landowner in the city into a potential entrepreneur and turned the city into a working 'factory'.[9] Through the introduction of *antiparochi*, the city authority withdrew its strict control over the market, effectively deregulating the construction sector by ceding control through master-plan or zoning regulations. In a sense, through *antiparochi*, the state aided in the creation of a semi-informal urbanism and the unplanned expansion of the city. Following the end of the Greek Civil War (1946–49), Athens experienced an unprecedented migration of people from surrounding rural areas, resulting in a construction boom of *polykatoikia* through *antiparochi*.[10] Until 1967, the beginning of the Regime of the Colonels (the Greek military junta of 1967–74) *antiparochi* was the main funding apparatus of the city, which evolved almost independently of any private or public credit system.

Within this context, Doxiadis's apartment building problematises the understanding of an architect's 'house' as consciously designed, philosophically enriched, well-assembled, and well-articulated. Built through *antiparochi*, Doxiadis's apartment building had multiple owners and stakeholders who, over time, altered parts of it. For Doxiadis, it was important to conceive the 'house' as an ongoing, incremental process of development – a process known in Greece

4
Literature on Doxiadis's involvement in various development projects in the Middle East, Africa, and South Asia is a growing body of scholarship. For a quick reference, see Daechsel, 'Misplaced Ekistics'.

5
Woditsch, *The Public Private House*; Theocharopoulou, *Builders, Housewives*.

6
Dragonas, 'An Obituary'.

7
Angelidakis, 'Unauthorized'.

8
Kalantidou, 'Westernizing the Semi-Orient'.

9
Aureli, Giudici, and Issaias, 'From Domino to Polykatoikia'.

10
For a detailed discussion of the production of *polykatoikia*, see Emmanuel, *The Growth of Speculative Building in Greece*.

11
Magouliotis, 'Learning from "Panosikoma"'.

12
For a critique of *polykatoikia*, see Issaias, 'On Conflict, Generic and the Informal'. Also see Issaias, 'Domestic, Production, Debt'.

13
Aureli, Giudici and Issaias, 'From Domino to Polykatoikia'.

14
Moatsu, 'Polykatoikia'.

15
Conversation with Hadjopoulos, a retired senior architect of Doxiadis Associates, at his residence in 2017.

16
Fessas-Emmanouil and Marmaras, *Twelve Greek Architects*.

17
Deane, *Constantinos Doxiadis*.

as *panosikoma*, in which an 'incomplete house' will be gradually developed through self-help, eventually completed when the owner has accumulated sufficient capital to do so.[11] Incompleteness in this sense was not a sign of economic weakness, but rather represents the centrality of entrepreneurial family in the production of architecture. Doxiadis's idea of the building was thus not a finished product but an accumulative phenomenon.

Antiparochi, when first conceived, was a pragmatic response to an immediate need, but, once unleashed, the enormous development drive of *polykatoikia* assumed a life of its own. The long-term negative effect of *antiparochi* and *polykatoikia* has been the loss of public space, extreme fragmentation and commodification of land, and the exclusive private life of citizens, as noted by Platon Issaias.[12] Aureali, Giudici, and Issaias also describe *polykatoikia* as a 'violent biopolitical project' that disintegrated the collective fabric of the city through an unchecked, extreme form of individualism,[13] while Olga Moatsou labels the latest iteration of *polykatoikia* as an 'object of hedonistic consumption'.[14] During the 1950s, however, *antiparochi* was widely considered a progressive means for development, and Doxiadis welcomed its central tenet, for it agreed with two of his fundamental design principles that he believed would resist the homogenising force of global capitalism. First, a self-help family was the basic entrepreneurial force of society and the central agent of change and development.[15] This view was connected to the traditional value system of southern Europe, in which homeownership was seen as an important attribute of personal empowerment. Second, folk spirit resisted state hegemony by nurturing bottom-up entrepreneurship. Folk, in this context, was not an exotic source from which a romantic, national past could be extrapolated, rather, according to architects, it was an open-ended, pragmatic theory in the face of economic scarcity during the interwar and post-Second World War times.[16] Doxiadis later expanded this idea of folk power in his works for various global development projects.

Doxiadis built the *polykatoikia* immediately on his return from Australia, where his idea of self-help and entrepreneurial family had been strengthened. Philipe Deane, a contemporary journalist, wrote about Doxiadis's apartment:

> In the days when he was rehabilitating Greece, the envious had said that Doxiadis could build only the brutal, functional and utilitarian. His apartment is his answer, a monument to his arc, big enough for a large audience, yet an intimate, pleasant home at the same time; the home of a highly successful man, the most lavish flat in Athens [...] The flat is part of Doxiadis's re-emergence and a mild form of revenge. With no apparent effort, he has extended friendship to those who struck him down, [...] He has demonstrated that his antagonists could not keep him down. In a literal sense, he sits above them, and they have come to realise he matters more to the world day by day. He makes his income and reputation mostly outside Greece and he is safe therefore from the historic rage of Greeks at the successful among them.[17]

While in Australia, Doxiadis was unable to obtain a license to practice architecture. His professional degree from the National Technical University of Athens and doctorate from the Technical University of Charlottenburg, Berlin, were deemed inadequate. He managed to get a builder's license but was unsuccessful in securing any projects. Having failed to practice either as an architect or as a builder, he and his wife started a tomato farm. Although Doxiadis's family-run farm eventually began to thrive, he was always eager to return to Greece. Being in a distant, English-speaking country where his children were often bullied in school for not speaking proper English while he was working in the tomato fields under the hot summer sun dwarfed his creative ego and instilled in Doxiadis three important principles that continued to influence him throughout his entire career. First, family was the basic core of any development project. Second, he compulsively relied on data to model development projects and project the future of landscape as a total system. Third, he nurtured a desolate sense of emptiness and a distrust in aesthetic monumentality almost to the point of psychotic nihilism.

Doxiadis's idea of the entrepreneurial family began to take shape in three unpublished manuscripts that he wrote while in Australia: a manual on the scientific production of tomatoes, a book on the future of Australia entitled 'The Coming Invasion of Australia', and another book on the future of Greece entitled 'Greece as an Element of an Emerging World'.[18] 'The Coming Invasion' is a grim prophecy about Australia's future and how millions of immigrants from all over the world would pour into this empty and unexplored land, and would corrode the country's economic base if the immigrant's skills and working potential were not well integrated with the existing economy. Doxiadis suggested harnessing the potential power of the immigrant families while placing restrictions on uncontrolled immigration to counter the forces of globalisation. He also explained how Australia could scientifically steer its economic development through the systematic organisation of its agricultural and mining industries. The small booklet on how to grow tomatoes more efficiently demonstrates his confidence in the power of personal scientific inquiry even in the apparently trivial job at a family farm cultivating tomatoes,[19] while 'The Coming Invasion' aimed to balance the global forces that control migration and strengthen national development by tapping into the power and capacity of incoming families.

18
'The Coming Invasion', vol. 34, 1952, Constantinos A. Doxiadis Archives (hereafter CADA); 'Greece as an Element of an Emerging World', CADA.

19
Report by Dr. Doxiadis, 9 March 1953. 29288, CADA.

Folk architecture, nationalism, and the failure of development

Doxiadis's first serious encounter with the idea of a self-help, bottom-up approach occurred during his tenure in the Greek reconstruction programme. During that time, Doxiadis edited a semi-clandestine periodical entitled *Chorotaxia* (regional planning) that published pragmatic and non-utopian essays for a readership of technical experts. In *Chorotaxia*, Doxiadis published a lengthy article, 'Folk Art and Architecture' by architect Angeliki Hadjimichali, that emphasised the value of self-help construction as the creative role of the non-professional, peasant-

Fig. 2 Doxiadis sitting in his office with a view of the Parthenon. (© Constantinos and Emma Doxiadis Foundation, Photographs 32591)

20
Tzonis and Rodi, *Greece Modern Architectures*, 144.

21
Daeschel, *Islamabad*, 103.

22
Doxiadis, *Architecture in Transition*.

technician.[20] For Doxiadis, the aesthetic of folk architecture corresponds to its socioeconomic condition, and thus suggested a way to unleash the power of bottom-up architecture.

Doxiadis thought that incorporating a folk sensibility in modern architecture was a way to decentre the hegemonic authority of the architect in the design process for folk, who, in Doxiadis's interpretation, embodied the collective wisdom of the marginal. This self-effacing process of personal authority, as historian Markus Daeschel explained, was at the heart of Doxiadis's later role as global development consultant.[21] A quintessential example of appropriating folk in modern architecture is the balcony of his apartment. A continuous narrow balcony wraps around the apartment block. Doxiadis called this balcony 'double skin', as a continuous and movable canopy over the balcony protected the house from the summer heat and low sun. Doxiadis wrote: 'This space [the balcony] is of different quality [. . .] the search for contemporary solutions leads to age-old patterns.'[22] The double skin, which according to Doxiadis has been derived from vernacular design practice, maintained a continuation between 'tradition' and 'modernity'.

He further explained:

> [W]hen I tried to purge the architecture of my own flat of everything that was inherited or inspired from outside, so as to make it as rational a dwelling-place as possible, I found myself back in the forms which are the old traditional forms that created the classical style and Byzantine style, and which can still be seen in Greek villages and monasteries: the interplay of lighter and darker surfaces, together with the rhythmical formation of the lightened ones.[23]

The idea of the *erker* – a continuous and enclosed balcony that alludes the vernacular Athenian house – was representative of Greek folk architecture and was considered by many architects the perfect element to establish a continuity between the vernacular, or past, and the modern, or future, thus legitimising modernism as a natural course of history.[24]

This idea of searching for an essential past and purging historical styles to capture the true meaning or folk consciousness of architecture was not uncommon at that time.[25] Folk, according to Doxiadis, manifested the inner essences of human civilisation; folk was the most effective concept to understand human collectivity and therefore, irrespective of differences among societies around the world, commonality can be found in folk architecture.[26] For Doxiadis, folk appeared as an archetypical human spirit. The cultural specificity of folk, Doxiadis argued, should not be seen as divisive but as unifying. Folk architecture cannot be theorised through kinship or nationalism; it goes deeper than the political condition of nation-states or socioeconomic conditions of kinship. Doxiadis argued that folk architecture lay beyond this imagined structure of nation-state. For him, it was reasonable to understand the essentialist nature of folk architecture through the agency of 'family', which, according to Doxiadis, existed and endured beyond the framework of nation and nationalism. In a sense, nationalism and the nation-state was an obstruction for the natural growth of the folk. To this end, Doxiadis imagined folk as a unifying force that resisted the homogenising force of international capitalism.

Folk as opposed to nation-state and autonomous family as opposed to kin-based politics cloaked in the rhetoric of nationalism was deepened from Doxiadis's experience as a technocrat in the Greek reconstruction programme and his subsequent termination from the position, which was the pretext for his exile in Australia.[27] Doxiadis's imagination left out individual architects from history, considering folk in lieu of the nation-sate as the exclusive arena within which historic dynamics played out. The apparently powerless architects, in Doxiadis's interpretation, could gain agency only if they complemented the collective subconscious of folk wisdom and thus laboured to give folk its due contemporary expression. This understanding of contemporary architects as the initiator of folk-wisdom can be recognised in Doxiadis's doctoral dissertation, which argues that the apparent disorderly arrangement of the ancient Greek sites was actually based on the principle of visual

23
Doxiadis, *Architecture in Transition.*

24
During the dictatorship of Ioannis Metaxas (1936–41), a former military officer and a great admirer of Hitler, Mussolini, and mid 1930s authoritarian regimes, the *erker* was seen as politically threatening for one could observe the street without being seen. In 1937, the Ministry of the Administration of the Capital banned not only the *erker* but also any other type of enclosed porch overlooking the street. At the end of the German-Italian occupation (1941–45), this building element was reintroduced into building practice. As such, Doxiadis's argument of connecting tradition with modernity was not at all apolitical; a specific political rhetoric and history was embedded in its form.

25
Aris Konstantinidis and Dimitris Pikionis were two prominent architects in this genre. See Tsaimbaos, *From Doxiadis' Theory*; Fessas-Emmanouil, 'The Architect and the Planner: Modernity and Tradition in the Work of Aris Konstantinidis and Constantinos Doxiadis', unpublished manuscript of a lecture given at the School of Architecture of Milano Technical University on 9 May 2012.

26
Pakistan Volume 2, DOX 2, diary, 12 October–23 November 1954, volume 3, report DOX 21, *Pakistan Ekistics,* CADA.

order, meaning that all buildings in the site were deliberately composed and connected through a complex web of invisible sightlines conditioned by and originating from a person's position within the building site.[28] In his thesis, Doxiadis claims that he found the hidden order of Greek 'folk architecture'. The 'Greek order', representative of an accumulated folk knowledge as argued by Doxiadis, was ontologically much deeper and thus created a stronger psychological effect. Consider the siting of Doxiadis's residence and how one's approach to this building reflects his conviction in the transferability of the ancient principle of hidden order in a modern situation **(Fig. 6)**. Doxiadis believed that as one approached a building, the temporal and visual experience of the observer was crucial for establishing a spiritual connection between the site, the architecture, and the observer.[29]

In a way, Doxiadis's imagination of folk was ambivalent: on the one hand, folk was considered as the true repository of human spirit; but, on the other hand, this spirit was politically unconscious and incapable of self-expression and thus required architects to intervene. Folk could only become relevant if the architect recontextualised its archetypal pattern in the contemporary time. This role of architects as animators of historic forces and thus preservers of historic order was communicated through Doxiadis's self-image in his home and office (which are both located on the same street). They were strategically placed on Mount Lycabettus in a way that the Acropolis and Parthenon could be seen directly from both his house and his office **(Figs. 2 and 3)**. For Doxiadis, a visual connection with the Parthenon would provide an ideological framework to position himself as a historical being, to present the idea of family as an essential unit of common folk and to underscore his personal agency at the heart of historical change. The photograph shows Doxiadis sitting in his office, pretending to write, with the Parthenon in the background. The picture was choreographed to evoke a sense of historical continuity in which Doxiadis claims his place. Similarly, in a series of unpublished family portraits by a *Life* magazine photographer, Doxiadis family poses on the rooftop balcony of his apartment with the Parthenon in the background.[30]

For Doxiadis, the Parthenon, and for that matter the entire swath of classical Greek architecture, was the emblem of folk architecture, which seems a little awkward because we usually understand folk architecture to be non-monumental and anonymous. Doxiadis contended that the Parthenon, a quintessentially monumentalised folk spirit, was produced through a democratic process of social participation. Ironically, while Doxiadis imagined a universal existence of empowered vernacular, his philosophy of history was colonial. In his *Pakistan Ekistics* report, written in 1955, Doxiadis identified Mughal monuments in India as mere 'egocentric' architecture of an 'empire builder' and pleaded with Pakistani bureaucrats and military generals to look for inspiration from their folk architecture.[31] Doxiadis imagined a fixed point of the origin of history – Athenian democracy – and an ideal form – the Parthenon.[32] By staging the Parthenon as the backdrop for his office and his residence, he dissolved the

27
Doxiadis's conflict with the local elite factions even went back to his working experience with Ionnis Metaxas and Konstantinos Kotzias (the Minister Governor of the Capital) on Athens' pre-war development. Doxiadis and Kotzias failed to negotiate with the multiple forces of the local elite. Doxiadis realised even an apparently centralised bureaucracy created by Metaxas failed to contain the heterogeneous local forces. Doxiadis thus became more convinced than ever for the need for a strict hierarchy of order, mutual relationships, networks, a flexible administration, and above all the abolishment of all kin-based political conflicts. See Tzonis and Rodi, *Greece: Modern Architectures in History*.

28
Doxiadis's dissertation was entitled *Raumordnung im griechischen Städtebau*; Jacqueline Tyrwhitt translated and edited it in English under the title *Architectural Space in Ancient Greece*.

29
Houston, *The Place of the Viewer*.

30
Contemporary architects of Athens criticised the location of Doxiadis's office and residence for blocking the view of Mount Lycabettus. Conversation with Hadjopoulos.

31
Pakistan Volume 3, Report Dox 21, *Pakistan Ekistics*, 1955, CADA.

32
Doxiadis, 'The Ancient Greek City'.

Fig. 3 View of Parthenon from the Doxiadis apartment. (Photograph by © Farhan Karim)

Fig. 4 The Doxiadis family posed for *The New York Times*. (Source: Reif, 'The Acropolis Is Backdrop for Modern Setting in Architect's Home', *The New York Times*, 13 December 1961)

Fig. 5 Interior view of the Doxiadis apartment. (© Constantinos and Emma Doxiadis Foundation)

Fig. 6 The road approaching the Doxiadis apartment on Mount Lycabettus. (Photograph by © Farhan Karim)

concept of grand history within the constant friction between his private and public life. He promoted the images of himself and his family **(Fig. 3)** to demonstrate that he was not just a modern individual who was working in a unique post-war, post-colonial condition. Indeed, he was more than an individual; he was a universal 'builder', who embodied the dynamic forces of history by bridging the ancient and the modern.[33]

33
Reif, 'The Acropolis Is Backdrop'.

34
Doxiadis, 'Architect in Evolution', 162–70.

The 'confused' architects and the question of agency

In 1960, Doxiadis delivered a lecture at the annual discourse of the Royal Institute of British Architects (RIBA) where he clarified his position as an architect and planner:

> We do not know whether the architect is supposed to create buildings or neighbourhoods or cities [...] Can the Design be an end in itself, and can the architect be justified in limiting himself to design?[34]

He then went on to explain that architects in the modern world had been reduced to service providers who had lost their political responsibility. Modern architecture, according to Doxiadis, had a style, but modern architects were 'confused' because of their loss of political agency. Doxiadis further explained that aesthetics have little value in exercising the political authority of the architect and could be turned into a political project only when they work as a medium or tool to transform the abstract reality into a concrete expression through visual graphics. Doxiadis eventually conceptualised his professional role as the agent of universal modernisation based on the power of folk. In his mind, an ideal, all-encompassing world composed of the free flow of resources through a worldwide network of information, and a spatial infrastructure was not a utopia but a concrete possibility. Although, in his imagination, the true agents of history are the anonymous folk animated only by the power of the autonomous family, architects and planners nevertheless had a tremendous responsibility to facilitate that animation. To this end his multifamily, multiowner apartment made a strong statement that an architect was essentially an 'international person', a representative of the folk who work against the forces of parochial kinship and divisive nationalist and regionalist forces. However, Doxiadis's post-nationalist, global worldview bypassed the *realpolitik* of the time, and eventually his political architect surrendered under the very world he wanted to resist.

Bibliography

Angelidakis, Andreas. 'Unauthorized', e-flux architecture, https://www.e-flux.com/architecture/positions/151178/unauthorized/. Accessed 4 May 2021.

Aureli, Pier Vittorio, Maria S. Giudici, and Platon Issaias. 'From Domino to Polykatoikia'. *Domus* 962 (October 2012). https://www.domusweb.it/en/architecture/2012/10/31/from-dom-ino-to-em-polykatoikia-em-.html. Accessed 24 April 2020.

Constantinos A. Doxiadis Archives (CADA), Benaki Museum, Athens.

Daeschel, Markus. *Islamabad and the Politics of International Development in Pakistan*. Cambridge: Cambridge University Press, 2015.

Daechsel, Markus. 'Misplaced Ekistics: Islamabad and the Politics of Urban Development in Pakistan'. *South Asian History and Culture* 4, no. 1 (2013): 87–106.

Doxiadis, Constantinos. *Architectural Space in Ancient Greece*. Translated and edited by Jacqueline Tyrwhitt. Cambridge, MA: MIT Press, 1972.

Doxiadis, Constantinos. *Architecture in Transition*. London: Hutchinson, 1968.

Doxiadis, Constantinos. 'The Ancient Greek City and the City of the Present'. *Ekistics* 18, no. 108 (1964): 346–64.

Doxiadis, Constantinos. 'Architect in Evolution', *RIBA Journal*, (September/October 1960): 429–38, 469–79. Republished *Ekistics* 11, no. 64 (1961): 162–70.

Doxiadis, Constantinos. *Raumordnung im griechischen Städtebau*. Berlin: Kurt Vowinckel Verlag, 1937.

Dragonas, Panos. 'An Obituary for the Greek City of Repetation'. *MAS Context* 21 (2014): 83–97.

Emmanuel, Dimitris. 'The Growth of Speculative Building in Greece: Modes of Housing Production and Socioeconomic Changes.' PhD dissertation, London School of Economics and Political Science, 1981.

Fessas-Emmanouil, Helen and Emmanuel V. Marmaras. *Twelve Greek Architects of the Interwar Period / Δώδεκα Έλληνες Αρχιτέκτονες του Μεσοπολέμου*, Herekleion, Crete: Crete University Press, 2005.

Fessas-Emmanouil, Helen. 'The Architect and the Planner: Modernity and Tradition in the Work of Aris Konstantinidis and Constantinos Doxiadis', unpublished manuscript of a lecture given at the School of Architecture of Milano Technical University on 9 May 2012.

Houston, Kerr. *The Place of the Viewer: The Embedded Bohlder in the History of Art, 1764–1968*. Leiden. Boston: Brill, 2019.

Issaias, Platon. 'On Conflict, Generic and the Informal: The Greek Case'. *Very Vary Veri* 2 (2016).

Issaias, Platon. 'Domestic, Production, Debt: For a Theory of the Informal'. In *This Thing Called Theory*, edited by Teresa Stoppani, Giorgio Ponzo, and George Themistokleous. New York: Routledge, 2016.

Issaias, Platon. 'From the Flat to the City: The Construction of Modern Greek Subjectivity'. *Joelho* 8, (2017): 127–39.

Issaias, Platon. 'The Absence of Plan as a Project: Notes on the Planning Development of Modern Athens, 1830–2010'. In *The City as a Project*, edited by Pier Vittorio Aureli, 292–331. Berlin: Ruby Press, 2013.

Kakridis, Andreas. 'Rebuilding the Future: C. A. Doxiadis and the Greek Reconstruction Effort (1945 – 1950)'. *Historical Review/La Revue Historique* 10 (2013): 135–60.

Kalantidou, Eleni. 'Westernizing the Semi-Orient and De-Westernizing the Semi-Occident: The Past, Present, and Future of Athens (Greece)'. *Design Philosophy Papers* 12, no. 2 (2014): 105–18.

Kyrtsis, Alexandros-Andreas, ed. *Constantinos A. Doxiadis Texts: Design Drawings Settlements*. Athens: Ikaros Publications, 2006.

Moatsu, Olga. 'Polykatoikia: the Popularization of a Status Symbol'. In *Proceedings of the 2nd International Conference of the European Architectural History Network (EAHN)*, edited by Hilde Heynen and Janina Gosseye, 494–7. Contactforum, 2012.

Magouliotis, Nikolaos. 'Learning from "Panosikoma": Atelier 66's Additions to Ordinary Houses'. *Architectural Histories* 6, no. 1 (2018): 1–15.

Reif, Rita. 'The Acropolis Is Backdrop for Modern Setting in Architect's Home'. *The New York Times*, Wednesday, 13 December 1961.

Theocharopoulou, Ionna. *Builders, Housewives and the Construction of Modern Athens*. London: Artifice Books, 2018.

Tsaimbaos, Kostas. *From Doxiadis' Theory to Pikionis' Work: Reflections of Antiquity in Modern Architecture*. London: Routledge, 2017.

Tzonis, Alexander and Rodi, Alcestis. *Greece: Modern Architectures in History*. London: Reaktion Books, 2012.

Woditsch, Richard. *The Public Private House Modern Athens and its Polykatoikia*. Zurich: Park Books, 2018.

Communal Living and Collective Action

The fourth section of the book focusses on communal living practices and collective action as tools to question engrained social and cultural norms on the one hand, and to upend deep-seated political and economic systems on the other. This section gathers five chapters that not only highlight the potential of the collective, but also reveal the tensions and challenges that alternative, communal living practices can encounter and engender.

The first two chapters in this section – 'Housing the Farmers of Enlightenment' by Lee Stickells and 'Living as a Guest' by Oscar Andrade Castro and Patricio Cáraves Silva – focus on two radical experiments in communal living that were conducted during the 1970s; one in Australia, the other in Chile. In 1977 Bodhi Farm was established on Australia's east coast, with architect Peter Hamilton as one of its founding members, and in 1970 the Ciudad Abierta (Open City) was founded sixteen kilometres north of the city of Valparaíso by a group of professors and students associated with the School of Architecture and Design at Pontificia Universidad Católica de Valparaíso. Both these countercultural communes, in their own way, rejected the social codes and cultural conventions of mainstream society in favour of a freer, more egalitarian and cooperative form of living. However, as the chapters by Stickells and Castro and Silva demonstrate, even if these communities eschewed mainstream society, they were confronted with the inevitability of that society's deeply engrained structures in various ways. In the case of Bodhi Farm, Hamilton had to negotiate zoning regulations and building codes when a demolition order was imposed on the community, while those who participated in the experiment in radical hospitality in the Open City – where everyone is considered a guest – struggled to depart from the innate settledness of domestic life.

The final three chapters in this section all in various ways present forms of resistance 'from within'. The contributions by Stylianos Giamarelos and Max Ott demonstrate how the collective actions of architects – through the design of their own homes – can challenge existing profit-driven and/or reactionary town-planning policies and urban development frameworks by squarely (and quite subversively) inserting themselves within such policies and frameworks. Giamarelos's chapter 'Building Before Theorising Resistance', focusses on the home that Greek architects Suzana and Dimitris Antonakakis built for themselves, to great acclaim, in Athens in the 1970s. Realised within the city's post-war urban development framework of *antiparochi* and *polykatoikia*, this collaboratively constructed collective dwelling – it was home to four families – presented an alternative to the run-of-the-mill, anonymous, developer-driven mode of production of apartments that was taking place in the Greek capital at that time. In his chapter, 'Creating a "We"', Max Ott describes how around the turn of the twenty-first century in a similar manner – by means of collective housing typologies that emerge through a collaborative building process – young architects in Berlin challenged the reactionary townhouse-based urban design framework that Hans Stimmann, Berlin's director of urban planning, had put in place after he took office in 1991. In this chapter, Ott uses the prosaically named 'R50' project, which was initiated by two architectural offices – ifau and Heide & von Beckerath – and which currently houses approximately forty people, including ifau's founding partners, as a case in point.

Valeria Federighi's contribution, 'Resisting from Within', presents a different form of resistance from within. Her chapter focusses on the work of Taiwanese architect Hsieh Ying-Chun whose practice, Atelier-3, rose to fame in the late 1990s when it became involved in the post-earthquake resettlement of the Hakka minority in the area of Sun Moon Lake in Taiwan. A large majority of this community, which had been residing in Dehua Village, was left homeless after the 1999 Jiji earthquake. Hsieh Ying-Chun suggested that they exploit the possibilities offered by national post-disaster schemes to relocate to their original settlement site, from which they had been forcibly removed fifty years earlier. Federighi postulates that this resettlement contributed to the official recognition of the rights of this aboriginal community, as she highlights the important role that Hsieh Ying-Chun's decision to make his home and office part of the new Ita Thao settlement played in bolstering and asserting these rights.

Federighi's chapter also examines the concept of self-building and collective construction as a form of resistance; an aspect that is also touched upon in the chapters on Bodhi Farm and the Open City. In the establishment (or re-establishment) of the Ita Thao settlement, the cooperative activity of self-building was seen not only as a way to cut costs, but also as a form of social activism. Instead of consumers, inhabitants become the producers of their own homes, and in this act of construction, they reclaim a plot of land to which they assert a pre-existing right of use.

Living as a Guest: The *hospederías* of Ciudad Abierta, Chile

Oscar Andrade Castro and Patricio Cáraves Silva

At the core of this chapter lies the question of how to live as a guest and, connected to this, what shape a life of hospitality takes, both in terms of living practices and architectural space. The chapter addresses these questions by looking at the *hospederías* (guesthouses) of Ciudad Abierta (Open City), a community of poets, architects, designers, and artists that was founded in 1970 by the members of the School of Architecture and Design at Pontificia Universidad Católica de Valparaíso (PUCV) in Chile. In Ciudad Abierta, hospitality was proposed as a form of everyday life and the *hospederías* as domestic spaces to accommodate its members so that they could receive others. This chapter looks at the example of the *hospederías* in order to discuss the rearticulation of the conventional relationship between domesticity and publicness, and the constant negotiation between the unsettled condition of the guest and the innate settledness of domestic life. The paper concludes by reflecting on the radicality of the guest and proposes that the members of Ciudad Abierta experience hospitality not as a contingency or condition subject to an event, but as a fundamental inner disposition. It is for this disposition that the architects of Ciudad Abierta have constructed the *hospederías*, to accommodate the other and in this way give course to public life, which constitutes the heart of the city.

The foundation of Ciudad Abierta

Many of the collective living practices that were implemented in Ciudad Abierta were first experienced in the community of Cerro Castillo, which was formed by the families of the founding professors of the PUCV School of Architecture and Design.[1] In 1952 this group of professors rented four newly built houses in the neighbourhood of Cerro Castillo in the city of Viña del Mar. In these houses, they developed a communal life that included study, seminars, celebrations, and even a domestic economy based on the shared use of their salaries. In Cerro Castillo the group of professors put into practice and experienced the dissolution of the borders of life, work, and study, bringing a sense of unity that was transferred to the school and crystallised in Ciudad Abierta years later.

Two characteristic practices of the community in Cerro Castillo were the rotation of the houses and the central presence of the figure of the guest. With regard to the rotation, the community was organised around a flexible system of shared spaces that allowed them to switch from one house to another according to the changing needs of the different families. As for the figure of the guest, this was fundamental to the life of the community, which practised commensality as a way to receive regularly other intellectuals and friends in the domestic spaces of the houses. The table thus

1
The group was formed by the Argentinian poet Godofredo Iommi, the Chilean architects Alberto Cruz, Miguel Eyquem, Fabio Cruz, José Vial, Arturo Baeza, Francisco Méndez, Jaime Bellalta, and the Argentinian sculptor Claudio Girola, who joined sometime later.

became a protagonist that stood out in the sober domestic interiors, which the poet and professor Godofredo Iommi described as 'completely white, all the tables were completely white, and nothing was hanging from the walls.'[2] The system of rotation and the central figure of the guest characterising the community in Cerro Castillo are both elements that later reappeared in Ciudad Abierta.

Ciudad Abierta was founded as the result of a university reform movement initiated by the professors and students of the PUCV School of Architecture and Design in 1967. The reform movement sought the complete 're-origination' of the university; that is to say, rather than seeking to change the existing university, they conceived of it as extending beyond the framework of an institution.[3] This idea was supported on two fundamental pillars: the opening towards a Latin American reality and the transformation of the university into a real community which united life, work, and study.[4] To accommodate this vision, the members of the school founded Ciudad Abierta in 1970 on a 270-hectare area that was located sixteen kilometres north of the city of Valparaíso.[5] The first group of inhabitants that settled on this land were the families of a young generation of professors and students. Since then, many of the initial residents have continued to live on the grounds, while others have left; some were born there, while others died there and are buried in the Ciudad Abierta cemetery.

The construction of Ciudad Abierta

The construction of Ciudad Abierta has been an intergenerational endeavour by its residents – today numbering around forty – together with the professors and students of the PUCV School of Architecture and Design. The projects are built and financed by its members through their own efforts and resources. While this autonomy may entail scarce resources and a slow pace of construction, it also ensures that the group's creative freedom is retained. This is also balanced by the collective nature of the group, which has shaped the figure of the architect as a plural being through a collective working format referred to as 'work in round' (*trabajo en ronda*).[6] Thus, Ciudad Abierta is a collective endeavour that, in the words of its founders, requires 'a people of architects that, with equality between crafts, build the city that will open up their destiny.'[7] Moreover, although the crafts of architecture and design are more present within the members of Ciudad Abierta, this place was intended to accommodate all human crafts, as it is only through such multiplicity that the city can reach its complexity.

The projects at Ciudad Abierta are built by the architects' own hands, inch by inch, with the help of students and workers from nearby. This empirical and hands-on approach has introduced the dimension of craftsmanship as an inherent characteristic of the group's modus operandi, manifested in their recognition of the 'intrinsic equality of intellectual and manual activities'.[8] As a result, the parity and interdependence between thinking and doing experienced by the architects of Ciudad Abierta led them to redefine

2
Iommi, 'Taller de América de 1987'. All quotations are translations by the authors.

3
Iommi, 'Manifiesto del 15 de Junio 1967'.

4
The school members put Latin America and the question about the American being at the centre of their reflections after formulating a poetic vision of the continent called 'Amereida, the Aeneid of America'.

5
The initial legal construct of Ciudad Abierta was that of a cooperative of professional services constituted in the year 1969, which years later changed to its current form of a cultural corporation.

6
Cruz and Iommi, 'De la Utopía al Espejismo'.

7
Cruz and Iommi, 'De la Utopía al Espejismo'.

8
'Estatutos Cooperativa de Servicios Profesionales Amereida LTDA'.

Fig. 1 The architect and resident Boris Ivelic working in the Hospedería de la Entrada, 1984. (© Archivo Histórico José Vial Armstrong)

9
Cruz and Iommi, 'Ciudad Abierta – Agora 7.1.1971'.

10
The poetic act – or *Phalène* (mot) – is a collective poetic game led by the poets of Ciudad Abierta in which everybody is called on to participate.

the figure of the architect as an architect-craftsman. Thus, the architectural works at Ciudad Abierta are constructed by its inhabitants and reflect the craftsmanship of a materialisation process made by many hands.

The construction of Ciudad Abierta does not follow any master plan. The architects regulated the site through an urban planning instrument entitled 'Cultural and Recreational Coastal Park', which defines the land boundaries and establishes zones and occupancy rates. However, this urban planning instrument did not emerge from a logic of planning but was carried out precisely to maintain openness with regard to what the community might eventually determine. Thus, in Ciudad Abierta, planning is not understood as a directive outlining one possible future to the exclusion of all others. Conversely, at Ciudad Abierta, there is a unique orientation known as the 'axis-stake', which is a poetic indication that does not impose any criteria but opens up fields of possibilities.[9] The orientation of the axis-stake bursts forth as a single point with the celebration of a poetic act that indicates – each time – the gratuitous singularity that emerges when the word and the place are crossed, giving origin to every construction at Ciudad Abierta.[10] Accordingly, the orientation of the axis-stake 'represents a detachment, so that each time different points might be affirmed by a poetic act, which builds that what has been called the unpunctual'.[11] In this way, the construction of Ciudad Abierta unfolds as an open figure shaped by the unpunctual.

Public life from hospitality

From its inception, Ciudad Abierta was intended to accommodate public life, and its founders believed that the primary condition supporting public life was hospitality: 'to live publicly is to talk and to talk is above all having the capacity to hear another. In this way someone may truly become the guest of another. This simple but radical hospitality demands architecture, as it demands the splendour of every craft.'[12] Accordingly, in Ciudad Abierta hospitality was advanced as a form of quotidian life, opening up the possibility for public life to exist as a consequence of living as a guest. Ciudad Abierta thus welcomes anyone who has the disposition to live as a guest, and its members affirm that 'one can enter without merit and leave without guilt, as many times as one wishes. The availability is real. The only requirement is consent. This radical consent of being a guest.'[13] In this light, the city reveals itself to be the convergence of multiple human crafts, which together construct the hospitality that enables the accommodation of the other. Consequently, to live as a guest and accommodate the other, the architects of Ciudad Abierta conceived the agorae and the *hospederías*.

> However, where could that kind of hospitality take place in full? Perhaps in what, for lack of a more adequate word, we could call 'agora', because hearing is not the same as listening when you have already decided but rather allowing the other to interrupt your own discourse with decision or scission. Could not this be the space, the apparition, the mirage, where so-called 'public life' could be extended?[14]

The Agora of Ciudad Abierta is the place of public discourse that enables citizens to govern themselves. Today, there are four agorae: the Agora del Fuego, the Agora de Tronquoy, the Agora de los Huéspedes, and the Agora de la Conmemoración. These are all open-air spaces that provide common ground where the community can gather. During gatherings at the agorae, the community discusses topics that concern the course of events and the construction of Ciudad Abierta, such as the incorporation of new members or the construction of new *hospederías*.[15] Decisions are made through consent and unanimity rather than by voting because consent does not deny the other in pursuit of a majority; conversely, it welcomes other, differing opinions. The Agora is then the place 'where we consent to being what we are: guests'.[16] In this way, the starting point for Ciudad Abierta is its agorae, which place the spoken word at the centre of the city.

Accommodating the public in the domestic

Apart from the agorae, the architect-residents of Ciudad Abierta also built accommodation that could provide hospitality. These dwellings were named *hospederías*, or guest houses, as they were designed for the residents

11
Cruz, 'Fundamento del Seccional'.

12
'Exposición 20 años Escuela de Arquitectura UCV'.

13
Iommi, 'Notas a propósito de vida'.

14
Cruz and Iommi, 'De la Utopía al Espejismo'.

15
Although the Agora is the highest form of government at Ciudad Abierta, there is also a directive that administers and manages the normal functioning of the terrain and the cultural corporation, and carries out the decisions reached by the community.

16
Iommi, 'Notas a propósito de vida'.

17
'Las Hospederías de la Ciudad Abierta'.

18
Cáraves, *Arquitectura desde la Hospitalidad.*

19
Cruz and Iommi, 'De la Utopía al Espejismo'.

20
Cáraves, *Arquitectura desde la Hospitalidad.*

21
Reyes, 'El Pueblo de las Mesas'.

to receive others. The figure of the guest – 'the ones who are heard, and for whom the necessary distance is created so they can speak' – is a crucial element informing the design of each *hospedería*.[17] This necessary distance, which can have many interpretations and measurements, is the space that guarantees hospitality. Today, there are eleven *hospederías* at Ciudad Abierta. All of them share the core idea of providing that necessary distance to accommodate the other, so that 'the public can occur together with the domestic when inhabiting'.[18] Nevertheless, this does not mean that all the projects follow the same spatial strategy. Rather it implies that they all consider the question of how to articulate hospitality in their spatial arrangement. For example, the first *hospederías* considered in their design a void at their core that could accommodate public life by acting as an inner public square. This void was seen as the nucleus and the starting point of the *hospedería*, while the rest of the project was left undefined. After the construction of the core void, the perimeter shape was determined by extending through the construction site to encounter the diverse conditions of the place and define its limits in the process.

The key element in the central void of the *hospedería* is the table. As in the community of Cerro Castillo, the table is the place where guests are received and heard. The table is also a quotidian place that accommodates dialogue between citizens about the present and contingency of Ciudad Abierta. That is why the residents of the *hospederías* 'always keep free places at the table [...] so others can arrive to talk about the peripety of the foundation: initiate proposals, finalise comments about acts, projects, funding, issues of a public nature, the arrival of guests, new agorae, concerns regarding intimacy, health, children, and also to talk about nothing'.[19] The architect-residents of Ciudad Abierta 'conceived the table as an architectural space, that is, thinking and projecting the void of the room from the table'.[20] Moreover, beyond the domestic realm of the *hospederías*, the element of the table is also present in many public projects of Ciudad Abierta to encourage commensality, which takes the form of a weekly communal lunch. The table has acquired such a central place within Ciudad Abierta that the poet and professor Carlos Covarrubias has referred to the group as 'a people of the tables'.[21]

In order to accommodate the other, the residents of the *hospederías* avoid claiming ownership over their interior spaces. They strive for neutral interiors that eschew signs of appropriation and thus possess a certain sobriety. Nevertheless, rather than being the antithesis of domesticity, these *hospederías* open another register of domestic design that prioritises hospitality. In other words, they are not designed to welcome guests into 'our' home, but into 'a' home. The design of the *hospederías* is thus centred on shaping availability – for instance, by always keeping an empty seat at the table. The common understanding of the public space as a place to meet the other and the domestic realm as a personal space are thus rearticulated in the *hospederías,* which promote new figures such as the domestic-other and the public-self.

Fig. 2 As-built plans of the Hospedería del Banquete *(left)* and the Hospedería de los Motores *(right)* with their respective core voids to accommodate public life. The table of each *hospedería* is in the core void. (© Archivo Histórico José Vial Armstrong)

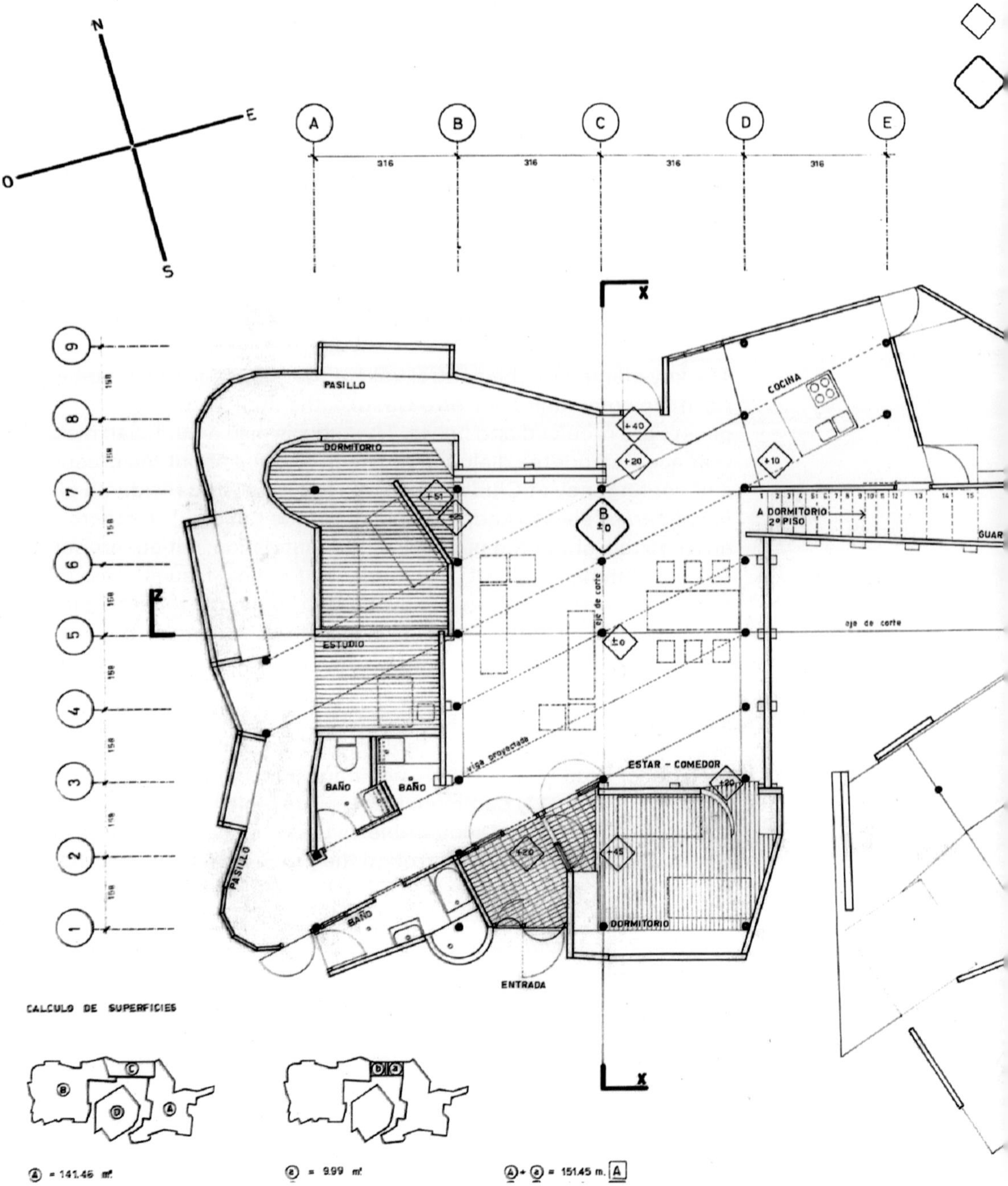

a cada una hospederia

mbas hospederias

COOPERATIVA DE SERVICIOS PROFESIONALES AMEREIDA LTDA. PARQUE COSTERO CULTURAL Y DE RECREACION				
OBRA : DOS HOSPEDERIAS	PROPIETARIO : COOP. DE SERVICIOS PROFESIONALES AMEREIDA LTDA.	ARQUITECTO : COOP. DE SERVICIOS PROFESIONALES AMEREIDA LTDA. V. BOSCOVIC ICA 2377	MATERIA : PLANO DE ARQUITECTURA PLANTA ESCALA 1 : 50	2

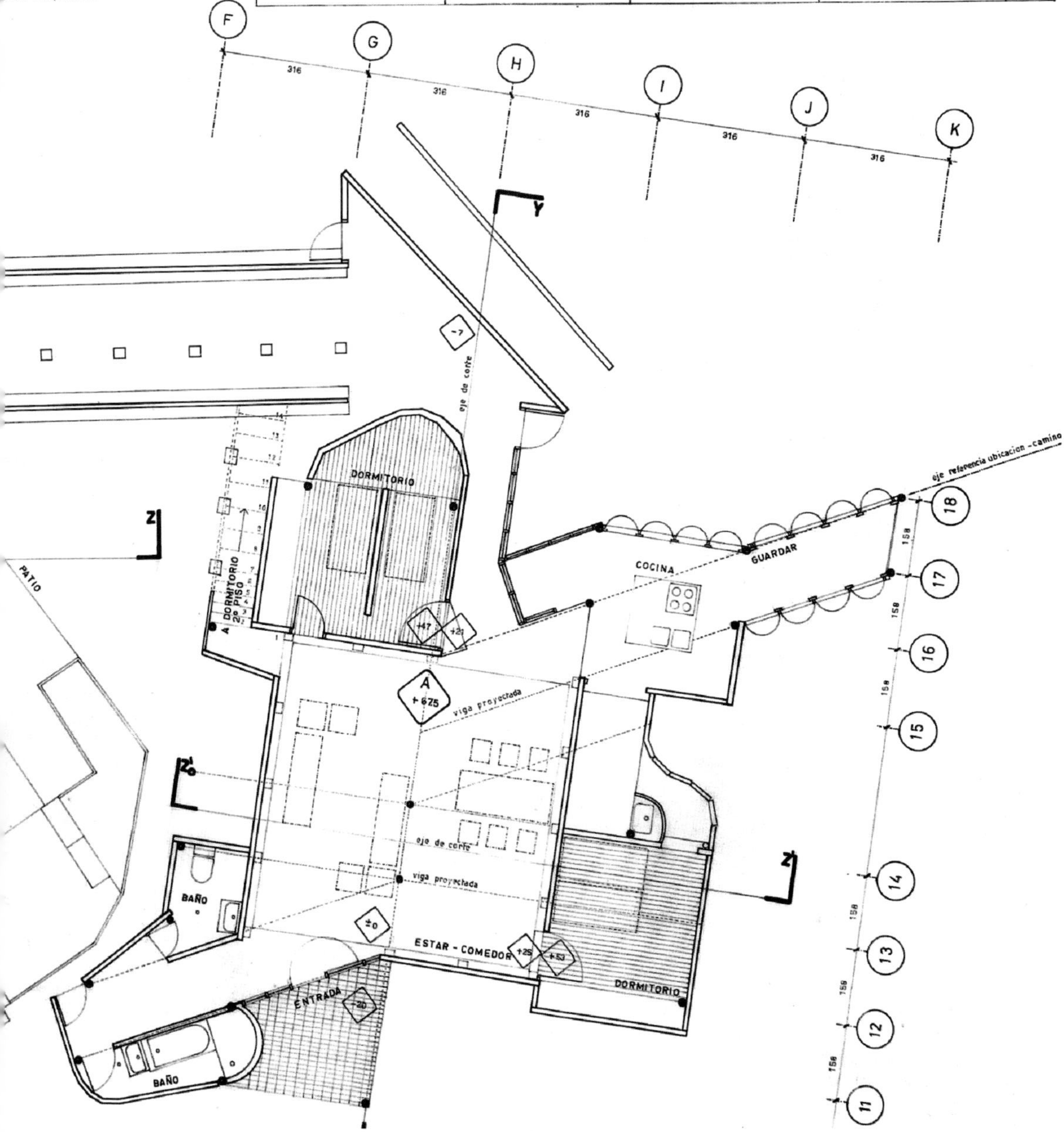

Fig. 3 Communal lunch at the Hospedería del Errante, 2009. (© Archivo Histórico José Vial Armstrong)

Fig. 4 Gathering in the Hospedería del Taller de Obras, 2010. (© Archivo Histórico José Vial Armstrong)

22
'Las Hospederías de la Ciudad Abierta'.

23
Iommi, 'El Pacífico es un mar erótico'.

Negotiating between settledness and unsettledness

Living in a *hospedería* requires constant negotiation between settledness and unsettledness, between permanence and impermanence. While the members of Ciudad Abierta sought a permanent residence that would be able to receive others, they also looked to develop an impermanent way of inhabiting; 'no open citizen is a permanent resident', and as such, in Ciudad Abierta, everybody is a guest.[22] One of the most concrete expressions of the pursuit of impermanence is embodied in a unwritten law of Ciudad Abierta: that of non-private property.[23] The absence of private property implies that even if a member funds the construction of a *hospedería* with their own resources, that member will not own the building; it becomes openly available to others if the resident decides to move. In this way, a *hospedería* is not understood as a domain to perpetuate, but as a residence of passage, which cannot be sold, transferred, or inherited. Accordingly, anyone who erects a *hospedería* does so as a gratuitous act.

In order to create a situation of impermanence, the group proposed a rotation system for the *hospederías* similar to that used in the houses of Cerro Castillo. The initial proposal was that the residents would exchange spaces every six months. However, this extreme quest for unsettledness turned out to be untenable, as the habits of domestic life inevitably impose a certain permanence. A new mode of rotation thus emerged, which is not defined by predetermined periods but follows the more natural tempo of the course of life. Accordingly, the redistribution of spaces occurs according to the changing needs of residents and families; they might rotate *hospederías* every few years, but only if required. Hence, the community simply makes it possible to exchange spaces but people are never forced to move out. For example, rotations take place when children leave the parental house; at this point, the parents may choose to move out of the *hospedería* to allow a larger family to move in.

To reconcile settledness and unsettledness, the architect-residents of Ciudad Abierta have shaped a mode of dwelling marked by lightness, which in turn has led them to develop an architecture characterised by its ephemerality and material volatility. This approach to building necessitates constant renovation, with permanence being regarded as a pulse that is sustained only by the constant reiteration of light, impermanent traces. Nevertheless, this act of retracing is not about repetition but rather reinvention; it does not approach the material renovation of the projects as a reconstruction but rather as an opportunity to creatively rethink the building. Accordingly, the *hospederías* are characterised by their open-ended nature, permanently changing in materiality and in spatial organisation; they are continual works-in-progress, oscillating between more dynamic or more consolidated phases. That said, fifty years on from its foundation, the architect-residents of Ciudad Abierta have come to understand that living in a condition of permanent departure, continually reinventing the traces

Fig. 5 Architects of Ciudad Abierta constructing the Hospedería de La Alcoba, 1977. (© Archivo Histórico José Vial Armstrong)

24
Cruz and Iommi, 'De la Utopía al Espejismo'.

25
Cruz and Iommi, 'De la Utopía al Espejismo'.

26
Iommi, 'Notas a propósito de vida'.

of every day, is an unreachable quest. They realise that to make a place of residence means to tame the outdoors and to leave permanent traces because to reside is to put down roots.

The radicality of the guest

The question arises as to whether aspects such as longevity, population size, or its constructed infrastructure can reveal the nature of Ciudad Abierta. Or it is precisely hospitality as a form of everyday life that holds the keys to understanding this city? A fundamental characteristic of such hospitality is that it is a generosity that expects nothing in return 'because, in essence, it is incoercible, it opens only with free mutual consent'.[24] Because of this, the experience of Ciudad Abierta – far from being measured in terms of successes and failures – abides by its intimate invitation of consenting to be a guest. This is because the generosity does not respond to fulfilments of any kind, but instead appears as an opening, which can certainly be denied, but also consented to.

Furthermore, in Ciudad Abierta, consent to be a guest has proven to its residents to be a possibility beyond contingency; that is, not as a condition subject to an event but a fundamental inner disposition. This radicality of the guest means that in Ciudad Abierta, one is a guest not because the situation or circumstances make it necessary but because it is a particular form of life. It is from that form of life that hospitality is experienced in Ciudad Abierta as that radical opening, 'a way of being oneself in the other'.[25] Thus, living as a guest – that consensual state of being together with the other – is both the foundation and the heart of Ciudad Abierta, as it represents an opening from which public life can unfold, which is the starting point for the city.

The architect-residents of Ciudad Abierta gave the disposition of hospitality as a form of life a spatial position by creating the *hospederías*; this was possible because the architect and the resident converged in one person who came to experience hospitality for themself. This meant that their experience of hospitality was not gained from literature or the words of third parties but from life itself. It is also precisely from living in the spaces that they themselves have conceived and built that the architect-residents of Ciudad Abierta have come to know their craft, making the role of thinking and doing architecture a praxis that happens together with dwelling in the direct experience of the space. Because of this, the architect-residents of Ciudad Abierta understand architecture as a craft and not as a profession. This distinction means that their practice is not oriented by external aspects of the discipline but by making the discipline an interior exercise of life. Therefore, the practice of architecture has unfolded in isolation from any action seeking for external change; on the contrary, those who built Ciudad Abierta have opted not to change life but for a change in life.[26] In this way, Ciudad Abierta is built primarily as an internal experience that is not individual but instead is the collective inner experience of a people of architects.

Bibliography

Cáraves, Patricio. *Arquitectura desde la Hospitalidad*. Barcelona: Universidad Politécnica de Catalunya, 2007.

Cruz, Alberto. 'Fundamento de Seccional'. Circa 1970. Manuscript document. Archivo Histórico José Vial Armstrong.

Cruz, Alberto, and Godofredo Iommi. 'Ciudad Abierta – Agora 7.1.1971'. https://wiki.ead.pucv.cl/Ciudad_Abierta_-_Agora_7.1.1971_Apertura_de_los_Terrenos. Accessed 20 June 2019.

Cruz, Alberto, and Godofredo Iommi. 'De la Utopía al Espejismo'. Santiago: *Revista Universitaria,* no. 9 Pontificia Universidad Católica de Chile, 1983.

'Estatutos Cooperativa de Servicios Profesionales Amereida LTDA'. Archivo Histórico José Vial Armstrong, Escuela de Arquitectura y Diseño PUCV.

'Exposición 20 años Escuela de Arquitectura UCV'. https://www.ead.pucv.cl/1972/exposicion-20-anos-escuela-de-arquitectura-ucv/. Accessed 12 January 2018.

Iommi, Godofredo. 'Manifiesto del 15 de Junio 1967'. https://wiki.ead.pucv.cl/Manifiesto_del_15_de_Junio_1967. Accessed 2 December 2019.

Iommi, Godofredo. 'Notas a propósito de vida, trabajo, y estudio y el real sentido contemporáneo de la hospitalidad como forma de vida cotidiana en la Ciudad Abierta'. Viña del Mar, 1971. Biblioteca de Amereida.

Iommi, Godofredo. 'Taller de América de 1987. Clases de Godofredo Iommi'. https://wiki.ead.pucv.cl/Taller_de_América_de_1987._Clases _de_Godofredo_Iommi. Accessed 12 January 2018.

Iommi, Godofredo. 'El Pacífico es un mar erótico'. https://wiki.ead.pucv.cl/El_Pacífico_es_un_mar_erótico. Edición_anotada. Accessed 12 January 2018.

'Las Hospederías de la Ciudad Abierta'. Original series of documents composed of seven sheets with drawings, plans, and text. Archivo Histórico José Vial Armstrong, Escuela de Arquitectura y Diseño PUCV.

Reyes, Jaime. 'El Pueblo de las Mesas'. https://wiki.ead.pucv.cl/El_Pueblo_de_las_Mesas. Accessed 12 January 2018.

Housing the Farmers of Enlightenment

Lee Stickells

For the counterculture of the 1960s, an ethos of self-production was critical.[1] This gave self-built dwellings particular significance as a means to attempt the building of material and symbolic alternatives to dominant systems and practices. The communal homesteading of the counterculture's back-to-the-land movement stands out in this regard, with its rejection of the individualistic and materialistic ethos of mainstream society and associated cultural mores, in favour of attempts to establish more egalitarian, cooperative, sexually liberated, and peaceful communities. The Australian community Bodhi Farm's foundational period offers a compelling example by virtue of the significance of counter-architectural practices for its everyday utopianism: the determined attempts to perform daily life differently, through a contingent process rather than realised ideal.[2] As those architectural efforts met resistance, the architect Peter Hamilton, founding member and resident of Bodhi Farm, emerged as a mobilising figure for the dynamic sharing of architectural expertise and innovative professional networks underpinning the community's attempts to put notions such as property, work, and kinship into practice in counter-normative ways. The episode contributes to the ongoing shaping of a more complicated historical picture of countercultural architecture than simple escapism or indolent refusal.[3] A running project of active social engagement and collectively oriented hard work was needed to sustain (and adjust) Bodhi Farm's unconventional dwelling practices. Paying attention to its architectural production vividly reveals ways in which actualising counterhegemonic practices means grappling with rules, routines, and commonplace concerns, developing an ethics of maintenance.

At the beginning of 1973, Peter Hamilton was teaching architecture at the University of Sydney, immersed (via encounter groups) in the human potential movement and experimenting with transcendental meditation.[4] The array of activities reflected a history of digressive personal exploration and an adventurous career path. During the Second World War, Hamilton trained as a pilot but afterward went on to study architecture and sculpture. He also hung out with the nonconformists and libertarians of the Sydney Push, organised film festivals, and established a record label. By the late 1960s he was a PhD candidate at the University of Sydney under the ground-breaking architectural anthropologist Amos Rappaport. Hamilton's doctoral research involved innovative field work in Aboriginal Australia, living with his family for eighteen months in a remote traditional camp of the Yankuntjatjara people.[5] As the 1970s dawned he remained intellectually, physically, and spiritually restless.

Hamilton was approached early in 1973 by some students keen to attend the upcoming Aquarius Festival – a ten-day countercultural

1
Farber, 'Self-Invention in the Realm of Production'.

2
Cooper, *Everyday Utopias*.

3
See, for example, Castillo, 'Counterculture Terroir'; Maniaque-Benton, *French Encounters*, 27–71; Sadler, 'An Architecture of the Whole'; Scott, 'Episodes in the Refusal of Work'; Stickells, 'Negotiating Off-Grid'.

4
Hamilton, 'The Nine Lives of Peter Hamilton – Part 2'.

5
Memmott and Keys, 'The Emergence of an Architectural Anthropology', 220.

Fig. 1 First Aquarius Festival, Nimbin, 1973. The first hippie festival in Australia was a mixture of back-to-earth skills laced with idealism and pot. Here, festival-goers harvest materials for self-built shelters. (Photograph by © Lee Pearce)

Fig. 2 Bodhi Farm house interior, c. 1980. (Photograph by © Colin James)

6
'The May Manifesto' reproduced in: Dunstan, 'Nimbin'.

7
Jiggens, *Rehearsals for the Apocalypse*, 8.

8
Metcalf, *Co-operative Lifestyles in Australia*.

9
Munro-Clark, *Communes in Rural Australia*; Cock, *Alternative Australia*; Jennings, 'Creating Feminist Culture'.

10
Fisher, 'Living Alternatively: Bodhi Farm', 49.

11
'Multiple Occupancy – How it Works'; Munro-Clark, *Communes in Rural Australia*, 136–8.

12
Cooper, *Everyday Utopias*, 219–22.

experiment being organised at the isolated rural village of Nimbin in north-eastern New South Wales – as part of their architectural studies. He followed the students' lead and the event would critically alter his life path. While the 1972 Sunbury Pop Festival is often seen as 'Australia's Woodstock', the 1973 Aquarius Festival was deliberately different. It was not a commercial rock music festival, nor simply an escapist carnival. The organisers framed it as a consciously unprogrammed experiment where 'architects and the like could develop new styles in community organisation.'[6] John Jiggens's gonzo journalism recounted walking through scenes 'that might have been pages ripped out of the Whole Earth Catalogue among people who looked like the cast of Hair.'[7] As with thousands of other festival-goers, Peter Hamilton looked subsequently to sustain that intense communal experience.

In 1977 Hamilton and twelve others established Bodhi Farm. It was a rural communal living experiment and part of a proliferation of such communities in Australia during the 1970s. They clustered not only in the Northern Rivers region of New South Wales, in the wake of the Aquarius Festival, but also in Western Australia's south-west and in the rural hinterlands behind Queensland's Sunshine Coast, as well as further north near Cairns.[8] The countercultural back-to-the-landers (referred to as 'new settlers') bought cheap land in remote backwaters, steep valleys, and shorelines of wild coastal districts, which enabled them to explore unconventional modes of living. Beyond protest movements and outside of conventional political activity, they often looked to cultivate ecologically and ethically centred modes of living and to build autonomous spaces of resistance to hetero- and homonormativity, to compulsory consumerism, and to entrenched hierarchies of race, class, and gender.[9]

Peter Hamilton and his fellow communards at Bodhi Farm shared a commitment to Buddhist practices, voluntary simplicity, consensual decision-making, and, as one member put it, 'walking gently on the earth.'[10] The sixty hectares of land they purchased – largely regrowth forest – were held in trust, with members retaining shares and all structures belonging to the community. Ad hoc collective labour was the default construction mode, with an understanding that occupation of structures was according to members' needs. The buildings used for sleeping, cooking, eating, and so on, were described as 'dwelling segments' and given names such as 'Effortless' or 'The Glade' to disassociate them from individual ownership. 'Expanded house' was the nomenclature used by the Bodhi Farmers and other nearby communities to describe this way of living in close proximity to each other using common facilities.[11] These prosaic domestic adjustments were vital moves in the community's unsteady actualisation of their communal living ambitions.[12]

The first years of building the farm's dwelling segments saw its members living in tents and caravans as they began slowly to fashion an array of structures conditioned by austerity, patchy construction knowledge, and desires for environmental harmony. Mud bricks were pressed manually on-site. Timber was often sourced from windfall trees or scraps from the local commercial mill that were considered too poor to grade (and became known as 'hippie grade' timber). By 1980, a hexagonal community centre was being constructed from timber milled on-site and mud-brick infill. Peter Hamilton's own sleeping shelter and storage comprised some small geodesic domes just large enough into which to crawl. The domes were clad with aluminium printer's plates obtained from the local *Northern Star* newspaper; the connectors were broomsticks (discovered to be an ideal length, uncut) and agricultural polyethylene pipe.[13] Working from published guides, idiosyncratic visions, and community effort, a countercultural vernacular developed. Alongside a spatial and conceptual enlargement of the house, this architectural future-primitivism was keyed to the Bodhi Farm community's attempts to rethink ownership, kinship, and dwelling practices. A culture of consumer affluence and planned obsolescence, insular families, and regulated time was consciously opposed through scavenging, craft production, ecological consciousness, tribal community, and circadian rhythms.

By the late 1970s, Bodhi Farm was at the centre of a region rife with makeshift countercultural living experiments and its residents were active in land-sharing, owner-builder, permaculture, home-birthing, and ecology movements. One resident reflected that 'in our more arrogant moments we can call ourselves farmers of enlightenment.'[14] While the first few years of building were conducted in relative anonymity, the involvement of the new settlers with the radical environmentalism of local anti-logging actions brought their growing communities into sharper view. The emerging conflict revolved around two basic issues: communal settlement and unauthorised construction.[15] At the time, there was no legislative recognition of communal living, and planning regulations permitted only one house per forty hectares on rural land (by the early 1980s Bodhi Farm had around twenty adults and fourteen children living in about fourteen structures). Unauthorised buildings also posed problems through their noncompliance with health and building regulations.[16] Other residents of the region were often affronted by what they saw as the threats to public health and order, and the new settlers were denounced as, for instance, 'the leeches of society'.[17] Local governments varied in their enforcement of planning and building regulations but the code wars over compliance with regulations fundamentally escalated. Lismore City Council began to carry out aerial surveys to discover unauthorised settlements, and at one point had issued as many as fifty demolition orders across perhaps a dozen communities.[18] This included Bodhi Farm, where around a dozen structures were determined as illicit.

Having worked without regard to building and zoning regulations, outlaw builders now took on a struggle to expand the permissible. The response to the precarious situation was to lobby government and resist the actions of local councils. Peter Hamilton became active in establishing a pressure group – the Rainbow Region Home Builders Association – and agitating alongside other new settlers to reshape state planning and building regulations. The activism took

13
The domes eventually collapsed and Hamilton lived on the farm in a series of caravans from the early 1980s onward. John Seed, conversation with the author, 29 September 2018.

14
Stuart Anderson, interview at Bodhi Farm, 5 December 1992, MLOH 103: Richmond-Tweed Oral History Group – Under the Rainbow, State Library of New South Wales.

15
James, *Lismore Report*, 136–8.

16
As specified in Ordinance No. 70 under the Local Government Act of 1919. Holland, Building Regulations'.

17
Invoking the durable counterculture stereotype of the lazy hippie. *Northern Star*, 10 October 1979, 5.

18
Taylor, *Retreat or Advance*, 39.

advantage of contacts in the environmental movement – such as the barrister Murray Wilcox, who was elected president of the Australian Conservation Foundation in 1979 and gave pro bono representation to the anti-logging protestors. These kinds of contacts, and the visibility they gave the struggles over the illicit communal building in the Northern Rivers, perhaps explain the state minister for environment and planning, Paul Landa, accepting an invitation to visit Bodhi Farm. There he observed that:

> A lot of architectural nous has gone into the Bodhi Buildings: they capture light and sun, are minimal energy users, have total reliance on the indigenous materials that are within carrying reach, can be built at low cost, are airy plus very functional and take advantage of the captivating views in the environment that they have here.[19]

The comments indicated surprising support for communities that were otherwise taking flight from the oversight and regulation of the state. Landa's statement offered a counter-reading to that of detractors who saw places like Bodhi Farm as 'Third-World' shanty towns. Rather, he suggested the settlement had an empirical rationale (solar performance), was modern (functional), and informed by indigenous (that is, national) precedent. The State Planning and Environment Commission subsequently held a hamlet seminar in Lismore in December 1979, after which it was announced that experimental building areas would be established – spaces for innovative self-build housing, where relevant building and health regulations could be further negotiated.[20] The development of communities such as Bodhi Farm, and their new living forms, was now permitted in areas behind what was colloquially referred to as 'the hippie line'.[21] A new countercultural geography was being legitimated – its territories and boundaries encoded into law – divergent from the initial imaginings of the communities involved. The architectural shaping of their countercultural dreaming exposed political pressure points relating to property, health, and dwelling norms.

Despite the successes, Bodhi Farm was still in court. While the community had carried out remedial building work, two dwelling segments still faced demolition orders. At issue were a mezzanine area considered unfit for habitation and elevations deemed insufficiently impervious to weather and pests. In late 1983, the Bodhi Farmers appealed the demolition orders in the Land and Environment Court of New South Wales, seeing the case as a critical test for the future development of similar communities.[22] Peter Hamilton undertook significant research and analysis to prepare Bodhi Farm's submission to the court. In his guideline notes for an expert witness, he declared: 'We are not interested in a settlement which compromises our principle.'[23] Hamilton was writing in this case to his friend the architect-planner and University of Sydney lecturer, Colin 'Col' James. James was also the chair of the technical assistance group that had been engaged by Landa to produce a handbook to both assist the new settlers in low-cost home building and assist councils in more liberally interpreting the relevant building codes.[24] Over months, Hamilton strategically deployed such personal and

19 Paul Landa quoted in Archer, 'Bodhi Farm', 18.

20 NSW Planning & Environment Commission, *Hamlet Development in NSW Seminar Proceedings.*

21 Fisher, 'The Future for Rural Landsharing Communities', 57.

22 Nicolson v. Lismore City Council, 20519 of 1983, 5. (NSW Land and Environment Court, 1984).

23 Peter Hamilton 'Guideline Notes', 1984, 'Bodhi Farm v. Lismore Council' folder, Colin James Papers, private collection.

24 The technical assistance group and its research were another outcome of the hamlet seminar. The group produced the alternative building guide: *Low Cost Country Home Building: A Handbook on the Essentials of Low Cost Construction for the Guidance of Rural Homebuilders* (Sydney: Dept. of Environment and Planning, 1981).

Fig. 3 Dwelling segment at Bodhi Farm, c. 1980. (Photograph by © Colin James)

professional connections, seeking to understand and review the legal basis for the orders. Apart from drawing in Col James's expertise (which also provided access to technical advice from James's colleagues), Hamilton interviewed employees of government departments related to the production and oversight of building standards, and authorities on the relevant published standards. He also corresponded with members of industry and professional advisory committees as well as his home builders association co-founder Sonia Atkinson.[25] This critical and collaborative hard work began to build knowledge and networks oriented toward sustaining the new settlers' alternative building culture, and it highlights the creative negotiation as well as blunt challenging of sociolegal frameworks that the new settlers used to defend their experimental dwelling practices.

A series of arguments were raised in court against the demolition orders. In some areas, it was contended that definitions in the building ordinance were ambiguous or inapplicable to the situation of the expanded house. In his briefing notes, Hamilton suggested: 'I find it useful to consider an expanded house as a cluster of structures connected by "corridors without walls".'[26] In other aspects, it was argued that the house performed adequately even if its

25
Peter Hamilton 'Guideline Notes', 1984, 'Bodhi Farm v. Lismore Council' folder, Colin James Papers, private collection.

26
Peter Hamilton 'Guideline Notes', 1984, 'Bodhi Farm v. Lismore Council' folder, Colin James Papers, private collection.

Fig. 4 Dwelling segment plan drawn during the land and environment court appeal case, c. 1983. Note the open facade protected by a sunken garden. (Drawing by © Colin James)

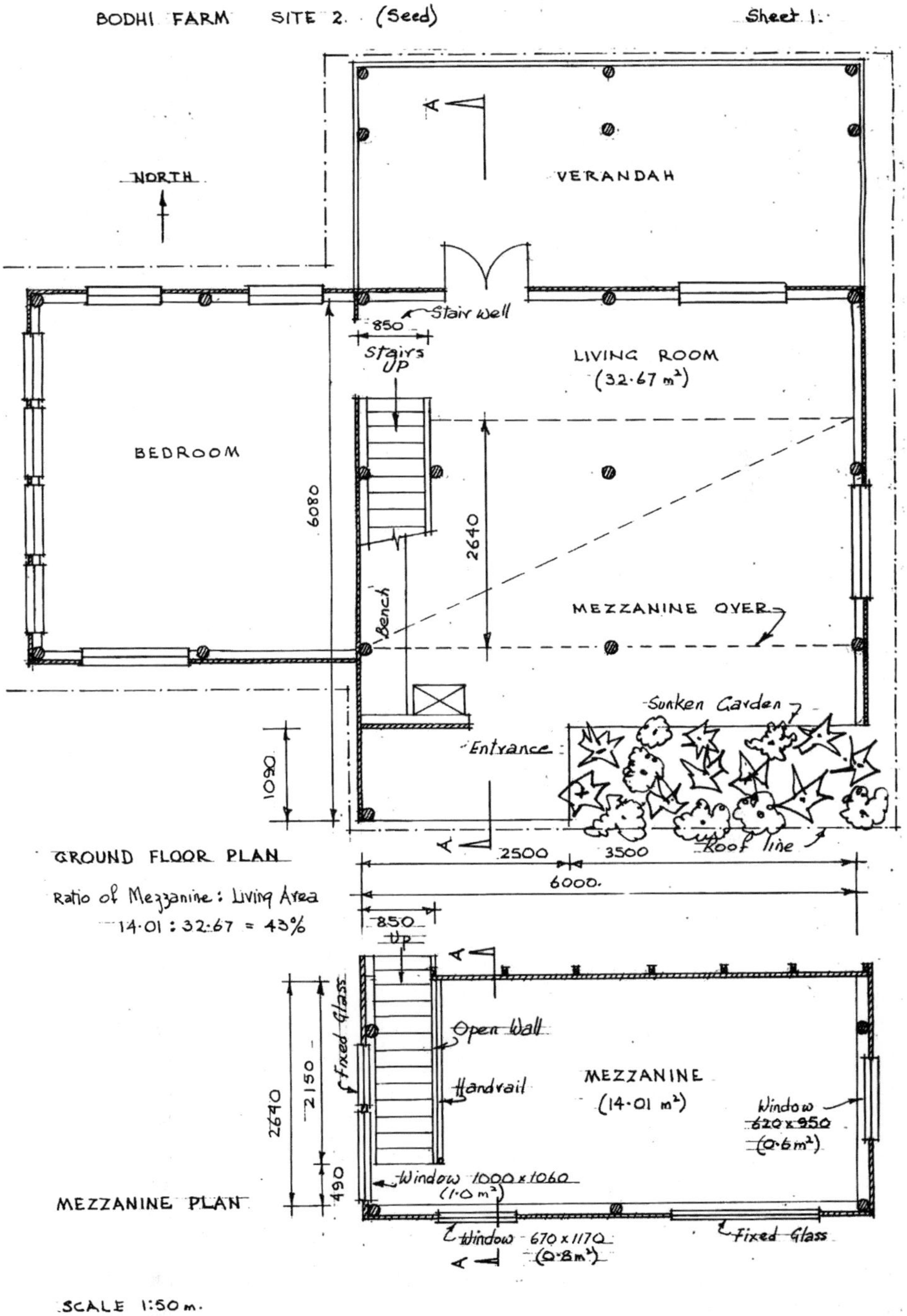

Fig. 5 Overleaf: A mud-brick section of a self-built house constructed between 1991 and 1993. Photographed in 2019. (Photograph by © Heather Faulkner)

dimensions did not meet the standards. For example, the technical assistance group spent considerable time calculating air volume and air movement in the living space containing the mezzanine sleeping platform in order to demonstrate its safety.[27] Hamilton also argued:

> Large roll up blinds are not uncommon in the area and found to be an efficient system to open a large area of a dwelling for air circulation in the hot summer and to aid fast drying of the interior of the dwellings after prolonged periods of rain.[28]

These arguments positioned the environmental performance of the dwellings not as an independent condition but as produced through the integration of the structure with its site, including the surrounding vegetation, microclimate, and specific living practices. Bodhi Farm's countercultural architecture was being legitimated through an epistemological re-encoding as a kind of climatic modernism.

In its 1984 judgement, the court largely upheld the arguments made by the Bodhi Farmers. The council was directed to set aside the demolition orders. While assessor Fitz-Henry pondered the likely difficulty of undertaking indoor stretching exercises in such small rooms, and the need that open elevations might create for extra clothing in wintertime, she also considered the desires of the Bodhi Farmers to 'live so close to nature' as part of a fringe lifestyle unlikely to provide a significant precedent.[29] Bodhi Farm celebrated. Their countercultural experiment was beginning to seem far from foolish idealism – in the same year as the successful appeal, the Australian prime minister, Bob Hawke, publicly speculated about the possibility of a government-sponsored kibbutz scheme inspired by communities like Bodhi Farm.[30] Four years later, new state planning policy came into effect legalising multiple occupancy.[31] By that time Bodhi Farm had added more dwelling segments, a community centre, and meditation retreat. As Aquarian pioneers they were the advance guard of a migration that continues to this day and has reinforced understandings of what is often called the 'Rainbow Region' as symbolic and material countercultural terroir – open to experimentation and possibility.[32]

Peter Hamilton would spend around thirty years living on Bodhi Farm. He continued to be an important actor in the shared building culture and related struggles to gain legislative recognition for the post-Aquarius communal living experiments. He worked as a 'bush lawyer' for many years, providing informal advice in dozens of planning law cases, and in 1983 produced a pamphlet entitled 'How to Play the Planning Game'.[33] He also helped found the Pan Community Council (Pan Com), with the aim of: 'promoting social interaction between communities; assisting in dealings with councils and government bodies; fostering economic initiatives; and supporting environmental repair and enhancement.'[34] By the time of his death in 2014 he had a regional reputation as a campaigner for environmental conservation.[35]

Tracking Peter Hamilton's imbrication in networks of self-builders, politicians, architects, planners, building inspectors, and others –

27
James to Hamilton, 1984, 'Bodhi Farm v. Lismore Council' folder, Colin James Papers, private collection.

28
Peter Hamilton 'Guideline Notes', 1984, 'Bodhi Farm v. Lismore Council' folder, Colin James Papers, private collection.

29
Nicolson v. Lismore City Council, 7–8.

30
'Nimbin Droogs', *Sydney Morning Herald*, 16 July 1984, 13; 'Hawke Call on Alternative Lifestyles', *Sydney Morning Herald*, 3 December 1979, 3.

31
NSW State Environmental Planning Policy No 15 – Rural Landsharing Communities, 1988 (since repealed).

32
Wilson, *Belonging in the Rainbow Region.*

33
Hamilton, *How to Play the Planning Game*. 'Bush lawyer' is Australian slang for an unqualified person who attempts to explain legal matters.

34
Peter Hamilton, ed., 'Background to and Features of Rural Landsharing Intentional Communities', 1999, Pan Community Council Reference Papers, private collection.

35
In 2002 the Byron Shire Council named him an 'Earth Champion.' http://www.earthchampions.org/about1-c10co. Accessed 4 October 2017.

36
Farber, 'Building the Counterculture'.

acting as an architect, builder *and* resident of Bodhi Farm – underscores a potential for rethinking relationships between countercultural architecture and broader society. The innovative organisations, practices, and institutions American historian David Farber has identified in countercultural striving for 'handmade lives' come into sharper focus.[36] Bodhi Farm's expanded houses became pivotal in code wars over ways of living, property regimes, and institutional recognition. Within this context, its alternative dwelling modes were established and reshaped through a collectively fostered and asserted self-build culture. The tools developed (from consensus decision-making processes to DIY construction guides) and outcomes (legal victories and new state planning instruments) expand our understanding of countercultural building and its valency, and of the rusticating counterculture's better-known ideological refusals and resolutely outlaw architectural culture. Bodhi Farm's design insurgency offers a rich example of an architectural activism reflecting the counterculture's organisational forms and ethics. The work carried out to sustain its building practices of everyday utopianism demonstrates a more dynamic relationship between imagining and actualisation; one that points toward an unsettling of commonplace assumptions about the amateurism and isolation of the counterculture's outlaw territories.

Acknowledgements: Research for this chapter was supported by the State Library of New South Wales' 2017 Nancy Keesing Fellowship.

Archer, John. 'Bodhi Farm'. *The Owner Builder*, no. 8 (June 1982): 18.

Bodhi Farm Archives, private collection.

Castillo, Greg. 'Counterculture Terroir: California's Hippie Enterprise Zone'. In *Hippie Modernism: The Struggle for Utopia*, edited by Andrew Blauvelt, 87–102. Minneapolis: Walker Art Center, 2015.

Cock, Peter. *Alternative Australia*. Melbourne: Quartet Books, 1979.

Cooper, Davina. *Everyday Utopias: The Conceptual Life of Promising Spaces*. Durham, NC: Duke University Press, 2013.

Dunstan, Graeme. 'Nimbin: The Vision and the Reality'. In *The Way Out: Radical Alternatives in Australia*, edited by Margaret Smith and David Crossley. Melbourne: Lansdowne, 1975.

Farber, David. 'Building the Counterculture, Creating Right Livelihoods: The Counterculture at Work'. *The Sixties: A Journal of History, Politics and Culture* 6, no. 1 (2013): 1–24.

Farber, David. 'Self-Invention in the Realm of Production: Craft, Beauty, and Community in the American Counterculture, 1964 to 1978'. *Pacific Historical Review* 85, no. 3 (2016): 408–42.

Fisher, Kath. 'Living Alternatively: Bodhi Farm'. *Social Alternatives* 26, no. 1 (2007): 49.

Fisher, Warwick. 'The Future for Rural Landsharing Communities in Far North Coast New South Wales'. *Southern Cross University Law Review* 8 (2004): 51–72.

Hamilton, Peter, ed. *How to Play the Planning Game: Being Guidelines for the Preparation of a Multiple Occupancy Development Application in N.S.W.* Nimbin, NSW: Home Builders Association (Rainbow Region), 1983.

Hamilton, Peter. 'The Nine Lives of Peter Hamilton – Part 2'. By Claudia Taranto, *Verbatim*, ABC Radio National, 13 November 2004.

'Hawke Call on Alternative Lifestyles'. *Sydney Morning Herald*, 3 December 1979: 3.

Holland, Graham E. 'Planning and Building Regulations and Alternative Lifestyles: Conflict and its Resolution in New South Wales Australia'. *Journal of Architecture and Planning Research*, no. 3 (1986): 65–77.

James, Colin. *Lismore Report*. Sydney: School of Architecture, University of Sydney, 1979.

James, Colin. Papers, private collection.

Jennings, Rebecca. 'Creating Feminist Culture: Australian Rural Lesbian-Separatist Communities in the 1970s and 1980s'. *Journal of Women's History* 30, no. 2 (2018): 88–111.

Jiggens, John. *Rehearsals for the Apocalypse: The Aquarius Festival, May 12–22, 1973*. Brisbane: self-published, 1982.

Letter to the editor. *Northern Star*, 10 October 1979: 5.

Maniaque-Benton, Caroline. *French Encounters with the American Counterculture, 1960–1980*. Farnham: Ashgate, 2011.

Memmott, Paul and Cathy Keys. 'The Emergence of an Architectural Anthropology in Aboriginal Australia: The Work of the Aboriginal Environments Research Centre'. *Architectural Theory Review* 21, no. 2 (2016): 218–36.

Metcalf, Bill, ed. *Co-operative Lifestyles in Australia: From Utopian Dreaming to Communal Reality*. Sydney: UNSW Press, 1995.

'Multiple Occupancy – How it Works'. *Owner Builder*, no. 7 (March 1981): 18–21.

Munro-Clark, Margaret. *Communes in Rural Australia: The Movement Since 1970*. Sydney: Hale and Iremonger, 1986.

Nicolson v. Lismore City Council. 20519 of 1983, 5. NSW Land and Environment Court, 1984.

'Nimbin Droogs'. *Sydney Morning Herald*, 16 July 1984: 13.

NSW Planning & Environment Commission. *Hamlet Development in NSW Seminar Proceedings*. Grafton: NSW Planning & Environment Commission, 1980.

NSW State Environmental Planning Policy No 15 – Rural Landsharing Communities, 1988.

Rainbow Archives, State Library of New South Wales.

Sadler, Simon. 'An Architecture of the Whole'. *Journal of Architectural Education* 61, no. 4 (2008): 108–29.

Scott, Felicity D. 'Episodes in the Refusal of Work'. *Archis*, no. 24 (2010): 34–8.

Stickells, Lee. 'Negotiating Off-Grid', *Fabrications* 25, no. 1 (2015): 104–29.

Taylor, Alison Louise. *Retreat or Advance: New Settlers and Alternative Lifestyles in the Rainbow Region*. University of New England, Armidale, Research Series in Applied Geography, 1981.

Technical Assistance Group. *Low Cost Country Home Building: A Handbook on the Essentials of Low Cost Construction for the Guidance of Rural Homebuilders*. Sydney: Dept. of Environment and Planning, 1981.

Wilson, Helen, ed. *Belonging in the Rainbow Region: Cultural Perspectives on the NSW North Coast*. Lismore, NSW: Southern Cross University Press, 2003.

Building Before Theorising Resistance: 118 Benaki Street beyond critical regionalism

Stylianos Giamarelos

The camera pans to capture, in 1978, the modern city of Athens as it covers the undulating landscape between the Philopappou and the Acropolis hills. It then zooms in to register specific moments in this seemingly endless urban mass, as four-to-six-storey apartment buildings (a typology known as the Athenian *polykatoikia*) succeed one another in invariable repetition. But as the camera moves closer to the foot of Strefi hill, it is suddenly attracted by a four-storey apartment building that differs from the rest. The viewpoint immediately shifts to the level of the street to inspect the main elevation of this unique piece of Athenian architecture on 118 Benaki Street. It then follows a young man who enters the building to visit the apartment on the first floor. He is the son of Suzana Antonakaki and Dimitris Antonakakis, the architectural couple who designed the building, and have lived and worked there since 1974. Tracing his visit to the apartment, the camera showcases its exceptional architectural features **(Fig. 1)**. The eye behind it belongs to Alekos Polychroniadis, a fellow architect in Antonakakis' collaborative practice, Atelier 66, which occupies the ground floor of the same building.

Resistant architecture

Summarising their ideas in a series of five sketches in the manner of Le Corbusier's five points for a new architecture, Suzana and Dimitris Antonakakis contrast the 'conventional' with 'another strategy' for the *polykatoikia* **(Fig. 2)**. Framing the visit to the building in juxtaposition to the city around it, the film records the two Antonakakis critique of the standard Athenian apartment building typology and the generic post-war development of the Greek capital. The camera inspects the main elevation to allude to the unique spatial arrangement behind it. It clearly shows that this is not the facade of a standard Athenian apartment building, with the wet spaces and the stairwells at its dark core, the living rooms extending to the horizontal symmetrical balconies at the front and the bedrooms at the back **(Fig. 3)**. There is no typical floor plan on 118 Benaki Street. Apparently sculpted rather than stacked on top of one another, most of the apartments span two floors. They can be clearly identified within the overall building structure even from the street level, as each of them has its own architectural identity. The camera returns to the visitor who enters the building. As he opens the door, he does not find himself in a luxurious lobby, but in a stone-paved courtyard. To get from the urban public space to the private sphere of the apartment on the first floor, he does not disappear into the building's interior but traverses a series of successive enclosed and semi-enclosed thresholds. These also serve as occasions for seeing and meeting with the other tenants, as they circulate in and out of their apartments. As the visitor enters the

Fig. 1 Selected stills from 118 Benaki Street video by Alekos Polychroniadis, 1978. (© Suzana and Dimitris Antonakakis private archive)

1
See Clogg, *A Concise History of Modern Greece*, 148–9.

2
See Emmanuil, *Η κοινωνική πολιτική κατοικίας στην Ελλάδα.*

apartment, the camera moves to showcase the architects' concern for cross-ventilation and natural light, and the gradient interplay of private, semi-public, and public spaces on different levels. When the visitor arrives at the heart of it, the apartment presents itself as a city within four walls, with similarly interlocking degrees of privacy and publicness. The double-height living room turns the apartment inside out. When Suzana Antonakaki leans out of her bedroom window, an internal window that gives on to the living room, this interior space echoes the outdoor piazza of a Greek island settlement within the four walls of a metropolitan apartment. This recourse to 'tradition' forms the resistant core of the Antonakakis architecture, which does not rely on mere formal replication but carries over the memory of spatial qualities of life in the open-air environment of the vernacular settlement. It is from this context that most Athenians originate anyway, following the unprecedented growth of the urban population in the early post-war decades.[1]

Their work on 118 Benaki Street in the early 1970s enabled Suzana and Dimitris Antonakakis to systematise their five-point critique to the Athenian apartment building typology in sketches and film later in the same decade. But as an essentially retrospective process, this narrowly defined architectural critique overlooks equally crucial ways in which the building resists and subverts existing design conventions, standard modes of production, and everyday practices of sharing a life within the same Athenian apartment building. It is the lived history of 118 Benaki Street, from the moment of its initial conception to the present, that foregrounds its agency as a resistant experiment of communal living in Athens. Revisiting this history unveils the multifarious, resilient, and dissipating aspects of resistance on 118 Benaki Street – from the dominant development model of the *polykatoikia* to communal life and its aesthetics. But it also highlights the tensions that gradually rise between the originally resistant intentions and their long-term implementation in practice over four decades.

Resistant mode of production

Post-war Athens was an essentially provincial capital that struggled to manage the massive influx of population from the rest of the country without the state funds to satisfy the rising demand in housing. In Greece, public housing represents less than three per cent of the total surface of residential space.[2] The production of new housing, therefore, seemed virtually impossible without the participation of the small-scale private sector, from landowners to contractors. To incentivise such partnerships, the Greek state eventually institutionalised the informal mechanism of the *antiparochi,* a quid-pro-quo agreement between landowners with limited budgets and contractors who did not own plots of land. Through *antiparochi*, the landowners got the best apartments they would not have been able to build themselves, while the contractors who constructed the buildings covered their expenses and profited from selling the remaining apartments to third parties. This 'win-win' mechanism proved especially effective for Greece's small-scale housing market, serving as the motor of the construction boom from the 1950s onwards.

Fig. 2 118 Benaki Street as a critique of the Athenian apartment building typology in five points. (© Suzana and Dimitris Antonakakis private archive)

Block of apartments

Not The Conventional Approach – But Another Strategy

(1)

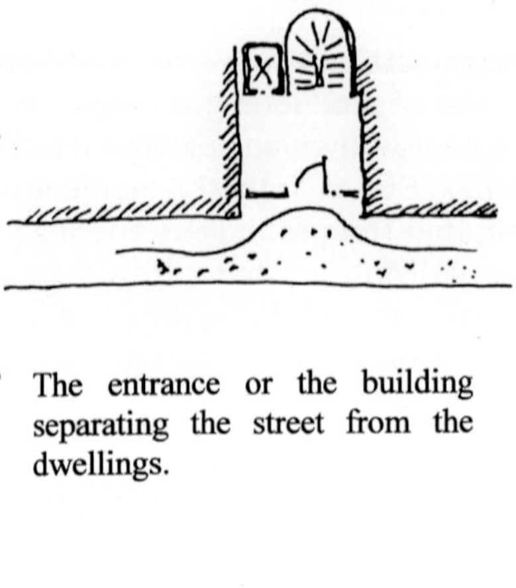

NOT The entrance or the building separating the street from the dwellings.

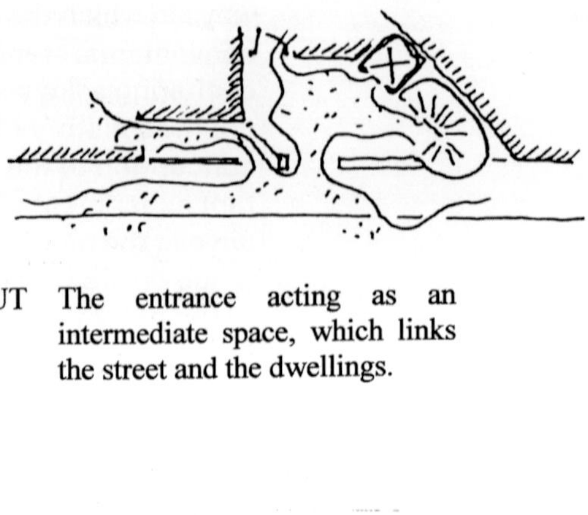

BUT The entrance acting as an intermediate space, which links the street and the dwellings.

(2)

NO Narrow, dark and repelling shared public spaces.

BUT Common spaces, which follow the entrance and are sunlit, inviting and open air.

3

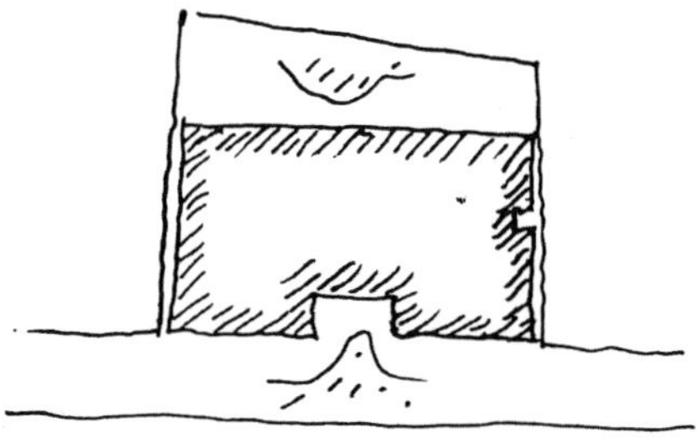

NO Disused outdoor space, which belongs to nobody, is used by nobody and is cared for by nobody.

BUT Outdoor space containing a yard on the ground floor which is planted with trees and flowers, cared for and used by private owners.

4

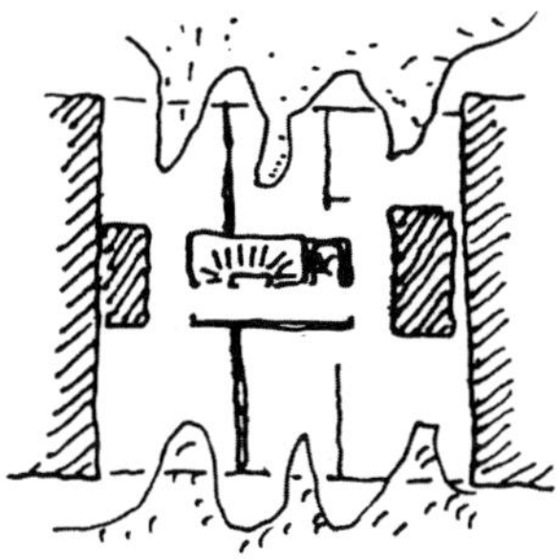

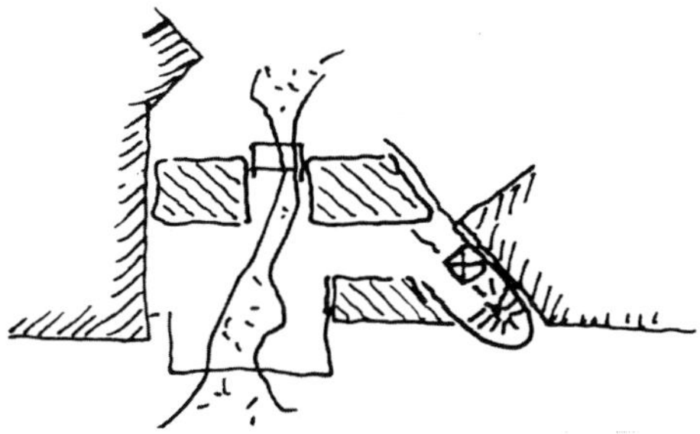

NO Spaces ventilated and lit only from one side with a dark intermediate zone of service spaces.

BUT Spaces, which are transparent and ventilated from all sides, allowing nature to penetrate in and including light service spaces.

5

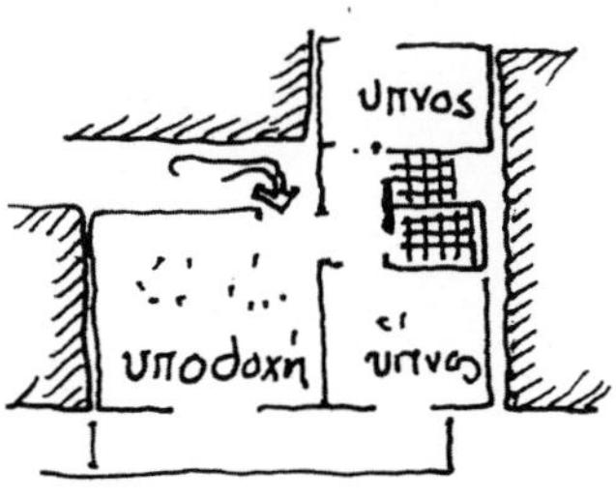

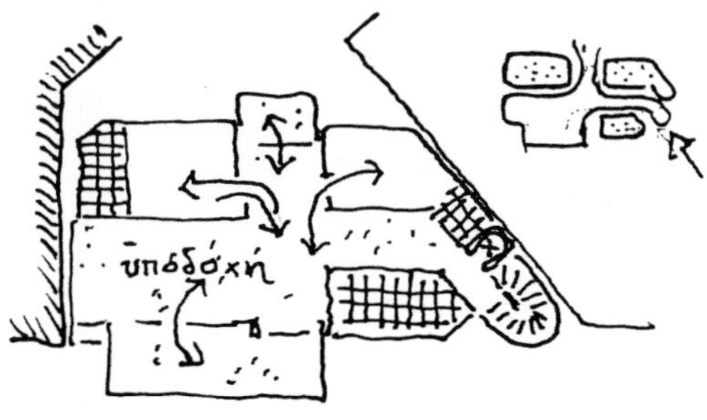

NO Separated activities in order to receive guests

- Dwelling divided in two.
- Outdoor spaces which become corridors
- Underserved privacy.

BUT Guests who participate in the activities.

- Spaces organized in small entities with larger grades of privacy.
- Outdoor spaces comfortable, protected and familiar, acting as an extension of the indoor spaces.

Fig. 3 Main elevation. Suzana and Dimitris Antonakakis, 118 Benaki Street apartment building, Athens, 1975. (© Suzana and Dimitris Antonakakis private archive)

3
See Woditsch, *The Public Private House*.

4
Pattie Dolka, interviewed by S. Giamarelos, 9 June 2014.

The other significant state intervention in the early post-war years appeared in 1955, when a new building code aimed to regulate the flourishing housing market through prohibitions and prescriptions. These ranged from the specified contours of new constructions (including the overall height, number of individual floors, window heights, setbacks, and penthouses) to architectural details (including the width and extensions of balconies and terraces).[3] Contractors added their own layer of requirements to this typology. To maximise profit, they aimed for simple, standardised floors with the maximum possible number of rooms, impressive facades, and luxurious lobbies. To suit the needs of projected but unknown clients, their architects in turn had to ensure their designs were flexible enough. The standard apartment building typology of booming post-war Athens was effectively prescribed by these practices and the new building code. But the indiscriminate repetition of this same building type across the Athenian basin created an urban environment that was deemed faceless by the 1970s.

It is this commodifying mode of production of the small-scale construction sector that Suzana and Dimitris Antonakakis opposed. Resisting the quantitative urges of the developers, they not only promoted the qualitative aspects of their architecture, but they also attempted to give a wider meaning to the notion of state-supported 'participation' of the small-scale private sector in the 1950s that went beyond its exclusive interpretation in economic terms. The two Antonakakis aimed to nurture unmediated and personified relations with the future residents of their project. These ties spanned from the design to the construction process and the subsequent sharing of a communal life within the building. In so doing, the two architects also explored the alternative possibilities for agreements between interested parties that remained latent in the legal mechanism of the *antiparochi*.

118 Benaki Street is indeed the product of a collaborative process that subverted the established hierarchies in the design, construction, and use of space in the standard Athenian apartment. Each of the four families involved contributed what was necessary for the realisation of the communal project: land, labour, and capital. The land was offered by the Dolkas and Kannas families. The labour was shared in accordance with each party's professional expertise (the two architects, Suzana and Dimitris Antonakakis, designed the building; the lawyer, Pattie Dolka, established the tenants' unmediated partnership through *antiparochi*; the mechanical engineer, Lampis Dolkas, devised the central ventilation and heating system). The remaining capital was offered by the Nezis (and later by the wider Antonakakis family when they stepped in to buy the ground floor and use it as the main office space of Atelier 66).[4] Starting their own one-off partnership with the other families to erect this building enabled the architects to keep their safe distance from the dictates of the Greek construction sector of the period. It was this move that enabled them to prioritise the architectural qualities they valued, and put them into practice in their complex building typology.

Each apartment of 118 Benaki Street is a bespoke piece of architecture. From the phase of the first sketches, the architects established a feedback loop with the future residents. The Antonakakis shared their initial architectural proposals, the tenants suggested modifications that led to a revised proposal by the architects, and so on, for about a year. The architects knew and shared friendly bonds with all the parties involved in the project. When I interviewed them in 2014, the other residents of the building emphasised its conception as an experiment in collaborative living. They referred to it as 'a four-storey single-family house', while children from different families described 'growing up like sisters' in the building.[5] They also described collective cooking sessions in kitchens on different floors, sharing meals with the other families, how the doors of their apartments usually remained unlocked, enabling their children to go up and down the stairs at will **(Fig. 4)**. These and other instances of their shared life across the building's four stories further reinforced the resistant aspects of communal living on 118 Benaki Street.

5
Myrto Nezi, interviewed by S. Giamarelos, 9 June 2014.

6
Myrto Nezi, interviewed by S. Giamarelos, 9 June 2014.

Knowing the future tenants to design residential spaces that would fit their specific needs was the two Antonakakis' personified response to the 'anonymous' generic approach of the Greek contractors. 118 Benaki Street is the product of a household economy. In the absence of intermediaries, the tenants' partnership ensured that the design decisions were affected only by those who intended to share their lives in this building. These social bonds were crucial for the completion of the project. It was only through the connective tissue of social relations that this more 'traditionally' collective way of life could be retained and developed in the transition from the agrarian to the metropolitan condition of atomised anonymity. These embedded social relations that were also transposed to the mode of production of the building formed the second significant layer in the Antonakakis holistic conception of 'tradition'. In addition to the spatial typologies that condense the insights of a long-standing relation of dwelling in the region, for the Antonakakis 'tradition' also signalled a specific aesthetic language as its significant third element. It is only when one considers these three registers (spatial typologies, social bonds, aesthetics) together that the resistant core of the Antonakakis architecture is fully revealed.

Resistant aesthetics

If the recourse to tradition in the anonymous context of a modern metropolis was to be fully realised, the residents would also have to ascribe to the architects' modernised 'traditional' aesthetic language. If a tenant did not share this mentality, an architectural project like this could not work. The residents of 118 Benaki Street were conscious of their decisions. They knew they were living in an unconventional apartment building. They therefore felt they also had to follow the architects' taste in the interior spaces, to avoid an aesthetic dissonance with the Antonakakis's overarching vision.[6] In the residents' eyes, the final word on the overall aesthetics could only belong to the expert architect.

Fig. 4 New Year's dinner in Suzana and Dimitris Antonakakis apartment with Atelier 66 architects and Benaki Street tenants, 1991. (© Lucy Tzafou-Triantafyllou's private archive)

Fig. 5 First-floor apartment, living room. Suzana and Dimitris Antonakakis, 118 Benaki Street apartment building, Athens, 1975. (© Suzana and Dimitris Antonakakis private archive)

Fig. 6 Atelier 66 architects, 1975. (© Suzana and Dimitris Antonakakis private archive)

But it was not long before the architects noted discrepancies between theirs and the other residents' aesthetic preferences. Tenants did not want their apartments as simple and austere as Suzana and Dimitris Antonakakis had originally designed them with their limited collective budget in the early 1970s. Aesthetic considerations aside, tenants had to settle for the most economic options available at the time: roughcast plaster for the walls and Sifnos stones for the floors. Despite their initial fascination with these materials as reminiscent of Greek island life, in the late 1990s and early 2000s the other residents of 118 Benaki Street replaced the Sifnos stones on the floor of their apartments with marble or timber. For some tenants, this was also a case of following the style of the times.[7] Constructed in the early 1970s, the aesthetic language of the interiors was aligned with the wider turn to Greek folk art of the time. The carpets, rugs, and other small objects that originally covered the floors or decorated the apartments were meant as a cultural expression of this return to folk culture **(Fig. 5)**. They represented an authenticity that resisted the superficial recuperation and kitsch abuse of Greek 'tradition' by the authoritarian military regime of the period (1967–74). This was especially the case for Suzana and Dimitris Antonakakis and their collaborative architectural practice, Atelier 66. From their non-hierarchical ways of collaboration to the ways they designed architectural interiors or dressed themselves, their holistic revisit of tradition aimed to re-

7
Pattie Dolka, interviewed by S. Giamarelos, 9 June 2014.

8
Antonakakis and Antonakaki, 'Το ιδανικό σπίτι'. *To Vima*. The quote has been translated from the Greek by the author.

9
See Antonakakis, Προβλήματα κατοίκησης. Πολυκατοικία: Τυπολογική πολυπλοκότητα ή σύνθετη τυπολογία, 98.

10
Yannis Roussos, interviewed by S. Giamarelos, 6 July 2014.

11
Alekos Athanassiadis, interviewed by S. Giamarelos, 8 July 2014.

gain it as an active cultural agent in the present **(Fig. 6)**. In so doing, it also signalled a political act of resistance to the junta.

Residual hierarchies

However, the actual life of the residents in the building proved that the architects' original intentions were short-lived. These increasingly sounded like the dying echo of a provincial tradition that could not survive the advance of the Athenian metropolis and the individualist urban lifestyle. The unconventional aspects of the tenants' shared life gradually faded. When the four families started locking their doors, and central heating was autonomously managed by each individual apartment because of their differing needs during the day, life on 118 Benaki Street increasingly resembled that of the typical Athenian apartment building in the early 1990s. Today each storey functions in isolation from the others, and the interiors of the other tenants' apartments have all been modified. The two architects were sceptical about the refurbishments instigated by the tenants. In a newspaper article they published in 2000, they refer to these decisions as 'irrelevant to the intentions that were once regarded as preconditions'.[8] Suzana and Dimitris Antonakakis could not bear losing control of their work after its completion. They were reluctant to entrust it unconditionally to the life and preferences of its residents. This in turn meant that the superior position of the architects in the design hierarchy was not practically subverted.

This was also the case for their collaboration with other professionals in the construction industry. The architects constantly remained at the helm of the design process. For them, collaboration practically meant getting the craftspeople to understand the architects' intentions and the overarching rationale of their designs. These went beyond the standardised solutions of banal apartment buildings. They therefore challenged the skills of their craftspeople. The design philosophy of the Antonakakis posited that this inability to standardise the design details of their work preserved a crucial architectural quality from being lost.[9] In an era of industrial standardisation, it harked back to the subtle qualities of 'traditional' human craft and manual work. The architects had developed their own good sense of the use, qualities, and properties of various materials. They prepared drawings and models specifically for their craftspeople. Through these drawings and models, they instructed them. They laid out the full details needed for construction.[10] For the structural design of their buildings, the civil engineers also had to retain the Antonakakis architectural intentions intact. They thus engaged with the architectural brief, to solve the problems that arose from the architects' design intentions. Again, the engineers started working on these details from a preliminary version of the structural design provided by the architects. This draft structure was already aligned with key design elements and architectural intentions.[11] Despite the Antonakakis repeated rhetoric of creative contribution of the parties involved, the architects' superior role in the design hierarchy was not practically challenged on this front either.

Finally, Suzana and Dimitris Antonakakis non-standard approach to the apartment building did not go unobserved by the Greek contractors of the period. Some of them charged the Antonakakis with elitism.[12] When Suzana Antonakaki reused and further developed some of the Benaki project features in the subsequent Doxapatri apartment building in the late 1970s, the future tenants of this building also formed a similar partnership, but they found it more difficult to cooperate as they did not share the friendly ties of the parties involved in the Benaki Street cooperative. Generalising a design process that rested on personified interaction with the involved parties proved inherently difficult.

Ioanna Theocharopoulou's recent work on the construction of modern Athens adds nuance to this bigger picture. From builders to housewives, her historical account of the post-war apartment building traces the rise of an aberrant way of making that is specifically Athenian.[13] This does not only contextualise Antonakakis work. It also suggests the substitution of their agrarian-inspired conception of 'tradition' with its urban equivalent by the 1980s. And this might in turn be another reason why the architects' original resistant intentions proved short-lived and many of the 'traditional' aspects of their work soon dissipated.

Today's architectures of resistance might therefore need to follow different genealogies of their own that address this concrete Athenian condition and its gradual formation in the late twentieth century. It is only through this sort of nuanced historical engagement that politics can be significantly retained at the heart of architectures and discourses of resistance today.

Retheorising resistance

Tensions that are only revealed when one turns to the lived history of the building over four decades challenge the standard ways in which this project has been appropriated to theorise architectural resistance by critical regionalism and other related discourses.[14] As they bypass the nuanced history of this resistant project, theoretical appropriations like Kenneth Frampton's offer only a frozen idealised image of architectural resistance. This cannot be informative for resistant practices today. It is only a return to the fullness of the original historical image, to the social world as the architects wanted to see it transformed alongside the contingent fate of their actions, that helps foreground the political core of these resistant architectures and discourses for the present.

The history of an exemplary signifier of architectural resistance like 118 Benaki Street shows how the resistant aspects of the project have also been interpreted differently from its historically variable audiences. These are not limited to the idealising critics, but also include unconvinced residents and deriding contractors. The architects' original intentions foreground the centrality of challenging specific modes of production to establish novel forms of collaborative living. But the short lifespan of these intentions in their practi-

12
Antonakakis, Προβλήματα κατοίκησης, 83.

13
Theocharopoulou, *Builders, Housewives and the Construction of Modern Athens*, esp. 111–45.

14
See, for instance, French, *Key Urban Housing of the Twentieth Century*; Tzonis and Rodi, *Greece: Modern Architectures in History*, 208–9; Frampton, *Modern Architecture*, 313–27.

15
Cohen, *Why Not Socialism?*

16
Issaias, 'Beyond the Informal City'.

cal implementation also highlights the contradictions involved in architectural pursuits that attempt to orchestrate unconventional ways of living. Their historical fate is more emphatically informative if one wishes to go the extra mile to envision these changes on a broader scale. Especially the Greek contractors' reactions to the architects' intentions show how an architecture of resistance can also be received as its exact opposite, a generator of elite circles of the happy few and their indulgent idealisations. In other cases, problems might emerge from residual hierarchies and operative modes that remain unchallenged or resist change.

Whenever an apartment building like 118 Benaki Street is posited as a microcosm of an envisioned social change at a larger scale, the temptation to enter into another circle of idealised discourse is also present. In significant respects, the concrete experiment of 118 Benaki Street echoes Gerald A. Cohen's thought experiment of the camping trip that explores how desirable, feasible, and difficult it would prove to expand the principles of equity and community from a group of friends to a wider societal scale.[15] Since projects like 118 Benaki Street still form part of legacies and genealogies of more recent attempts to rethink the city of Athens as an urban common,[16] the challenge lies in resisting to turn these exemplars into supposedly self-evident images, but engage with the full spectrum of their historical contingency.

Acknowledgements: I would like to thank Suzana and Dimitris Antonakakis, Alekos Athanassiadis, Pattie Dolka, Myrto Nezi, and Yannis Roussos for agreeing to be interviewed for this project, and the Bartlett School of Architecture Research Fund for supporting it.

Bibliography

Antonakakis, Dimitris and Suzana Antonakaki. 'Το ιδανικό σπίτι'. *To Vima*. 25 June 2000.

Antonakakis, Dimitris. Προβλήματα κατοίκησης. Πολυκατοικία: Τυπολογική πολυπλοκότητα ή σύνθετη τυπολογία. In Έξι διαλέξεις για την κατοίκηση: Κατοικία, αστική πολυκατοικία, συλλογική κατοικία, edited by N. Marda, M. Papavasiliou, and S. Tsiraki, 55–99. Athens: NTUA School of Architecture, 2014.

Clogg, Richard. *A Concise History of Modern Greece*. Cambridge: Cambridge University Press, 1992.

Cohen, Gerald, A. *Why Not Socialism?* Princeton: Princeton University Press, 2009.

Emmanuil, D. Η κοινωνική πολιτική κατοικίας στην Ελλάδα: Οι διαστάσεις μιας απουσίας. Athens: National Centre for Social Research, 2006.

Frampton, Kenneth. *Modern Architecture: A Critical History*. 2nd ed. London: Thames & Hudson, 1985.

French, Hilary. *Key Urban Housing of the Twentieth Century: Plans, Sections and Elevations*. London: Laurence King, 2008.

Issaias, Platon. 'Beyond the Informal City: Athens and the Possibility of an Urban Common'. PhD dissertation, Technische Universiteit Delft, 2014.

Theocharopoulou, Ioanna. *Builders, Housewives and the Construction of Modern Athens*. London: Black Dog, 2017.

Tzonis, Alexander and Alcestis Rodi. *Greece: Modern Architectures in History*. London: Reaktion Books, 2013.

Woditsch, Richard, ed. *The Public Private House: Modern Athens and its Polykatoikia*. Zürich: Park Books, 2018.

Creating a 'We': When architects build for themselves, others, and a city in transformation

Max Ott

(No) collaboration

In November 2010, the journal *Arch+* published an open letter from a group of Berlin-based architects,[1] who refused an invitation to contribute to a book project on contemporary inner-city housing in Berlin, entitled *Stadthäuser* (Townhouses).[2] Their rejection was provoked by the fact that the publisher Philipp Meuser had announced that Berlin's former director of urban planning Hans Stimmann was to be the editor of the book. After the reunification of Berlin, Stimmann had commissioned the Planwerk Innenstadt, a huge framework for the once-divided historical city centre that had been officially established as a guiding principle in 1999. This framework drew strong criticism from many professional planners, academics, and journalists, who considered it an outcome of its initiator's sharp attacks on modernist urban-planning rationalities.[3] Since he took office in 1991, Stimmann had consistently accused modern architecture and urban design of a conscious destruction of dense and networked urban spaces and had insisted on the necessity of regaining what he called the 'memory of the European city'.[4] Stimmann promoted the reconstruction of Berlin's pre-war urban fabric with perimeter blocks on parcelled plots within a close grid of streets and squares, and favoured a housing scheme consisting of individually owned townhouses with a neoclassical appearance. In his view, this was the only means to revitalise a bourgeois 'urban identity'[5] that both the socialist and Fordist regimes in East and West Berlin had supposedly tried to overcome **(Fig. 1)**.

The authors of the open letter opposed Stimmann's anti-modernist conviction of only one legitimate way to (re-)create urbanity, and then made another point why they did not want their projects to be displayed in his book. They stated that during the Stimmann era – which had lasted until 2006 – their campaigning for the actual heterogeneity of Berlin's urban spaces had mostly been excluded from official decision-making processes. Although the Planwerk Innenstadt was of a rather recommendatory nature and sometimes even bypassed by administrations of the relatively autonomous city districts, architects who were at odds with its proposals had limited chances to win competitions or receive public contracts within the framework's perimeter. In the early and mid 2000s, the architects who would later sign the open letter began to develop a different path, thereby benefitting from a particular spatial and economical constellation.

More than a decade after Berlin's reunification, many former border territories in inner-city areas outside the scope of Planwerk Innenstadt were still shaped by fallow land or interstitial sites.

1 'Offener Brief'.

2 Stimmann, *Stadthäuser*.

3 Hain, 'Berlin's Urban Development Discourse'.

4 Düwel and Mönninger, *Von der Sozialutopie zum städtischen Haus*, 167–75. Translated from German by the author.

5 Hertweck, *Der Berliner Architekturstreit*, 191. Translated from German by the author.

Fig. 1 Townhouses in Berlin's historical city centre. (Photograph by © Max Ott)

6
Colomb, *Staging the New Berlin*.

7
'Offener Brief'. Translated from German by the author.

8
'Offener Brief'. Translated from German by the author.

As private investments had significantly declined after 2001 due to a stagnating population trend, such properties were relatively affordable.[6] In this context, several architects assembled stakeholders to collectively finance the purchase of land and the construction of buildings which were often their first projects in Berlin. It is therefore not surprising that 'self-initiative' was the decisive term these architects used when pointing out to Philipp Meuser the difference between their concepts and Stimmann's townhouses.[7] But they did more than describe self-initiative as just a pragmatic means of self-help by early career architects. 'We understand architecture as the organisation of social relationships through built structures', they stated, adding that this organisation often resulted from 'building with various clients at once' – a process including all residents and users of the houses, among them often the architects themselves, who argued: 'This is how we integrate the responsibility of every single participant for the development of the architectural project and the city.'[8]

This way of addressing the city turned Stimmann's ideas upside down. Instead of supporting the top-down implementation of a large-scale master plan composed of individually owned townhouses and inspired by selected parts of Berlin's history, the open letter

Fig. 2 Exterior shot of building R50.
(Photograph by © Andrew Alberts)

9
'Offener Brief'. Translated from German by the author.

10
Quotations from architects Tim Heide and Susanne Heiss in this article are taken from an interview conducted by the author on 24 September 2015 and were translated from German by the author.

signatories argued in favour of the divergent small-scale realities of the present city and celebrated the potential of bottom-up planning to create 'social spaces within a Berlin made of stone perimeter blocks as collaboratively organised space in-between.'[9] In doing so, the open letter confronted the normativity of an established urban development policy with an explicitly ethical positioning. It emphasised self-initiated collaboration as the core value of their architectural practice, and the fundamental principle to ensure responsible action towards a city in transformation.

The architects' statements invite a closer look at an example of those kinds of 'social spaces' described in the letter, in order to gain a better understanding of the relationships constituted by collaborative planning. On the one hand, it helps to explore how built structures resulting from collaboration may actually organise concrete ways of living together and support the creation of connections to a broader urban context. On the other hand, and with particular relevance to *Activism at Home*, it is fruitful to look into planning together 'with various clients' to illustrate how architects who are both commissioned professionals and future coresidents deal with an interplay of ethical ambitions, pragmatic considerations, varying degrees of individual expertise, and both the wish and need for joint action.

Minimised standards

Actually, we wanted to know: 'how simply can we live?' [...] The people, who are now living here, are not poor [...] That is why I believe this project was rather 'culturally' driven, and here, the experiment was to ask: 'How far can we go in minimising the standard?' – Tim Heide, interview with Max Ott (2015)[10]

In this quote, the architect Tim Heide introduced R50 by making a short reference to the core idea of a co-housing project whose name does not evoke strong images, as it is just a pragmatic reaction to an inner-city address. R50 was completed in 2013 and is a detached building with six full storeys, a basement and an attic, located on Ritterstrasse 50 between a modernist social housing development from the 1950s and a residential block from the 1990s. The neighbourhood is heterogeneous in terms of spatial structure as well as social composition, both of which are historical remnants of a section of West Berlin's border territory. Although the property size of roughly 2,000 square metres would have made it possible, R50 is not set back from the street but instead is directly placed on it in order to create an immediate proximity to Ritterstrasse and a generous open space around the adjacent buildings. In accordance with this decision, the property does not have a fence and now merges into the green spaces of its surroundings, an 'achievement of [...] avoiding the impression of a closed community', as Heide put it. This measure is accompanied by an 'offer to the city': one corner of the building is occupied by a glazed common room, one-and-a-half storeys high, which is accessible from the street via a long ramp to the subterranean level. Heide's colleague Susanne Heiss described this intervention as a 'small element' for creating a 'connection' between R50 and the neighbourhood. From time to time it is open to people living in the area, for instance, when homework supervision is offered or for meetings of neighbourhood initiatives.

When approaching R50, everyone can get an impression of an architecture resulting from the idea of simplicity. The appearance of the building is defined by narrow circumferential galleries consisting of ordinary prefabricated metal components set in front of a facade made of light wooden panels and floor-to-ceiling windows. The building thus looks somewhat unpretentious, resembling an office building more than a townhouse, as one of its architects depicts it.[11] But the galleries are neither a smoking area for office workers nor a simple private extension for the residents in the building's nineteen apartments. Instead, these galleries can become performative in terms of collaborative living because they provide one continuous space, allowing residents to walk around the entire house and meet coresidents. At the same time, the limited depth of the gallery space suits only temporary private appropriations: while everyone may hang out the washing or place small flowerpots outside, there is never enough space for individual parties to claim this area more permanently, for example, by placing a large table or a heavy sun lounger in the space **(Fig. 2)**.

R50 houses roughly forty people and was initiated by two architectural offices – ifau and Heide & von Beckerath – and the architect and design theorist Jesko Fezer, who currently lives in the building in Ritterstrasse 50 as do ifau's founding partners. In 2010, the architects had outlined a preliminary concept for a co-housing project, gathered a group of people from a 'wider circle of friends',[12] most of them working in the creative industries, and then bid for a property offered by the federal state of Berlin at a fixed price. Soon after, the architects presented R50 at a public lecture series hosted by *Arch+*.[13] Instead of displaying drawings that would have represented a completed project, like overall sections, floorplans, or elevations, they focussed on letters, emails, diagrams, working models, and preliminary sketches; that is, they demonstrated the ongoing process of collectively negotiating the future architecture of R50 **(Fig. 3)**.

It was in this process that the multiple meanings of 'minimising' building standards became manifest. On the one hand, this approach was not just expressing a common desire for an architectural experiment in accordance with an ethical ideal of simplicity. It was also a quite pragmatic means to reduce the building's construction costs to 2.350 euros per square meter – an important factor for a group whose members were depending on private loans to finance their share.[14] On the other hand, keeping down the costs for the whole building also kept down the prices for individual apartments, which enabled the fulfilment of one of the co-housing group's central wishes, the creation of common spaces. In July 2011, Jesko Fezer reflected on the significant impact that minimis-

11
Fezer, 'Stadtentwicklung und Stadtpolitik'.

12
Heiss and Heide, interview.

13
'R50. Ifau und Jesko Fezer, Heide & von Beckerath'.

14
Käpplinger, 'Individualität in Gemeinschaft ist möglich'.

15
Fezer, interview. Translated from German by the author.

16
'R50. Ifau und Jesko Fezer, Heide & von Beckerath', 2–5.

17
These quotes and the following from the interview with Fezer.

18
'R50. Ifau und Jesko Fezer, Heide & von Beckerath', 11. Translated from German by the author.

ing standards thus had on both the design process and its three-dimensional result.[15] He stated two different but simultaneous 'phases', in which negotiations either took place between single members of the co-housing group and the architects or within the whole group. The former applied to the design of the apartments. In a first step, the architects only determined a primary structure consisting of one staircase, several walls, and two installation shafts, and agreed with the whole group on basic rules for the apartment floor plans – rough concrete ceilings and load-bearing walls, for instance, as well as standardised bathrooms and kitchen elements. Then they started an intensive discussion with every single party of the house. In close communication with the future users, they designed the layout of every apartment, but left the decision up to the users as to where to position window elements, whether to have an open floor plan, whether to integrate further partitioning walls themselves or whether to make use of construction companies.[16] This resulted in nineteen highly individualised floor plans, which are nonetheless based on the same minimised standards **(Fig. 4)**.

The common spaces in turn – including the subterranean level, the garden, the gallery, as well as the staircase, a workshop, a laundry room, and a roof terrace – result exclusively from negotiations within the whole group of coresidents. Fezer explained that the architects always aimed at delaying decision-making for as long as possible, seeking only for a 'minimum consensus' on a 'situational standard' of how something could look and how it eventually could be used.[17] Specifying as little as possible was meant to create a maximum of options for redefining spaces during the planning and construction phase, and to enable further collective negotiation processes on desired changes once the building was completed. Moreover, Fezer linked the peculiarity of 'not making decisions, as long as you do not know what is the point of making them' to both his belief in the need for professional planners to 'deprofessionalise' in favour of enabling collaboration and his observations of the planning process itself. Some participants urged the architects to 'decide, because you are the architects', while others insisted on 'things to be done like this and not like the architects want'. Delaying or 'not making decisions' also served the purpose of underlining that architects are not necessarily 'offering the right solution' and that, as soon as architects act as if they are 'experts for life', their expertise must be contested.

This is best illustrated with the common space, which eventually incorporated the group's initial idea to have a variety of shared rooms with different functions on the upper floors of the building into one large volume on subterranean level **(Fig. 5)**. Flooded with daylight and accessible both from outside as well as from the staircase on the first floor, the subterranean space is an example of how to accommodate emerging new concepts during the planning process. It represents the 'wish for more programmatic openness and flexibility, spatial density, and efficiency by superimposing uses as well as for spatial generosity'.[18] Facing the public street level, this

Fig. 3 A collection of concepts and proposals for common spaces in R50. (Diagrams by © ifau and Jesko Fezer, Heide & von Beckerath)

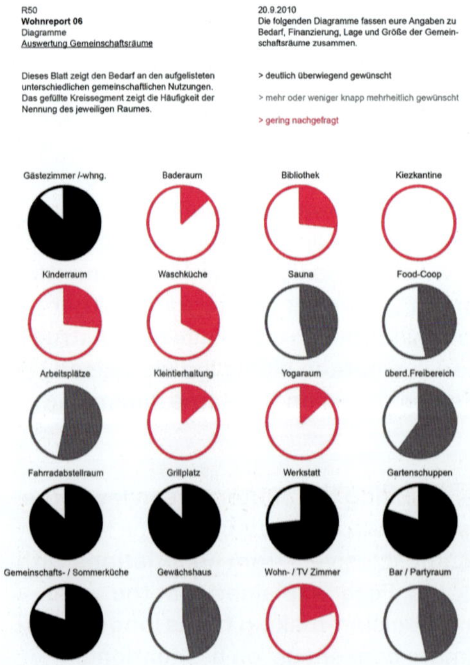

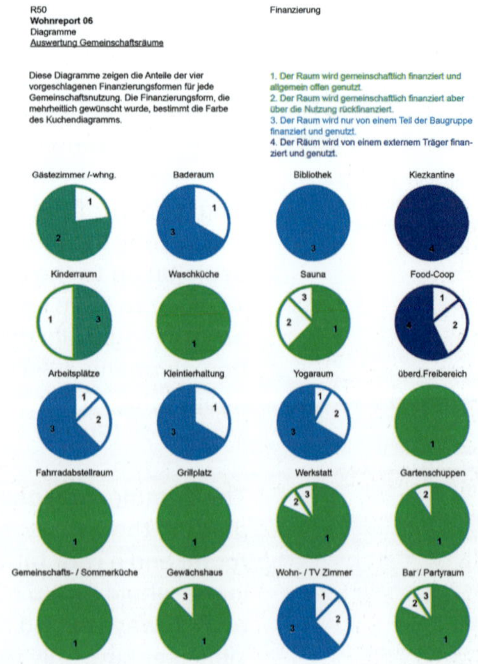

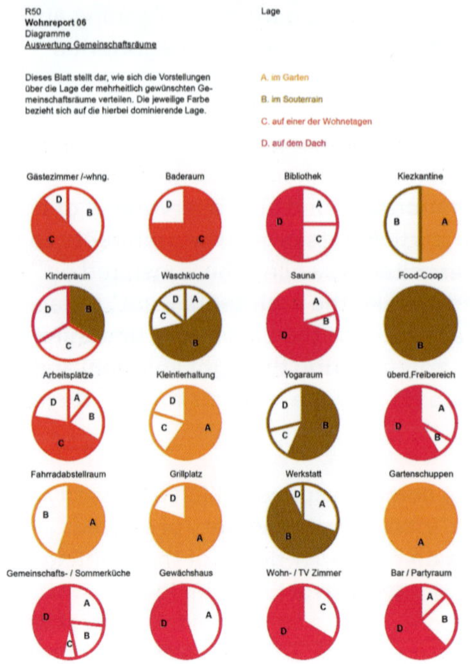

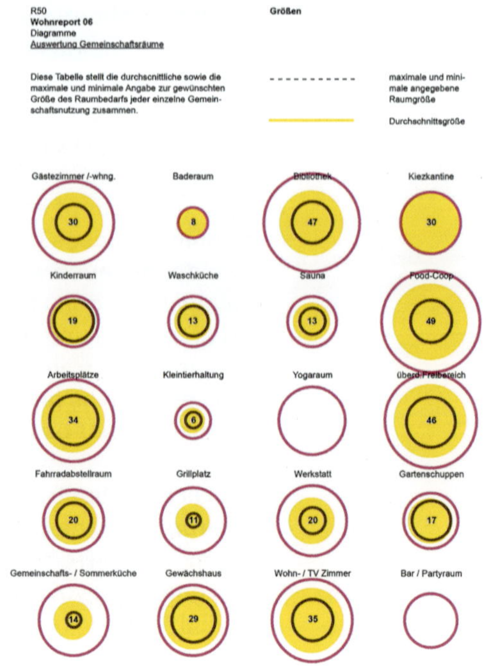

Fig. 4 Interior shot of apartment R50. (Photograph by © Andrew Alberts)

19
'R50. Ifau und Jesko Fezer, Heide & von Beckerath', 14.

20
Heiss and Heide, interview.

space provides a 'stronger disclosure' of collective ways of living.[19] While its current uses include being a space for public gatherings, a place for residents to meet with friends, and a playroom for children, that may well be modified in the future, as might be its current architectural configuration. It is possible to integrate a gallery to enlarge the usable space with interventions that can be carried out by the residents themselves and completed within a few days – another result of the collective decision to design spatial structures with minimised standards that facilitate future adjustments.

From activity to activism

Two years after moving into R50, one of its architects, Susanne Heiss, described ongoing discussions about extending the functions of the large room on subterranean level by occasionally using it as a cinema, for exhibitions, or as a temporary guest room with a table tennis table. She made clear that the latter idea could cause some friction, but a kind of friction that the residents actually embraced.[20] More than four years later, Christoph Schmidt, Heiss' partner at ifau and also a resident of R50, stood in the common space with a group of students from Munich and shared his views on ideas and realities of living in a cohousing

Fig. 5 Interior shot of community space R50. (Photograph by © Andrew Alberts)

21
Participatory observation on 10 January 2020.

22
de Carlo, 'Architecture's Public', 17.

project.[21] Asked about the dual role of being an architect of R50 *and* a coresident, Schmidt took a somewhat different stance than his colleague Jesko Fezer. Fezer underlined the need for architects to deprofessionalise in order to pave the way for what design theorist and architect Giancarlo de Carlo once called '(t)he discovery of the users' needs',[22] and he highlighted the importance of returning the responsibility of determining the spaces needed for collective living back to the whole group of residents. Schmidt, instead, considered different degrees of expertise not only an undeniable fact, but also an indispensable factor to guarantee the desired outcome of a design project. It didn't matter if an architect-as-coresident was perceived as a ruling expert who might be tempted to act in their own favour as a future resident; they still had to bear the legal responsibility for inevitable planning decisions. Their knowledge on technical issues, building law, or questions of construction costs committed them to claim certain responsibilities that others could not claim. This was a prerequisite to getting any building built and to ensure that it would meet the expectations of as many people as possible in the best possible way, Schmidt explained. Moreover, he also saw certain opportunities in having the building's architects as coresidents. Firstly, they could provide specific support, for instance, by explaining how to do necessary work on the house on one's own, such as the refurbishment of the waterproofing of the wooden facade panels. Secondly, this constellation might enhance the quality of communication: as they were all coresidents who knew each other quite well, most people did not hesitate to tell them if there was something they did not like, Schmidt said. And they could directly refer to a critique, agree or disagree, discuss possible solutions to a problem, and question whether there actually was a true problem or not.

Christoph Schmidt presented yet another interesting point of view, one that illustrates a sociomaterial quality of space that also helps to shed the dualism 'architect-resident'. When a student asked him how often the common space was used by all of the residents simultaneously, Schmidt answered that this only happened once or twice a year and that there were also long periods during which nobody made any use of it at all. In Schmidt's view, a regular collective use of this space could never be forced, and if someone tried to do so, the room would probably end up as a representation of an obligation to live in common. Instead, he described it as an optional space with a potential to trigger individual or joint actions, which could help to widen one's own perspectives and even provide a chance to slip into other roles. Schmidt gave three distinct examples in this regard. First, he told how he occasionally found himself cooking huge amounts of pasta for sixteen children in the common space since a resident built a kitchenette for the room. Then he spoke about a recent initiative of two or three coresidents, who organised monthly public concerts and that he liked to 'play the guy' who stood at the entrance of the room to welcome guests and to collect donations for the musicians. And finally, Schmidt mentioned that, a few years ago, the co-housing group had agreed on a proposal of some of its members to turn the common space into a temporary shelter for refugees for a period of roughly one year. Taken together, the depictions of R50's architects reveal the processual nature of co-housing as an activity of both reflecting or even questioning and redefining the role of its participants, as well as imagining and creating social relationships, and they illustrate how such activities may be stimulated by the adoptability of its spatial structure. However, if co-housing is not only a specific activity, but also an expression of activism and thus a conscious positioning towards sociopolitical questions, it is the architects' emphasis on R50's 'connections' and thresholds as an 'offer to the city',[23] and the strong examples in this regard, that seem to be particularly noteworthy. On the one hand, this leads back to the open letter which was the subject of the first section of this essay and its claim of 'integrating the responsibility of every single participant' of co-housing projects 'for the development of [. . .] the city'.[24] Here, architects argued both as people who had been subjected to a top-down decision-making process that had threatened to become an impediment to their professional careers, and as acting subjects who tried to generate more public attention for their own architectural projects and for self-initiative and collaboration as the proper means to develop the city. On the other hand, as soon as such architects are also residents in a co-housing project they initiated, this project is more than just a showcase of planning professionals. It becomes the very place where architects, in view of the public attention they wished for, may have to prove that they truly live the claimed responsibility 'for the development of the city'. It is thus not surprising that Jesko Fezer, in speaking of the ambition to create 'new social types of housing', pointed out an aspect that brought his role as a resident into play.[25] He contextualised the middle-class members of R50 within a city that since the end of the 2000s had experienced an enormous pressure of growth and ever-rising costs for housing, and he explained, that relatively privileged people, who could afford to build their own house and possess their own apartments in a neighbourhood characterised by lower income groups should become aware of how they take part in a process of gentrification and respond to it. Against this background, the common space on subterranean level may be understood as an attempt to give something back to the city and its inhabitants after having taken one of its properties – and in this sense, this space results from reflecting both the possibility and necessity of creating a broader 'we' with collaborative housing.

23
Heiss and Heide, interview.

24
'Offener Brief'.

25
Fezer, interview.

Bibliography

Colomb, Claire. *Staging the New Berlin: Place Marketing and the Politics of Urban Reinvention Post-1989*. Abingdon, Oxon: Routledge, 2012.

de Carlo, Giancarlo. 'Architecture's Public'. In *Architecture and Participation*, edited by Peter Blundell Jones, Doina Petrescu and Jeremy Till, 3–22. Abingdon: Spon Press, 2007.

Düwel, Jörn, and Michael Mönninger, eds. *Von der Sozialutopie zum städtischen Haus: Texte und Interviews von Hans Stimmann*. Berlin: DOM publishers, 2011.

Fezer, Jesko. 'Stadtentwicklung und Stadtpolitik – Gespräch zur Baugruppe R50 in Berlin'. Interview by Christian Berkes. *Urbanophil, Netzwerk für urbane Kultur*, 10 July 2011. http://www.urbanophil.net/stadtentwicklung-stadtpolitik/gesprach-zur-baugruppe-r50-in-berlin/. Accessed 1 June 2021.

Hain, Simone. 'Berlin's Urban Development Discourse: Symbolic Action and the Articulation of Hegemonic Interests'. In *The Berlin Reader: A Compendium on Urban Change and Activism*, edited by Matthias Berndt, Britta Grell, and Andrej Holm, 53–65. Bielefeld: transcript, 2013.

Hertweck, Florian. *Der Berliner Architekturstreit. Architektur, Stadtbau, Geschichte und Identität in der Berliner Republik 1989–1999*. Berlin: Gebr. Mann Verlag, 2010.

Käpplinger, Claus. 'Individualität in Gemeinschaft ist möglich – Wohnhaus R50, Berlin'. March 2014. https://www.dbz.de/artikel/dbz_Individualitaet_in_Gemeinschaft_ist_moeglich_Wohnhaus_R50_Berlin_1946554.html. Accessed 1 June 2021.

'Offener Brief Berliner Architekten'. *Arch+: Zeitschrift für Architektur und Städtebau*. Last modified 8 November 2010. https://www.archplus.net/home/news/7,1-4947,5,0.html. Accessed 1 June 2021.

'R50. Ifau und Jesko Fezer, Heide & von Beckerath'. *Arch+: Zeitschrift für Architektur und Städtebau*, no. 201/202 (March 2011): 1–16.

Stimmann, Hans. *Stadthäuser. Handbuch und Planungshilfe*. Berlin: DOM publishers, 2011.

Fig. 1 Hsieh Ying-Chun's house and the Atelier-3 office in Ita Thao, 40 YiDa Thao Road. (Photograph by © Valeria Federighi)

Resisting from Within: The Ita Thao house and settlement as breeding ground for design innovation

Valeria Federighi

40 YiDa Thao Road

Atelier-3, the practice founded by Taiwanese architect Hsieh Ying-Chun, is known for its work in post-disaster reconstruction. The office designs and builds houses by the hundreds for ethnic minorities across China and Taiwan, employing a technique that allows local communities to take part in the construction process. The construction of the Ita Thao settlement was a turning point in Hsieh Ying-Chun's career. Before that, he had been conducting what he now refers to as a conventional practice, with a number of publicly commissioned designs dedicated to the Hakka culture, such as the Hsinchu Cultural Center and the Meinung Hakka Cultural Museum in Taiwan.

Because of his previous work dedicated to the Hakka minority, after the 1999 earthquake hit Taiwan, Hsieh Ying-Chun was contacted by anthropologist Fred Y. L. Chiu, who was working with the Ita Thao community in the area of Sun Moon Lake in central Taiwan. The members of the community had been residing in Dehua Village, but a large majority of them had been left homeless after the earthquake. Hsieh Ying-Chun insisted they exploit the possibilities offered by a national-scale, post-disaster situation to relocate to their original settlement site, from which they had been forcibly removed fifty years earlier. On 5 December 1999, Hsieh moved his office and home from Taichung to Dehua, and by the following February the construction of the whole Ita Thao settlement had been completed.

The settlement now occupies about one hectare of publicly owned land, extending south to north along a sloping terrain, on the southeast shore of the lake. Strategically, Hsieh's home and the Atelier-3 office sit at the far end of the settlement. Whoever visits the office – clients, employees, sympathisers – comes face-to-face with its social implications and with the role it has played in the life of the small community. Since the land is occupied illegally, the registered address of Atelier-3 is still in Taichung, although the Taiwanese address listed on the website is no. 40 YiDa Thao Road. The address does not officially exist even though the tribe has paid around 9000 yuan every month in electricity bills[1] since it established the settlement and are now negotiating a formal utility with Taipower, the national provider of electric power in Taiwan.[2]

After the initial period of post-disaster emergency was over, the authorities repeatedly but unsuccessfully attempted to evict the community in order to develop the site as tourist resort.[3] Since then, the political standing of the Ita Thao appears to have improved noticeably: in 2001, the tribe was recognised as independent Aboriginal Community of Taiwan rather than a subset of another community

1 Shih, 'Electricity costs 9.000 a month'.

2 Interview with Shao-yi Chiang, designer at Atelier-3, January 2019.

3 Interview with Hsieh Ying-Chun, January 2016. Where not otherwise specified, the information provided comes from these two main interviews and from a site visit carried out in January 2016. Although I wasn't able to retrieve any specific information regarding the tourist resort, the name of the Garden Peacock Hotel comes up repeatedly in local media as the proposed object of development for the site.

as had been the case before; in 2006 the Thao Community Parliament was instituted;[4] and, finally, in early 2018, the Han Chinese-imposed name 'Dehua' (德化 – a term originating from the phrase 'civilizing the aborigines with virtues'[5]) was removed from the police office of the village.[6] Currently, Atelier-3 feels quite confident that the community is not in immediate danger of forced relocation as policies towards aboriginal cultures have improved over time.[7] The role that the building of the settlement played in the recognition of this aboriginal community is hard to assess objectively. However, it cannot be denied that the re-establishment of the community through a clear spatial definition of its boundaries (where) and, thus, its members (who) coincided, in terms of time, with the beginning of a larger and more official recognition of its rights as a specific and independent minority group. For a historically dispossessed people, the demarcation of land appears here as the foundational act through which to claim further recognition. For the architect, this allows for a very specific narrative in which the project – broadly intended as a process (identification of the land, development and refinement of the technological elements, design of the houses, process of construction) – boldly enforces a specific set of rights and allows for a public discussion to be carried out over a built set of objects (the settlement) rather than over abstract values (for instance, the legal ownership of the land versus the legitimacy of the aboriginal community's claim).

The only non-Thao household belonging to the community – the house and office of Atelier-3 – now stands as a political statement, as a signifier of a type of practice that takes a clear stand and wholly and unapologetically upholds a specific set of values as non-negotiable, even in the face of institutional contempt. In their continuing work with dispossessed communities and post-disaster relief reconstruction, Atelier-3 consistently refers to that initial project through the location of their office and everything it stands for. The Ita Thao settlement and house is the first project of this kind, and is to this day the most significant among the projects carried out by the office, as it worked as a breeding ground for a technological element later to become a signature of their work, as well as offering a house where the architect and his office have resided now for almost twenty years.

Who builds [whose] architecture

In an oft-quoted passage, Edward Ford explains the main difference in approach between socially engaged practitioners in the nineteenth and twentieth centuries: 'Insofar as twentieth-century architects have concerned themselves with the social consequences of their work, they have focused on the way in which buildings affect the behavior of their occupants. Insofar as nineteenth-century architects concerned themselves with the social consequences of their work, they focused on the way in which buildings affect those who build them.'[8] The particularity of Atelier-3's activity is that it allows these two social concerns to overlap. For Hsieh Ying-Chun, 'everyone should be the producers of their own house, instead of the consumers.'[9] In the office's

4
Huang, 'Sixteen years after the disaster, the Thao are still in crisis'.

5
Pin-chuan, 'Police station renamed for Thao'.

6
The 'Dehua' denomination was the last of a series of colonial tags assigned to the tribe from their original displacement under the Qing Dynasty, through the Japanese domination, and the Han-Chinese Nationalist Party (KMT) government. Cheung, 'Taiwan in time'.

7
Still, newspapers did report in 2016 that the authorities made a few attempts to evict the community. See for instance, Shih, 'Electricity costs 9.000 a month'.

8
Ford, quoted in Deamer, 'Introduction'.

9
Chen-Yu and Ying-Chun, 'People's Architecture', 2.

Fig. 2 Diagram of the Ita Thao settlement agreement-in-action construction process. (Drawing embedded in diagram, © Atelier-3)

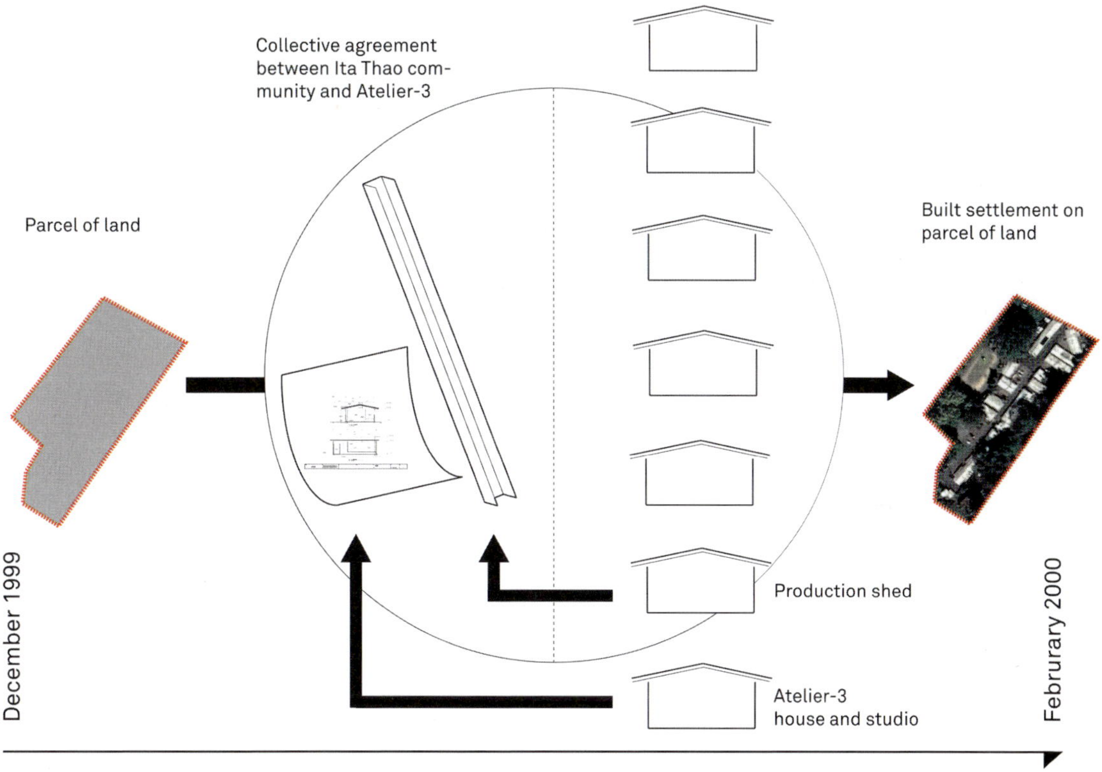

10
Quoted from a statement describing the work of the office, produced for the recent exhibition *Acts Without Effort: The Societal Architecture of Hsieh Ying-Chun*, dedicated to the work of Atelier-3, running from 21 September 2018 to 10 February 2019 at the Kaohsiung Museum of Fine Arts. This method described is reminiscent of a long tradition of an open-building approach based on the idea that buildings are actions rather than products and should act as collectors of communal energies, allowing for a direct involvement of end users to various degrees. The first project of this kind to be constructed in China was the Wuxi Experimental

'eight core values', this approach is referenced to as 'open-building approach' and rests on a distinction between skeleton and infill: 'Under the premise of [reinforced light-gauge steel], the "supports" are made with the light-gauge steel framework, ensuring [an] adequate and safe structure, while allowing various "infills" to attach to such as local craftsmanship, scavenged local materials and various spatial needs.'[10]

When faced with the necessity of resettling the tribe after the earthquake, the architect decided to work closely with community members to expedite construction times and reduce costs. As the narrative goes, the tribe members did not want houses made of bamboo; they would rather have ones made of concrete. Thus, Hsieh managed the construction of a model house to show what the final result would be. In the process, the technological details for the use of the lightweight steel frame were developed and ultimately refined, allowing for the use of widely available and cost-effective hardware, tools, and steel. A small production shed was set up at the lower end of the slope, where steel members were delivered, and then punched and cut according to the drawings.

Fig. 3 Diagram of the continuing practice of Atelier-3. (Drawing embedded in diagram, © Atelier-3)

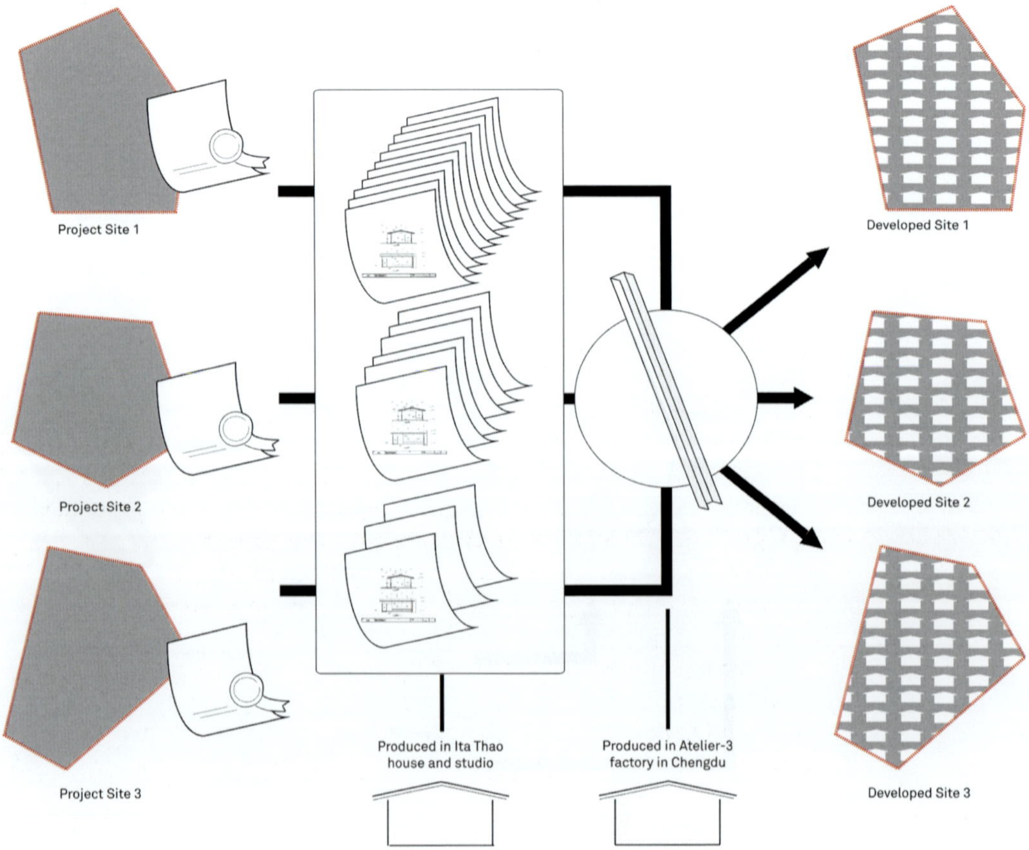

The fact that steel members allowed everyone to participate in the construction process proved to be strategic on two counts. On one hand, it expedited the building process and allowed the tribe to occupy the land in a matter of weeks. On the other, it effectively engendered a new collectivity around the act of building, one that included all those taking part. Building is a communal act, allowing participants to be in a constant process of agreement-in-action, and revolves around the sociotechnical objects of construction drawings and steel members, both accessible to end users/builders and both necessary to carry out the work.

[Big] scale, [big] change

Contemporary socially engaged architecture usually retreats from testing its effectiveness on a measure of scale, preferring to explore the possibility that small-scale projects may ultimately engender larger-scale effects, and resisting as dangerous the modern-scented notion that architecture might obtain social relevance through large-scale transformations. 'Tactical' design and 'acupunctural' urbanism work in such a way,[11] and

Project, dating back to 1981 and designed by Bao Jiasheng (Li 2015), of which Hsieh Ying-Chun is likely aware. Atelier-3's strategy is different from this particular tradition of open-building approach in that it is is framed around a narrative of sheer technical feasibility. The focus is on the lightweight steel member, its flexibility and its adaptive configurations, as well as the social inclusivity of the building process it generates.

11
Brenner, 'Is Tactical Urbanism an Alternative to Neoliberal Urbanism?'

12
Federighi, 'The Informal Stance: Representations of Architectural Design and Informal Settlements'.

13
Interview with Shao-yi Chiang; many websites speak of up to three thousand units altogether.

14
Ying-Chun, 'The Reconstruction of the Housing after the '88 Flood in Taiwan'.

curatorial endeavours such as the MoMA exhibition *Small Scale, Big Change* demonstrate the resonance – disciplinary and otherwise – of the trend. The small scale is employed as a way to politely mediate the institutional and normative nature of architectural work: the smaller the intervention, the less intrusive on local conditions which are by definition unknowable, or at least not fully knowable, to the architect. Disciplinary discourse around socially engaged architecture superimposes large-scale design with deterministic and top-down interventions; this engenders a paradoxical but enduring divergence between the constant and ever-active search for a renewed social relevance of disciplinary tools and a wider loss of faith in the project – the disciplinary tool par excellence – as a way to envision societal change.[12]

Atelier-3 employs around thirty people in design and sixty in production; its total number of built units, at the time of writing, amounts to 623 in China and 1,087 in Taiwan.[13] This is a high number and is testament to the fact that the office's stance is not one of polite reductionism in the face of delicate ethical issues, but rather one of steady growth in line with a consistent social project. In general terms, the legitimation of such a project rests on the body of work carried out over time by the office: as figure 3 shows, the aspiration to quantitative relevance makes it necessary to follow a more conventional process, one where the work of negotiating norms and rights is carried out by other actors – often NGOs involved with local minorities – and where the office can focus on the design and construction phase. The act of collective building still offers a moment of agreement-in-action, but one that is inserted into a priori defined boundaries. Since the building of the Ita Thao community, the office has continued to develop the steel-member technique, although the degree to which it is possible to involve future inhabitants in the construction process varies from time to time.

The building code in China, especially in rural areas and in post-disaster situations, commonly allows for some degree of participation. In 2008, Atelier-3 was hired by the NGOs World Vision Taiwan and Red Cross Taiwan to manage the reconstruction of five hundred houses for three different minorities after the Sichuan earthquake.[14] In order to participate in the bid, Atelier-3 had to borrow a bigger contractor's license, and later hired the communities as subcontractors, thus allowing them to legally carry out construction work and paying them by the day. Other times, Atelier-3 has carried out the building of the structures and leaves the construction of partitions and minor details up to the inhabitants.

In 2009, after Typhoon Morakot hit Taiwan, Atelier-3 managed the construction of almost one thousand houses for aboriginal communities in remote areas across the south and east of the island: in Taiwan, though, building codes are more restrictive than in China and the future inhabitants could not be involved in the process of construction at all. In order to sidestep this issue and guarantee some form of community involvement in the construction, in the

Fig. 4 Diagram of the Ita Thao house and settlement as site of resistance. (Drawing embedded in diagram, © Atelier-3)

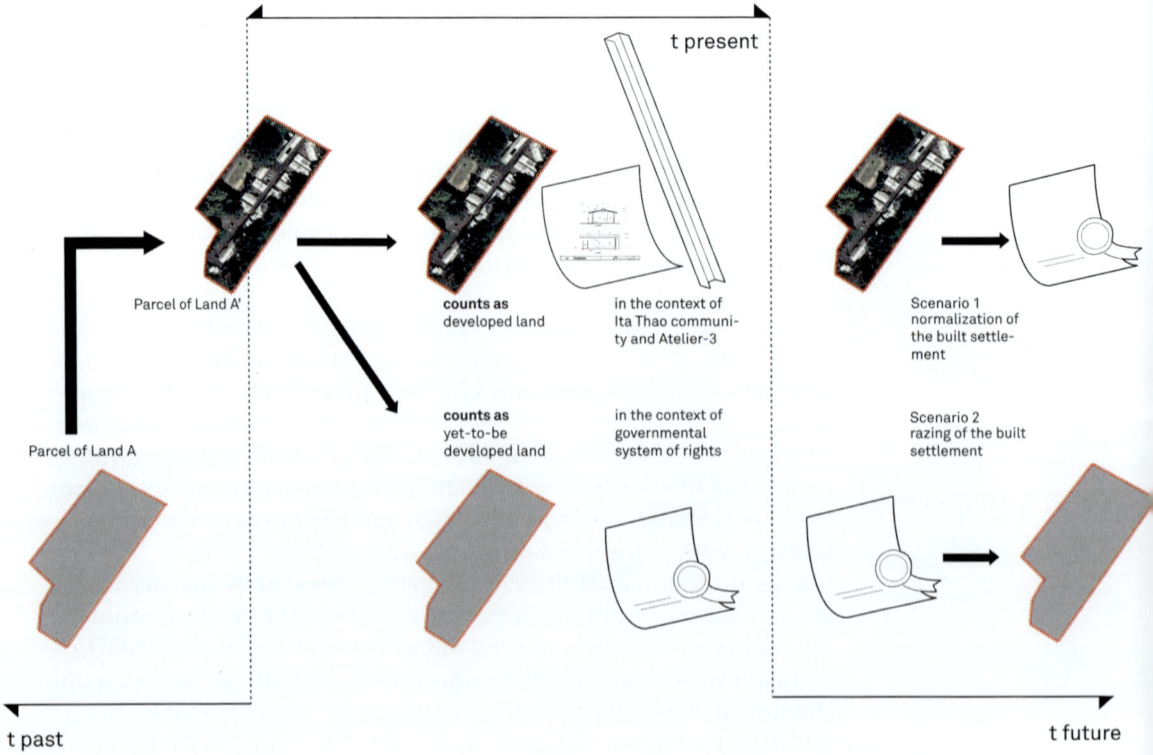

2014 project for Ari Mountain, the space of the foundations was left bare as a possible basement extension to be added later, although the houses were handed to the inhabitants as fully completed units.

For the Curry Stone jury, awarding Hsieh Ying-Chun the Curry Stone Design Prize in 2011 in recognition for his humanitarian work with Atelier-3, the involvement of villagers in the reconstruction of their own homes was particularly significant, and was further enhanced by the decision to employ them during agriculturally idle months, when construction work wouldn't 'conflict with farming cycles'.[15] The cooperative activity that self-building involved was seen as 'therapy' and praised as a pragmatic way to cut costs drastically, together with the use of inexpensive construction material. According to the office, 'the simplification of techniques [...] flattens the value of labor in certain areas, reducing technical boundaries in a highly professionalized society.'[16] Although this is certainly nothing particularly new, as it is clearly reminiscent of a number of experimental practices in developing countries spanning the whole of the twentieth century, the scale to which these processes have been applied is nonetheless impressive. The deliberate coupling of a specific and well-mastered technology with a specific ethical mandate was instrumental in achieving large-scale effectiveness – which is, indeed, something new when it comes to socially engaged architectural practices.

15
'Hsieh Ying-Chun'.

16
Ying-Chun, 'The Reconstruction of the Housing after the '88 Flood in Taiwan'.

17
A notable exception is to be made with reference to the work that Hsieh Ying-Chun carried out, on different occasions between 2004 and 2009, as part of the collective *Weak!* together with architects Marco Casagrande and Roan Ching-Yueh. The work of *Weak!* explored the role of architects as piratical actors, balanced between their institutional role and the choice to resist top-down actions. In this sense, and on the part of Hsieh Ying-Chun, *Weak!* can be read as an attempt to continue exploring the more subversive side to the Ita Thao house and settlement project.

18
Chen, quoted in Wu, 'Enabling Solidarity into the Steel: Rethinking Innovation from East Asian Cases'.

A trajectory of design innovation

The Ita Thao house and settlement are sites of ongoing resistance, a peculiar resistance in that a relevant part of it is being carried out by a professional whose role would conventionally entail mediating between clients and institutionalised norms. In moving his house and office to the settlement, Hsieh Ying-Chun makes a bold statement: so bold, in fact, that he need not (or cannot) make it again. From this moment on, his work is carried out within the boundaries of norms; his house and office are still in Ita Thao, and his work is dedicated to the improvement and development of the values – both technical and social – that that first project marked as defining of his practice.[17]

Thus, the use and adaptation of widely available lightweight steel members is the device through which Atelier-3 reaches social effectiveness, as it allows a merger of two social categories – builders and users – that benefits both. Hsin-Hsing Chen calls these rebuilding efforts 'the first large appropriate technology project' in Taiwan, for it consciously designs progressive social values into technological innovation and social organization.'[18] In the building of the Ita Thao house and community, the lightweight steel member works as a social aggregator. A specific kind of political and design activism takes place as a consequence of the application of a technological element allowing the inhabitants to successfully and cheaply occupy a plot of land to which they claimed a pre-existing right of use in the course of three months. By looking at the trajectory of the firm's work, it is possible to assess the progression from initial disruption (invention) in the use of the lightweight steel member as bred within the Ita Thao settlement construction – as a way to reach agreement-in-action and allow for a necessarily expedited building process – to the consolidation of such disruption as innovation within the day-to-day work of the practice and its wider objectives.

Atelier-3's use of the steel member is innovative in that it combines three converging trajectories: first, the technology itself has been simplified as much as possible (according to the office, they have progressively cut down the number of joints needed to build complex structures to ten per cent of the number of joints present on the market); secondly, the number of construction drawings needed for each unit decreased from three hundred drawings per unit in the first settlement projects to five drawings per unit in 2015; and thirdly, the design and logistical apparatus revolving around the simplified technology was progressively enhanced. While a small shed was set up for production purposes during the construction of the Ita Thao settlement, during the 2009 reconstruction job in south and east Taiwan, Atelier-3 set up another makeshift production site, or 'factory', where steel members were collected, cut, punched and, if necessary, underwent a first assembly through welding. Finally, in Chengdu, for the post-earthquake reconstruction, a stable production site was set up which exists to this day and is employed for most jobs in mainland China and beyond. During the reconstruction project in Nepal, steel members for the

Fig. 5 Makeshift production site, 2009.
(Photograph by © Atelier-3)

whole development were prepared in the laboratory in Chengdu and then transported over the mountains to the job site.

The case of the Ita Thao house and settlement is necessarily unique, as it requests a long-term involvement that can be hardly replicated – the office still resides there and still produces working drawings for other jobs there. It allowed the office to test the full performative power of a sociotechnical process of collective building, as well as gain lasting legitimation for the pursuing of a social project over time. Subsequently, the innovation element gradually shifts from the (politically and otherwise) disruptive application of the lightweight steel member, to its normalisation within large-scale processes of inclusive building. Thus, in the firm's most recent work, a narrative of scale substitutes a narrative of political engagement, in a necessary move from a non-replicable, long-term political involvement to the measurable effectiveness of a large number of houses built through minimal design and economic effort.

Altrock, Uwe and Sonia Schoon. 'Conceded Informality: Scopes of Informal Urban Restructuring in the Pearl River Delta'. *Habitat International* 43 (2014): 214–20.

Boyarsky, Nicholas. 'Reconstruction Solidarity: The Thao Tribe'. *Architectural Design* 73, no. 5 (September/October 2003): 86–9.

Brenner, Neil. 'Is tactical urbanism an alternative to neoliberal urbanism?' In *Critique of Urbanization*, edited by Neil Brenner , 128–46. Basel: Bauwelt Fundamente Series, Birkhäuser Verlag, 2016.

Chen-Yu, Chiu and Hsieh Ying-Chun. 'People's Architecture: Architect HSIEH Ying-Chun and His Post-Disaster Reconstruction Work in East Asia'. 6th International Alvar Aalto Meeting on Contemporary Architecture: Technology and Humanism, 14–15 September 2017. Seinäjoki, Finland. https://www.alvaraalto.fi/content/uploads/2017/08/chiu_chen-yu_hsieh_ying-chun.pdf. Accessed 11 May 2021.

Cheung, Han. 'Taiwan in time: a community that needed to "change"'. *Taipei Times*, 14 October 2018.

Deamer, Peggy. 'Introduction'. In *The Architect as Worker: Immaterial Labor, the Creative Class, and the Politics of Design*, edited by Peggy Deamer, xxvii–xxxvi. London: Bloomsbury, 2015.

Dutton, Thomas A. and Lian Hurst Mann. 'Introduction'. In *Reconstructing Architecture: Critical Discourse and Spatial Practices*, edited by T. A. Dutton and L. H. Mann, 1–26. Minneapolis: University of Minnesota Press, 1996.

Federighi, Valeria. *The Informal Stance: Representations of Architectural Design and Informal Settlements*. San Francisco: Applied Research+Design, ORO Editions, 2018.

Huang, Yi-ying. '[回家]災後十六年 邵族仍然面對危機' ('[Home coming] Sixteen years after the disaster, the Thao are still in crisis'). *Public Television Service News Network* (14 September 2015).

'Hsieh Ying-Chun', Curry Stone Design Prize 2011, https://currystonefoundation. org/practice/hsiehying-chun/. Accessed 8 January 2021.

Pin-Chuan, Liu. 'Police Station renamed for Thao'. *Taipei Times*, 5 October 2018.

Riano, Quilian. 'Relearning the Social: Architecture and Change. A Review of the MoMA Exhibition Small Scale, Big Change'. *Places: Design Observer* (October 2010).

Roan, Ching-Yueh. 'Xie Yingjun yi shehuixing de jieru zhiyi xiandai jianzhu de fangxiang (Hsieh Ying Chun challenges modern architecture with its social engagement)'. *Shidai jianzhu* (Time Architecture) 4, (2007): 38–43.

Shanshan, Li. 'Post-Occupancy Evaluation of Two Open Building Projects'. *Open House International* 40, no. 4 (2015): 94–100.

Shih, Hsiu-Chuan. '電費每月9000塊、住17年沒地權邵族人「不存在」的伊達邵街' ('Electricity costs 9.000 a month, Thao people who have lived without land rights for 17 years "don't exist" on Yida Thao Street'). *The Storm Media*, 17 March 2017.

Wu, Chia-Ling. 'Enabling Solidarity into the Steel: Rethinking Innovation from East Asian Cases'. *East Asian Science, Technology and Society* 3, no. 1 (2009): 1–3.

Ying-Chun, Hsieh. 'The Reconstruction of the Housing after the '88 Flood in Taiwan'. In *Illegal Architecture*, edited by Wang Shu and Hsieh Ying-Chu, 22–3. Taipei: Gardencity, 2012.

Resisting Socioeconomic Norms and Regulations

The four chapters included in this section demonstrate how architects have sought to formulate alternatives to exclusionary housing markets, social norms, and oppressive planning systems through the design of their own homes. Here, architects use their own houses to test novel approaches towards construction and building manufacturing processes. In the case of House in Butantã, as discussed by Michele Gentile; the C.E.C.A. House, which is the subject of Peter Swinnen's chapter; and Interloop architects, discussed in Scott Colman's contribution; architects' houses were part of a larger ensemble of, respectively, two, eight, and an undefined number of homes (Interloop's house was part of a larger collaborative development effort involving also other architectural offices). This facilitated experimentation with standardised production methods and prefabrication aimed at affordability through economy of scale.

Michele Gentile's chapter, 'House in Butantã', revisits the house that architect Paulo Mendes da Rocha designed and built for himself between 1964 and 1966, a time of political turmoil in Brazil. While some architects of the time accused Mendes da Rocha and others of accepting commissions from a politically oppressive regime, his own home, built as one of a pair of identical homes, was intended to expose some of the political and social issues of this difficult historical period for Brazil. The architect subverted the internal configuration of programmes and the relationship with the city as expected by bourgeois domestic norms. Also, Gentile argues, his choice for reinforced concrete was a political/economic gesture as it provided employment for the rural immigrants in search of work. The C.E.C.A. House, which was a prototype developed by architects Willy Van Der Meeren and Léon Palm in the mid 1950s in Belgium and is discussed in Peter Swinnen's chapter, 'C.E.C.A. House', targeted more affordable housing solutions for working class families. Struggling to find a way into mass production, the house did find implementation in an experimental co- housing project just outside Brussels composed of eight units, one of which inhabited by Van Der Meeren himself. Although in this setup the house was culturally appropriated by the middle classes and its affordability compromised, it still offered an opportunity for the architect to continue experimenting with the potentials of this prototype in terms of materiality, spatial configuration, and communal living through co-housing around communal gardens. Also, in the more contemporary setting of mid 2000s Houston in the US, efforts towards affordable housing can be found in the experiments by Interloop Architecture, as discussed by Scott Colman in his chapter 'Pliable Praxis House'. Interloop shows how architects, while being fully immersed in the dominant political economies governing architecture, can also resist the cultural expectations tied to such economy; for instance, through spacious single-family homes in sprawling suburbs. In response to the increasingly volatile nature of that political economy, Interloop offers instead a 'pliable praxis', a way of working and producing that accepts contingency and the need for flexibility. As Colman shows, the architects' modestly sized own home-cum-office offers a testing ground for such an approach, including experimental collaborations between a collective of architects and the modelling of architectural production on the used-car market and off-the-shelf components industries.

The final chapter in this section, 'Good Fences Make Good Neighbours (So They Say)' by Kirsty Volz, wraps up this discussion by adding an important note of caution. Volz brings a compelling case of her own house built together with her partner in Brisbane, Australia, prompting the question: How much resistance can an individual home shoulder? Volz's house straddles a very narrow plot, restrictive planning regulations obsessed with neighbourly privacy, and mortgage requirements abiding by the rules of a financialised housing market. In navigating these various 'clients' and resisting regulations and requirements that sacrifice important spatial qualities for the sake of absolute privacy, the house opted for an opening up towards the neighbours. Intended to expose the shortcomings of urban planning regulations and instead emphasising the importance of redefining priorities for architectural quality, their gesture was met with resistance. The Volz house demonstrates the limits of how much resistance a single project can sustain.

House in Butantã: The politics of the villa, beyond the privateness of the domestic space

Michele Gentile

Paulo Mendes da Rocha's House in Butantã, designed between 1964 and 1966, can be regarded as the cornerstone of extensive research conducted by the Escola Paulista (São Paulo School) on the theme of the single-family villa.[1] The dwelling, intended for the Mendes da Rocha family, exemplifies all the themes connected with the critique of the bourgeois domestic environment that, from the 1950s, were introduced in São Paulo's architectural scene by Vilanova Artigas.[2] This text intends to offer an explanation about how the domestic space of a middle-class, single-family villa became a political project. Beginning with an overview of the complex historical period in which the House in Butantã was conceived, the text examines how its architectural features reacted to the politics and culture of the time.

The São Paulo School and the Brazilian political context during the military coup

The construction of the House in Butantã started in 1964, the year of the military coup in Brazil, which removed the left-wing government of João Goulart and established a military dictatorship that lasted until 1985.[3] Over the following twenty years, ideas of modernisation, economic development, and industrialisation were pursued with liberal policies backed by foreign investment, to the detriment of freedom, democracy, and social justice. Politicians, intellectuals, artists, and regular citizens were persecuted, exiled, tortured, or assassinated and architects weren't excluded from this. Artigas and Mendes da Rocha were both affected by these acts of persecution and both were forced to leave their teaching positions at the Faculty of Architecture and Urban Planning at the University of São Paulo (FAU-USP).[4] Artigas, a member of the Communist Party spent the first years of the dictatorship in Uruguay and then returned clandestinely to Brazil. Mendes da Rocha was less politically exposed, and therefore was affected later and less violently by state repression and continued to live with his family in São Paulo.

Even though the political repression, which escalated from 1969 to 1979, continued to keep Artigas and Mendes da Rocha far from any academic role, it didn't prevent them from receiving assignments for the design of some public buildings like schools and social housing. The regime seemed more concerned about the ideas that architects could transmit to younger generations through their teachings than about the possibility of influencing citizens' behaviour through the design of buildings.[5]

In designing public buildings, Artigas, Mendes da Rocha, and other members of the São Paulo School were severely criticised

1
Escola Paulista, or the São Paulo School, refers to a movement of intellectuals and architects born within the Modern Movement around 1950s and close to the academic environment of the Faculty of Architecture and Urban Planning at the University of São Paulo (FAU-USP).

2
Vilanova Artigas (1915–1985) was the greatest exponent of the São Paulo School and primary mentor of Paulo Mendes da Rocha. He was the one who promoted a programme of radical teaching reform at the FAU-USP.

3
For a detailed discussion about the cultural and political context between the military coup and the affirmation of the dictatorship, see Schwarz, 'Culture and Politics in Brazil'.

4
FAU-USP was built in 1968 as the meeting point of the engineering excellence of the technical school of São Paulo and the humanistic background from the Faculty of Literature and Philosophy. The aim was to create a new academic environment where the students would become professionals able to fight for the development of the country with both technical and humanistic competencies.

5
León, 'Designing Dissent'.

by the most politicised fringes within FAU-USP. The group called Arquitectura Nova publicly accused Artigas and his collaborators of being at the service of the regime, having betrayed the original resistance ideals.[6] Although the position of these architects might appear contradictory, because they collaborated with the regime, their political ideals were strong. They repudiated acts of public contestation or the use of violence in resisting the regime and, instead, opposed it through the only means at their disposal, their architecture. The political function of architecture and the social accountability of the architect were the common ground on which the entire São Paulo School was founded. The architectural project was understood beyond simple formal composition and became an essential element of the resistance. Artigas, interviewed on this topic, said, 'São Paulo School is not a lexicon, a set of vocabulary [...]; instead, it is the propensity to resolve the issues that a community, as the Paulistana one, has.'[7]

Certainly, the progressive left-wing ideology, propagated in those years by the Brazilian Communist Party (PCB), was decisive and it defined the background for academic and professional practice. In Brazil, the PCB differed from the ideals of the majority of communist parties overseas. They did not consider the working class as the undisputed protagonist of the revolution. Rather, they saw in the bourgeoisie and in the entrepreneurialism of the emergent middle class the only force capable of leading the country towards a reversal of the dominant power and towards a change of the social order. The PCB thought that it was only by shaping the upper classes that it would be possible to influence and lead the rest of the population towards revolution, obtaining a more egalitarian society and more modern Brazil.[8]

During the years of the so-called Brazilian Miracle (1968–1973), the entrepreneurial middle class was on the rise and led the economic development of the country, together with the bourgeoisie. The country experienced extraordinary growth – the average annual GDP grew at a rate of ten per cent and rural–urban migration increased from three million people in the 1940s to seventeen million in the 1970s.[9] This sudden development led to a frenetic urbanisation process in which cities continued to expand following the foreign urban model imported at the beginning of the Portuguese colonisation. The resultant urban growth was characterised by the proliferation of residential building types, constructed not only to house the many workers migrating from rural communities, but also to offer better housing conditions for the growing middle class. The single-family house and especially the villa was the typology predominantly chosen to domesticate the upper-middle classes.

In a few years this type of accommodation became widespread. However, rather than being enriched by Brazilian vernacular housing models, it was built following European domestic space patterns. In the old country, the house of the bourgeoisie was articulated in a series of private environments (bedrooms) connected through corridors to the other service spaces of the house (kitchen

6
Arquitectura Nova was founded in 1962 at the FAU-USP and composed of Sergio Ferro, Flavio Imperio, and Rodrigo Lefevre. All pupils of Villanova Artigas, during their university careers, they developed more radical political positions, collaborating with a more direct form of contestation the military regime.

7
Artigas, quoted in Sarno, 'L'architettura della scuola Paulistain Brasile', 129.

8
Skidmore, *The Politics of Military Rule in Brazil.*

9
Skidmore, *The Politics of Military Rule in Brazil.*

10
Navarro Martínez and Blanco Lage, 'Traspasando las fronteras del espacio privado'.

11
Navarro Martínez and Blanco Lage, 'Traspasando las fronteras del espacio privado'.

12
Gallanti, 'Architectura e trabalho libre'.

and bathroom), and both in turn connected with the unique common and representative area of the home (the living room). The number and dimensions of these rooms depended on the family's wealth, but the spatial organisation of the house was a constant.

In Europe the process of domestication of the upper-middle class, which led to the development of this model, was slow and accompanied the Western society for centuries. It was strictly influenced by the absolute predominance of the familiar model on any other types of human association. In Brazil, the process of domestication was somewhat more rapid, imposing itself on a completely different society with dissimilar uses, traditions, and forms of dwelling than those of the Europeans.[10] Historically, both colonial and indigenous housing in Brazil had less marked distinctions between public and private space. These dwellings, compared to the European tradition, offered few possibilities for inhabitants to exclude themselves because the majority of the space was shared by more people, who usually were connected beyond the relationships typical of the nuclear family.[11] Although São Paulo School references originate in the modern movement, elements of the Brazilian tradition can be recognised in single-family villas designed in São Paulo by this group of architects.

Obviously, materials and technologies used to build this type were far from those used in the precolonial tradition. The modern housing production system, based on the use of concrete cast in situ, was conceived as an instrument of direct political action. If in Europe architects suffered the influence of the industrialisation process and had adapted to it, in Brazil the São Paolo School sponsored, through the use of reinforced concrete, the development of the country. In this way, concrete became more than a simple aesthetic choice and actually represented clear political ideals connected with labour. The work to make the reinforced concrete was conceived as a way to offer employment to the high number of unskilled workers that arrived in the city to escape from the poor conditions of the countryside.[12]

The widespread use of the concrete, together with all the other architectural features of the single-family house, make this type a device capable of summarising the political and social issues of this difficult historical period. The House in Butantã, particularly, as well as the way in which it reinterpreted through concrete local technologies for the dwelling, subverts the classical relationship between the city and the house and revolutionises the domestic internal configuration, making itself a model for São Paolo's next generations.

House in Butantã

The villa, located on a corner plot on a hill west of São Paulo in the district of Butantã, was built together with an almost identical replica, intended for the architect's sister. The possibility of achieving two twin houses allowed the design process to become an experiment in prefabrication. Hidden behind that

Fig. 1 External view of the house with the earthworks in the foreground, House in Butantã. Paulo Mendes da Rocha, São Paulo, 1964. (Photograph by © Nelson Kon)

Fig. 2 View from the street of the space below the first floor, House in Butantã. Paulo Mendes da Rocha, São Paulo, 1964. (Photograph by © Nelson Kon)

13 Pisani, *Paulo Mendes da Rocha.*

experiment are both a critique of the bespoke construction of the single-family villa and an attempt to advance Brazilian industrialisation through the development of the prefabrication process. Although, in the end, the two houses were completed with beams and pillars cast in situ, they were designed as a set of modular elements that could, in theory, be produced in the factory and assembled on site. Therefore, each part of the dwelling was composed with precise modularity, perfectly related with an equally accurate structural setting that defined the composition of the entire project. As often happened with buildings that emerged out of the São Paulo School, the structure has a fundamental role in defining the entire project. The House in Butantã is the space contained between the two slabs, and how these two elements react with the artificial topography configured around them. The higher slab projects over the lower on two sides of the building and both rest on two main beams, each of which is supported by a couple of pillars higher than the street level. The shadow produced by the volume on the earthworks encircling the dwelling gives the building a sense of suspension, that it seems to float in mid-air **(Fig. 1)**.

The gesture of raising the volume automatically generates an intimate place above that still maintains an urban character. This porous threshold, which makes the approach to the home a spontaneous process, is defined by the earthworks obtained from the excavation of the building's foundations **(Fig. 2)**. These two elements, like an artificial geography, replace the barriers conventionally utilised to border the bourgeois villa and make this space part of the street and the city. The sense of private property is weakened and, in this, appears to be a clear critique on building speculation that in those years fragmented the city of São Paulo into a multitude of isolated parts. In addition to having softer boundaries surrounding the property, the House in Butantã also has an unusual perimeter; representative facades are absent and the walls seem to lose their principal function of separation thanks to all the elements designed by the architect to add connections with the outside of the villa. The long ribbon windows on the short sides of the building, together with all the smaller openings on the long sides and the skylights on the roof, generate a continuous space that breaks the ordinary distinction between the internal and external space.

From the area below the floating volume, stairs, placed on one of the short sides of the building, provide access to the main level of the house. The entire programme, except for the technical room and the car park on the ground floor, is located on this floor. The plan is organised in three strips that run perpendicular to the primary axis of the circulation, and architectural devices dedicated exclusively to circulation, like corridors, are eliminated **(Fig. 3)**.[13] Bedrooms are concentrated with the other service spaces like the kitchen and bathrooms in the core of the building, subverting completely the classical organisation of the villa, where all the representative spaces were located at the centre of the plan, clearly separated from the rest of the functions. In the House in Butantã,

Fig. 3 First-floor plan, House in Butantã. Paulo Mendes da Rocha, São Paulo, 1964. (© https://www.atlasofplaces.com/architecture/casa-butantae/#figure-5)

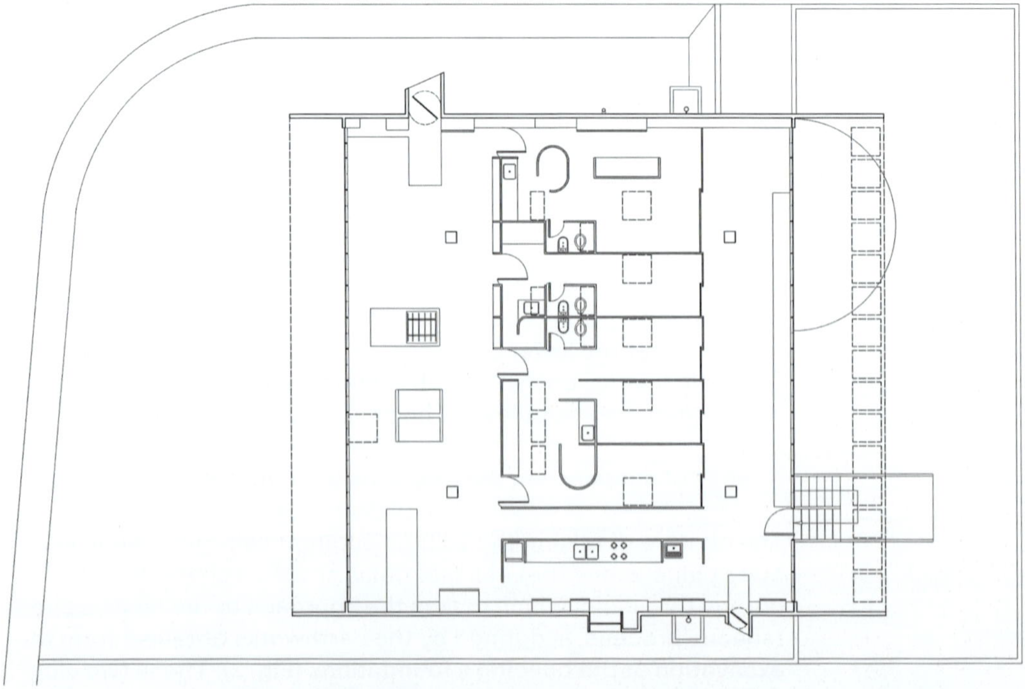

Fig. 4 View of the living room, House in Butantã. Paulo Mendes da Rocha, São Paulo, 1964. (Photograph by © Nelson Kon)

Fig. 5 View from the entrance, House in Butantã. Paulo Mendes da Rocha, São Paulo, 1964. (Photograph by © Nelson Kon)

instead, the central strip is compressed between the other two communal areas and divided by very skinny internal partitions which do not reach the ceiling. This feature, together with the minimal dimensions of the bedrooms and ability to cross through the house from one side to the other make complete isolation impossible. For Paulo Mendes da Rocha, 'There is no private space, only degrees of public space.'[14]

14
Spiro and Snozzi, *Paulo Mendes da Rocha*, 252.

The impossibility of isolating oneself suggests a constant sense of belonging to a community that was physically represented in the house by the two strips on the sides of the plan. These are spaces and occasions for the family and guests to cohabit and share common practices.

The first strip, opposite the stairway, is characterised by the presence of some concrete furniture such as the table, the sofas, and the chimney, which together organise the environment around some recurrent practices of domesticity **(Fig. 4)**. The second stripe, facing the entrance, is devoid of a specific function, which means almost a fifth of the house is occupied by this indefinite space, characterised just by a long strip window under which runs a long horizontal raised plane. All the bedrooms have sliding doors that can fully open on this area, fusing the central stripe with this part of the dwelling **(Fig. 5)**.

It is not easy to define this space, nor other areas of the house, using as a guide the types of function common to the European dwellings. The use of these spaces goes beyond strictly defined functions; it doesn't impose precise roles for each family member. Therefore, the kitchen is not a detached space dedicated to the labour of the housewife; the children's bedrooms are not isolated from the rest of the family; and the living room is not the place in which bourgeois habits find their perfect representation. The domestic space, instead, seems to have a character that is more urban than domestic. Apart from some common needs for living like cooking, eating, and sleeping, the rest of the space looks like a city environment where the flows, uses, and the occasions to meet each other multiply, leaving room for chance and indeterminacy.

The widespread use of concrete, which is everywhere in the house, not only augments this sense of urbanity, but it plays also many other roles. First of all, it has a structural function. It is also the enclosure material and used to build many of the furniture in the house. Last but not least, it is an aesthetic feature. Leaving the concrete face uncovered creates an opportunity to show the labour of the workers through the impressions on the material surface. In this way their work is clearly imprinted on the bourgeoise domesticity, acquiring its own dignity. Mendes da Rocha had clear political reasons in his choice of exposed concrete as a material. He wanted to move the condition of the bourgeois dwelling closer to that of the poorer classes in order to reduce the disparities that the Brazilian economic growth had accelerated in those years.

15
Arendt, *The Human Condition*, 199.

16
Flavio Motta, quoted in Mendes da Rocha and Artigas, *Paulo Mendes da Rocha: Fifty Years 1957–2007*, 18.

The philosopher and historian Flávio Motta defined the House in Butantã as expressing the idea of living in a rationalised favela. The austerity of its finishes, together with the indetermination of its spaces, are all features that recall São Paulo's suburbs, but also the architecture of indigenous tribes and vernacular dwellings developed in rural Brazil. In both these contexts, dwellings go beyond the canonical relationships connected to the nuclear family. The great common spaces that characterise the core of many rural house typologies, or the labyrinthic streets that are natural extensions of favela houses, become places where the individual disappears into the community.

Paulo Mendes da Rocha, together with other São Paulo School architects, seemed to recover these models to rediscover this communitarian way in which the Brazilian people interpreted domestic life for centuries.

Kenneth Frampton similarly described the empty space of the House in Butantã as a 'space of public appearance', borrowing a term put forward by Hannah Arendt. Namely, it was a place that originated in a prepolitical experience of 'being together', that potentially exists only when people meet constructing actions and speeches, 'but only potentially, not necessarily and not forever.'[15] The space of public appearance according to Arendt's view is the life-blood of the human artifice; it is in this place that humans build their ancestral relationships.

Frampton's and Motta's arguments help us to understand further the fundamental political and social role that the house played for Mendes da Rocha. Convinced about the reasons at the base of his project he sought to experience it with his family members, constructing that spatiality to have that relationship with them. Mendes da Rocha took the rigidity of the bourgeois villa and moved it towards a collective and public perspective where 'the liberty of everyone depends on the freedom of others'.[16] The dwelling was no longer an intimate place, a shelter from the city; the domestic space lost its privacy and the typology of the single family villa becomes political. From a passive space or, better, an imposed space, the house becomes active in the education of human behaviour, with the goal to encourage community formation, to fight individualism, and to challenge disparity promoted by the Brazilian dictatorship.

Bibliography

Arendt, Hannah. *The Human Condition*. Chicago: University of Chicago Press, 1998.

Frampton, Kenneth. *The Unfinished Modern Project at the End of Modernity: Tectonic Form and the Space of Public Appearance*, Soane Medal Lecture 2019. London: Sir John Soane's Museum, 2019.

Gallanti, Fabrizio. '"Arquitectura e trabalho libre": The Use of Concrete in the Escola Paulista and the Reorganisation of Labour in Brazil'. Architecture and Labour Space and the Production of Subjectivity Symposium, City/Architecture PhD programme, Architectural Association, London, 13 November 2015.

León, Ana María. 'Designing Dissent: Vilanova Artigas and the São Paulo School of Architecture'. In *Architecture and the Paradox of Dissidence*, edited by Ines Weizman, 74–88. London: Routledge, 2014.

Mendes da Rocha, Paulo and Rosa Camargo Artigas, eds. *Paolo Mendes da Rocha: Fifty Years 1957–2007*. New York: Rizzoli, 2009.

Navarro Martínez, Héctor, and Manuel Blanco Lage. 'Traspasando las fronteras del espacio privado: manipulación de los límites del espacio de la arquitectura doméstica por Vilanova Artigas y Paulo Mendes da Rocha / Crossing the Borders of the Private Space: Manipulation of the Limits of the Space in the Domestic Architecture by Vilanova Artigas and Paulo Mendes da Rocha'. *Rita: Revista Indexada de Textos Académicos*, no. 7 (April 2017): 144–53.

Pisani, Daniele, ed. *Paulo Mendes da Rocha: tutte le opere*. Milano: Electa architettura, 2013.

Sarno, Francesca. 'L'architettura della scuola Paulistain Brasile. Necessidade e desejo'. PhD dissertation, Sapienza University of Rome, 2013.

Schwarz, Robert, 'Culture and Politics in Brazil, 1964–1969'. In *Misplaced Ideas: Essays on Brazilian Culture,* 126–59. London: Verso, 1992.

Skidmore, Thomas E. *The Politics of Military Rule in Brazil, 1964–85*. New York: Oxford University Press, 1997.

Spiro, Annette and Luigi Snozzi. *Paulo Mendes da Rocha: bauten und projekte / Paulo Mendes da Rocha: Works and Projects*. Zürich: Niggli, 2002.

Weizman, Ines. *Architecture and the Paradox of Dissidence*. Hoboken, NJ: Taylor and Francis, 2014.

C.E.C.A. House: Expediting the un-private client

Peter Swinnen

The primary responsibility of the architect is not one of representing the interest of the client, but representing the public interest.
– Wouter Vanstiphout, 'The Self-Destruction Machine' (2014)

On 24 March 1954, Léon Palm delivered a seminal lecture at the Brussels Chamber of Commerce entitled 'Immoralité du gaspillage dans les constructions dites "A bon marché"' (The immorality of waste in so-called 'cheap construction'). Palm, a young, entrepreneurial architect, formulated a fundamental critique of the ruling practices of post-war housing construction. According to the architect, both industry and national housing policy advocated an all too dogmatic and traditional take on building technology, causing a needless inflation of material consumption and labour. As a provocation, Palm suggested in his lecture that he could build an all-mod-cons family house of 100 square meters at less than half the market price; an idea he pitched as 'a house at the price of a FORD car!' Furthermore, the housing unit's ensuing mass production could bring about a shift in output velocity, which was necessary to resolve the country's housing deficit, then estimated at more than 250,000 dwellings.

Bluff

Annoyingly intrigued by Palm's provocation, the Brussels Chamber of Commerce decided to challenge the architect by offering him a stand at the upcoming Coal and Steel Exhibition in Liège. Confronted with an impossible time frame (the exhibition was to open in less than a month), Palm decided to team up with architect Willy Van Der Meeren, whose architecture he had positively reviewed in a recent article published in the journal *Beaux Arts,* but whom he had never met. Legend has it that the architects arranged a meeting at the Brussels Central Station's buffet, where Van Der Meeren sketched the house's principle on a beer felt: a two-bay square plan with a steel portico structure and a centralised heating system.[1] The weeks following the buffet session, Palm's bluff was moulded into a partial one-to-one scale model and, on 24 April 1954, the concept was put on display. Baptised the 'C.E.C.A. House', a reference to (and acronym of) the Communauté Européenne de Charbon et de l'Acier, the prototype expressed the architects' will to promote modern affordable homes for working class families.[2] The accompanying billboard at the Liège show read: 'MAISON C.E.C.A.? HABITATION OUVRIÈRE MODÈLE ...– ECONOMIE N'EST PAS MEDIOCRITE MAIS QUALITE DES MATERIAUX – SIMPLICITE DE CONCEPTION – FABRICATION INDUSTRIELLE – RESULTAT: CETTE MAISON POUR LE PRIX DE 148.000 F – AVEC: CHAUFFAGE GENERAL – SALLE DE BAIN COMPLET – CUISINE EQUIPE – ARMOIRES PLACARD DANS LES CHAMBRES.'[3] The Liège exhibition was soon followed by a second fair, the Exposition Inter-

1
Historical facts relating to the initial conception of the C.E.C.A. House have been based on rare live interviews with Willy Van Der Meeren conducted by Emiel De Kooning, as well as the Ziggurat TV documentary, edited by Jurgen Persyn (BRT 1995). Emiel De Kooning's work has been reproduced in: De Kooning, *Willy Van Der Meeren*; De Kooning, 'Willy Van Der Meeren'.

2
The C.E.C.A. name was somewhat provocatively chosen by Van Der Meeren and Palm since Belgium had the poorest level of housing facilities for steel and coal workers within the future European Union (Ziggurat, BRT 1995, televised interview with *Willy Van Der Meeren*, conducted by Jurgen Persyn).

3
'C.E.C.A. HOUSE? A MODEL WORKERS' HOUSE ... – ECONOMY DOESN'T EQUAL MEDIOCRITY BUT QUALITATIVE MATERIALS – CONCEPTUAL SIMPLICITY – INDUSTRIAL FABRICATION – RESULT: THIS HOUSE FOR THE PRICE OF 148,000 F – INCLUDING: GENERAL HEATING – FULLY EQUIPPED BATHROOM – FULLY EQUIPPED KITCHEN – BUILT-IN BEDROOM CUPBOARDS' (Translation by the author).

nationale Technique et Industrielle at the Palais des Expositions in Charleroi, enabling Palm and Van Der Meeren to gather a staggering 4,500 clients in only six months.[4]

The key to the C.E.C.A. House's instant success was its straightforward logic and sense of economy, both in volume and materiality. However, C.E.C.A.'s true invention – beyond the advanced socioeconomic ethos – was its capacity to link thousands of individual households (private house owners) in a shared longing for a generous and affordable dwelling. Palm's bluff and Van Der Meeren's simple design – originally intended to house workers' families – managed to tap into an architectural middle ground, fluidly bypassing the antagonistic doctrines of both the bourgeois post-war house and the (social) apartment slab. In a stealthy manner, C.E.C.A. aimed at 'un-privatising' the individual homeowner by guaranteeing the right to a compact private property while maximising the potential for social placemaking and local community creation. Due to the house's extremely light facades and its nuanced transparencies, the private naturally affected the (semi-)public realm and vice versa.

Boycott

Like many experimental housing architectures of the twentieth century, the C.E.C.A. House failed to outgrow its prototype phase. Influential precursors like the Eames House (1949), the lightweight shelter programme by Atelier Jean Prouvé (1944), or Le Corbusier's M.A.S. programme (1940) are fine examples where intriguing prototypes were conceptualised, sometimes even built, without ever reaching, in a convincing manner, the necessary level of mass production.[5]

In Belgium, fellow architects like Peter Callebaut or René Heyvaert were interested in similar socioeconomic housing experiments, though they were devoid of any active ambition for serial reproduction. In C.E.C.A.'s case, the final push away from mass production was given by the Belgian National Housing Company (NHS). The idea that two young daredevils could effortlessly merge social ethics and astute economics didn't go down well with the ruling traditionalist housing companies. Instead of being hailed as a fresh and urgent complement to post-war housing industry, the C.E.C.A. project unleashed fierce opposition. The NHS refused to approve the prototype's structural principle, falsely claiming that the central steel portico would be too weak. The unilateral veto caused construction companies to withdraw and overnight the project's prime mission – *construire pour le plus grand nombre* – became its fundamental weakness. Any chances for mass production dissolved and 4,500 potential orders had to be cancelled.

The NHS's veto silently cancelled another innovative C.E.C.A. trait. The architects aimed at a rather revolutionary system for design fees. In the minds of Palm and Van Der Meeren, the C.E.C.A. type was developed as a building kit that could be adopted by other architects or housing companies, making them, in effect, 'ghostwriters'

4
Ziggurat, BRT 1995, televised interview with Willy Van Der Meeren, conducted by Jurgen Persyn.

5
M.A.S. or Maisons Montées à Sec, was a never-executed housing programme based on complete standardisation, offering a steel construction with steel facade cladding and a centralised heating equipment. http://www.fondation-lecorbusier.fr/. Accessed 4 August 2020.

Fig. 1 C.E.C.A. house no. 7, 2019. (Photograph by © Leonard Streich)

Fig. 2 C.E.C.A. house no. 6, 2019.
(Photograph by © Leonard Streich)

of the projects. In order to render such ghostwriting profitable, the architects planned to implement a royalty arrangement instead of claiming a regular designer's remuneration. Such a shift on authorship was crucial if mass production was to be possible. Unfortunately, the financial concept was never seriously developed or tested. The truth of the matter is that C.E.C.A. was never adopted, or even copied for that matter.

Afterlife no. 1

A couple of weeks after C.E.C.A.'s initial failure, a new and unexpected opportunity arose. Benoît Verhaegen, one of the original 4,500 applicants, asked Palm and Van Der Meeren to rethink C.E.C.A. and develop an 'XL version' with three instead of two bays to accommodate his large family. Verhaegen owned a sizable piece of land near Brussels, named Clos des Quatre Vents. The generous plot with its undulating topography convinced the architects to imagine not one but eight C.E.C.A. units, all fluidly arranged around a communal garden and playground.

Verhaegen and the architects invited tenants for the remaining seven houses, based on the Liège and Charleroi applicants' lists. Hence, the *Clos* became home to a medical doctor, a politician, a civil servant, a writer, spaced ellipsis: . . . and an architect (Van Der Meeren himself). By means of this social rearrangement, the Clos des Quatre Vents made an abstraction of two of the prime C.E.C.A. creeds: mass production and an economically weaker, working-class clientele. Middle-class families and intellectual peers, hungry for a comfortable living experiment, had silently traded places with the intended working classes. Because only eight units were produced, the price per house skyrocketed above the foreseen 'price of a FORD car' by fifty per cent, thus costing nearly as much as a 'normal' post-war house.

Even so, the contextual concept and extremely rapid completion of the Clos did produce new insights. Even in its bourgeois version, the C.E.C.A. type continued to un-privatise the architectural client, both economically and socially. The un-privatising effect was particularly discernible on levels of ownership, material consumption, and social interdependency. Without the C.E.C.A. opportunity, all eight homeowners would have built their own individual houses, presumably on a private plot without any form of communality. Moreover, for all C.E.C.A. units an absolute minimum of construction materials was used, using only a fraction of that typically required for a typical post-war house. But most importantly the community's careful arrangement – the subtle distances between neighbours – allowed for an untapped modern practice of social interdependency. Arranged in three blocks (one block contained two homes and two others accommodated three homes) and surrounded by varied green spaces, the compact C.E.C.A. principle gave rise to a continuous social experiment, of which the first decade proved to be unique, since Willy Van Der Meeren and his family lived there at the time and thus 'watched over' the evolution of the co-housing's reality.

Embedded

Together with the new inhabitants, Van Der Meeren continued to push the boundaries of the C.E.C.A. type, boasting an intriguing catalogue of 'personalised' versions, including different interior finishings, varying colour schemes, and alternative facade arrangements. Such differentiation strategies, which were crucial within the un-privatised realm of cohabitation, allowed the inhabitants to retain their own identities. In his own house (no. 6) Van Der Meeren went beyond aesthetic variation and altered the spatial organisation of the C.E.C.A. type by introducing a double-height space. This scale move, fundamentally reconceptualised C.E.C.A.'s spatial potential from an economical prototype into a cultural one, whereby the compact private interior and the generous semi-public exterior merge into an un-private continuum, cancelling out any form of public/private dichotomy.

The presence of Van Der Meeren in the young community proved vital. The experimental cohabitation required guidance as well as punctual recalibrations. Despite the presence of a protocol on how communal spaces and amenities should be used (*acte de base*), the minutes of the Clos's community meetings reveal day-to-day frustrations on how to live together. On 25 June 1958 the minutes read:

> The main purpose of the meeting is to draw up a development plan for the common and private parts insofar as these concern all the owners. In particular, each owner is requested to make known the modifications and derogations that he wishes to make in his lot either to the specifications or to the current situation, for example: construction or development of a pond, claustra, grid, special type of fence or even no fence at all, plantations overflowing onto the undivided lot, etc.[6]

On 28 July 1962, Willy Van Der Meeren (acting as syndic) noted: 'I am obliged to remind you that the intentions of the architects Palm & Van Der Meeren were to reserve the common garden exclusively for pedestrians and children's playgrounds. For some time now people have had the unfortunate habit of loading their cars in front of the door.'[7] After Van Der Meeren's departure in 1964, cohabitation continued to be challenged by outlandish wishes such as house extensions or simple neglect. A report, dated 7 November 1969, stated: 'As you can see, it is difficult to please everyone [...] and one's neighbour. By now, the common garden has adopted the appearance of a wasteland.'[8]

The brittle balance between private and communal profits haunted the Clos from the start. Over the years, new tenants and owners continued to challenge this un-private equilibrium, either out of simple ignorance or out of a clear disinterest to maintain the unique formula of this wayward neighbourhood. So far, this development is best illustrated by the curved extension of House no. 1, executed in 1998. Willy Van Der Meeren, who was then seventy-five years old and no longer living at the Clos, was alerted by the cohabitants that House no. 1 was being enlarged without respecting the

6
'l'Objet principal de l'assemblée est d'établir un plan d'aménagement des parties communes et privées dans la mesure ou celles-ci concernent l'ensemble des propriétaires. En particulier chaque propriétaire est prié de faire connaître les modifications et derogations qu'il desire apporter dans son lot soit au cahier des charges, soit à la situation acuelle, par exemple: construction ou aménagement de bassin, claustra, grille, clôture de type spécial ou même abscence de clôture, plantations débordant sur le lot indivis, etc.'. Excerpt from the Clos's minutes archive, stored on-site at House no. 5.

7
'Je me vois obligé de vous rappeler que les intentions des architectes Palm & Van Der Meeren étaient de réserver le jardin commun exclusivement aux piétons et jeux d'enfants. Depuis quelque temps, on prend la malheureuse habitude de charger sa voiture devant la porte.' Excerpt from the Clos's minutes archive, stored on-site at House no. 5.

8
'Comme vous pouvez le constater, il est difficile de contenter tout le monde... et son voisin. Il s'ensuit donc, la partie commune est destinée à presenter sous peu, l'apparence d'un terrain vague.' Excerpt from the Clos's minutes archive, stored on-site at House no. 5.

Fig. 3 C.E.C.A Houses nos. 7 and 8, 2019. (Photograph by © Leonard Streich)

Fig. 4 C.E.C.A Houses nos. 6, 7, and 8, 2019. (Photograph by © Leonard Streich)

Fig. 5 C.E.C.A Houses nos. 4, 5, and 6. Still from documentary *Cursus Bouwen en Wonen*. (© VRT archive, 1955–56)

architectural ensemble or the colour scheme (a white curved extension adjacent to the initially red end wall).

In a letter dated 20 September 1998 Van Der Meeren addressed the mayor and aldermen of Tervueren, stating that this curved extension read as an 'aggressive groin rupture', destroying the balance of the whole site.[9] Importantly, Van Der Meeren wrote the letter in the name of the co-owners of the Clos. Unfortunately, the extension was already well on its way. In his letter Van Der Meeren suggested, presumably for the first time, that the Clos des Quatre Vents, being an internationally recognised example of modernist architecture, should be listed as a monument. The split between the original 'ghostwriting' stance to allow for potential mass production (1954) and the architect's seemingly over-protective patronage forty-five years later clearly reveals a contradictive stance. Nonetheless, heritage listing could be deemed the last possible recourse to safeguard C.E.C.A.'s cleverness and social potential.

9
Based on a copy of the letter, part of the C.E.C.A. listing file, archived at the Agentschap Onroerend Erfgoed, Dept Vlaams Brabant, Leuven.

Afterlife no. 2

It took another decade before Van Der Meeren's hint at listing the Clos was picked up by heritage officials. On 10 October 2008, the Van Der Meeren family house was formally acknowledged as a monument, and on 15 October 2010 the entire estate was recognised as architectural heritage. Surprisingly, this listing was contested by most co-owners. In a letter dated 3 December 2007, the inhabitants of some of the houses claimed that listing would be an unnecessary burden on the Clos's autonomy. Their objection was not upheld by the heritage department. So, in a regrettable reaction, ahead of the presumed 'heritage sclerosis', some owners replaced the slender steel facades with 'energy-efficient and user-friendly' PVC frames. If anything, the new facades prove how quickly the DNA of C.E.C.A. can be subverted and even erased. The removal of the lightweight filters had a fundamental effect on the communal central space, virtually dissociating it from the three houses.

The C.E.C.A. House was never meant to last for more than one generation. Hence, the original choice for 'poor' materials and euphemistic stability calculations. The prefab construction had to be easy to dismantle and recycle. This specification was in line with Van Der Meeren's belief that human amenities shouldn't put a permanent claim on the limited space at hand. After one or two generations, new societal insights will rule and thus architecture shouldn't burden these unpredictable evolutions. In this respect, the listing of the Clos fundamentally opposed C.E.C.A.'s original ephemeral intentions. At the same time, it also gave rise to other necessary freedoms. Today, exactly sixty-five years after C.E.C.A.'s inception, the Clos des Quatre Vents is welcoming its fourth generation of inhabitants. The past decade, the Clos has primarily turned into a cultural good, bearing witness to what could have been (the mass production), what has been (an unencumbered modernist cohabitation), and what currently is (a listed dwelling environment within urban sprawl).

Perhaps the most interesting feature of the Clos, post-listing, is the fact that it has become a rule-avoiding mechanism. Listed monuments are absolved from complying with generic urban and ecological regulations. In an era obsessed with 'eco-correctness' and compact urban living, the C.E.C.A. House has become a prime offender. The project is in effect one huge thermal bridge – the dwellings are hardly insulated, limiting temperatures to a maximum of eighteen or nineteen degrees Celsius in winter, while in summer requiring all windows to be opened for air flow and cooling. By today's housing standards and aggressively lobbied energy guidelines, the C.E.C.A. House fails on all levels. Updating the C.E.C.A. House to comply with these top-down rules would simply end the project forever. Its original frail materiality and economy of means have proven to be the ideal catalysts for a generous and informal communality.

Postscript

Living at the Clos is a challenging pleasure. Since May 2017, my family and I have had the chance to reside in Houses no. 6 and no. 7. House no. 7 is the unit closest to the original 100 square-metre plan, partially composed of elements from the 1954 prototype, and comprising the originally intended steel portico structure. House no. 7 was the architect's original home. Despite its many contradictory episodes, the Clos remains a societal exemplar project. As fourth-generation inhabitants we see ourselves as an enhanced version of the un-private client. Not only do we actively participate within the co-housing ensemble, we consciously invest in community creation and social placemaking, act as syndic of the Clos, and progressively restore the common infrastructure and gardens based on their original economy of means. Perhaps, the true genius of Palm and Van Der Meeren resides in C.E.C.A.'s promise – that through reformatting the smallest entity imaginable – the affordable house – society and its predominantly static political policy system could be subverted and opened up. The fact that this never truly happened is probably not that important. The promise has installed a joint – almost immaterial – responsibility within the Clos. To curate C.E.C.A. on a daily basis is what should be understood as our current and future un-privatised nature. C.E.C.A.'s ultimate lesson is one of taking private responsibility seriously while simultaneously producing an original communality.

Architecture serves society – the public – through the inevitable agency of a client. Independent of the client's inclination (private, public, semi-this, semi-that, . . .), the architect should always venture to un-privatise the architectural client, making the project, again and again, relevant to public interest. Ultimately, with Palm and Van Der Meeren in mind, the architect should perform as a producer, not as a divine creator.

Bibliography

Agentschap Onroerend Erfgoed, Departement Vlaams Brabant, Leuven. C.E.C.A. listing file.

De Kooning, Emiel. *Willy Van Der Meeren. Vlees En Beton*, vol. 21–24. Damme: Laat-XXe-Eeuws Genootschap, 1993.

De Kooning, Emiel. 'Willy Van Der Meeren. Architectuur. Stedenbouw. Design. Research. Onderwijs'. PhD dissertation, Faculty of Engineering and Architecture, Ghent University, 1997.

Vanstiphout, Wouter. 'The Self-Destruction Machine'. In *Real Estates*, edited by Jack Self and Shumi Bose, 57–66. London: Bedford Press, 2014.

Pliable Praxis House

Scott Colman

'In Houston, where bigger means better and suburbanites in SUVs dominate the highways, architects Dawn Finley and Mark Wamble are anomalies: Their domestic lives fit into 1,200 square feet [110 square metres], and their commute to work is but a walk downstairs.'[1] This quote, from a 2007 article in *Dwell*, featuring the 48' House (2004–06; 14.4 metres) by Interloop—Architecture, presents the architects' home as the embodiment of an anomalous lifestyle and, implicitly, an enviable alternative to the norm in Houston, world capital of the energy industry and infamous for its sprawling suburbs of inflated (spacious and air-conditioned) single-family houses, dispersed by ever-more tenuous circuits of congested freeways **(Fig. 1)**. On the eve of the global financial crisis, precipitated by the collapse of the mortgage futures market, lifestyle journalism succinctly transformed the figure of the architect and the idea of the architect's house into an avant-garde lifestyle, dissolving pressing political economic and environmental concerns through the consumptive lens of cultural envy. But these concerns – live-work, housing size and financing, the organisation of the domestic and urban economy, and the relationship between design and political economic systems – are fundamental to Interloop's practice and the architectural objects it produces.

Acknowledging that the factors affecting the design and fabrication of buildings are no longer as clearly delimited or stable as they were assumed to be in the twentieth century, in their experimental architectural practice and academic research in the School of Architecture at Rice University, Finley and Wamble consciously seek to reconceive the architectural design process and rearticulate the architectural object in advance of and response to the fluid and fickle protocols and processes of the disruptive neoliberal political economic system. The discourse of architecture at Rice University in the late 1990s and early 2000s concerned expanding the context of architectural design beyond the organisation, appearance, and materiality of the built fabric to include the legal structures, financial flows, environmental systems, logistical sequences, and research agendas of contemporary architectural production. This discourse lent Houston – with its NASA-oriented frontier spirit, high-tech medical industry, oil-driven economy, and lack of zoning, planning, and public infrastructure – international prominence as the paradigmatic neoliberal city.[2] In recognition of and resistance to this volatile context, Finley and Wamble have developed a practice that considers procedures of architectural production contingent and the relationship between the design, fabrication, and use of buildings open to constant reconsideration.

Of central importance for Finley and Wamble is the redesign of the protocols of design practice and the articulation of the architectural object to allow both their own practice and the life- and work-practices of their clients to more deftly negotiate this fluid political

1
Gustin, 'Greetings from Houston, TX', 190.

2
This discourse includes the writings of Lars Lerup, Albert Pope, and Sanford Kwinter in addition to those by Finley and Wamble, as well as Rem Koolhaas's unjustly infamous reference to Marshall Berman's statement about surfing the wave of modernisation: Kwinter, *Rem Koolhaas*, 64. On Houston as the paradigmatic neoliberal city, see Bell and Leong, *Slow Space*, including Mark Wamble, 'Knee Play'; and Kwinter and Fabricius, 'Houston™'.

Fig. 1 Rear facade, 48' House. Interloop—Architecture, Houston, Texas, 2004–06. (Photograph by © Daniel Hennessy)

3
All project information is drawn from www.interlooparchitecture.com. Accessed 15 February 2019.

and economic condition. The result of this effort is a particular aesthetic, comparable to the transformable interfaces that resulted from the contemporaneous development of 'applications' in the tablet and smartphone industries. The architectural object is conceptually 'disarticulated' to produce a choreographed assemblage of discrete knowledge-objects, each possessing an autonomy that allows them to circulate in the architect's own practice and, potentially, the rapidly transforming building components market. As an aggregate of applications, in its hybrid programming and innovative siting, and as a product of and tool for invention, the 48' House reconceives the twentieth-century suburban context as a space of production rather than consumption, reconstituting the infrastructures of life, work, and material culture in the contemporary political economy.

Staging financing

In a departure from the normative understanding of architectural practice as a professional service distinct from building, the 48' House was conceived as a marketable *objet-type* in the contemporary housing market **(Fig. 2)**. It became part of the Hometta project, a collaboration between a group of young architects and the developer Mark Johnson to produce a web-based platform that expands the availability of affordable, high-quality house designs. With architects such as David Clovers, James Evans, Doug Garofalo, Wes Jones, Keith Krumweide, Blair Satterfield, and Brett Zamore, the venture was promoted in exhibitions in Houston, San Francisco, Boston, Chicago, and New York in late 2009.

An effort to rethink the design and delivery of residential architecture, the 48' House can be understood as a development of Finley and Wamble's earlier efforts to reconceive the domestic architectural object as a means of transforming the financial apparatuses that structurally impede home ownership. In a predominantly suburban city and a political climate in which public-supported or -provided housing remains a rare or distant dream, their 1999 Klip House project, a housing system they call a 'platform or infrastructure', is comprised of modules that, leased or purchased incrementally and built-up over time, could allow low-income residents to accrue housing equity while avoiding the large and risky investments required by the current mortgage system.[3] Standardising connections between modules and pre-installed foundations and between the modules themselves, the architects invented a mechanism for liberating consumer agency and choice. Finley and Wamble presented this potential in a fictitious invoice, listing a series of brand-name modules and components distributed from a catalogue, to emphasise that the project is more concerned with the system of housing than any particular embodiment. The after-market renderings of the project, some of which extend beyond housing to accommodate urban services, suggest the flexible, accretive system could result in buildings comprised of units aggregated from multiple sources and manufacturers **(Fig. 3)**. While Interloop's model was the used-car market, in which off-the-shelf or remodelled objects and parts can be traded or resold, subsequent

Fig. 2 Plans, 48' House. Interloop—Architecture, Houston, Texas, 2004–06. (From the Hometta catalogue)

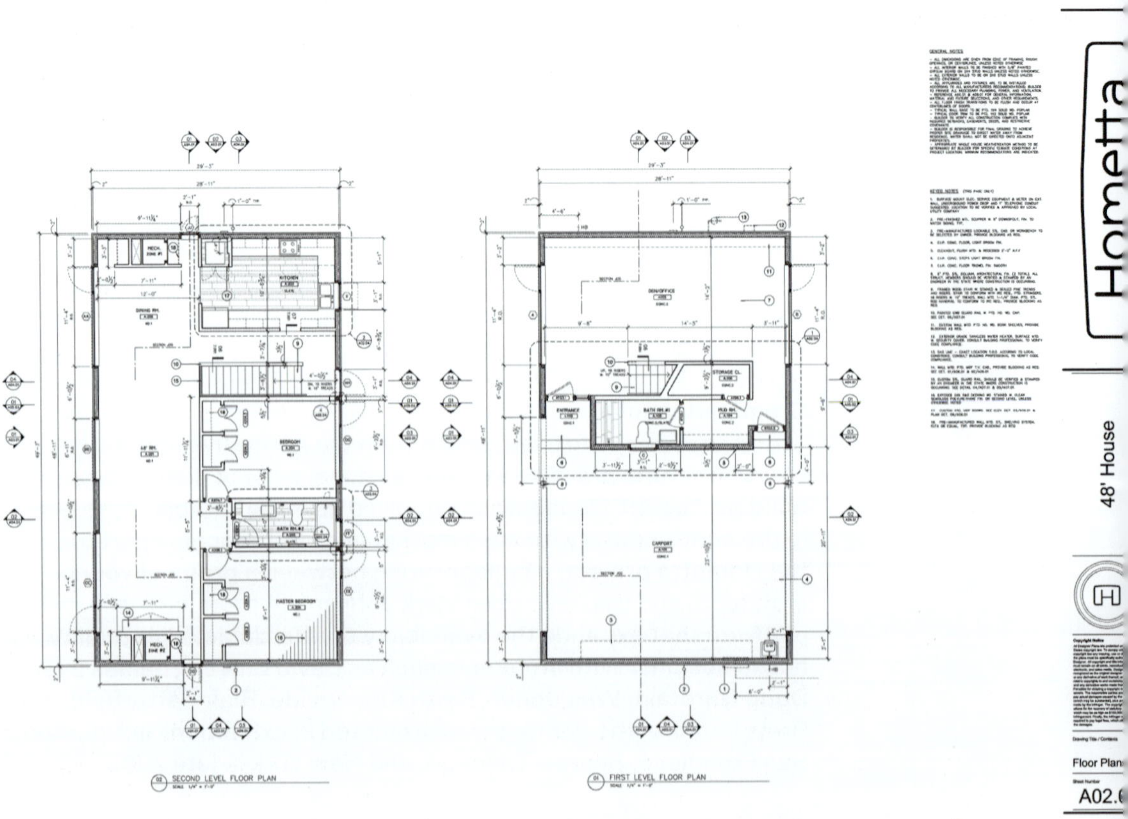

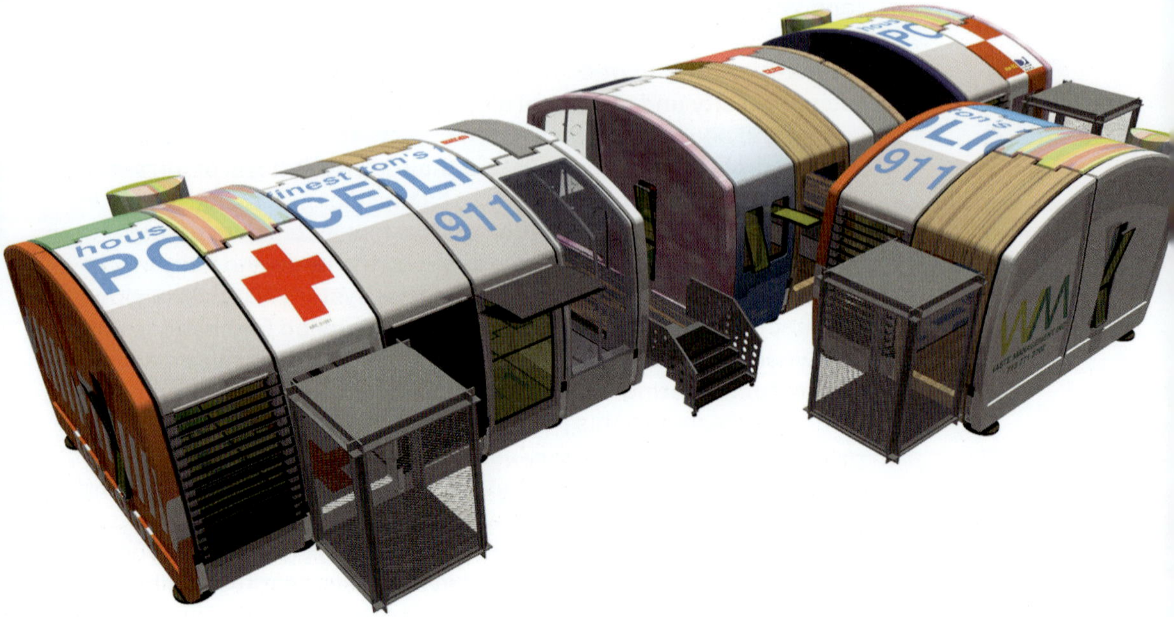

Fig. 3 'Aftermarket' potential, Klip House, project. Interloop—Architecture, 1999.

4
For subsequent works on learning and urban environments incorporating these ideas, see Interloop's Global Energy Learning Center (2008) and Open Transfer (2012) projects, respectively. On the Symonds Teaching Labs see Wamble, 'Globalism and the New Interior'.

developments in the smartphone industry highlight the potential for such a platform to disrupt the construction industry by encouraging the development of building applications. Such potential runs throughout Interloop's practice, which consistently shifts the critical locus of architectural work from the scale of the building to the scale of the building component, conceiving the architectural object as physically situated yet participant in the building market and the so-called market of ideas.

Very different in appearance to the Klip House project, the 48' House nevertheless embodies its intent for the benefit of the architects and their children. In this relatively modest house Finley and Wamble have established a home and office that, employing an underlying modular order, anticipates accretion over time **(Fig. 4)**. As the name of the project indicates, the house is specifically dimensioned. Divisible into 4' × 8' (1.2 × 2.4 metre) panels for plywood sheathing, the design minimises waste and – with its use of standard construction practices and materials, minimal detailing, efficient planning, and mix of custom and store-bought fixtures (such as IKEA kitchen cabinetry) – cost.

The (domestic) user interface

The planning of the 48' House, like the Klip House, disassociates the logics of the architectural platform from its functional applications, allowing programme to change. While the large ground-floor room was initially programmed as a workspace, it is conceived as a multipurpose room that by specifically designed built-in and mobile furnishings can be transformed into a playroom, formal living area, library, or other use. Similarly, the upstairs plan is dominated by a long hall that accommodates multiple and shifting uses, such as dining, sitting, and lounging, as well as spillover from the office directly below **(Fig. 5)**. This space acts as a connector into which specific, more functionally oriented components (a kitchen, stair, bathroom, and two bedrooms) are 'plugged'. Understood as an open horizontal volume connected to specific functional components, this plan is a domestic application of the firm's work incorporating information technologies into learning (Symonds Teaching Labs, 1995–2001), production (Houston Products Lab, 1997), and urban environments (Do Post, 2001; projects for the First Architecture Biennale in Rotterdam, 2002). These projects develop the observation that we now constantly move between defined nodes (usually vertical information interfaces) and horizontal fields of less-defined physical activity.[4]

In their project for the Houston Products Lab, a specialty engineering and fabrication company, the architects distinguish between the enclosing envelope of the building and what they call 'boundary objects' organising the programme. Constituting the interstices between major spaces, each of these devices is a bespoke hybrid, nesting selected technologies, such as display and tack boards, drawers, cabinets, filing systems, specialty tools, computer screens and processors, shelving, and display cases. Rendered a unified whole through the deployment of precise detailing, formal

Fig. 4 Front facade, 48' House. Interloop—Architecture, Houston, Texas, 2004–06. (Photograph by © Daniel Hennessy)

Fig. 5 The upstairs 'hall', 48' House. Interloop—Architecture, Houston, Texas, 2004–06. (Photograph by © Daniel Hennessy)

articulation, and colour, these assemblages of ready-made components and systems are contingently synthesised into a conceptual and visual unity. Optically differentiated from the tectonically articulate spatial enclosure that accommodates them, these objects have a quasi-autonomous character, both with respect to the spaces they define and the actions they engage. Through these physical devices, Finley and Wamble assert architecture's role in managing the organisation and internal communications central to this small firm's operations. In lieu of the usual practice of naming architectural spaces by reference to a commonly used gerund (e.g., dining, living) or noun (e.g., bedroom, laundry, kitchen), Finley and Wamble label plan diagrams of the Houston Products Lab with actions – for example, an area for manufacturing: 'cut / mill / cast'; another for the packaging and distribution of products: 'schedule / crate / wrap / tag / label'; the loading dock: 'lift / pick / stack / sort'; and an informal outdoor space: 'greet / gather / meet'. As a consequence, a broad range of activities – like manufacturing, cooking, design, and administration – are equated. Categorical distinctions customarily drawn between primary, secondary, and tertiary economic sectors and between isolated realms of production and consumption are eliminated, building typologies become moot, and programme 'retoolable'.

This object-oriented programming also appears in Interloop's 'houses', where the architects' emphasis on activity undermines the normative typological understanding of the domestic in a political economic context where the distinction between life and work has become, usually to the benefit of capital, obsolete. For example, in a project completed three years after the 48' House, an accessory dwelling unit – behind a single-family house on an inner-suburban Houston lot – functions as a garage and small guesthouse, but also as a small yoga studio that supplements the owners' income. The joinery at the centre of the upper-story plan demarcates and screens space, and through the integration of devices – bathroom fixtures, plumbing, and cabinetry on one side, and a murphy bed, closets, drawers, storage for yoga mats and other exercise equipment on the other – allows the space to be programmed as a bedroom or exercise room. The immediate prototype for this joinery, not quite built-in nor fully autonomous, is the cabinetry at the end of the long upper-story room of the 48' House. In both objects, a white surface unfolds into a deep hue as it opens: contents become available with a beckoning visual depth.

This active relationship between surface and object, object and user, is carried into the design of the 9º House (2006–09), which integrates a collection of 'apps' at varying scales. The joinery of the built-in plywood double bed reads as mobile furniture and the white cabinetry near the fireplace as a wall. Similarly, grey cabinets form a sitting area and pink bookshelves blur the distinction between object and room. These various applications, differentiated by their individuated coloured surfaces, render the 9º House an aggregation of autonomous components that cohere as a result of the underlying geometric order apparent in the plan. In this regard, the proportional

Fig. 6 Plans, 9º House. Interloop—Architecture, Houston, Texas, 2006–09.

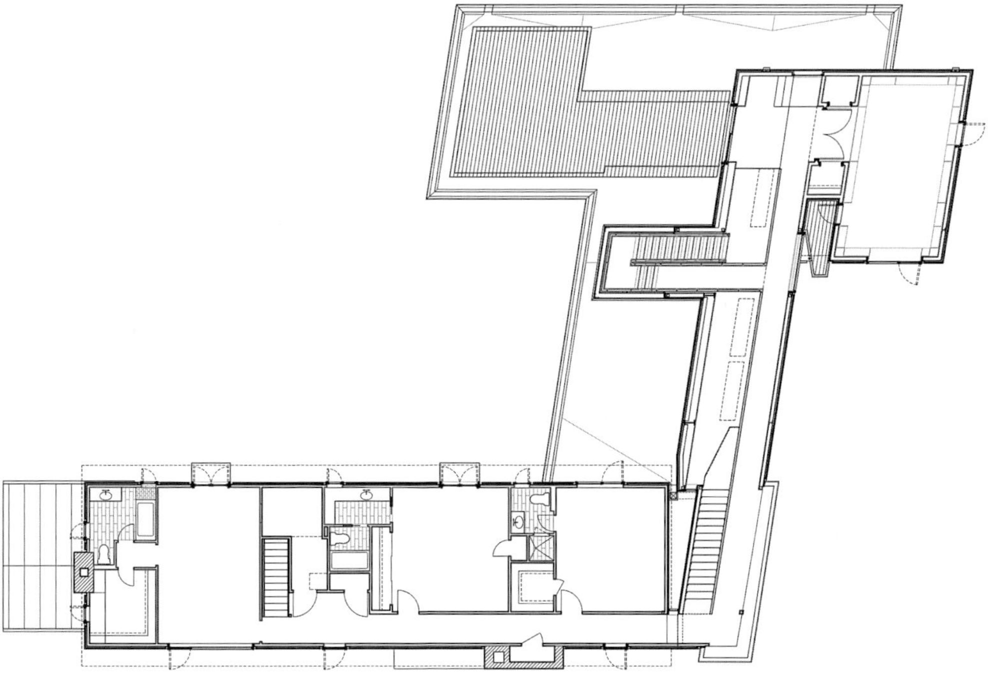

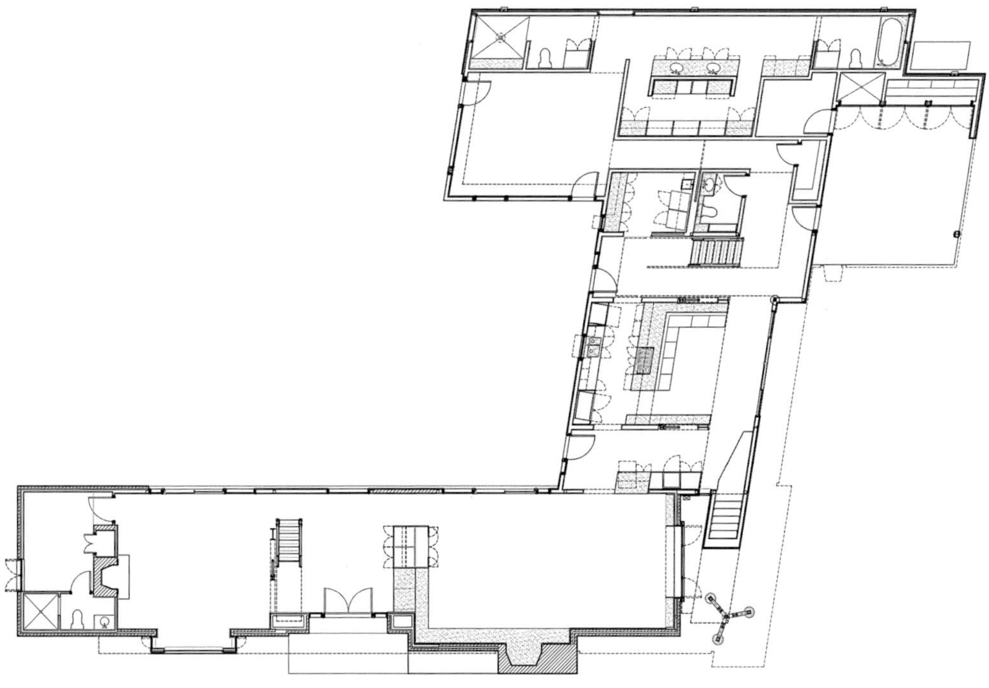

rigor of the 48' House appears instrumental. With an emphasis on minimal cost, the 48' House is an essay in rectilinear standards. By contrast, in the more elaborate 9º House, in the intersection of the normative grid of the remodelled house and the skewed grid of the addition, Finley and Wamble make critically legible the graphic schema implicit in the relationship between architecture and building **(Fig. 6)**. If the right angle is the standard facilitating the integration of building components by ensuring the correspondence of design, fabrication, and assembly, it also prejudices architectural intent toward the convenient offerings of the building products industry. Much of the pleasure of the 9º House is the unfolding realisation of the extent to which the normal pervades our assumptions, experiences, and apperception and has infused our technologies and environment. Navigating the building for the first time, the extent of this pervasion builds in a concatenation of details, as the visitor rediscovers the objects of our everyday domestic landscape – furnishings, fittings, machines, components – obliquely redefined.

Calibrating the domestic and broader economy

In its modular logic and dissociation of form and function, the 48' House, anticipating future expansion, calibrates architectural design to the vicissitudes of planning a family, financial realities, career changes, and the organisation of domestic labour and material life in a context in which 'disruption' has become an ideological mantra. Taking advantage of lax planning ordinances and integrating urban and architectural concerns, the house defies the conventional setback. The deep siting preserved an existing oak tree and light and views for the neighbouring dwellings, but, most importantly consolidated as much open space as possible into a single area on the site for future expansion. The recently completed 54' Addition (2018; 16.2 metres) to the 48' House, employing the modular proportions of the original dwelling, now occupies the western half of the front garden. With the installation of a new application – a media wall replacing the wall-length workbench – the ground-floor space in the 48' House has been converted with minimal investment into a formal living room. The carport has been enclosed to form a third bedroom. The addition accommodates a larger office space, kitchenette, and bathroom on the upper floor and, below, a new carport and, adjoining the original house, workshop for activities Interloop have been performing in rented space for over a decade. With these changes, the suburban site houses the expected domestic economy, less-expected tertiary-sector work, and entirely unexpected secondary production in the form of Interloop's ongoing fabrication of specialty architectural components.

Intervening in the building products industry

The design and fabrication of architectural components is an unusual venture for an architectural practice. Interloop's E-X-I-T sign, conceived when the architects were administering the construction of Renzo Piano's Nasher Sculpture Centre in Dallas (1999–2003), is in the collection of the Museum of Modern Art in New York. In a process of prototyp-

5
Finley, 'Assuming Risk'.

ing, testing, and licensing, requiring substantial and risky investment by a small firm, this sign, developed under the name LELU, has become a spin-off business for the architects.[5] In the design and production of this and other architectural components Finley and Wamble have sought to reconceive architectural practice in the context of a radically transformed building products industry. While twentieth-century architects made more or less successful, but incremental, attempts to engage and transform the industrial system of building production, that sphere of activity has been much more radically destabilised in recent years by changes in technology. Instantaneous and inexpensive communication, 'just-in-time' production, global supply chains, the flexible manufacturing allowed by retooling, the seamless interface between digital design and manufacturing, and the emergence of distributed digital fabrication have made it easier to reconceive received assemblies and procedures. As the Internet has subsumed the building products catalogue, architects have gained unmediated access to a world of producers, including 'artisanal' manufacturers hitherto unable to compete with large operators. Rather than accepting off-the-shelf, predetermined wares, components, and systems, Interloop have sought to leverage this newfound capacity to directly engage production and transform architectural knowledge and practice. Rather than a late- and postmodernist 'design by choice', Interloop seeks opportunities for 'design by invention'.

While the majority of the 48' House is standard construction and deploys off-the-shelf materials and components, such as corrugated metal siding, Finley and Wamble engage the specialty industries characteristic of Houston's energy, medical, and aerospace sectors in the delivery of certain elements, such as the metal laundry cabinet doors and stair guardrail, fabricated by a manufacturer of off-shore drilling equipment. Similarly, the exposed steel columns at the junction of the ground-floor entryways and carport is an exception to the building's otherwise normative structure. Subsequently, this distillation of the architectural enclosure into standard and exceptional elements has become a central strategy in Interloop's practice, as the prominent tripod column of the 9º House makes evident. In an effort to lower costs for both themselves and their clients, the architects and their collaborators have experimented with fabricating and sometimes installing these props themselves, such as the steel frame that constitutes the basic structure of the 54' Addition.

Reconstituting the building delivery process

This interest in the fabrication of architectural components fundamentally implicates the design and building processes. The apportionment of the building fabric between off-the-shelf and specialty components and between elements constructed by the contractor and the architects themselves means the articulation of the architectural object is intrinsically related to the manner of its design, production, and delivery. In Interloop's work, it is impossible to divorce an understanding of the architectural object – the particular way in which

Fig. 7 Plug—On. Interloop—Architecture, Houston, Texas, 2002–03.

6
Finley and Wamble, 'Notes on System Form'.

the building is divided into systems, components, and details – from its processes of design and production, but also from the way in which the architectural object operates under the given contingencies and constraints operative in a particular situation. A clear example is Interloop's Plug—On project (2002–03) **(Fig. 7)**. Its off-site production, packaged delivery, and installation required bespoke contractual agreements and the development of new collaborations, construction schedules, and fabrication processes, all of which allowed the accretion to cantilever from the existing slab to facilitate spatial expansion where extension of the building footprint was prohibitive given site regulations and constraints. Applied to an existing 1960s dwelling, this eight-foot, stainless steel and glass cube – evidencing the quality finishes, exacting tolerances, and integration of components factory production allows – transforms both the spatial organisation and aesthetic of the house. Provisionally yet perpetually suspended from the extant dwelling, Plug—On constantly updates the existing home, with the contemporaneity apparent in a visibly acquired, high-tech application.

The result of Interloop's systematically contingent engagements are products with a life of their own: packages of knowledge embodying newly defined protocols of resourcing, production, fabrication, testing, and assemblage, developable in subsequent iterations. The conceptual division of the architectural object into a manifold of parts allows Interloop to isolate particular components and use the commission to develop proprietary knowledge. Systems like Plug—On, details of which appear as the feature element of the 9º House and in the Yoga Studio, become recurring elements in Interloop's designs.

'It just arrived'

As the principal juncture between their design ambitions and their own domestic, professional, and academic activities, the 48' House embodies many of the ideas central to Interloop's larger practice and reflects the capacities of architectural labour in the contemporary political economic system. While the 48' House clearly embodies Interloop's broader ambitions, it often does so in a financially restrained form and *in nuce*. Historically, architect-designed houses have been a crucial locus of architectural invention because an alternative, avant-garde lifestyle is implicated in their design. But Finley and Wamble recognise that, in the context of a neoliberal economy, dwelling is rarely conceivable beyond mutable and pressing realities. They craft the design process, the building delivery method, and the articulation of the architectural object to the given conditions of each commission. Finley and Wamble have characterised this contingent emphasis on delivery and performance with a figure they dubbed 'the Scrounger', based on Hendley, the character played by James Garner in John Sturges's film *The Great Escape* (1963).[6] Trapped in a Second World War prison camp, Hendley furnishes his compatriots with the materials necessary to effect efforts at escape. Seemingly out of thin air, the Scrounger identifies available means, procuring and repurposing them for desired ends.

Realising constraints and opportunities, Finley and Wamble integrate experimentation into their commissions by developing an architectural praxis that questions established norms of architectural design and building production. Some might be concerned this approach abandons radical propositions and fundamental reform for neoliberal 'research and development'. But, in the face of given reaities, where projecting and embodying an alternate mode of dwelling – as though conditions are infinitely and readily plastic – is unrealistic, Finley and Wamble engage the systems, technologies, procedures, and requirements we contingently confront, seeking to identify and take advantage of where and how they are pliable, so their clients, the practice, and the discipline might engage with greater agency the fickle currents of the prevailing political economic condition, however long it lasts.

Inseparable from this approach is Interloop's aesthetic. The articulation of the architectural object into a system of applications – be it structural props, graphic objects, wrapping enclosures, plugged-on spaces, or packaged dwellings – produces, despite contingency, a remarkably fresh and positive temporality. Unconsciously thought, if not spoken, today, as a book, song, or app is seamlessly delivered to your device, 'It just arrived' is a powerful cultural phenomenon. As our world becomes more intricate, our knowledge more specialised, our lives more interconnected yet no less remote, the 'just arrived' announces – rather than suppresses – the organisation of a complex background into a graspable interface: timely, available, and ready for use.

Bibliography

Bell, Michael and Sze Tsung Leong, eds. *Slow Space*, New York: Monacelli Press, 1998.

Finley, Dawn. 'Assuming Risk'. *Log* 5 (Spring/Summer 2005): 37–9.

Finley, Dawn and Mark Wamble. 'Notes on System Form: The Rest of the World Exists'. *Perspecta* 34 (2003): 110–17.

Gustin, Georgina. 'Greetings from Houston, TX' *Dwell* 7, 10 (10 October 2007): 190–7.

Kwinter, Sanford and Daniela Fabricius, 'Houston™' In Koolhaas, Rem, Stefano Boeri, Sanford Kwinter, Nadia Tazi, and Hans Ulrich Obrist. *Mutations*. Barcelona: Actar, 2000.

Kwinter, Sanford. ed. *Rem Koolhaas: Conversations with Students*. Houston: Rice School of Architecture, 1996.

Wamble, Mark. 'Globalism and the New Interior'. *Arch+* (April 1997): 44–6.

Good Fences Make Good Neighbours (So They Say)

Kirsty Volz

Introduction

Private housing can be thought of as somehow insulated from broader social, political, environmental, and economic discussions. Each house is contained within an individual plot of land, standing a silo of secluded domesticity. But architects designing private detached dwellings can, and do, contribute to communities and neighbourhoods by making houses that are inclusive, affordable, sustainable, and accessible. To create a house that extended the concept of domesticity beyond privately held boundaries was precisely the approach that my partner David Toussaint and I had in mind when we designed our family home in Brisbane, Australia. However, in testing the established narratives of uncompromised privacy through the physical and visual separation between private dwellings, we found ourselves testing the patience of our neighbours. After receiving formal complaints lodged with the local city council, the removal of plants from our property, and verbal abuse over our common fence, we knew that we had a lot to learn from our decision to design a house that challenged the pursuit of absolute suburban privacy. Or perhaps it was the wrong neighbourhood that we challenged? The following chapter tells the story of the house – we call it the 'Two Pavilion House' – that David and I designed for our family. It also reflects on the architectural exemplars and theories that influenced the design and how some of these ideas materialised, for better or worse.

David and I had limited experience with private housing. Much of our careers had been spent working in the employment by large firms on institutional buildings. We were struck by the high levels of regulation and legislation involved in building a house, leaving us perplexed by how institutionalised residential architecture in Australia is. Working with a challenging, narrow site (5.5 metres wide) we were intrigued by local planning laws for designing houses. In particular, the emphasis placed by local government planning legislation on privacy achieved through private space and visual separation between private dwellings, manifesting the sentiment of 'good fences making good neighbours'. The saying originates from Robert Frost's 1914 poem, 'Mending Walls', in which he fictively quotes his neighbour using the phrase, 'Good fences make good neighbours'.[1] In the poem, Frost questions this phrase, pondering who he would be walling in or out of his fence and who would be so offended by his presence next door?[2]

The spatialisation of privacy via arbitrary dimensions for setbacks from site boundaries and the location of windows and openings was something that we questioned through our design for the Two Pavilion House.[3] Perhaps informed by our experience of working on judicial and correctional facilities, we believed that, while some

1
Frost, *The Poetry of Robert Frost*, 44.

2
Frost, *The Poetry of Robert Frost*, 44.

3
Residential architecture in Australia is regulated by three levels of government: national, state, and local. The national level sets out standards for general construction quality such as water proofing and structural integrity. It also sets out general rules for the location on dwellings from boundaries such as street fronts and neighbours. The state level of legislation outlines more detailed planning requirements, including how neighbouring houses should relate to each other in terms of setbacks and the location of windows. The local level of government provides the most detailed information about location of adjoining rooms as well as doors and windows in neighbouring houses. Where there are discrepancies between the three levels of building legislation, the more local level of planning supersedes the least local; that is, the local government planning supersedes the national.

Fig. 1 The narrow front facade of the Two Pavilion House. (Photograph by © Scott Burrows)

Fig. 2 Ground- and first-floor plans for the Two Pavilion House.

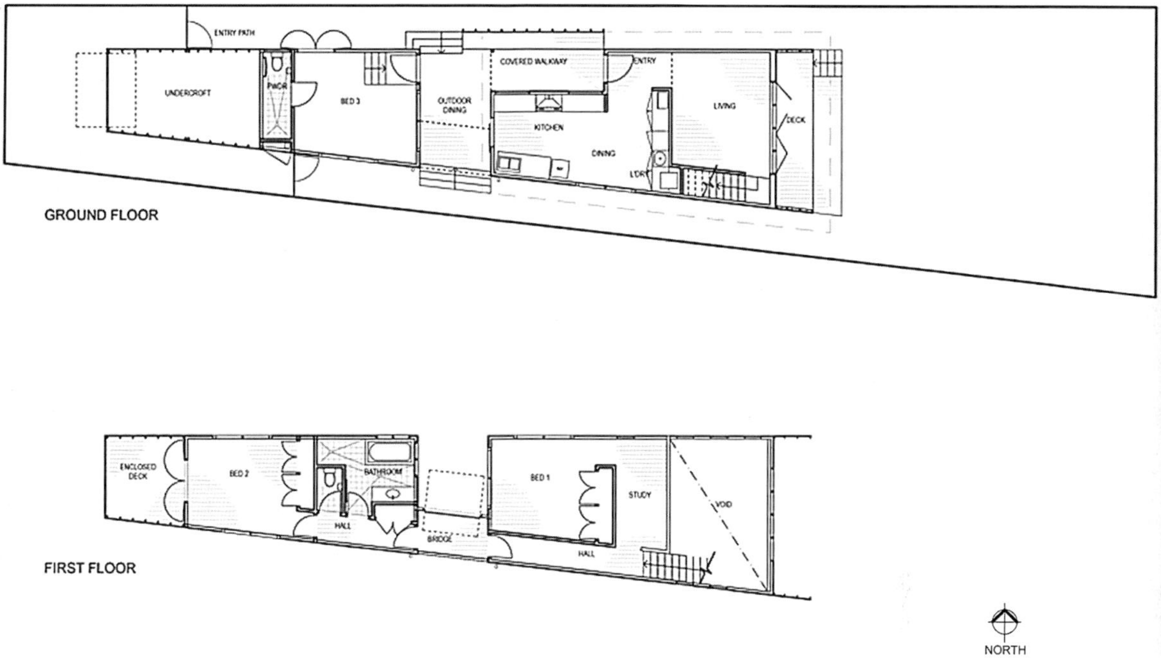

privacy is always needed, too much privacy only acts to create isolation, seclusion, and segregation. For a number of practical reasons, especially in response to a difficult site, the form of the Two Pavilion House challenged conventions of absolute privacy between us and our neighbours. The design intent also sought to engage with our neighbours in what might be considered an unconventional way for post-war planned suburbs. In an age of increasing social isolation, we endeavoured to design a house that contested the prioritisation of privacy over other spatial qualities.

The Two Pavilion House

There were many physical challenges to address in designing a house for the narrow site we purchased. The narrow entrance to the block is west-facing and overlooks a train line that runs parallel to the long edge of the site. All of these factors made the block affordable for two young architects. It also presented an opportunity to flex our designer capabilities and create something workable. As well as a difficult site, we had to work within the means of our own limited funds. Like most Western countries in the twenty-first century, Australian housing has been financialised. It has become a commodity that is valued by its components, like cupholders and electric windows in a car. The value of housing is determined by the number of bedrooms, bathrooms, and how many cars it can accommodate – rather than the incalculable value that

Fig. 3 The southern elevation shows how the house is split into two pavilions. (Photograph by © Scott Burrows)

good quality housing provides to both individuals and societies.[4] What this meant for us is that we had to design the house for a secondary client, the financial institution from which we borrowed money for the build. To make a viable case for funding from the bank, we needed to meet their formula for financial value, which resulted in the inclusion of a third bedroom and car parking, despite neither of these being necessary for our family's housing needs. However, this requirement inspired some creative thinking and was the main driver for splitting the house into two.

Splitting the house into two pavilions meant that the house could be occupied as either a three-bedroom dwelling or used in two sections, with a self-contained flexible compartment (the third bedroom). The configuration in which we use the house is that the third bedroom is our office, and we inhabit the two-bedroom house on the second floor, with these spaces connected by a raised internal courtyard. The space between the two pavilions acts as a foyer that both joins and separates the two units of the house. The flexibility of this plan, allowing for various configurations of living and working at home, was the defining concept behind the design of the house. Flexibility was a method for minimising risking personal investment in the post-global-financial-crisis housing market.[5] Prior to 2008, regulatory and legislative changes led to excessive risk borne by households and mortgage holders, which was exposed by the financial crisis. In response, we designed a house that could accommodate various programmes as a way of future-proofing the suburban detached dwelling.[6]

This space between the two pavilions also works like the breezeway in a 'dog trot' (or 'possum trot' in Australia) house, providing good air movement and ventilation, which is necessary for houses in the subtropics and tropics. The bridge on the second floor that connects the two pavilions is clad in a translucent material that provides diffused daylight to the long corridor that runs along the southern side of the house. The walls on this bridge also open out, like an awning to further ventilate the second-floor spaces on hot and humid days. All of this means that the very middle of the house is completely open and that instead of having a street-facing entrance, the house opens out to the neighbouring property. The entrance being located in the middle of the house was also a response for incorporating car accommodation within such a narrow street-facing facade. With no space left for an entrance, this became another reason for locating the entrance adjacent to our neighbour instead of the street. But it has also facilitated much of the flexibility inherent in the design, by acting as a foyer between the two pavilions.

Good intentions drove the idea to open the centre of the house to the neighbouring property. We felt that we could provide a better microclimate to our neighbour in terms of access to natural daylight, air movement, and ventilation. Rather than looking at a long continuous wall, our neighbour could look through the opening between the pavilions to the view beyond. Most importantly, it

4
Cheng, 'Future Proofing the Suburbs', 56

5
I have explored this topic in a short article for *The Conversation*. In this article, Ulrich Beck's concept of the 'risk society' was used to analyse how the Two Pavilion House and The One Room Tower by Phorm Architects and Antony Moulis and Silvia Micheli were responses to the risk borne by the housing market in twenty-first-century living. Volz, 'We Need More Flexible Houses'.

6
There is a significant amount of literature on the risk society and housing. For a concise overview and a clear articulation on how housing and mortgages were at the centre of the global financial crisis, see Horváth, 'Risk Society in Housing', 129.

Fig. 4a The operable wall of the second-storey bridge in the Two Pavilion House. (Photograph by © Scott Burrows)

Fig. 4b The operable wall of the second-storey bridge in the Two Pavilion House. (Photograph by © Scott Burrows)

provided us with the opportunity to be actively private or social with our neighbours. However, opportunities to socialise with neighbours may have not been as desirable as we imagined, causing us a considerable amount of stress in the months after we first occupied the house. In designing the Two Pavilion House, we found that we could not simultaneously provide complete privacy via the prescribed separation of outdoor spaces found in local planning guidelines, and also provide access to ventilation and daylight to our neighbours. The dominant approach found in town planning guidelines for Australian cities was to prioritise absolute privacy over other spatial qualities such as access to daylight, ventilation, and opportunities for socialising.[7]

Brisbane City Council, the jurisdiction under which the Two Pavilion House was built, required that 'the building must be oriented to the street to facilitate casual surveillance of the street and provide visual interest.'[8] We were able to address this requirement by using screens of CNC-routed circles in shiplap boards at the front of the house, which is also a significant part of the front facade's visual expression to the street. These permeable screens were incorporated throughout other sections of the house to mediate spaces that open onto public areas. The screens allow for us and our neighbours to choose between socialising or to retreat behind the screens for privacy. We wanted to challenge the notion that socialising with neighbours was restricted to passive surveillance over the street and create opportunities for more ad-hoc, semiprivate interaction to occur between neighbouring houses. The element of choice, being able to choose to socialise with your neighbour, is one aspect of the design that we could have developed with more care by consulting with them on the design and intent of this space more thoroughly.

Influential Australian Houses

Of course, we are not the first, or only, architects to contest concepts of privacy in domesticity. There were two Australian houses that were completed while we were students at university that we critically studied as exemplars for this project. One was Sean Godsell's Kew House (1997), which was named after the Melbourne suburb in which it is located and built for his family. The second exemplar was D House (1998) designed for a private client by architectural firm Donovan Hill in the Brisbane suburb of New Farm. Both of these projects offered very different lessons in our pursuit of challenging notions of privacy in domestic architecture.

Sean Godsell is an internationally esteemed Australian architect whose work has been described as having, 'a reputation for being uncompromising, tough and difficult'.[9] His Kew House is a modernist glass-and-steel dwelling, with glass facades mediated by operable steel shutters that shade the north and west elevations. In describing the limited privacy provided by the house, Godsell stated that '[if] you don't feel good about yourself, you won't like the building. There's nowhere to hide in that sense.'[10] In an interview

7
Guidelines stipulating casual or passive surveillance over the street was mentioned in all planning guidelines for small lots (those under 350 square metres) in all local government planning guidelines for major cities along the east coast of Australia. For example, in Sydney, the Liverpool City Council outlines these same provisions: Liverpool City Council 'Development Control Plan 2008, Part 3.5 Dwelling houses on Lots less than 400sqm', (Liverpool City Council, 2014), 19.

8
Brisbane City Council, 'Chapter 5: Small Lot Code', 12.

9
'No Guts, No Glory'.

10
***In the Mind of the Architect: Keeping the Faith*, (Episode 2), Australian Broadcasting Commission, 1998 [documentary].**

Fig. 5 Looking out from the bridge over the open space between the two pavilions. The neighbour's house is behind layers of screening. (Photograph by © Neil Burton)

Fig. 6 The front window of the D House, which can be opened or closed to the street so that occupants can socialise or be private. (Photograph by © L. Jenkins)

in the 1998 documentary *In the Mind of the Architect*, Godsell's partner, Annemarie Kiely, described how this lack of privacy affected her daily routines of inhabitation.

> Living here is accepting the fact that you're living in a very public domain [...] and I remember one of the first nights we stayed in here, I became incredibly aware of the fact that there were no blinds in the front bedroom and that I'd have to get into the cupboard and change, which I did and after a short space of time, I got very used to getting changed in the cupboard.[11]

Keily's reflections on living in the Kew House reveal Godsell's uncompromising approach to architecture. From studying this house, we learned that even if privacy was to be managed by operable screening devices, the design had to walk a fine line of providing an equal exchange between being seen in the house and to see out of the house. If the house allowed for someone to look out onto the street or neighbours, they had to be able to do this without feeling as though they were constantly being watched. People from either inside or outside of the house need to feel as though they can exert control over what they can see, and how much they are seen themselves.

Perhaps a more successful example that we studied, which, like our house, was built in Brisbane, was the D House by Donovan Hill. Built in 1998 in the suburb of New Farm, the house was designed for a private client with the architects occupying a section of the house for their studio after its completion. The Two Pavilion House shares a very similar approach to this house in its versatile programming and its provision for a multitude of methods for inhabitation. Timothy Hill commented: 'If you were going to the trouble of making a building it ought to have another use and that she [the owner] could lease it as a business if circumstances required it.'[12] This approach was influential to the concept that underpinned the Two Pavilion House, where designing for multiple functions was a method to minimise the financial risk of an investment in the housing market. Additionally, Hill felt that houses with layered and varied functions, such as small businesses or other community-oriented programmes, would promote village-like communities within the suburbs.[13] The house negotiated its relationship with the street via a garden wall and a large window that opened out onto the street. This window can be opened or closed, be private or social, depending on how or by whom the space adjacent to the street was occupied.[14] Now D House is widely celebrated as a significant work of Australian architecture; however, it required a significant amount of discussion with the local council.[15]

D House was built on a 300-square-metre plot of land, the same size as the site of Two Pavilion House, which meant working with the same overlay of planning laws for small lots, even though these two houses were built fifteen years apart. Timothy Hill also sought to challenge local planning laws. In an interview Hill described how the planning application process was argued over a period of two years. He said that he felt 'the application process was arduous

11
In the Mind of the Architect.

12
McCartney, *80/90/00 Iconic Australian Houses*, 156.

13
Fraser, 'Brian Donovan and Timothy Hill of Donovan Hill'.

14
Hill and Donovan, 'D House', 11.

15
Donovan Hill's D House was awarded the Robin Boyd Award for House of the Year in 2001 by the Australian Institute of Architects, the highest honour awarded to Australian residential architecture. For more information on this award, see the Australian Institute of Architects' Robin Boyd Award site: https://dynamic.architecture.com.au/i-cms?page=5611. 1. Accessed 5 July 2021.

16
Interview with the architect, Timothy Hill, 4 February 2019.

17
Interview with the architect, Timothy Hill, 4 February 2019.

18
Feagins, 'Geraldine Cleary'.

19
Cockayne. *Cheek by Jowl*, 36.

20
Cockayne. *Cheek by Jowl*, 23.

but was fought on very earnest grounds, i.e. the building presented as a garden wall to the street (which was promoted as a reasonable and precedented idea).'[16] Fortunately, Hill and his client prevailed and not only has this house won many awards, it has been an influential work of Australian architecture, and a house from which we drew inspiration. Hill commented on how it was one of only a few houses in the area that encouraged socialisation. He stated, 'As it has turned out the house quickly became an amenable contributor to the street edge since it is one of few openable windows in the street.'[17] The original client and current owner and occupant of D House, Geraldine Cleary, reflected on how successfully the house facilitated its public presence while providing a private residence. She said in a recent interview that she appreciated how the house promoted 'the feeling of being in a sequestered zone while being so close to the activity of the street.'[18]

While the D House was successful in managing the interaction of activities associated with the public and private spheres of the house, the Two Pavilion House was not as well received by the neighbourhood at first. On reflection, the section of our house that opens to our neighbours might have been accepted more easily if we had engaged and consulted with our neighbours more thoroughly throughout the design and construction processes.

Housing creates neighbours

Historian Emily Cockayne has written a detailed history of neighbourly relations in her book, *Cheek by Jowl: A History of Neighbours* (2013). Much of the book is dedicated to analysing changing expectations of privacy between dwellings, especially in the post-war era. Cockayne articulates that creation of housing is also the creation of neighbours, writing, 'Designing houses involves creating neighbours. Build one house and you might build the conditions for as few as one or two new relationships between existing and new residents in a street.'[19] She also argues that architects have the capacity to amend the worrying trend of social isolation in our cities and communities. She writes:

> Architects are in an unusually privileged position of being able to help to ameliorate the decline of neighbourliness by creating homes that accommodate modern requirements without isolating people in hermetic boxes. Sensitive architecture allows occupants to regulate their privacy – sometimes cultivating relations with people living nearby and at other times allowing retreat. When neighbours can meet each other casually and routinely in the street or glimpse each other in less private parts of the house, friendly familiarity can flourish.[20]

Contrary to Cockayne's optimistic view of how opening up public spaces of a house to neighbours could assist in friendly neighbour relations, our experience was something quite different.

What began as some terse exchanges during the construction of the house escalated to verbal death threats over the fence. When we tried to address the tension by planting tall bamboo along the

Fig. 7 Screens and planting in response to complaints from neighbours. (Photograph by © Scott Burrows)

shared boundary, these were promptly cut down and pulled out of the ground. Then finally, a formal complaint about the design of the house was submitted to the council, and after review, the council found in our favour. All in, it was twelve months of stressful exchanges between neighbours. The one relief I draw from that experience is that we did not inflict this situation onto a client and that we have learned so much from this experience. In particular, the need for regular, consistent consultation with neighbours from an early stage of the project. If you intend on designing a house that addresses issues beyond your private boundary, then you better make sure that everyone affected is on board with the idea. I would recommend that every young architect design their own house and live with their own mistakes.

Conclusion

Is it the architecture that facilitates social interaction between neighbours or do we need neighbours with existing friendly relationships and then architecture that is designed in response to this? In the case of the Two Pavilion House, the answer to this question was the second scenario. More broadly though, greater neighbourhood cohesion requires both, but it needs to start with the kind of soft infrastructure that facilitates neighbourly relations and then architecture that assists and maintains these relationships. For us, we learned that an architectural concept needs to be executed beyond the drawing board and we should have engaged those soft skills by talking with our neighbours from the very beginning. However, with time our neighbourly tensions have subsided, and we have started to appreciate the benefits of the open centre of our house. Of course, good access to daylight and ventilation have proven advantageous to the efficient running of the house and quality of internal spaces, but we have also been able to gradually build a relationship with our neighbour via this space.

Encouraging neighbourhood relationships is not just about the physical interactions that residential architecture frames. It can also be encouraged through the layering of other activities within houses, such as home-based businesses, as discussed in the design of Donovan Hill's D House as well as the Two Pavilion House. We were motivated to do so in response to the 'risk society' in the post-financial-crisis housing market. However, in light of the pandemic in 2020, where working from home has become normalised and people have been living almost entirely within their suburbs, it will be interesting to note if approaches to planning for residential architecture evolve with these requirements. For us, the flexibility of the planning for the Two Pavilion House has assisted in so many ways while we work, school, socialise, and live, all within our home, during these extraordinary times.

Bibliography

Brisbane City Council. 'Chapter 5: Small Lot Code'. https://www.brisbane.qld.gov.au/sites/default/files/chapter5_rdsmalllot_code.pdf. Accessed 6 June 2019.

Cheng, Linda. 'Future Proofing the Suburbs: Toussaint and Volz', *Houses*, no. 126 (February 2019): 56–7.

Cockayne, Emily. *Cheek by Jowl: A History of Neighbours*. London: Random House, 2012.

Donovan, Brian, and Timothy Hill. 'D House' *UME* 15 (2002): 10–9.

Feagins, Lucy. 'Geraldine Cleary'. *The Design Files*, 13 February 2013. https://thedesignfiles.net/2013/02/brisbane-home-geraldine-cleary/. Accessed 6 June 2019.

Fraser, Margie. 'Brian Donovan and Timothy Hill of Donovan Hill', *ArchitectureAU*, 24 January 2012. https://architectureau.com/articles/brian-donovan-timothy-hill-of-donovan-hill/. Accessed 1 June 2019.

Frost, Robert, 'Mending Walls' (1914). In *The Poetry of Robert Frost*. London: Random House, 2001.

Horváth, Vera Csilla. 'Risk Society in Housing'. *Corvinus Journal of Sociology and Social Policy* 8, no. 2 (2017): 123–30.

Liverpool Development Control Plan 2008, Part 3.5 'Dwelling houses on Lots less than 400sqm in the R2, R3 and R4 Zone', 19 February 2014. https://www.liverpool.nsw.gov.au/__data/assets/pdf_file/ 0014 /111830/Part-3.5-Dwelling-houses-on-lots-less-than-400sqm-PDF-copy-linked-to-webpage-19-February-2014.pdf. Accessed 1 June 2019.

McCartney, Karen. *80/90/00 Iconic Australian Houses: Three Decades of Domestic Architecture*. Sydney: Allen & Unwin, 2007.

'No Guts, No Glory'. *The Age*, 24 September 2003. https://www.theage.com.au/national/no-guts-no-glory-20030924-gdwebr.html. Accessed 4 June 2019.

Volz, Kirsty. 'We Need More Flexible Houses for 21st Century Lives', *The Conversation*, 14 September 2018. https://theconversation.com/we-need-more-flexible-housing-for-21st-century-lives-102636. Accessed 1 June 2019.

Nature, Naturism, and Lived Resistance

The chapters gathered in the sixth and final section of this book all in some form draw connections between nature, the body, and lived resistance. In doing so, the architects' homes discussed in this section not only subvert established sociocultural mores and conventions and decry economic systems by which the right to a good home is afforded to the few rather than the many, but they also make statements about ecology and a concern for the environment in architecture.

The first chapter in this section focusses on La Baumette, a holiday retreat that Belgian architect Jul De Roover created for himself and his family in the 1960s in the south of France. In their chapter, 'The Home as Refuge', Els De Vos and Selin Geerinckx address the apparent paradox that existed between De Roover's social-utopian (even communist) beliefs, and the rather bourgeois practice of having a holiday home. Through an analysis of De Roover's writings and conversations with those who knew him personally, they point out that De Roover himself did not regard this as a paradox, as he – like many of his modernist colleagues at that time – believed that a more primitive existence in close connection to nature was a way of living a truer life and opposing conventionalism in society. For De Roover, it was, as De Vos and Geerinckx put it, a balm for the soul.

In 'Naturism at Home', living in close proximity to nature is also a central theme; one which in the case of furniture designer Bruno Mathsson, who is the subject of this chapter, became intricately entangled with Swedish health and fitness culture. In the 1960s Mathsson built a small one-level summerhouse for himself and his wife in Frösakull in southern Sweden. In her text, Helena Mattsson describes how this house was set up in such a way to allow its residents to lead an ascetic naturist life, which was anti-consumerist and self-disciplining. Viennese architect Bernard Rudofsky also aspired to such an existence. As Pierre Chabard describes in his chapter 'Between Sparta and Sybaris', Rudofsky practised a naturist lifestyle, and advocated for a return to nature, vegetarianism, equality between the sexes, clothing reform, etc. In his text, Chabard focusses on the embodied resistance of the famed author of *Architecture without Architects*, as he explores how Rudofsky in his various homes – including the project for a patio-house on Procida Island in Italy, and La Casa, which he built near the end of his life in Frigiliana near Malaga in Spain – questioned all facets of the art of living: the way of sitting (preferably on the floor), of sleeping (not necessarily in a bed), of bathing (separated from washing), and of dressing (or not dressing). In doing so, Chabard argues, Rudofsky took a clear stance against the capitalist and techno-industrial way of life.

Lived resistance is also at the heart of Xiang Ren's chapter 'A Bare Form of Practice', although in this case it is performed in the name of environmental protection, understood both in the sense of natural and cultural ecology. The protagonist of Ren's story is Weizhong Ren, a Chinese farmer, whose commitment to creating a truly ecological environment made him into a self-taught, 'barefoot architect'.

From the early 2000s, Weizhong Ren opposed the increasing financialisation of rural land in China as well as the market-driven promotion of certain architectural styles that negate traditional forms of dwelling and adversely affect local environments through their use of industrialised materials. In response, he proposed a different mode of architectural and urban production; one that makes use of local materials, such as earth, clay, and wood, and respects traditional patterns of dwelling. Naturally, Weizhong Ren used his own home as a case in point.

The final chapter is by Australian architect Robert Riddel, who is today perhaps best-known for his work in heritage conservation and adaptive reuse. In 'A Secret Life', Riddel tells the story of one of his first endeavours in adaptive reuse, when he made a home for himself in early 1970s London inside a second-hand milk delivery van. Riddel's choice to live inside what he calls 'an urban bolt-hole' was a direct response to contemporary housing conditions in the British capital. With vast slum clearance projects underway in an effort to make space for grandiose new urban schemes, affordable and good-quality housing was scarce. Rather than join the squatter movement, Riddel sought inspiration in the pages of *AD* (*Architectural Design*) to give shape to his own living experiment – a minimum dwelling for maximum freedom.

The Home as Refuge: Jul De Roover's Cave House in Les Baux, France
The paradox between modernist socialist thought and the bourgeois refuge

Els De Vos and Selin Geerinckx

Introduction: the role of the refuge in the life of modernist architects

Little is known about the different homes of Belgian modernist architect Jul De Roover (1913–2010), a CIAM member, a writer on modern home culture, and a founder of the first full-time interior architecture programme in Antwerp.[1] Although this may be unsurprising, considering that De Roover lived in rental homes, we do know that his 'cave', which was called La Baumette and was located in the village of Les Baux-de-Provence in France, formed an essential part of his life. It was a place where he could seek refuge from the stress of the world. In this cave, he received students, relatives, and his inner circle, including his brother-in-law, the leading Belgian post-war modernist architect and urban planner Renaat Braem (1910–2001). Braem, who designed several iconic modernist buildings in Belgium, is known as an engaged advocate of modernist urbanism.[2] De Roover also realised some iconic buildings in Antwerp, such as the Silvertop social housing towers and the public library of Deurne.

1 De Vos, Somers, and Eeckhout, 'Three Profiles of "Interior Architects" in Postwar Flanders'.

2 Braeken, *Renaat Braem 1910–2001*.

De Roover was a social-utopian architect who flirted with Marxism. Like his modernist contemporaries (including Braem), he advocated a more equal society and the democratisation of architecture, which he believed should be accessible to everyone and not just to the privileged few. A testament to his engagement for the working classes is the fact that De Roover had a column on home culture education for the journal of the Socialistische Vooruitziende Vrouwen (forward-looking socialist women) that was mainly published for female (socialist) blue-collar workers in Flanders. So how can we reconcile the fact that De Roover had a holiday house – essentially an expression of a rather bourgeois lifestyle – with his strong leftist ideas? The possession of an individual refuge as a second home seems to go against De Roover's broader social and communal ideas, namely his belief in modernist rental social housing as a vehicle to emancipate the masses. On the one hand, De Roover argued against bourgeois concepts of the home such as the parlour, a room that held all the best furniture and was intended to receive prestigious visitors, while on the other hand, he possessed a home in which to spend his holidays, clearly a bourgeois concept. Was De Roover aware of these contradictions? If so, how did he justify the purchase of the cave house?

We shed light on La Baumette's significance in terms of both space and meaning by means of a site visit, archival material, and some interviews. The most important archival sources were De Roover's memoirs as well as photographs and letters by De Roover, Braem, and their wives, Frida and Elza Severin, respectively. We conducted interviews with a graduate of De Roover who later bought his refuge as well as with De Roover's son Jan and his brothers Walter, Luc, and Herman De Roover.[3] An analysis of the layout of the cave and its dwelling practices enables us to have a better understanding of how the cave house fits into De Roover's life and ideology. As we will argue, De Roover used arguments of authenticity, simplicity, contemplation, and connection with nature as a way to justify his cave house; while at the same time, his way of life had more in common with a bourgeois life than with the poor, who couldn't afford a (second) home and didn't have a choice as to how they wanted to live. The study of La Baumette illustrates the tension between the ideas of modernist architects and their way of life.

The discovery of the refuge, La Baumette

In his unpublished memoirs, written in 1988, De Roover reported how during a 1967 trip to the south of France, some members of his family saw a 'for sale' sign for a cave house in the wilderness of Les Baux-de-Provence. For some years already, De Roover and his wife Frida Severin, daughter of the painter Juliaan Severin, had been looking for a holiday retreat.[4] They had initially targeted the region of the Ardennes, the French-speaking southern part of Belgium, but prices were too high. When contacted by his father Albert, Jul De Roover dropped his activities to visit Les Baux with his wife.[5] The couple was immediately won over. They arranged the sale and the cave was theirs. The troglodyte-shaped La Baumette was originally a shelter for shepherds and their sheep, offering protection from the rain and mistral winds. These *maisons troglodytes*, as these cave houses are called in French, are typical of the region. La Baumette is situated among expressive rocks and wild nature. A single path leads from the village towards a quite imposing wooden fence **(Fig. 1)**. On the left side, the garden is bordered by a low stone wall which encloses a balcony facing the valley. The outside space shows different sections with green flora as well as a Janus statue by Renaat Braem. From the stone table in the front garden there is a marvellous view of the Val d'Enfer, which was sketched innumerable times by De Roover and Braem **(Fig. 2)**. From the outside, the house is no more than a facade with a small roof **(Fig. 3)**.

Inside, the house contains three rooms **(Fig. 4)**. The central, multipurpose living room is arranged around a centrally placed table with four chairs; there are two beds against the wall. To the right is a kitchen with a shower in a corner and to the left a small bedroom with a bunk bed. The furniture is sober and convenient, limited to the essentials, and with a mix of second-hand objects gathered from Belgium and the local region. For example, the rattan chairs were bought by his son at a flea market in Ghent. The bunk bed, two single beds, a low cupboard, a wooden table, four Thonet chairs, and a free-standing coat rack were bought second-hand. In contrast to the largely mobile furnishings, only three cupboards in the kitchen and one in the main room are fitted. The small bedroom

3 Interviews with Richard Blomgren, alumnus of Jul De Roover, Antwerp, 22 June 2017; Richard Blomgren and Willem-Jan Nys, Les Baux, 3 July 2017; Jan De Roover, son of Jul, 23 June 2010; Herman De Roover, brother of Jul, Ghent, 10 March 2017; Luc De Roover, brother of Jul, Berchem, 16 May 2017; Paula Braem (mother of Renaat Braem) and her son Paul De Roover, Antwerp, 25 July 2014.

4 Frida was the sister of Elza Severin, the wife of architect Renaat Braem, and daughter of painter Juliaan Severin. Both spellings, Frieda and Frida, occur, but according to the cousin Paul De Roover, Jul De Roover insisted that it should be written as Frida Severin (email from Paul De Roover on 22 February 2019).

5 Jul De Roover, unpublished memoirs, private collection (Walter De Roover).

Fig. 1 Entrance to the premises of La Baumette with the text 'Segues lou benvengou' (Welcome). Date unknown. (Private collection, s.d.)

Fig. 2 A marvellous view of the valley of Les Baux (Val' d'Enfer) from the stone table in the front garden, 2017. (Photograph by © Selin Geerinckx)

Fig. 3 View of the frontage of the cave house, 2017. (Photograph by © Selin Geerinckx)

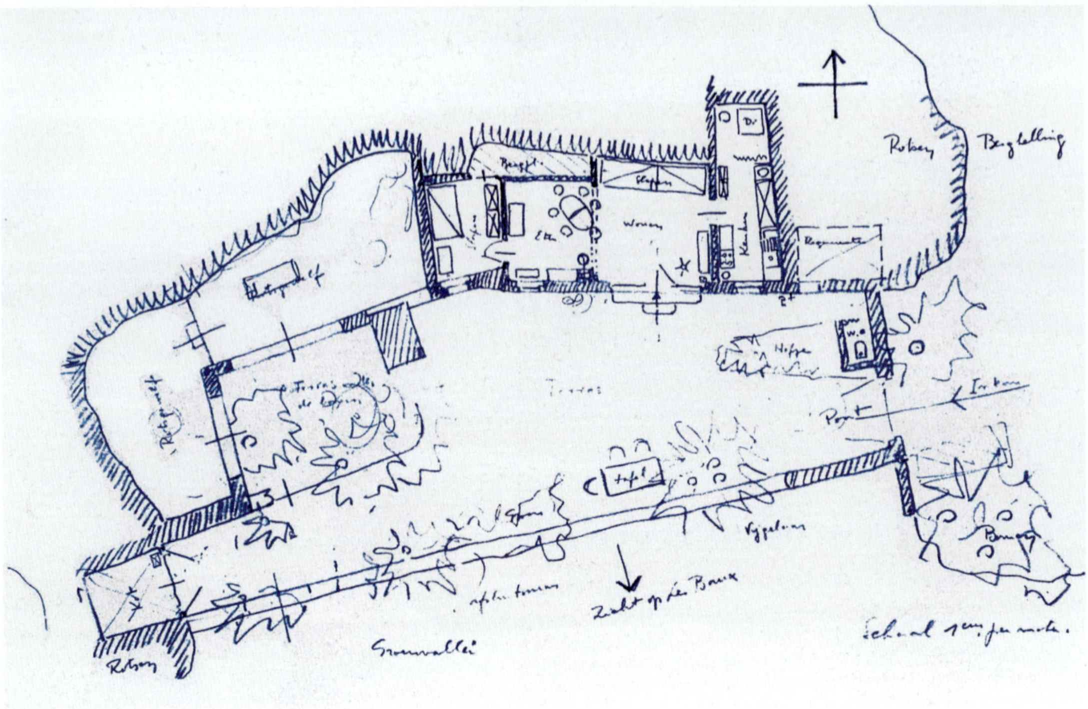

Fig. 4 Floor plan of the cave house and garden. (Undated drawing by Jul De Roover, private collection)

houses two then-fashionable Kewlox cupboards with the typical sliding doors. The toilet is outdoors, in a space with no door.

In the early days especially, De Roover and his wife had to do up the house considerably. During their first holiday, at Easter in 1967, they worked hard on their house – 'like devils', as De Roover recalled – while staying in a hotel in Les-Baux.[6] They had to strip the house, remove the collapsed ceiling, and clean up the dust and debris. De Roover created a new wood-slat ceiling and contacted local carpenters to replace the windows.[7] He was charmed by the fact that the carpenters seemed to treat them as fellow villagers, not demanding to work with a contract and unhurried when it came to sending the bills after completing the work. As the house had no water supply, one of the first tasks was to install a rainwater reservoir. Although the village had promised to provide a water supply, it took four years before the De Roovers could tap water from the village. The family also used a stove with a gas bottle and gas lamps until at least the end of 1992, when negotiations about the installation of electric pipes and a telephone cable were concluded.[8]

In sum, the cave house was, as its name suggests, a cross between a cave and a house, situated in a place of wilderness. It was quite hard to reach and it was minimally furnished and equipped. However, the magnificent view, the roughness of the spaces, and the house's integration with nature gave it a high sensorial quality. For De Roover and his family, it was a place in which to seek shelter from everyday life and to recharge their batteries. Their daily activities encompassed fixing up and painting the house (especially in the beginning), cooking meals, enjoying and observing the natural environment, making numerous sketches and sometimes also sculptures. They regularly took trips to the local shops, the theatre in Avignon or the baths in Saintes-Maries-de-la-Mer, which were fifteen kilometres away by car.[9] They also enjoyed the casual interactions with locals.

The leftist ideas of Jul De Roover

Notwithstanding the statue of the Virgin Mary in a niche above the entrance door, De Roover was not Catholic. He was baptised into Catholicism like most Belgians, but his family turned socialist during the First World War. During their exile in the Netherlands, they met the leftist poet Henriette Roland Holst and Herman Gorter, who influenced their political opinions.[10] Jul's father, Albert, a violist and painter who taught at the Royal Academy of Fine Arts, initiated his son but also his other pupils, such as Renaat Braem, into socialism. Albert often joined the Joe English Guild, an association of Antwerp academy students founded in 1928 that aimed to contribute to the design of a contemporary Flemish culture. Every Saturday they went to the Kalmthout Heath to camp in the grassland and discuss politics. According to Els Spitaels and Stefan Goossens, 'the union with nature was considered by these young idealists to be a source of rejuvenation and a fracture with the "bourgeois culture", a romantic idea that Braem intertwined with his socialist ambitions'.[11] The

6
Translated from Dutch: 'we werkten iedere dag als duivels'. De Roover, unpublished memoirs, private collection (Walter De Roover).

7
For example, he contacted a glassmaker from St-Rémy as there was no glass in the windows. Felix Archives, Stadsarchief Antwerpen, Antwerp.

8
Frida De Roover, postcard to the Braem family, dated 1 August 1992, in which she reports on negotiations about getting electricity and a telephone line. Felix Archives, Stadsarchief Antwerpen, Antwerp.

9
Elza Severin, letter to Braem, undated; and Jul De Roover, letter to Elza Severin, dated 14 July 1971, both in the Felix Archives, Stadsarchief Antwerpen, Antwerp.

10
De Vos, 'Biografie. Jul De Roover', 164.

11
Spitaels and Goossens, 'Biomorfe vormen. De architectuur van de liefde', 234.

Fig. 5 *Top:* De Roover and Braem on a rock in Les Baux. *Bottom:* De Roover on the right and Braem on the left. (© Felix Archives, Stadsarchief Antwerpen)

same applies to Jul De Roover. His personal library included some classic socialist and communist books, such as a series of pocketbooks on communism and politics, written by Lenin and Stalin, *The Communist Manifesto* by Karl Marx and Friedrich Engels, and issues of the Flemish Marxist journal *Uilenspiegel*, besides several issues of the socialist journal *Mens & Taak* (Humankind & Work).[12]

De Roover mainly communicated his political ideas through lectures, public talks, and conversations with his clients. He refused to sign an administrative document that demanded 'neutrality' in his teaching. 'How can I behave "neutrally"? Then you become a mussel', he said indignantly. 'If I can't pass on my ideas, I can't teach, because you teach who you are.'[13] He wanted his students to be unruly, to be 'sharp', as he called it, since life, he claimed 'will wear them down enough as it is'.[14] His motto was 'You don't need to be angry, but you need to remain angry.' Architecture was a symbolic struggle against conventionalism in society. He was in constant opposition to conventional ideas and didn't want to follow blindly the popular and often bourgeois taste of the masses. De Roover, like Braem, belonged to an avant-garde found across Europe, which advocated a cultural attitude that courageously embraced modernisation, including its contradictions between progress and identity, and left behind the past with its traditions and habits.[15] By means of well-designed, unconventional houses, buildings, and interiors, De Roover aimed to contribute to a more rational and better way of living. But he was sceptical about home ownership, which he considered 'merely a way to be tied to the banks. It prevents humans from being really free.'[16] For these reasons, he championed the provision of public social housing.

Central to De Roover's ideas was authenticity. Simplicity – discarding all the unnecessary clutter – as well as a close connection with nature were seen as ways of becoming and being more authentic. De Roover liked to quote the French architect Charlotte Perriand to explain this: 'Faire le vide, afin de créer la possibilité de penser et de se mouvoir' (To clear out in order to create the possibility to reflect and to move). She used it to refer to monkhood, a religious way of life in which one renounces worldly pursuits to devote oneself fully to spiritual work.[17] By the same token, De Roover gave the following advice:

> Sit on the floor in your empty home and reflect on your real living needs. For example, if you lack something to sit on, you can conclude that you need a chair. Gradually, you need to build up a list with the elements you really need (equipment). Secondly, you may also sum up your irrational needs, but these are less important and should be placed in a second column. Between the two elements, a thick concrete wall should be constructed, while the architect needs to drill holes in the wall to connect the rational needs with some well-selected irrational ones.[18]

'That is precisely the task of the architect', he continued in his lectures, 'starting from the rational needs while taking into account some irrational needs and being able to translate these needs.'

12
Private archive Jul De Roover, private collection (Walter De Roover). The books in the Amsterdam: Pegasus series were the following: J.W. Stalin, *Enige vraagstukken van het Leninisme*, 1938; W.I. Lenin, *De linkse stroming: een kinderziekte van het communisme*, 1966; W.I. Lenin, *Staat en Revolutie*, 1933; W.I. Lenin, *Het imperialisme als hoogste stadium van het kapitalisme*, 1916.

13
Translated from Dutch: Orban and Thijssen, *Jul De Roover,* video.

14
Translated from Dutch: De Roover, 'Oudersbezoek afdeling Binnenhuis', 24 February 1951, Box 36, Archive De Roover, Architecture Archive of the Collection of the Flanders Architecture Institute.

15
This attitude is described in Heynen, *Architecture and Modernity*, 13–4.

16
Translated from Dutch: Orban and Thijssen, *Jul De Roover*, video.

17
De Roover, 'Terug naar NUL - Cr.er le Vide'. Quote taken from lecture summary entitled 'Vormgeving en woninginrichting' at the 'Contactdagen Scheppend Ambacht', held in Lommel, Belgium 3–4 July 1963. Archive De Roover, Architecture. Archive of the Collection of the Flanders Architecture Institute.

18
Translated from Dutch: Orban and Thijssen, *Jul De Roover*, video.

What clients should absolutely avoid, according to De Roover, was to fill their homes with all kinds of furniture, similar to or inherited from their grandparents. First, they needed to reflect on their rational needs, and only then should they look for an object or piece of equipment in order to meet their own demands. Above all, they could only understand their real needs if they know who they were, De Roover argued. He therefore considered Le Corbusier a great example because 'this master has opened the dwelling problem by means of developing the "free plan" and the "free space"'. Only 'people who have enough depth', according to De Roover, are able to live in a free plan. 'Only people with a rich inner life are able to live in an empty space without objects, because they have enough with their selves. These are the main lessons that Mies van der Rohe and Le Corbusier have given us', continued De Roover.[19]

Tensions between a second home and socialism

In his lectures, as well as in his way of life, we can discern several contradictions. Although it is a noble idea to empty your house of 'old-fashioned stuff' and reflect on your real needs, this is not possible for everyone. Many people don't have the time to contemplate their ideal home; some even struggle to find a home. Not everybody is free to choose their furniture, as some have to be satisfied with that which they inherit or receive from friends or relatives, even if it looks dated or is not completely in line with what they really want. Besides that, inherited objects also have an agency. Irrespective of their appearance, they may have an emotional value, as they can act as a key to remember a (deceased) loved one. This is an aspect that the modernists generally ignored. Although De Roover was a columnist for a socialist women's magazine, his writings and lectures in effect addressed the middle and upper classes. Also, his lifestyle was ambivalent. The cave house itself was rather primitive, because it was traditionally a place for shepherds to shelter their sheep from the weather and it was modestly furnished. However, a second home is of course typically for the privileged few and an element of the bourgeoisie.[20]

Although De Roover pleaded for authenticity and his cave house looked like the primitive, authentic home of a local, in fact it was not. It was the holiday home of a Belgian architect who resided elsewhere. Its symbolic reference to old rural community life was not matched by real-life participation in anything resembling village life, nor by a lifestyle that had anything to do with sheep farming. It was a base for touristic activities. Because De Roover was on good terms with the locals, he did not consider himself a tourist. But, of course, he was one of the first, before the development of mass tourism. When he purchased the home in 1967, comfort was limited, but that changed rapidly. De Roover sought from the beginning for the arrival of tap water, and the use of gas bottles and gas lamps was out of necessity than a conscious choice. However, the overall image that visitors remember from the cave is the beauty of the natural surroundings, its primitive look, and the view of the valley.[21] They don't really remember the lack of domestic comfort.

19
All quotations in this paragraph are translated from Dutch: Orban and Thijssen, *Jul De Roover*, video.

20
In England, the hut became the holiday home of the bourgeoisie from the mid-eighteenth century onwards. Guéné-Loyer, 'Grande-Bretagne: du cottage pittoresque aux cités-jardins', 134–7.

21
Interview with Paul De Roover, Antwerp, 25 July 2014.

Fig. 6 Sketch by Jul De Roover, Les Baux, 1983. (Photograph by © Els De Vos, 2019)

The cave and nature of Les Baux were experienced by visitors as well as by De Roover and his family as a stimulating environment in which to draw artistic inspiration and to remain in close contact with nature.

De Roover was of course not alone in having a refuge. Many of his contemporaries had one – most famously, Le Corbusier's Cabanon in Roquebrune-Cap-Martin and Elissa and Alvar Aalto's atelier and summer residence in Finland, Muursatsalo.[22] These modernist architects also needed an 'environment for communal spiritual renewal'.

As architectural theorist Hilde Heynen has noted, modern architecture found itself in a double bind in the West:

> On the one hand its protagonists continued to fight an ideological battle defending modern architecture's superior qualities against a popular taste that increasingly favoured other styles. To avoid an alignment with the politically 'bad' guys of communism, however, their arguments turned cultural, stressing more and more the issue of authenticity and less and less the social concerns that had been primordial in the pre-war period.[23]

Concerning their second homes, similar arguments can be distinguished in their talks to legitimise the refuge: its capacity for contemplation, its escape from a (bourgeois) society in favour of its connection with nature, and its authentic design.

22
Menin and Samuel, *Nature and Space*.

23
Heynen, 'The Jargon of Authenticity'.

What distinguishes De Roover's cave house from the retreats of the above contemporaries is its physical appearance. While the Cabanon and Muursatsalo were self-designed and contrasted with nature – particularly Le Cabanon, for which Le Corbusier employed platonic volumes, but also Aalto's refuge, which was white – De Roover hardly intervened in the authentic *maison troglodyte*.

Unlike with his housing projects for clients, he didn't create architecture. He bought a vernacular house that he just improved. In leaving the architecture untouched, was he afraid to be associated too much with a particular house? Or it is perhaps more likely that he considered modern architecture inappropriate for a second home, at least in a place like Les Baux?

As he seemed to consider himself a local who was completely accepted by, even integrated into local society, the decision to live in a vernacular home in order not to stand out seems completely acceptable. It was also in line with his vision of a good home; it was:

> not a machine for living. In the first place we should create a living environment where we gather with relatives and friends, where we show our personalities, where the small pleasures of life, such as flower arrangements, the placing and hanging of art objects and knick-knacks, reproduce the character of the inhabitants in the interior, and where the colours also reflect the mood of the inhabitants.[24]

The cave is a good representation of that vision of home culture, perhaps even more than the fine houses De Roover designed for his clients. De Roover's cave house was like a comfortable old coat that served its purpose: a place to withdraw from society and explore nature. It was a place in which to rejuvenate and to meet friends and relatives, like a sacred balm applied to the soul.

24
De Roover, written texts entitled 'Onze wooninrichting' (Our Design of Dwelling Interiors), 1959, Archive De Roover, Architecture Archive of the Collection of the Flanders Architecture Institute. All translations from Dutch are by the authors.

Bibliography

Archive De Roover, Architecture Archive of the Collection of the Flanders Architecture Institute, Antwerp.

Braeken, Jo. *Renaat Braem 1910–2001.* Antwerp/Brussels: ASA Publishers, VIOE, 2010.

De Vos, Els, Inge Somers, and Bart Eeckhout. 'Three Profiles of "Interior Architects" in Postwar Flanders'. *Journal of Interior Design* 40, no. 2 (2015): 37–57.

De Vos, Els. 'Biografie. Jul De Roover'. In *Van Academie tot Universiteit. 350 jaar architectuur in Antwerpen*, edited by Els De Vos and Piet Lombaerde, 164–5. Antwerpen/Brussel: UPA/ASP, 2013.

Felix Archives, Stadsarchief Antwerpen, Antwerp.

Gresleri, Giuliano. 'La Sainte-Baume: terre et ciel, ombre et lumière'. In *Le Corbusier et la nature*, edited by Marc Bédarida and Claude Prelorenzo, 166–71. Paris, Néotype/Éditions de la Vilette, 2004.

Guéné-Loyer, Hélène. 'Grande-Bretagne: du cottage pittoresque aux cités-jardins'. In *Le régionalisme, architecture et identité*, edited by François Loyer and Bernard Toulier, 134–7. Paris: Monum/Editions du Patrimoine, 2001.

Heynen, Hilde. *Architecture and Modernity: A Critique*. London: MIT Press: 1999.

Heynen, Hilde. 'The Jargon of Authenticity: Modernism and Its (Non)political Position'. In *Constructed Happiness: Domestic Environment in the Cold War Era*, edited by Mart Kalm and Ingrid Ruudi, 10–27. Tallinn: Estonian Academy of Arts, 2005.

Heynen, Hilde. 'Geborgenheid en ontheemding' (Security and homelessness). In *Wegwijs wonen (Guide for the home)*, edited by André Loeckx et al., 25–8. Leuven: Davidsfonds, 1993.

Menin, Sarah and Flora Samuel. *Nature and Space: Aalto and Le Corbusier*. London: Routledge, 2003.

Orban, Louis and Jolanda Thijssen. *Jul De Roover: een visie op wonen*, dvd. Antwerp, 1996.

Private archive of Jul De Roover, private collection Walter De Roover.

Spitaels, Els and Stefan Goossens. 'Biomorfe vormen. De architectuur van de liefde'. In *Renaat Braem 1910–2001* by Jo Braeken. Antwerp/Brussels: ASA Publishers, VIOE, 2010.

Strauven, Francis. *Renaat Braem: Architect*, Brussels: AMA, 1983.

Strauven, Francis. 'Vlaamsgezind en vrijzinnig, socialistisch en religieus bewogen'. In *Renaat Braem 1910-2001*, by Jo Braeken. ASA Publishers, VIOE (2010).

Fig. 1 Frösakull, Mikael Olsson – FK02.2000, chromogenic print. (© Mikael Olsson / Galerie Nordenhake)

Naturism at Home: Building for a new lifestyle

Helena Mattsson

1
Friedman, 'Notes on Swedish Design', 25.

2
'Ingen vill köpa formgivarens hus', 18.

3
For a detailed account of Bruno Mathsson's work, see: Böhn-Jullander, *Bruno Mathsson* and Hogdal, *Bruno Mathsson*.

In 1960, the Swedish furniture designer Bruno Mathsson constructed an experimental summer house, dubbed the House of Tomorrow, for himself and his wife Karin Swärd at Frösakull, Tylösand, a popular sunbathing spot on the west coast of Sweden. The house was designed to suit their lifestyle as nudists and naturalists. Since the house was not passed on to any relatives, it stood uninhabited and virtually untouched from when Karin died in 1999 until it was sold in 2000. Both international and Swedish architects have praised the house and highlighted its innovative architecture. As Martin Friedman wrote in *Design Quarterly* in 1965: 'Constructed over sand dunes and tucked into a forest of dwarf pines, it is undoubtedly one of the most remarkable buildings in modern Sweden' **(Fig. 1)**.[1] Outside the architectural scene, however, the house has been more sceptically received. The architect Thomas Sandell and his colleagues Ulf Sandberg and Joakim Übel bought the house in 2000, thereby ensuring its future existence. They initiated a process to get the building listed before they put it on the market for sale, but things were looking bleak – nobody seemed to want the house. To the estate agents it was a shed; to the owners, a burden; and to most potential buyers, something to be demolished. If Frösakull – as the house was more often called – was not considered a real house, perhaps it qualified as art? The owners decided to put Frösakull up for auction as art at Stockholms Auktionsverk. Bruno Broberg, who was still officially the estate agent, made a statement in the press: 'This is a derelict building, a shed, and now they're planning to sell it as a work of art. That's just bullshit.'[2] In November 2004, Frösakull was advertised among several lots of 1960s Danish furniture as 'House', but the estate agent was right; nobody made a bid over the reserve price and the house was returned to the commercial real estate market. It was eventually evaluated at zero Swedish kronor and sold in 2006, with all the original fittings and inventory included in the price of the land. Throughout its existence, the house in Frösakull has attracted attention, either as a useless house, not to be seen as a home; or as remarkable architecture.

Bruno Mathsson was a furniture designer who had started to study and work with architecture in the mid 1940s to become, in the 1950s, a designer and self-taught builder of homes and exhibition buildings.[3] These works reveal him to be an original designer working in a style influenced by his personal lifestyle, of which the summerhouse in Frösakull is the most distinct exponent. Here, exclusive post-war modernism meets rugged outdoor living verging on asceticism. In Mathsson's summerhouse you live your life outdoors, interacting with nature, the climate, and the light. This is a house that very concretely has dissolved many of the material and functional boundaries of architecture **(Fig. 2)**. The climate and light change throughout the day; the kitchen has no stationary location

Fig. 2 Frösakull, Mikael Olsson –
FK08.2000, chromogenic print.
(© Mikael Olsson / Galerie Nordenhake)

4
Böhn-Jullander, *Bruno Mathsson*, 157–60.

5
Widman, 'Bruno Mathsson: Slå sönder och gör nytt!', 6.

6
Banham, 'A Home Is Not a House', 56–60.

in the house but is distributed and mobile; the ceiling is transparent and lets in the sunlight. The windows cannot be opened but have an open passage between inside and outside. The walls are on rails and can be opened and closed to change the layout.

In 1948, Bruno and Karin went to the United States, invited by Edgar Kaufmann Jr, the then-head of the design department at the Museum of Modern Art (MoMA) in New York, and met several of the most prominent American architects of the time, including Ray and Charles Eames, Philip Johnson, and Frank Lloyd Wright.[4] Bruno Mathsson was deeply impressed by the American way of building with large glass sections, underfloor heating, and other highly developed services. After returning to Sweden he showed a picture of Johnson's recently completed house in New Canaan to a journalist at the magazine *Form*, commenting, 'We could live like this in Sweden too [...] we are hopelessly backward here in Sweden!'[5] Johnson's house consists of two elements – a heated brick floor and an upright unit that is a bathroom on one side and an open fireplace on the other, constituting an excellent example, according to Reyner Banham, of the 'anti-house': 'The "house" is little more than a service core set in an infinite space.'[6]

Almost certainly influenced by Johnson's house in New Canaan and the Case Study Houses – a range of experimental budget homes designed and built between 1945 and 1966 on the west coast of the US – Bruno Mathsson designed a series of glass houses exploring the potential of new building technology. In these houses, Mathsson used the same elements, albeit with some variations: the concrete platform resting directly on the ground, underfloor heating, triple-glazed walls, separate windows for ventilation, and a simple floor plan where the kitchen and living room are merged and the bedrooms are usually lined up along a hallway. A similar floor plan is found in Frösakull. The bedrooms are in a line, but the kitchen is not open-plan with the living room but instead dissolved and spread out over the communal areas of the house. Not only was Mathsson the first architect in Sweden to design and build glass houses on a larger scale; he also patented and produced an insulating glazed unit – named 'Brunopane' – consisting of three panes of glass with nitrogen in between. During the war and in the immediate post-war era, building regulations were rigid and it was hard to get building permissions. Since the process of constantly applying for permissions and exemptions was expensive, Mathsson ceased his activities in the field of architecture after less than ten years (he practised between 1950 and 1957), with rare exceptions such as Frösakull.

After the Second World War, the attitude to technology was dynamic and complex, opening the door to architectonic fantasies. Both in the US and in Europe numerous experimental housing projects were presented, demonstrating in various ways the potential of new technology. In the UK, for instance, Alison and Peter Smithson displayed the House of the Future in 1956 at the *Daily Mail*'s Ideal Home Exhibition; and in the US, the Monsanto House designed by

Richard Hamilton and Marvin Goody was exhibited at Disneyland's Tomorrowland between 1957 and 1967. Bruno Mathsson's House of Tomorrow, the experimental house he presented as an idea in 1956 in the newspaper *Värnamo nyheter*, belongs among them:

> First and foremost, I want to use the heat and energy from the sun. In this respect I have gone one step further by making the roof out of transparent corrugated and bent plastic, which resembles the waves on a lake. If you want, the house can be fitted with a sunscreen. The house will be heated by solar energy, so the warm air generated right under the plastic roof by the sunlight can be conducted down to the floor, where the heat will then rise upwards. Naturally, this needs to be complemented with the existing electric underfloor heating.[7]

The House of Tomorrow was partially materialised in the Frösakull summerhouse in 1960, four years after it was presented in *Värnamo nyheter*. Like most of Mathsson's glass houses, Frösakull consists of a base platform measuring ten by fifteen metres, supporting a galvanised iron structure. The walls are made of corrugated plastic, South American wood (parapine), and glass, all of which are attached directly to the structure. The roof is made by flexing translucent opal-white acrylic plastic between the rafters to form six barrel vaults running across the structure and closing the entire space except for the inner court. Under the transparent vaults and steel rafters a ceiling of angled and mounted wood slats is suspended, sifting the light like venetian blinds. The house has two yards – an inner court enclosed by corrugated plastic and thus screened from view, and a sun patio that is not on the platform but enclosed with the same corrugated plastic and thereby incorporated in the body of the building. The layout is very simple; the building consists of two parts: a closed part with north-facing walls of wood for the bedrooms and bathroom and toilet, and an open part with corrugated plastic walls and a roof covering half of the space, making up the living room and inner courtyard. The only part that is different is the little sun patio, added as an extension to one of the corners.

From the outside the building looks like a yellowish plastic box with translucent walls showing the bodies moving inside as silhouettes, keeping the privacy without hiding from the common. At night the building stands as a lamp on the sand dunes in the pine forest. The entrance is on the west-facing, short side and consists of a sliding segment in the corrugated plastic facade facing the street. It opens onto the large inner courtyard paved with Fjärås granite, the first space in a sequence ranging from the most public to the most private – the courtyard, the living room, the bedroom, and the sun patio.[8] The house lacks ordinary doors, usually placed where there is a clear boundary between functions and degrees of privacy, such as between the courtyard and the living room and the bedrooms. Instead, whole sections of walls can be opened and closed, giving the house a dynamic layout. There is no insulation, and the walls and the roof work more like a skin, like a canvas tent, creating the feeling of sleeping outside rather than inside a house.

7
Mathsson, 'Morgondagens hus', 7.

8
Part of the inner courtyard originally consisted of fine sand from Tylösand, but as the house has no thresholds and lets in a lot of air, the sand kept blowing into the house. The floor was subsequently changed to granite.

9
Tylösand is famous for its beach and is popular among sunbathers. Naturists have also frequented the area. The outdoor sports enthusiast Gösta Zadig was Bruno Mathsson's closest neighbour, having built a house there in 1949 out of several building huts positioned around a central courtyard and a separate, screened patio for nude bathing. Mathsson did not call on Zadig until he had built his own house, but he was inspired by Zadig's patio and added one to his own house. From a talk with Gösta Zadig, 27 July 2006, Frösakull.

The cooker is on wheels and can be rolled anywhere. A sink and draining-board unit is just outside the living room in the courtyard under the loggia. The house has evenly spaced electric sockets along the skirting boards, so electrical appliances can easily be moved around. Technology is installed to serve social life and specific but flexible requirements depending on the how the structure is being used – shifting between an ascetic naturist's home to a glamourous cocktail lounge. Frösakull differs from many of its antecedents, including Johnson's New Canaan house, in that it does not have a service core. Instead, technology and other services are spread throughout the plan, which means that the kitchen can be dissolved and mobile. This potential for change and built-in variability makes the building appear like a stage rather than a house divided according to functional purposes. The granite floor becomes a platform for different settings depending on the arrangement of the sliding walls and the mobile interior elements, such as the stove, tables, chairs, and so forth. The environment has no determined organisation; the scene is set according to the desires of the actors, or the inhabitants, and the social activities that unfold in the space.

The glass wall of the bedroom can also be opened to incorporate the landscape behind the house, leading down to the sun patio, which is for private naturism, a space of exclusivity that offers the maximal privacy for being nude in the sun without being seen. The patio has a sand floor and a shower. If the curtains between the living room and bedroom are closed, a private quarter is created, making the bathroom, bedroom, and sun patio private for nude sunbathing.[9] This architectural environment does not only express a societal utopia of naturism and health, but also a critical historiography through its pragmatic response to (Swedish) functionalism.

Professionally, Bruno Mathsson was influenced by the 1920s and 1930s, when the modern Swedish state was evolving. The mind that would populate the emerging welfare state would be egalitarian and ethically aware – and it would be shaped partly by a new architecture and new commodities. Like many others, Bruno Mathsson saw the buildings, commodities, and ideals of this new movement at the Stockholm Exhibition in 1930, where architectural modernism was introduced in Sweden. The exhibition applauded the new technology and the growing consumer and media society, parallel with the emergence of an anti-consumerist body culture centring on health and outdoor sports. Alongside the emergence of functionalism, another vital movement evolved – the fitness culture. The fitness enthusiasts helped build up 'public health' as part of the strategy towards creating a new, healthy, egalitarian human being governed by needs rather than by desires.

Although the legal holiday entitlement was not introduced until 1938, the first parliamentary bill on legislated holidays was presented as early as 1917. One reason why it took so long before it was introduced was the scepticism regarding the workers' capacity to utilise their free time constructively. Holidays must not become

Fig. 3 Frösakull, Mikael Olsson – FK09.2002, chromogenic print. (© Mikael Olsson / Galerie Nordenhake)

Fig. 4 Frösakull, Mikael Olsson – FK07.2000, chromogenic print. (© Mikael Olsson / Galerie Nordenhake)

10
Näsström, *Fritidens morgonrodnad. En epokbildande utställning i Ystad 1936*, 52. Näsström also points out that it was Gregor Paulsson who highlighted the concept of free time. In 1926 there were only two definitions of free time according to the Swedish Academy's dictionary: the time one is free from a periodic illness (especially fever) or the time when a student is not attending school.

11
Nilsson, 'Man måste härda sig', 196–221.

12
Waerland, 'Gammal vid 20, ung vid 60!', 14.

13
Böhn-Juhlander, *Bruno Mathsson*, 107.

demoralising free time used for, say, uncontrolled consumption. The Swedish Tourist Board's walks and hostels and the recreation exhibition that Gregor Paulsson participated in organising in 1936 in Ystad are examples of attempts to influence and fill free time with structured activities. Largely the same people were engaged in the Ystad exhibition and the debate about free time at the Stockholm Exhibition – Alva Myrdahl, Gotthard Johansson, Gustaf Näsström, and others – and, as Näsström wrote: 'They managed their assignments in the same spirit of pulling along the new welfare state that had inspired the men and women involved in the [Stockholm Exhibition] in 1930.'[10]

In the late 1800s, when the tuberculosis bacteria had been identified, 'evil' obtained a material form and a scientific definition, but it was not visible to the naked eye, giving rise to general, collective fear. The sun was considered to be a 'disinfecting oven' – and both the fitness addicts and the modernists were sun-worshippers, making them a good team.[11] In the late 1920s, sunbathing, or naturism, grew into a popular movement, and in 1928 the brochure 'Against the swimsuit culture' was published repudiating the swimming costume culture and prescribing nude bathing as an ancient Swedish custom. The skin specialist Johan Almkvist was the figurehead of the Swedish naturists, claiming that it was unhealthy to keep the body constantly covered, that we should be naked as often as possible and only use clothes when necessary as protection. Being naked at home was part of the naturist lifestyle, and it was also important to emphasise that nudity in itself was not immoral. From this perspective, naturism and nudism could be seen as a disciplinary self-practice part of the processes of modernity where individual desires are controlled in favour of more general needs.

Bruno Mathsson came in contact with the fitness movement in the mid 1930s when he read the health guru Are Waerland's articles in the magazine *Frisksport* and used to eat fibre and raw vegetables. Sun and oxygen were as important to the fitness advocates as light and air to the functionalists, and the transparency promoted by the modernists was expressed in very concrete spatial terms by fitness advocates who transferred certain domestic functions, such as sleeping and cooking, from the interior to the exterior. Are Waerland advocated outdoor sleeping and had two beds outdoors, one in an open alcove and one in a treetop, writing:

> I have estimated the gain in oxygen in one night to more than one-third of consumption indoors, since the depth of breathing itself stands in direct relation to the freshness, coolness, purity (low dust content) and humidity of the air. The dry, dust-saturated indoor air is one of the main causes of respiratory disease.[12]

Following a visit to Waerland's home, Bruno Mathsson built an outdoor bed shaped to fit his body. It was a sort of metal tub on wheels, light enough to be moved indoors and outdoors, and covered by a body-shaped plastic hood with a zipper that could be heated up with five litres of water in a demijohn.[13] The bed caused a stir when it was shown at the *Vår bostad* exhibition in 1941, and one critic in the magazine *Form* described it as 'a typical example, in its meticulous attention to detail, of this fitness furniture philosopher's eagerness to take his life philosophy and professional potential to their utmost consequences.'[14]

Among fitness enthusiasts it was not only the bedroom/bed that 'moved outdoors' to be 'disinfected' with air and sunlight, but also the kitchen was often built outdoors, and it was a simple meal that was to be prepared in simple cooking facilities. Simplicity and anti-consumerism are lifestyle objectives often supported by scientific discoveries, as in Are Waerland:

> Civilised man has completely forgotten that the pleasure of eating lies not only in the choice and preparation of food, but above all in the body's ability to absorb nutrition, or in the natural, healthy need for 'tissue regeneration', which always stands in direct relation to the functionality of the respective organs. If this functionality is first-rate, then every meal is a feast – no matter how simple. And here simplicity is the foundation of life.[15]

Bruno Mathsson also designed an outdoor kitchen in the form of a tent shed on the lawn outside his mother's house. Mathsson was a veritable 'health architect' who converted the plans of the health programme into a new lifestyle, new commodities, and new homes. He wrote:

> When I have created for myself, according to Waerland's plans, the perfect health, which I have set as my goal [. . .] I will start redesigning the interiors of Swedish homes. And not just the interior but also the *houses* themselves. This diet and approach to life that the fitness movement presents to people calls for *a fundamentally new style* – with new, simple, *beautiful* utensils, not least.[16]

Frösakull would become the primary example of this fundamentally new style that Mathsson was advocating. The house reveals a tension between elegant, sleek American mid-century modernism and brutalist anti-aestheticism, which combines elements of a luxury life with a simple do-it-yourself architectural style; it is a form of merger between the desire-driven consumer product that flirts with our dreams, and the concrete, immediate, brutal object that appears only in its real setting. The large, illusory window sections and the undulating, transparent ceiling coexist with recycled steel rafters, wood slats nailed on slightly askew, and the most basic steel draining board. The building oozes pragmatism rather than aestheticised design, and the builder underlines this with his affirmation that Frösakull was not built according to the drawing board but that a great deal was left to the builders to solve.[17] The design and the solutions are usually the simplest and cheapest possible, and they do not consistently adhere to predetermined notions of measurements, proportions, or aesthetics.

The ambivalence characterising modernism, the embracing of a modern commercial culture and desire-driven consumption on the one hand, and a restraining moralistic relationship to goods

14
Wettergren, 'Vår bostad 1941', 150.

15
Waerland, 'Gammal vid 20, ung vid 60!', 15.

16
Bruno Mathsson quoted in Windmark, 'Järnskruv genom trä', 25.

17
A conversation between the builder Åke Svensson, Helena Mattsson, and Mikael Olson, 28 July 2006, Frösakull.

Fig. 5 Frösakull, Mikael Olsson – FK11.2002, chromogenic print. (© Mikael Olsson / Galerie Nordenhake)

Fig. 6 Frösakull, Mikael Olsson – FK04.2005, chromogenic print. (© Mikael Olsson / Galerie Nordenhake)

Fig. 7 Frösakull 1960, Bruno Mathsson. (Drawing by © Carl-Johan Viklund. In Olsson, Mikael. *Södrakull Frösakull*. Göttingen: Steidl Verlag, 2010)

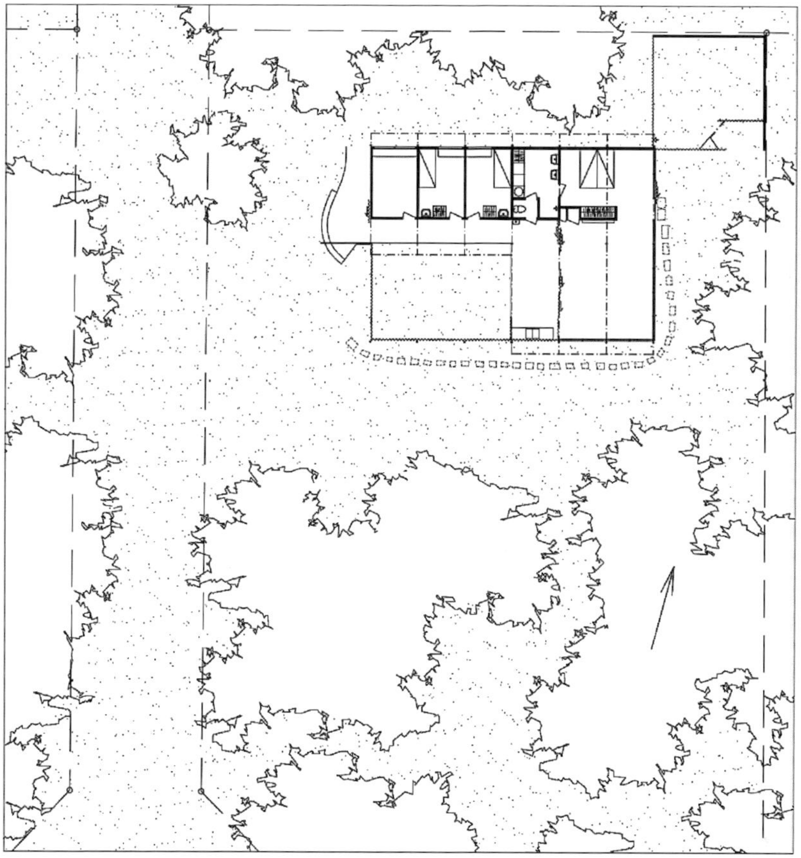

and architecture based on needs on the other, is nakedly evidenced here. The recreational free time that Frösakull opens up, to a life without work that can be devoted to desires – food, drink, and socialising – is constrained by a restrictive moralist lifestyle. Fitness and naturism involve a disciplined self-practice that, combined with innovative architecture, both allows and prevents extravagant living. The summer house in Frösakull points towards a trajectory of health, naturism, and body culture in the formation of Swedish modernism and functionalism. This influence was of great importance at the time. Still, its role in the historiography of Swedish architecture is not yet covered, which makes Frösakull a crucial example of Swedish modernism.

Bruno Mathsson used his own language – architecture and design – to create a material realisation of his philosophy of life. His architectural activism could be understood both as a resistance towards dominating ideas in society, including the contemporary architecture culture, and as a positive act – an act of affirmation of a 'new world'. It is an activism and resistance through constructions, where building elements, furniture, and everyday objects frame a living environment based on interaction with the local weather and where architecture is based on non-material services, such as light, sun, and heat. As Mathsson stated, he wanted to redesign the Swedish interiors and houses in a new style that responded to Waerland's fitness ideals, and his private house in Frösakull is one of his most radical attempts to realise this goal.

The text is a revised version of 'A Home Is Not A House: Swedish Ascetic Naturism Meets a Luxurious American Modernism' in Mikael Olsson, *Södrakull Frösakull* (Göttingen: Steidl Verlag, 2010). All images are part of Mikael Olsson's artistic work Södrakull Frösakull published with the same title.

***Södrakull Frösakull* is an investigation into ideas about perception and representation. The images taken between 2000 and 2006 oscillate between factual recordings and a personal account of an intimate relation and attraction to two of Mathsson's houses. The photographs of Frösakull are the result of a long-lasting engagement with the house at different intensities.**

Bibliography

Banham, Reyner. 'A Home Is Not a House'. *Art in America* (April 1965). Reprinted in *Design by Choice*, edited by Penny Sparke, 56–60. New York: Rizzoli, 1981.

Böhn-Jullander, Ingrid. *Bruno Mathsson*. Lund: Bokförlaget Signum, 1992.

Friedman, Martin. 'Notes on Swedish Design'. *Design Quarterly*, no. 65 (1966): 25.

Hogdal, Lisa, ed. *Bruno Mathsson*. Malmö: Bokförlaget Arena, 2006.

'Ingen vill köpa formgivarens hus'. *Göteborgs-posten*, 7 November 2004: 18.

Mathsson, Bruno. 'Morgondagens hus'. *Värnamo nyheter*, 4 February 1956: 7.

Näsström, Gustaf. *Fritidens morgonrodnad. En epokbildande utställning i Ystad 1936*. Ystad: Ystad Fornminnesförenings skrift, 1976.

Nilsson, Jan Olov. 'Man måste härda sig'. In *Möjligheternas landskap: nordiska kulturanalyser*, edited by Anders Linde-Laursen and Jan Olov Nilsson, 196–221. Copenhagen: Nordiska ministerrådet, 1994.

Olsson, Mikael. *Södrakull Frösakull*. Göttingen: Steidl Verlag, 2010.

Waerland, Arne. 'Gammal vid 20, ung vid 60!' *Frisksport*, no. 35 (1935): 13–5.

Wettergren, Erik. 'Vår bostad 1941'. *Form*, no. 8 (1941): 149–51.

Windmark, Agne. 'Järnskruv genom trä'. *Frisksport*, no. 25 (1940): 25.

Widman, Dag. 'Bruno Mathsson: Slå sönder och gör nytt!' *Form*, no. 1 (1950): 6–7.

Between Sparta and Sybaris: Bernard Rudofsky's endless search for the ideal home

Pierre Chabard

Regarding the issue of 'activism at home', the case of Bernard Rudofsky is anything but straightforward. Obviously, Rudofsky devoted a large part of his travelling life to speculating about domestic architecture in general and about his own house in particular.[1] However, he wasn't able to secure the favourable conditions for building his own house until the late 1960s, at almost sixty-five years of age. A location was ultimately found in Spain, far away from east Manhattan where this cosmopolitan émigré had predominantly lived from 1941 until his death in 1988, and where he had 'avowedly dwelt in an uprooting condition'.[2] So Rudofsky's Spanish house, no more than a summer retreat, appears to have been a later and imperfect embodiment of the radically reformed way of life that he adopted early on and which one could describe as a kind of activism.

1
His successive failed attempts to build his own house were listed in: Guarneri, *Bernard Rudofsky: A Humane Designer* and Rossi, *Bernard Rudofsky: Architect.*

2
Scott, 'Bernard Rudofksy: Not at Home', 233.

3
Ullan, 'Nerja: asamblea de pescadores e intelectuales'.

It is this dialogue between home and house, between activism in lifestyle and forms of domestic architecture, that this paper wishes to address. After examining the tension between the seemingly banal architecture of Rudofsky's holiday house in Spain and the alternative way in which he lived in his New York apartments, I will consider a much earlier house that Rudofsky designed for himself and his wife on the Italian island Procida in 1935. Perfecting the articulation between modern architecture and *lebensreform* (life reform), this aborted project would haunt Rudofsky's later work and become a latent driving force behind his work as a writer and a curator.

Resisting the American way of life from within

In the summer of 1969, Bernard Rudofsky acquired a plot in Andalusia, Spain, between Frigiliana and Nerja, near Malaga. At that time, this part of the Costa del Sol was still almost-virgin territory, quite cheap and frequented by a small network of avant-garde artists and intellectuals.[3] Nicknamed 'La Casa', Rudofsky's single-storey house was carefully built on the highest point of a secluded sloping plot facing the sea, shaped by terraces and planted with olive, pine, and carob trees.

Built during the summers of 1970 and 1971, the house looked rather ordinary, at least at first sight: lime-washed masonry walls, sloped roofs covered with roman roof tiles, floors paved with common terracotta tiles. Due to the climate, the architecture was sturdy, using thick walls and few windows. Long vine-covered pergolas provided shade. Straight walkways and stairways descended to a lower terrace where the pool was dug out. Fragmented in plan and section, the house was divided into three main parts (living rooms, study, and bedroom) only connected through outdoor or semi-outdoor rooms. Apart from the typological particularity of this intertwining of interior and exterior rooms, and the relative nudity of them – their deliberate lack of comfort – this seaside holiday house appeared as a rather inoffensive architecture.

To describe the long-meditated and resolutely alternative lifestyle of which this house was the setting, it is useful to move away from Andalusia and explore other areas of Rudofsky's life. La Casa was only a later and intermittent summer residence. Since the early 1940s, Rudofsky had mostly lived in New York: first in a small apartment on the seventeenth floor of an Art-Deco-style building on East 57th Street; then, from September 1960, back from a two-year stay in Japan, in a two-room apartment in the south wing of the Kips Bay Plaza residence recently built by Ieoh Ming Pei, near the East River.

Paradoxically, Rudofsky, who was a great explorer of non-Western cultures, lived in the heart of one of the largest cities of the dominant civilisation. This great advocate of vernacular and anonymous architecture lived in a modern and high-style one. In the early 1960s, while he was preparing his famous exhibition *Architecture Without Architects* (MoMA, 9 November 1964–7 February 1965), he resided in one of the best examples of American International Style architecture and one of the main targets of the exhibition (**Fig. 1**). The books on Rudofsky never showed any image of the interior of his New York apartments, but a few testimonies exist.[4] They describe a very spartan space, with very little furniture and no electrical or electronic appliances. In the most technologically advanced metropolis of that time, Rudofsky conceived his apartment as an island of resistance to a certain idea of American domestic comfort. The testimonies also evoke a space organised with careful precision, where each daily gesture was essentialised, almost ritualised. Manual preparation of meals, for example, took his wife Berta long hours every day. Following vegetarian and even macrobiotic principles, the food was little transformed, and very slowly cooked, preferably steamed. It was served in bite-sized portions in order to be consumed without the need for cutlery. Rudofsky considered knives and forks as weapons, as remains of the barbaric and anthropophagic origins of Western civilisation. In 1938 he wrote: 'Chinese do not put metal instruments in their mouths. Turkish peasants eat ably and enthusiastically with a piece of bread, never dirtying their hands.'[5] Drawing inspiration from both his first-hand experience and his bookish knowledge of non-Western civilisations or ancient states of Western ones, and 'radically decoupling any vernacular type from any strict identity with a geographical place',[6] Rudofsky questioned, in the same way, all facets of the art of living: the way of sitting (preferably on the floor), of sleeping (not necessarily in a bed), of bathing (separated from washing), or of dressing (or not dressing). Indissolubly linked to a critique of conventional forms of domestic architecture, this active life reform was, for him, a way to subvert the cultural and material stereotypes he attributed to capitalist and techno-industrial civilisation.

4
See Arquitectura-G, 'La Casa'.

5
Rudofsky, 'Non ci vuole un nuovo modo di costruire', 8; translated from Italian by the author.

6
Scott, 'Bernard Rudofksy: Not at Home', 228.

Fig. 1 View from Rudofsky's own apartment in Kips Bay Plaza building in Manhattan. (© The Bernard Rudofsky Estate, Vienna / Adagp, Paris 2020. Reproduced with permission from Bernard Rudofsky, *Streets for People: A Primer for Americans*, Garden City, NY: Doubleday, 1969, 18)

The view from the author's window over some of Manhattan's East Side is clouded with smoke and dust seeded by demolition crews. There is no civilized street life.

Fig. 2 Double-page with two contradictory images claiming the benefits of mediaeval collective bathing in the chapter 'Our Indecorous Bathroom' in Bernard Rudofsky's *Behind the Picture Window* (New York: Oxford University Press, 1955), 128–9. (Reproduced with permission)

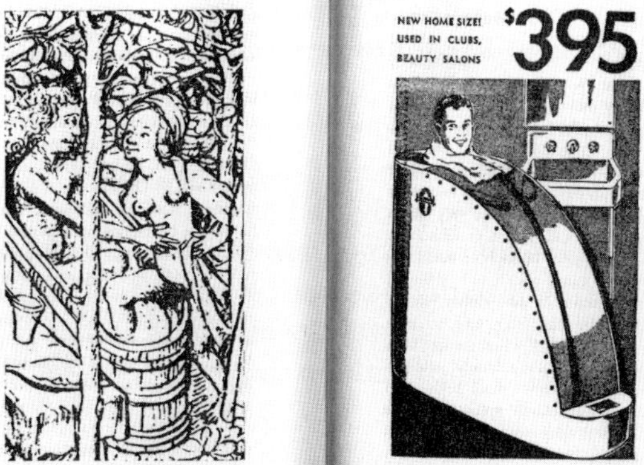

Detail from a sixteenth-century engraving.

In both cases the bathing was quite promiscuous; the abuse of the custom is indicated by the colloquial use of the Italian word *bagnio* (bath) for a brothel.' (The word is not Italian; bagnio, like braggadocio or cafeteria, is mongrel English. The Italian euphemism for bordello is casino.) Its sister publication, the *American Encyclopedia*, informs us without regret that 'how thoroughly the bath afterward [after the sixteenth century] fell into disuse, is a matter which historians have been unable to determine.' This is

128

Newspaper advertisement. Courtesy Gimbels' Department Store.

a curious statement in view of the notorious resourcefulness of historians. Recent centuries are without doubt less opaque than those which preceded them, and it rather seems that the historians themselves were shy of water and in about the same predicament as a confirmed teetotaler who is asked to write a treatise on French wines.

The estrangement between man and water reached its apex in the eighteenth century when bathing was valued, at best as a powerful medication, not to be undertaken

129

Developing this argument throughout his career, Rudofsky substantially adjusted his target after the Second World War. He passed from a critique à la Adolf Loos – of the narrow conventions of the bourgeois-industrial society still rooted in the nineteenth century – to a critique à la Lewis Mumford – of the alienating standardisation of lifestyles in the context of consumerist and suburban America. A skilled mediator and a brilliant and acerbic writer, Rudofsky developed his statements in a hundred articles and lectures, a dozen books, and half a dozen exhibitions, some of which were visited by large international audiences, thus making him an important protagonist of the New York cultural scene.

Withdrawal and exile: an ideal but failed project on Procida Island

For Rudofsky, the architectural and spatial issues were never separated from highly temporal and human ones. Biographers mentioned his intense transdisciplinary curiosity that had emerged in his formative years at the Vienna Technische Hochschule, between 1922 and 1928. During this time, Rudofsky found inspiration largely outside of school and outside of architecture, notably through his frequent summer trips.[7] Shaped by these experiences, his architectural culture articulated three main issues. The first one was an interest, quite usual among architects of his generation, in Mediterranean vernacular architecture that he discovered on the island of Santorini in 1929, and to which he devoted his PhD dissertation in applied sciences.[8] The second issue dealt with modernity. Rudofsky felt a certain ambivalence towards modern architecture, which affiliated him with other Viennese figures, including Adolf Loos or Josef Frank.[9] Rudofsky rejected the bourgeois stylistic eclecticism of the nineteenth century as much as he did the machinist and functionalist dogmas of the most radical avant-gardes. Close to certain protagonists of the Bauhaus, he followed a modernist and essentialist reinterpretation of tradition rather than its outright rejection. The third issue was Rudofsky's interest in the *lebensreform* movements that developed from the end of the nineteenth century in various places in the Germanic sphere, which he discovered when he lived in Berlin between 1928 and 1930. He found immediate connections with this compound ideology, difficult to define politically, that advocated alternately a return to nature, vegetarianism, naturism, solar cult, equality between the sexes, and clothing reform.[10]

Rudofsky found in remote islands of the Mediterranean archipelago, near Naples, a favourable place for exploring these three intertwined issues: return to origins, 'anxious modernism',[11] and life reform. He first spent the summer of 1931 in Capri, which had been, since 1899, a land of choice for some German *lebensreformers*. He settled there in March 1932, pursuing during the next two years a free and hedonistic lifestyle marked by many meetings in intellectual and artistic circles.[12] In the summer of 1934, on the nearby island of Ischia, he met Berta Doctor, an independent Viennese musicologist. They married in the winter of 1935 and then settled together on the more intimate island of Procida where the architect

7
de Wit, 'Rudofsky's Discomfort', 101–10.

8
Rudofsky, 'Eine Primitive Betonbauweise auf den südlichen Kikladen, nebst dem Versuch einer Datierung derselben'.

9
Platzer, 'Lessons from Bernard Rudofsky', 14–7.

10
Rossi, *Bernard Rudofsky: Architect*, 59.

11
Goldhagen and Legault, *Anxious Modernism.*

12
Rossi, *Bernard Rudofsky: Architect*, 63–6.

Fig. 3 Bernard Rudofsky, *Pianta di Orientamento* (orientation map) of Procida Island. (© The Bernard Rudofsky Estate Vienna / Adagp, Paris, 2020. Reproduced with permission from 'La Scoperta d'un Isola', *Domus* 16, no. 124 [April 1938]: 5)

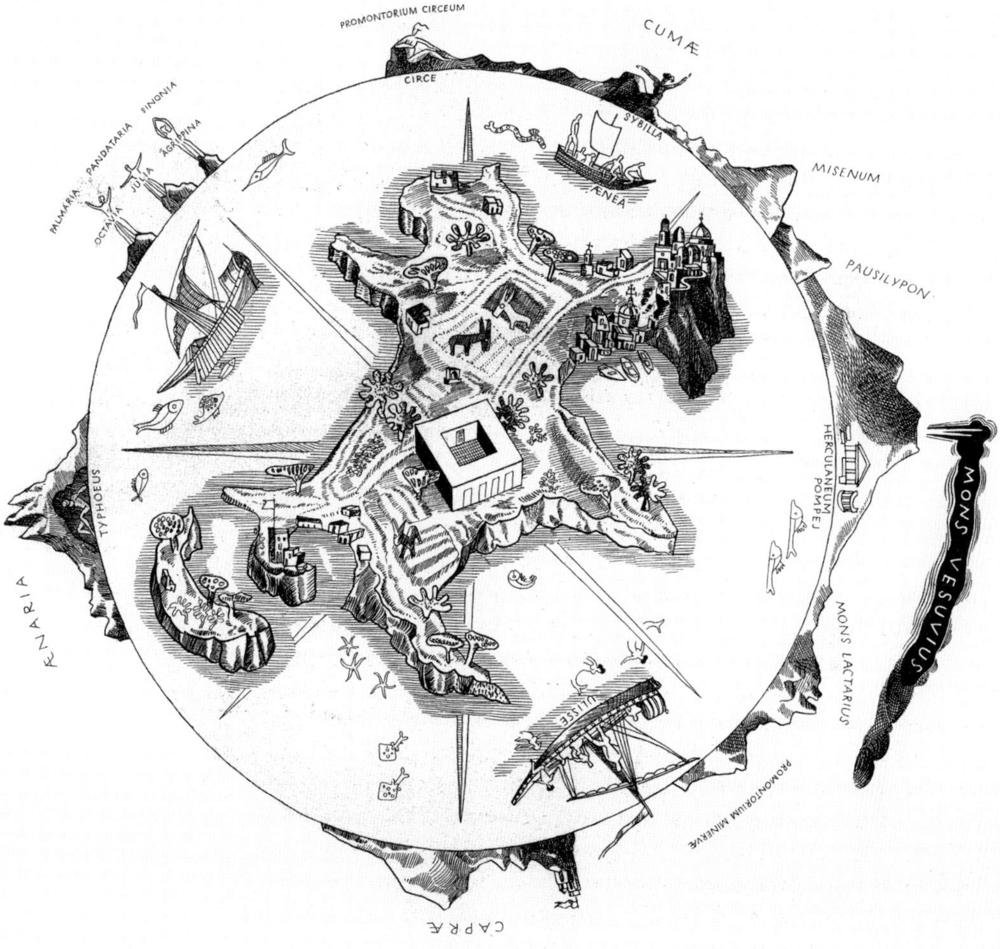

PIANTA DI ORIENTAMENTO

Disegno di B. Rudofsky

said he had found 'the site marked by his fate'.[13] This time of happiness was brief, brutally interrupted by their exile to America in April 1938 to escape the consequences of the Anschluss, including Rudofsky's obligation to join the army of the Third Reich. Just before this, in the winter of 1938, Rudofsky had succeeded his friend Gio Ponti as the editor-in-chief of the Italian magazine *Domus.* A series of articles for which Rudofsky produced the text, iconography, and layout encapsulated this short period of existential harmony. In the three *Domus* issues published under his direction, Rudofsky set out the main trajectories for his later work.[14] All these themes had already been crystallised in the architectural form of the house he designed for Berta and himself in Procida in the winter of 1935 (but which had been refused a building permit).[15]

This modern reinterpretation of the immemorial patio house was characterised by the straightness and the precision of its plan: a regular and symmetrical sequence of rooms around a square courtyard. The austerity, the spartan simplicity of this house in Procida resulted directly from the Rudofskian quest for the primitive truths of domestic architecture. He was seeking the 'Origine dell'Abitazione'[16] in the ancient villas of Pompeii, in the archaic houses of Santorini Island but also in the Procida fishermen's houses in the small port of Corricella with their thick walls and vaulted and terraced roofs. This search for the primitive house, in the past and present, led Rudofsky to question systematically every architectural element and accessory that cluttered the contemporary house and constituted what he would later call 'the ballast of the house'.[17] In his project for the Procida House, there was no bed but instead a room with padded flooring that allowed for sleeping in any direction, in any position. A simple mosquito netting hung from the ceiling transformed the room into an archaic tent. There was no staircase in this one-storey house as Rudofsky considered that the staircase was an element of a high style architecture and not of a vernacular and domestic one. There were no windows, but doors that allowed fluid circulation between the interior and exterior rooms. There was no bathroom but a large and bare room with a simple dug-out basin, large enough for collective bathing – the hygienic functions of the washing of the body were separated and relegated into a small adjacent room. There were neither tables nor chairs but instead three long horizontal slabs of stones modelled on the *triclinium*, the ancient dining room where one ate in a semi-reclined posture on three *klinē* (couches).[18]

The house as a garment for the naked body

This stripping bare of domestic space, where Rudofsky suppressed any superfluous accessory, was neither an end in itself, nor a purely aesthetic aim. Above all, it served the hedonist emancipation of the body in the house, which he conceived as a sensual and immersive space. In this regard, the floor materials were of prime importance to Rudofsky. In *Domus,* he talked about the delights of having his bare feet, 'brushed by sand, by freshly-mown grass, or by cool striated marble'.[19] In another text, he was excited about the many meanings

13
Rudofsky, 'Scopertia di un'isola', 3; translated from Italian by the author.

14
Domus 16, nos. 122, 123 and 124, respectively in February, March, and April 1938.

15
Guarneri, *Bernard Rudofsky: A Humane Designer*, 261.

16
Rudofsky, 'Origine dell'Abitazione', 16–9.

17
Rudofsky, *Behind the Picture Window*, 168.

18
Rudofsky later developed this topic in his exhibition *'Now I Lay Down to Eat': A Salute to the Unknown Art of Living* (Cooper-Hewitt Museum, New York, November 1980 – February 1981) and eponymous catalogue.

19
Rudofsky, 'Non ci vuole un nuovo modo di costruire', 6; translated from Italian by the author.

of the Italian word *pianta*, referring to both the sole of the foot and the floor plan of the architect.[20]

The solid and insular architecture of this house was that of a retreat, a hideaway, sheltered from the turmoil of a world sinking into fascism and war.[21] Its opaque walls redoubled the shores of the island itself. Rudofsky wrote: 'Our homes should be a cultural refuge, the aesthetic backdrop of our passions.'[22] However, despite – or thanks to – its thick facades, the house was conceived to fully open the body to the rhythms of nature, the ground topography, the solar geometry, and the flow of the climate. Its walls were not those of a fortress or a prison. They brought secrecy and intimacy more than defence and reclusion. The three main rooms were wide open, each in its own way, horizontally or vertically. For example, the patio was conceived as what Rudofsky later called a 'room without a roof'.[23] Although an introverted space, it was 'the real living room', of which 'the sky, with its endlessly changing appearance, serves as a ceiling'.[24] The architecture of this house created a paradoxical tension between distance and connection, insularity and openness, protection and nakedness, both in the literal and figurative sense.

Bernard and Berta both practiced naturism. Wherever possible, indoors or outdoors, they lived naked. In his abundant graphic production around this project, the architect represented the inhabitants of the house as ancient Greek figures, either undressed or draped with fluid and uncut pieces of fabrics, like the ancient toga or *himation*. In his writings, he often deplored, in half-words, the moral and police repression of naturism in these remote islands of the Mediterranean Sea: 'Only a few years ago, many peoples used to bathe in public without the aid of clothing. This custom, we are learning, is rapidly disappearing due to the protests of foreign travelers.'[25] In this respect, the house was conceived as a container, 'as a vessel for our lives'.[26] Its material thickness hid the naked body and subtracted it from the dominant moral conventions and the contingent laws of modesty. Rudofsky saw modesty as the principal lever of a suspicious eroticisation of the body and a perversion of its naturalness through the puritan mask of the garment. Against this hypocritical denial of anatomy, Rudofksy advocated nudity as a way to attain not only a full and intense relationship with nature but also a healthy and pacified relationship with the other's body. Rudofskian nudity was a contradictory synthesis between the lascivious and playful hedonism he attributed to the inhabitants of the Greek city of Sybaris and the evidence of a frank and innocent relationship to the naked body that he recognised among the inhabitants of Sparta. All his later thoughts on architecture and clothing were informed by this quest for an emancipation of the body, by the will to return to a primordial and innocent sensuality, open to pleasure and free of any perversion; in other words, a synthesis between neutralisation and celebration of the body.

20
Rudofsky, 'Variazioni', 14.

21
Regarding Rudofsky's critical consciousness of the political situation, see Scott, 'Bernard Rudofsky: Not at Home', 224–5.

22
Rudofsky, 'Panorama negativo', 2; translated from Italian by the author.

23
Rudofsky, *Behind the Picture Window*, 140.

24
Rudofsky, 'Non ci vuole un nuovo modo di costruire', 10; translated from Italian by the author.

25
Rudofsky, *Are Clothes Modern?*, 19.

26
Rudofsky, 'Panorama negativo', 2; translated from Italian by the author.

PIANTA DELLA CASA DI PROCIDA

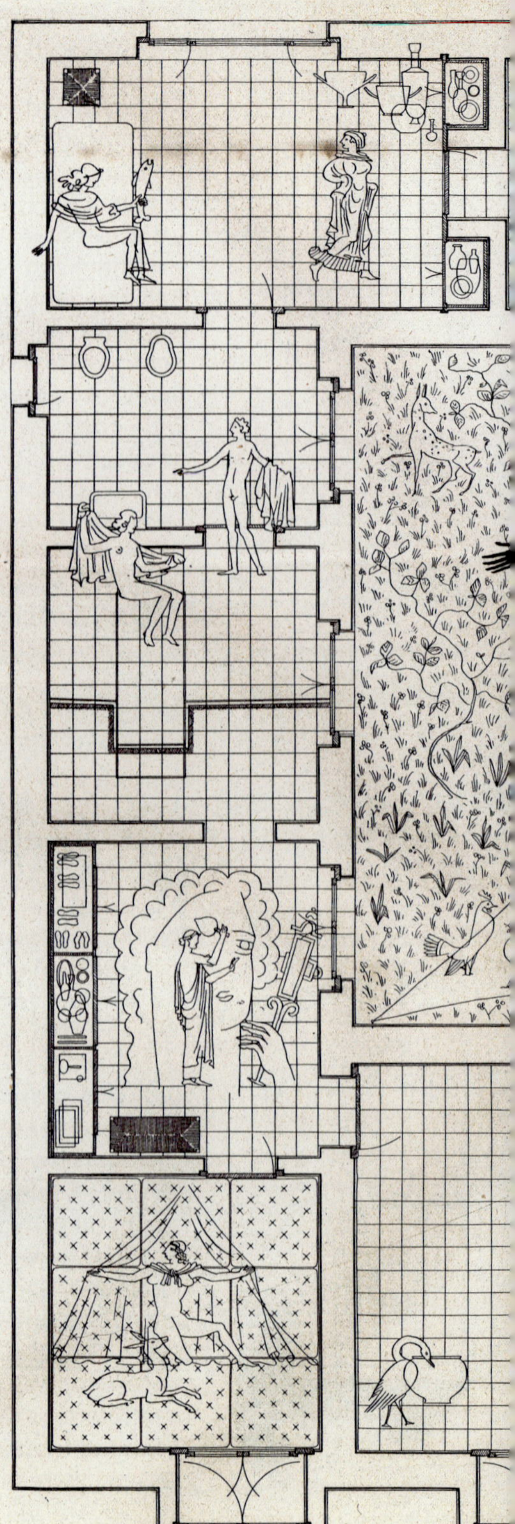

Camera dell'ancella prospiciente il sentiero che conduce all'entrata.

La camera da bagno non contiene nessun apparecchio. Nel pavimento c'è un abbassamento che accoglie l'acqua pel bagno. Attraverso la porta aperta entra il sole mattutino. Gli apparecchi igienici sono confinati nella camera accanto.

Il cortile è la vera camera da stare. Il suo pavimento è formato da erba rasata con margheritine e veronica; in primavera ci saranno violette ed orchidee. Il cielo coi suoi mille aspetti fa da soffitto. Contro il sole d'estate si può difendersi con una tenda a vela, color ruggine. Un cammino permette il soggiorno anche durante le sere di mezza stagione. Cani, gatti e colombe vi troveranno un rifugio.

Prima di entrare nella camera da letto ci si scalza nello spogliatoio, perchè il pavimento di quella è fatto interamente di materassi. Contro le zanzare e le mosche serve una zanzariera, che pende dal soffitto.

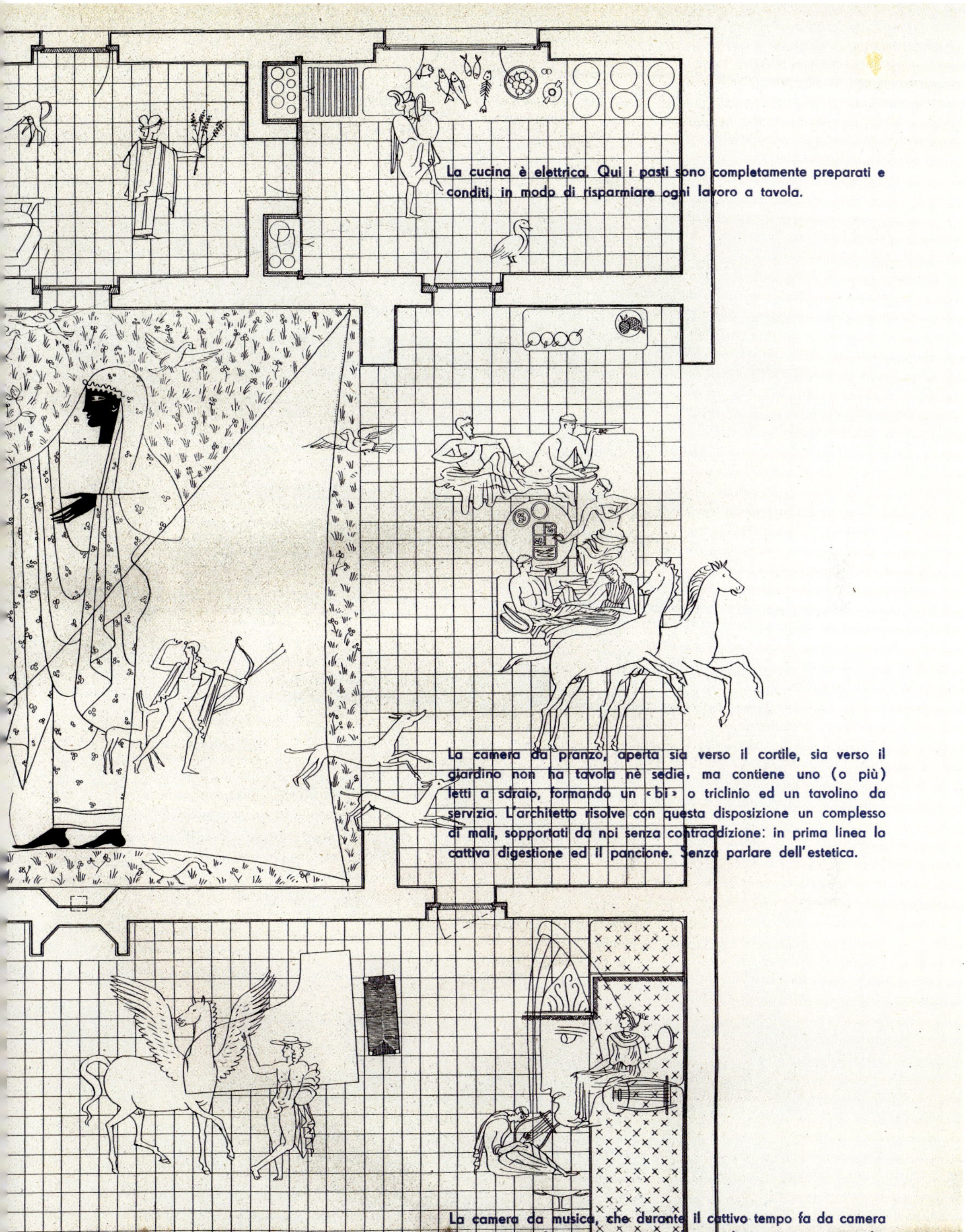

Fig. 4 Bernard Rudofsky, commented plan of the 'Casa di Procida'. (© The Bernard Rudofsky Estate Vienna / Adagp, Paris, 2020. Reproduced with permission from *Domus* 16, no. 124 [April 1938]: 10–11)

Fig. 5 Cover of *Interiors* 105, no. 10 (May 1946), designed by Bernard Rudofsky. He published the same drawing in his article 'Problema: Falsi e Giusti Concetti della Casa', *Domus* 16, no. 123 (March 1938): xxxiv. (© The Bernard Rudofsky Estate Vienna / Adagp, Paris, 2020. Reproduced with permission)

27
Rudofsky, *Behind the Picture Window*, book's back cover.

28
Rudofsky, *Behind the Picture Window*, 3.

29
Baudelaire, 'The Painter of Modern Life', 12.

La Casa a Procida: refuge or stage?

In what respect was the Procida house related to activism? If we define activism as a direct political action of a transgressive nature performed by minority actors at the margins of a dominant system, then Rudofsky's work did not perfectly coincide with this category. His activism was unusual in that it had, first of all, an individualistic and private horizon. It did not imply the collective organisation of a coordinated group for the purpose of acting in the public space. Instead it was home-centred and self-centred. This form of activism intended to subvert norms and conventions in the secrecy of the private domestic space. However, given the fact that it was never built, the house in Procida only existed through representations, publications, images, and texts. Paradoxically, having been conceived as an enclave, a hide-away, a retreat, the Procida House became quite the opposite. It became a manifesto, a medium, a virtual stage from which Rudofsky displayed a demonstrative and even prescriptive public discourse. One may wonder if Rudofksy would have felt the need to produce books and exhibitions if this house had been built. The house in Procida, and all the issues it embodied, constituted an inexhaustible source for Rudofsky's later editorial and scenographic work, including his first exhibition at MoMA, entitled *Are Clothes Modern?*, in 1944, and, in 1955, his first book on architecture, *Behind the Picture Window*, a catalogue of an aborted exhibition at MoMA. In this book, which was intended to be 'an examination of the contemporary house', Rudofsky developed and detailed every argument he had raised in *Domus* in 1938 and turned them into weapons against the American way of life.[27]

Nevertheless, he explicitly refused to assume the role of a guide: 'It is therefore neither a How To book nor a textbook for captive students. Indeed, no thought is more remote to me than that it fills a need, like a business directory or a mystery story.'[28] In this regard, one might conclude that Rudofsky's purpose was less political than ethical and aesthetic. In the manner of the industrial designers of the Ulm school that he admired, his aim was to devise the formal invariants that could become the ingredients of a reformed and modern domestic architecture. Actually, he was in quest of a timeless architecture, immune from the cyclical changes of fashion imposed by the industrial system. In the manner of the nineteenth-century French poet Charles Baudelaire, who proposed 'to distil the eternal from the transitory',[29] Rudofsky sought to extract from the infinite cultural variations of lifestyles in the present and in the past a primitive essence of the ideal home. It would be a paradoxical bastion of emancipation where architecture could at the same time protect the body from modernisation, defined as a pressing process of standardisation, and open him to the true modernity, conceived as the re-enactment of the virtuous simplicity of the origins in the present time. Regardless, he never really built it as a house. He only achieved this ideal on a small scale, in his temporary exhibitions, but with an extraordinary cultural impact.

Bibliography

Arquitectura-G. 'La Casa'. *Apartamento Magazine*, no. 19 (Spring/Summer 2017): 161–76.

Baudelaire, Charles. 'The Painter of Modern Life' (1863). In *The Painter of Modern Life and Other Essays by Charles Baudelaire*, translated by Jonathan Mayne, 12. New York: Phaidon Press, 1995.

Chabard, Pierre. 'La mode climatisée. Atours et détours de la modernité chez Bernard Rudofsky'. *Modes Pratiques. Revue d'histoire du vêtement et de la mode* 1, no. 3 (Autumn 2018): 304–23.

Goldhagen, Sarah Williams and Réjean Legault, eds. *Anxious Modernism: Experimentation in Postwar Architectural Culture*. Cambridge, MA: MIT Press, 2000.

Guarneri, Andrea Bocco. *Bernard Rudofsky: A Humane Designer*. New York: Springer, 2003.

Guarneri, Andrea Bocco. 'Bernard Rudofsky and the Sublimation of the Vernacular'. In *Modern Architecture and the Mediterranean: Vernacular Dialogues and Contested Identities*, edited by Jean-François Lejeune and Michelangelo Sabatino, 231–50. London, Routledge, 2009.

Platzer, Monika. 'Lessons from Bernard Rudofsky'. In *Lessons from Bernard Rudofsky: Life as a Voyage*, edited by Monika Platzer and Wim de Wit, 14–7. Basel: Birkhäuser, 2007.

Platzer, Monika, and Wim de Wit, eds. *Lessons from Bernard Rudofsky: Life as a Voyage*. Basel: Birkhäuser, 2007.

Rossi, Ugo. *Bernard Rudofsky: Architect*. Naples: Clean, 2016.

Rudofsky, Bernard. *Are Clothes Modern?* Chicago: Paul Theobald, 1947.

Rudofsky, Bernard. *Behind the Picture Window*. New York: Oxford University Press, 1955.

Rudofsky, Bernard. 'Non ci vuole un nuovo modo di costruire, ci vuole un nuovo modo di vivere'. *Domus* 16, no. 123 (March 1938): 8.

Rudofsky, Bernard. 'Eine Primitive Betonbauweise auf den südlichen Kikladen, nebst dem Versuch einer Datierung derselben'. PhD dissertation, Technische Hochschule, Vienna, 1931.

Rudofsky, Bernard. 'Origine dell'Abitazione'. *Domus* 16, no. 124 (April 1938): 16–9.

Rudofsky, Bernard. *'Now I Lay Me Down to Eat': A Salute to the Unknown Art of Living*. Garden City, NY: Anchor Press/Doubleday, 1980.

Rudofsky, Bernard. 'Variazioni'. *Domus* 16, no. 124 (April 1938): 14.

Rudofsky, Bernard. 'Panorama negativo'. *Domus* 16, no. 124 (April 1938): 2.

Rudofsky, Bernard. Cover art. *Interiors* 105, no. 10 (May 1946).

Rudofsky, Bernard, 'La Scoperta d'un Isola'. *Domus* 16, no. 124 (April 1938): 5.

Rudofsky, Bernard. 'Problema: Falsi e Giusti Concetti della Casa'. *Domus* 16, no. 123 (March 1938): xxxiv.

Rudofsky, Bernard. *Streets for People: A Primer for Americans*. Garden City, NY: Doubleday, 1969.

Scott, Felicity D. 'Bernard Rudofsky: Allegories of Nomadism and Dwelling'. In *Anxious Modernism: Experimentation in Postwar Architectural Culture*, edited by Sarah Williams Goldhagen, and Réjean Legault, 215–37. Cambridge, MA: MIT Press, 2000.

Scott, Felicity D. 'Bernard Rudofksy: Not at Home'. In *Émigré Cultures in Design and Architecture*, edited by Alison Clarke and Elana Shapira, 221–36. London: Bloomsbury Academic, 2017.

Scott, Felicity D. 'Primitive Wisdom and Modern Architecture'. *Journal of Architecture* 3, no. 3 (1998): 241–61.

Scott, Felicity D. 'Underneath Aesthetics and Utility: The Untransposable Fetish of Bernard Rudofsky'. *Assemblage,* no. 38 (April 1999): 58–89.

Ullan, José Miguel. 'Nerja: asamblea de pescadores e intelectuales'. *El País*, 24 August 1980: 14–5.

de Wit, Wim. 'Rudofsky's Discomfort: A Passion for Travel'. In *Lessons from Bernard Rudofsky: Life as a Voyage*, edited Monika Platzer and Wim de Wit, 101–10. Basel: Birkhäuser, 2007.

A Bare Form of Practice: The anthropology and activism of a barefoot architect's own house in a Chinese village

Xiang Ren

The figure of the 'barefoot architect' can speak in other and non-canonical ways to contemporary architectural discourse and deserves further theoretical development. Johan van Lengen first coined this term in the early 1980s in his handbook for an ecological construction,[1] following directly the emerging environmental consciousness in architecture since the 1960s, and indirectly the post-modern turn to the everyday and vernacular, which includes the discussions of 'architecture without architects'[2] and the celebrations of its own encyclopaedias.[3] These studies in vernacular architecture and the indigenous built environment, with its own conceptual contradictions, share a consistent ambition to trace premodern construction all over the world in order to make a complimentary archive to the dominant forms of architecture.[4] But this focus on the indigenous self-builder somehow weakens the conceptual depth of the barefoot architect as an 'other', bare form of architectural practice in active resistance to mainstream architecture. Borrowing Gyanendra Pandey's conceptual framework describing two types of 'others', those excluded from the archive (the 'mad'), and those exiled within it (the 'trifling'), the activist practice of the barefoot architect can be reframed, resisting the dominant mainstream in a way that is differentiated slightly from that of the vernacular architect, though both refer to those who are not professionally trained.[5]

This chapter presents an anthropology of a live, contemporary version of the barefoot architect through a study of the architectural practice embodied in his own house in a Chinese village, vividly demonstrating a live work and a bare form of resistance in a contemporary setting. Contemporary vernacular architecture in China was for a long time ignored by both the profession and academia because of its hidden process and living tradition inhabiting the blurred boundary between the designer and the builder, between the master-builder and the professional architect.[6] The vast territory of rural China and its contemporary legislative and economic conditions provide an opportunity for the revival of the barefoot architect. The individual introduced here is Weizhong Ren, an ordinary resident of Jianshan village in the eastern part of China. He is a farmer, and previously worked as an employee engaged in shipping administration. A lifetime volunteer for environmental protection, Ren first put forward his idea of eco-building in 2002. He was determined to make a truly ecological environment, not only in a physical sense but also at a mental level. Since 2005, he has employed almost all of his savings to fund the self-building of a series of houses and lodges. He has gradually come to be known as a barefoot architect for rural preservation and ecological construction in and beyond Jianshan.

1 For the introduction and promotion of the concept of 'barefoot architect' in architectural discourse, Johan van Lengen is a central figure. See Van Lengen, *The Barefoot Architect.*

2 Rudofsky, *Architecture without Architects.*

3 Oliver, *Encyclopaedia of Vernacular Architecture of the World;* see also Vellinga, *Encyclopaedia of Vernacular Architecture of the World*, second edition.

4 Richards, '"Vernacular" Accomodations'.

5 Pandey, *Unarchived Histories.*

6 Ren, 'Anonymous Process and Absent Architect'.

Fig. 1 Bird's eye of the barefoot architect's own house (in the middle of the picture) with two sloping roofs, which (to the left) faces the square piazza and (to the right) radically confronts the market-driven standardised form of the new housing scheme in Jianshan village, Zhejiang province, 2017. (Photograph by © Weizhong Ren)

7
For more clues and evidence of the government-led, modern tourism development in Jianshan village and other neighbouring villages in Anji county, see, for example, the following in the official newspaper: 'Jianshan village, Anji county, Zhejiang province – Creating an International Rural Life Benchmark'.

8
'Beautiful Chinese Village Construction' is a national initiative to beautify the rural villages in China, with a same-named milestone policy 'Beautiful Chinese Village Construction Guidance: A National Standard', officially published by General Administration of Quality Supervision, Inspection and Quarantine of the People's Republic of China and Certification and Accreditation Administration of the People's Republic of China on 1 June 2015. It is part of the larger rural policy initiative 'Constructing New Socialist Rural Area Movement'. For its architectural impact, see Ren, 'Socially Engaged Architecture'.

9
Interview with villagers by the author in April 2015 in Jianshan village, China.

10
Fan, 'Shanzhai'.

11
Interview with villagers by the author in May 2015 in Jianshan village, China.

Jianshan village has quietly stretched its development along its main road and waterway, which run from the northwest to the southeast. The stable condition of this village, home to four hundred families, has changed dramatically in the past two decades. Tourism and modernity have intervened,[7] partly as a result of it having been granted the title of 'Best Practice for Beautiful Chinese Villages' by its supervising township in 2008.[8] The linear areas alongside the waterway, once surrounded by large areas of reeds and bamboo that provided a collective place for washing, have now been developed into a commercial tourist park built in fake rural characteristic style to satisfy the demand for an increasingly urban aesthetic. Ironically, expensive and expansive golf courses were scattered as artificial 'green islands' in the existing natural environment, along with more forthcoming top-down development schemes.[9] The 'European Style', regarded as a more advanced 'modern' architectural style in residential buildings, was very rapidly applied into waves after waves of standardised housing developments. These have replaced villagers' traditional houses and affected most of the inhabitable land adjacent to Ren's site for his own house **(Fig. 1)**.

The financialisation of village land and assimilation of superficial 'Shanzhai' architectural styles made of industrialised materials displaced the traditional forms of living and exerted a negative impact on the environmental ecology.[10] Ren consciously noticed this and didn't follow the trend. His absence of professional architectural training did not prevent him developing firstly a strong design position and then an activism in and through architecture. He has argued against the application of top-down, tabula-rasa development practice for 'Beautiful Chinese Villages', in which even the basic source of construction materials remains unknown and is therefore unsustainable for the locality.[11] For this barefoot architect, the use of materials sourced nearby form the soul of a building that is in harmony with natural environment. Earth and clay are the bare form of the land and its primary material, as they will eventually return to their original state.

Design

The barefoot architect's own house **(Fig. 2)** occupies the gateway part of an L-shaped, semi-enclosed site. Oriented in a north–south direction, the house is designed to stand adjacent to an established bamboo forest, a natural filter of the summer sun from the west and a barrier to the winter wind from the north. Earth and wood form both the ecological building's concept and its low impact, as-found materials.

As the 'user-architect', Ren adopted the traditional 'two depths' of horizontal spatial organisation from the local vernacular architecture but separates the private sleeping part and the sem-public living part vertically. Spatially, articulation is created in the transition between the two depths, with a central courtyard as both an intimate space for arrival and an environmental mediator between the two floors. This arrangement is familiar to the local house type,

Fig. 2 External view of Ren's own house after a refurbishment in 2015. Timber cladding and a lightweight roof structure were added onto the original clay building. (Photograph by © Xiang Ren)

Fig. 3 A bare model of the house from the barefoot architect, which looks very different from the representational and expressive models from professionally trained architects. It became a key medium to communicate and collaborate with local carpenters and masons. (Photograph by © Weizhong Ren)

12 Interview with Weizhong Ren by the author in April 2015 in Jianshan village, China.

though it is rare to have the toilet and kitchen, rather than the bedrooms, on either side of the central courtyard. This design decision is largely driven by the focus on using earth for both the building's structure and material, as the toilet and kitchen require smaller openings in the earthwork than bedrooms. The durability of low-impact materials is also expressed in the structural decisions. Central to the house is a multifunctional hall sited at the end of the north–south axis and linking a series of spatial thresholds, including the entrance doorway, spaces under the eaves, a water pond, a wooden bridge, and the screened partition in the main hall. The hall is used for the family's dining, meeting, and socialising. The doorway tablet reads, 'Rural Self-Help House Design-Build Training Centre', indicating that this is not only a semi-public family space but also an empowering space for villagers to meet and share skills. This is evidence that the barefoot architect's larger ambition was to use his own house as a site of resistance to the increasingly disconnected community of Jianshan village. The barefoot architect's own house can be reinterpreted as a bare form of the village, a microcosm village-house.

Tectonically, the first depth, which includes the kitchen, courtyard, and toilet, is the services part of the house and is entirely built of rammed-earth structures that are both load-bearing and enclosing. The second depth, including the hall on the ground floor and three bedrooms above, has a wooden structural frame and rammed-earth enclosing walls. While the span of a wooden frame could be predicted, the most appropriate size and geometry of an earth wall had to be found through trials and errors on-site. Several mock-up tests were conducted based on Ren's experience of selecting, mixing, and compacting different types of soil, all by hand and without mechanical equipment. It is a learning-by-doing process from the very beginning. Understanding the properties of the soil and the performance of its construction was painstaking and time-consuming, but later proved worthwhile because it clarified the design position and supported Ren's resistance to those developer-led houses in mass-manufactured materials which have little sympathy with the environmental ecology of his village.[12]

Once the relationship between design-build strategies and practical limitations was clarified, a series of physical models were developed, from a wall-enclosure model and a wood structure model, to a final model with detailed roof articulations **(Fig. 3)**. The key problem with a rammed-earth house is the amount of light and ventilation. This was solved through two steps: firstly, the north wall's openings were enlarged to introduce natural light and cross-ventilation from the south-facing courtyard to the hall; and secondly, a glazed corridor enhances daylight on both floors and becomes a linear greenhouse in winter **(Fig. 4)**. Protection against direct sunlight is provided by the manually foldable wooden shades.

Construction

Ren teamed up with two local carpenters for the design development to optimise the way the wooden structure would support the roof. Later a mason was involved, too, working on the

Fig. 4 The south-facing transition space has a complex roof articulation between different heights and orientations, which not only acts as a glazed corridor to maximise daylight in spring and autumn, but also as a closed buffer zone to prevent overheating in summer and cold in winter, 2015. (Photograph by © Xiang Ren)

Fig. 5 The open plan and flexible use of the first floor is based on the structural independence between timber frame and the rammed-earth wall. An enclosed space can be used as a guest bedroom, communal lounge, or a study room, all with a good visual and spatial connection with the semi-outdoor roof terrace, 2015. (Photograph by © Xiang Ren)

foundation using pebbles sourced from the nearby waterway. Physical models again became a key medium for the barefoot architect to communicate with and coproduce with his team of craftsmen. One of the carpenters commented, 'I can't understand the drawings from professional architects but I could make it from looking at Ren's models!'[13] For the barefoot architect, there was no real distinction between design and construction; he worked with local tradesmen and oversaw and negotiated spatial strategies and social resources in and around a building, behaving like a traditional master-builder. The team returned to site to finalise the design details after the delivery of several wooden members and stone panels from a local supplier. With the exception of these items, all the construction materials were a pre-existing part of the site before the house was built. Working with these materials through trial and error, the team found an appropriate construction sequence to work out how the timber frame met the rammed-earth wall. The wooden frame was erected and assembled after completing the rammed-earth wall for the ground floor, which had two advantages: firstly, the frame prevented the wall from becoming offset when stacking the upper floor wall and plate; and secondly, the frame could itself act as a scaffolding for transporting materials to the upper floor. The construction took around four months in total, including two months spanning a hot summer. The low-cost water pond in the courtyard, strategically placed underneath the entrance bridge, successfully facilitated the construction, not only acting as a natural refrigerator for drinks, but also supporting the micro-environment within the building.

13 Interview with one of the carpenters working on Ren's house by the author in April 2015 in Jianshan village, China.

Use

Since taking up occupancy of the house, Ren and his family have developed a daily routine to use the house flexibly **(Fig. 5)**. The house has undergone a series of spontaneous micro-regenerations and small-scale physical transformations. These ordinary details represent an activist manifestation of the barefoot architect's own house: it will never be finished, either physically or conceptually.

The first round of refurbishments occurred a few months after the house's first 'completion', and included transforming the glazed roof of the top-lit corridor to one covered in traditional tiles to adjust the light. The second round took place a year later, in which Ren added a curved metal roof supported by four lightweight tubular steel columns to provide a sheltered roof terrace. The front facade was also changed from the original white-washed wall and wooden lattice windows to a more hybrid expression, to a mix of reclaimed timber panels and exposed rammed earth walls. A leaking problem due to the cold bridge of the connection joints between the steel columns and metal roof triggered a third round of repairs, which included adding a protective ceiling of reeds. Regardless of whether these transformations were products of the ageing process or aesthetic changes inspired by a desire to express the building's structural integrity, the fundamental position of this barefoot architect has been consistent: the building is not a finite built object but a transformative process which evolves through time. The

14
Blundell Jones, 'The Meaning of Use'.

15
Cupers, 'The Infrastructure of Participation', 15.

16
Interview with Weizhong Ren by the author in December 2014.

17
Visiting politicians included the deputy head of the province and the mayor, who were both accompanied by local village leaders and supervising county leaders.

18
Blundell Jones and Kong, 'The Case for an Oral Architecture'.

19
Ren, 'Hybrid Building and Hybrid Practitioner'.

constant changes to the original designated object are allowed and appreciated since there hadn't been an absolute design intention in the first place.

Activism

The activism in the barefoot architect's own house is manifest both in terms of its use and in terms of meaning,[14] in its rejection of the market-driven housing products and trends, and in the way it informs the larger idea of a 'house of the people'.[15] The 'Rural Self-Help House Design-Build Training Centre', based in the multifunctional hall, had a positive start, with more than ninety per cent of Ren's invited list of villagers attending.[16] The means by which it could sustain its function as a 'house for the people' has remained a challenge. Since 2008, it has attracted more visitors from the outside than from the village of Jianshan itself. There have been strategically important visits from high-level politicians, usually associated with event publications found in many local newspapers, which supported Ren's activism at home.[17] They have made Ren's house into a village-house which is socially constructed.

The house has provided an alternative, a contrast to the prevailing top-down residential development that puts users in uniform spaces and shells. It began and evolved in the absence of an overall master plan, and is instead based on a more progressive, user participatory, and site-specific approach. Without a written brief, which tends to be too thin in current professional architectural practice in rural China, Ren adapted the basic programme of the local vernacular house and ancestral hall, but gave it a new spatial meaning by reclaiming locally sourced, low-impact materials. Designing and budgeting were phased – not in the contemporary professional sense of phasing under strict planning – but in a loose-fit yet more resilient mode of interaction with the project's uncertainties and contingencies.

The house is not driven by norms and regulations. It does not comply with building regulations, which can be skipped in the rural Chinese context, nor does it consider the broadest notions of mainstream norms and frameworks, such as what a rural house should look like or symbolise. For this house, its appearance was not judged to be a priority; the priority is rather for a more layered, engaged, and messy process which engages with the specificities of site and sources.

The house points to a suppressed type of 'oral architecture' which is built from below, and radically confronts the drawing-based, visual-dominated architectural production process.[18] Design and construction overlap and even run in parallel on-site, through getting down to earth, getting hands dirty, and learning by doing. Everything was communicated through oral instructions in an aesthetically challenging but socially minded approach. Activism is also evident in the way that this approach has been transferred and disseminated through the barefoot architect's travelling practice in neighbouring villages.[19]

The house reflects the very specific conditions of its place: the given. The design-build activism is a constant process of constructing the site-specific, that 'the building had been, and is destined to remain, part of the site'.[20] The order of time nurtured by this barefoot architect overcomes the order of space imposed by mainstream professional architects. A larger and longer speculation on an ecological human habitat of the barefoot architect starts from this house, as a site of resistance to the ecologically destructive urbanisation undergone in the region.

Conclusion

The barefoot architect's own house illustrates an ecological and place-sensitive route that is against the contemporary Chinese rural housing production, which flows from neoliberal urbanisation. It suggests a radically different alternative. The house offers an approach not only based on building for people but also building for the land. Building becomes a bare form of its land, based on innovation in ecological materials. By embracing the long tradition of self-build, collaborative design and collective assembly, the barefoot architect has expressed a heroic version of a social model in the right to build, rather than simply branding a cultural model for an ecological rural reconstruction. The very hands-on, design-build process in this house project constantly cross-references those who design and those who build. In this sense the project's activism is a time-based assemblage, a state of being in the making. The non-stop, micro-scaled transformations show that the house was not a finite project but an ongoing activism. Better understanding always emerges from daily use, identifying both good construction points and errors alike. This approach needs the will and skill of repair, largely lost in contemporary architecture.[21] The barefoot architect blends the roles of architect-developer, user-architect, and architect-builder, and highlights the craftsman's individuality while turning the layperson into an architect in a coherent scheme. This making of an 'architect' and legitimisation of the practice of 'building' as 'architecture' occurs here through the expression of the right to design-build, the spontaneity inherent in it, and the temporal expression through it.[22] It lays a promising foundation for a more empowering form of architectural practice as resistance, as activism, countering top-down production and the reduction of richer life-worlds at home. To paraphrase Jeremy Till's statement, it leads not only to a revitalised form of contemporary architecture, but also to a revitalised, bare, and more relevant form of contemporary architectural practice.[23]

20
Interview with Weizhong Ren by the author in April 2015 in his house at Jianshan village, China.

21
For this argument see more details in Blundell Jones, *Architecture and Movement*.

22
Grubbauer and Streets, 'The Making of Architects'.

23
Till, 'The Negotiation of Hope'.

Blundell Jones, Peter. *Architecture and Movement: The Dynamic Experience of Buildings and Landscapes*. London: Routledge, 2015.

Blundell Jones, Peter, and Derong Kong. 'The Case for an Oral Architecture: Carpentry and Communal Assembly among the Dong of Southwest China'. *Architectural Research Quarterly* 20, no. 2 (June 2016): 145–58.

Blundell Jones, Peter. 'The Meaning of Use and Use of Meaning'. *field: a free journal for architecture* 1, no. 1 (2007): 4–9.

Cupers, Kenny. 'The Infrastructure of Participation: Cultural Centres in Postwar Europe'. In *Participation in Art and Architecture: Spaces of Participation and Occupation*, edited by Martino Stierli and Mechtild Widrich, 13–39. London: I.B.Tauris, 2016.

Fan, Kerry Sizheng. 'Shanzhai'. *Architecture and Culture* 4, no. 2 (2016): 323–9.

Grubbauer, Monika, and Silke Streets 'The Making of Architects: Knowledge Production and Legitimation in Education and Professional Practice'. *Architectural Theory Review* 19, no. 1 (2014): 4–9.

'Jianshan village, Anji county, Zhejiang province -- Creating an International Rural Life Benchmark'. http://www.xinhuanet.com/travel/2018 -11/14/c_1123712605.htm. Accessed 30 June 2019.

Oliver, Paul, ed. *Encyclopaedia of Vernacular Architecture of the World*. Cambridge: Cambridge University Press, 1997.

Pandey, Gyanendra, ed. *Unarchived Histories: The 'Mad' and the 'Trifling' in the Colonial and Postcolonial World*. London: Routledge, 2013.

Ren, Xiang. 'Socially-Engaged Architecture in a Chinese Rural Village: Xihe Village Community Centre'. *Architectural Research Quarterly* 20, no. 2 (2016): 119–30.

Ren, Xiang. 'Hybrid Building and Hybrid Practitioner: An Unbuilt Clan-Community Hall in a Chinese Natural Village', RIBA Publication (2017).

Ren, Xiang. 'Anonymous Process and Absent Architect: Behind the Scenes of Chinese Rural Regeneration'. *Architecture and Culture* 6, no. 1 (2018): 145–54.

Richards, Simon. '"Vernacular" Accommodations: Wordplay in Contemporary-Traditional Architecture Theory'. *Architectural Research Quarterly* 16, no. 1 (2012): 37–48.

Rudofsky, Bernard. *Architecture without Architects*. New York: MOMA, 1966.

Till, Jeremy. 'The Negotiation of Hope'. In *Architecture and Participation*, edited by Peter Blundell Jones, Doina Petrescu, and Jeremy Till, 23–41. London: Taylor & Francis, 2005.

Van Lengen, Johan. *The Barefoot Architect: A Handbook for Green Building*. Bolinas: Shelter Publication, 2007.

Vellinga, Marcel, ed. *Encyclopaedia of Vernacular Architecture of the World*, second edition. London: Bloomsbury, 2022.

A Secret Life ... Emerging from an urban bolthole

Robert Riddel

The 'house' described here – a Citroën H milk delivery van transformed into a mobile living cell – challenged many assumptions about a place to live, by being anywhere and mobile, invisible yet secure. It provided a solution to accommodation in central London which, during the 1970s, proved extremely difficult and expensive. The 'house' avoided regulation by assuming an acceptable disguise of an ordinary delivery vehicle; it was not questioned as a component of urban life, but it was in reality a mobile capsule home at an affordable cost. It offered an experiment in living on the street as a viable concept and an alternative to other solutions then in practice. Squatting in empty properties, for example, seemed much less secure by comparison, and it also lacked the freedom offered if one's home was hidden from view and capable of relocation.

The year 1968 was one of widespread dissent. Students were rioting in Paris, Belgrade, Britain, Warsaw, and even the US.[1] In Brisbane, Australia, where I was studying at the time, student activity was less focussed. The war in Vietnam, and the draft by lottery to be part of it, ensured there were visible demonstrations, which were invariably met with disproportionate brutality from an ultraconservative government.[2]

Although in Brisbane, architecture students took part in the marches and many were arrested, it was the theatrical Architectural Reviews held at the local Avalon Theatre that defined the era.[3] These productions contained not only political commentary, but also were mixed with generous servings of original music – one of the most famous songs was 'High on a Hot Banana' – as well as satire and comedy, which mostly took aim at the shortcomings of our local architectural education, something the student body (to which I belonged) sought to remedy with published manifestos, student magazines, and the organisation of student conferences. For these conferences, we invited international speakers whom we thought could better address the real needs of architecture.[4] With a core of activist students, I was involved in the production of a film in 1968 entitled 'Happiness is a Three-Legged Dog'. It portrayed the teaching of architecture in Brisbane as an endless parroting of the words 'truth, beauty, integrity' by students dressed in uniform, following the instructions of a robotic tutor.[5] Yet nothing changed; it was time to leave.

With two more years to complete my degree, I resolved to find something better. There were similar thoughts among a few of my peers, usually the more devoted students, and we began applying to go to other places. I submitted my portfolio to two schools that were then considered to be among the best in the world, both in London. It was going to be expensive but worth it. I applied to the

1
The first student protest at the Sorbonne in Paris followed the shutdown by the government of the Paris university on 2 May 1968. On the 6 May, 20,000 students, staff, and supporters marched toward the Sorbonne to a confrontation with police. The protest escalated from there after hundreds were arrested. By the end of May, after a general election was called, the protests subsided. Other cities followed the example and in London the Hornsey College of Art was occupied by students from 28th May–12th July. Tickner, *The Art School Revolution*.

2
The National-Liberal coalition government in Queensland, under Bjelke Petersen, was the most conservative in Australia. It was in power from 1968 until 1987. During the Vietnam War the Australian government instituted conscription by lottery for males aged twenty. Between 1964 and 1972, 15, 381 Australians were sent to partake in the war.

3
Architecture students in Queensland held theatrical reviews at the Avalon Theatre, St Lucia, between 1965 and 1970. See Gosseye and Macarthur, 'Angry Young Architects'.

Architectural Association and to the Royal College of Art and was accepted for both. I chose to first attend the RCA and entered into the Furniture Design School, under David Pye.[6]

Arriving in London in 1970, I was confronted with a whole new set of life experiences. At that time, a vast slum clearance and reconstruction program for London was underway. Thousands of terraced houses in inner London were deemed 'unfit' for habitation, scheduled for demolition, emptied of their occupants, boarded up by local councils and, in some cases, deliberately vandalised by councils to prevent reoccupation. A succession of grandiose London plans were published, aiming to restructure the city into zones and build new housing for the working classes in the form of council flats. However, these plans were slow to materialise, council house waiting lists became hopelessly long, and a squatting movement had appeared in London as a direct response to housing needs among young people and families.[7]

As one of the few foreign students at the RCA, I was initially offered a place in the school student hostel in Evelyn Gardens in South Kensington. My room was narrow – it was actually half a room – with a window, a work desk, chair, and a ladder to a bunk above a hanging rail for clothes, as there was insufficient space to have the bed at floor level. It was far from the environment I sought. After all, I was a designer and wanted to be able to adapt my space and experiment with and control my surroundings.

My experience in Brisbane with student accommodation had been in shared houses. My most recent house, shared with two colleagues, had been a formerly abandoned two-storey cottage on the edge of the Brisbane city centre. Although we did not squat it – we rented it from the company who owned it – we did adjust the building in multiple ways to suit our needs and to give us the liberties we sought in the contemporary ultraconservative Queensland political climate. The three of us drew straws to allocate bedrooms. I drew the shortest and was given the smallest bedroom, opening onto the back veranda. To make the most of it, I immediately explored ways to expand my domain and make it more appealing. As a result, I devised an intimate, Swedish-style, alcove-bedroom box addition, which hung over the top of the staircase and was accessed from the back veranda. Through a Perspex window it had a wonderful view of the city. As adolescent sex in the 1960s was not possible in the parental homes we had left, planning for it became an important functional requirement in any shared house. The new addition was a considerable success in this respect and was even borrowed on occasion, sometimes without my knowledge.

However, in London, suitable accommodation alluded me. As part of my work for the RCA, I was designing furniture that could occupy a central space and simultaneously become a room divider. I was commissioned through a friend to redesign the Notting Hill bedroom of a wannabe rock star. The chosen concept was a single piece of furniture placed in the centre of a room of generous proportions.

4
The Australian Architecture Students Association (AASA) had branches in each Australian state. National student conferences were held in Sydney/Canberra in 1964, Melbourne in 1965, Perth in 1966, Brisbane in 1967, Hobart in 1968, and Sydney again in 1969. Guest speakers at these conferences included Aldo van Eyck, Jaap Bakema, Buckminster Fuller, Gio Ponti, Cedric Price, and Tony Gwilliam. In terms of architecture student magazines, *Scarab* was the first of several architectural student magazines produced in the decade from 1966. Only three issues were ever printed.

5
A sixteen-millimetre film, 'Happiness is a Three-legged Dog', was made in Brisbane in 1968, directed by Tony Airey, with the backing of the Queensland Architectural Students Association.

6
David Pye (1914–1993) was head of the Furniture Design School at the Royal College of Art (RCA) from 1964 until 1974. I was a student at RCA from 1970 to 1973 and at the Architectural Association (AA) between 1974 and 1976.

7
Public housing was a chief plank of the post-war welfare state in Britain. The law existing to protect sitting tenants from eviction caused many property owners to keep buildings vacant to make them easier to sell for redevelopment. Chronic shortages in available rental housing encouraged illegal squatting in empty buildings.

Fig. 1 Bedroom furniture module on wheels which divided the available space as required. It contained a bed with side table, clothes storage, ladder, desk, and a full-length mirror. Designed and built by Robert Riddel, Notting Hill, 1971. (Photograph by © Robert Riddel)

Fig. 2 Alternative capsules for living in, as published in *AD*. 'The service module can provide control, information storage and communication, nutrition, waste and maintenance. A range of ancillary components give choice of enclosure, body support, diet, display etc.' (Source: *Architectural Design (AD)*, no. 7 (1969): 374)

Fig. 3 Technical specification for Citroën Type H 9 CV, showing extent of space available in the short wheelbase version. (1971 Citroën sales brochure)

Fiche technique

Transmission : Traction AV - Couple 6 x 29. Embrayage monodisque à sec à moyeu amorti.
Direction : A crémaillère - Rayon de braquage : 5,60 m. entre trottoirs.
Suspension : Barres de torsion à l'AV et à l'AR, différentes sur le 1000 et le 1600, 4 roues indépendantes, 4 amortisseurs hydrauliques.
Pneumatiques : 17 - 400 X - en option : 19 - 400 C et 19 - 400 X.
Freins : Frein principal : transmission hydraulique sur les 4 roues (surface de freinage : 1240 cm^2) - un doseur répartiteur équilibre l'action selon la charge, tambours à ailettes pour refroidissement. Frein de secours (à main) : transmission mécanique sur les 2 roues AV (surface de freinage : 714 cm^2).
Capacités : Carburant = 60 litres - Carter moteur = 4 litres.
Carter boîte de vitesses = 3 litres.
Système de refroidissement = 8 litres.
Options : Deuxième porte coulissante à gauche sur le fourgon.
Chauffage - dégivrage.
Peinture laquée bleu Week-end, blanc Paros ou rouge Masséna.
Sièges « Club ».

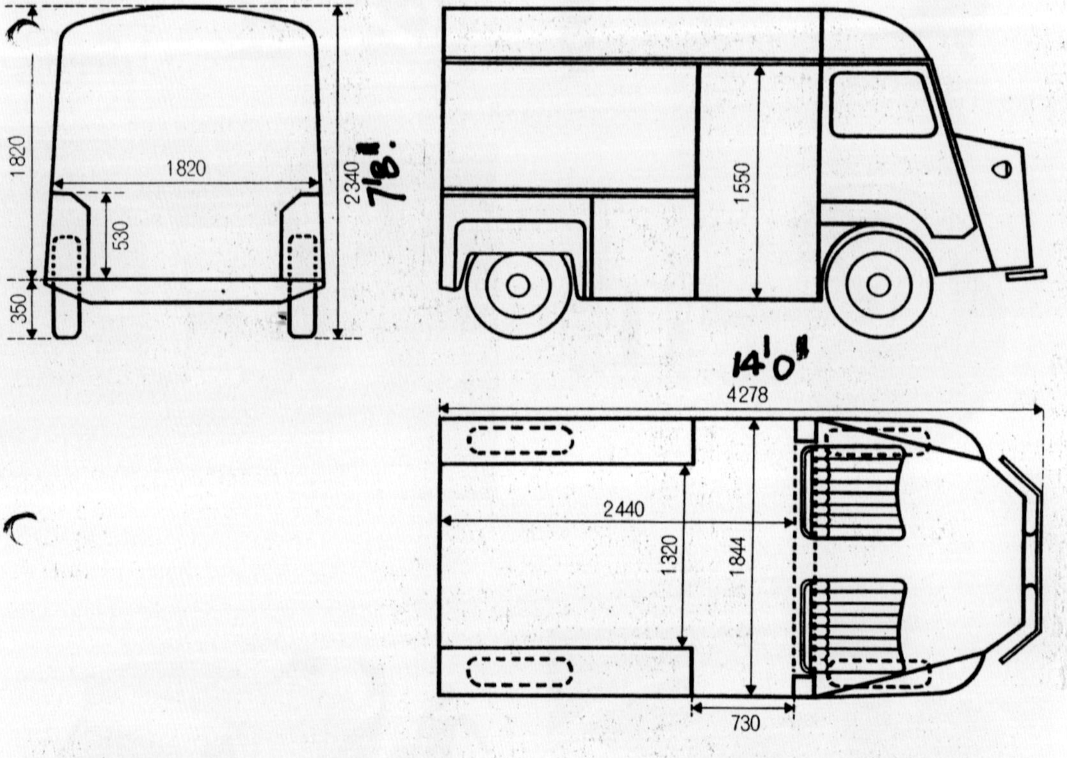

Type du moteur	Essence	Essence	Diesel
Puissance fiscale	9 CV	11 CV	8 CV
Cylindrée	1628 cm^3	1911 cm^3	1946 cm^3
Puissance maximum	45 ch à 4200 tr/mn	56 ch à 4000 tr/mn	57,5 ch à 4000 tr/mn
Vitesse maximum en charge Citroën 1000	92 km/h	105 km/h (101 km/h avec boîte « montagne »)	88 km/h
Citroën 1600	90 km/h	101 km/h	88 km/h
Consommation	10 à 13 l	11 à 13 l	7 à 9 l

Type du moteur	Essence	Essence	Diesel
Batterie	12 V 40 AH/CEI Alternateur	12 V 40 AH/CEI Alternateur	2 de 6 V 95 AH/CEI Alternateur
Citroën « 1000 » Citroën « 1600 »	PTC PTC	2440 kg 2975 kg	CU 1075 kg* CU 1605 kg*
1600 Spécial (seulement essence 11 CV et 8 CV Diesel)			
pour carrosseries agréées	PTC	3200 kg	CT 1900 kg*

* Avec moteur Diesel - 55 kg.

8
Architectural Design (AD), in particular, covered capsule living extensively. See Greene, 'Instant City Children's Primer'; Dawson and Stanton, 'Another Alternative'; *Architectural Design* 2, 63; Rabeneck, 'Hier Today'.

9
Jencks and Silver, *Adhocism.*

It was a mobile installation that housed a desk and, with clothes storage below, a queen-sized bed with a bedside bookshelf **(Fig. 1)**. It had the same components as my student hostel but made better use of space and (I believe) looked and worked infinitely better. This commission made me consider what might be the minimum space required for one's personal needs (the 'minimum-dwelling' if you like), but one which would offer the greatest possible freedom. As heating in Britain was a considerable expense, a smaller volume would be advantageous. Squatting, as I mentioned, was en vogue in London at the time, but this often meant sharing with a larger numbers of occupants and also inhibited the freedom that I sought. Small was better, but how small and where to find it? I had lived on yachts and travelled in sleeping compartments on trains, where space standards were pared down to the minimum. Capsule living was extensively discussed in journals like *AD (Architectural Design)*. Some of the projects published in *AD* at that time included Hans Hollein's telephone box fitted out for living (1965), Walter Pichler's tv helmet (1968–69) and several space capsule typologies. Archigram's David Greene had his Rockplugs and Logplugs as invisible service points for mobile dwellings. The car was recognised as 'a self-powered mobile room with limited support systems' **(Fig. 2)**.[8]

A student project that I did in Brisbane in 1968 for a single-person shelter had been influenced by these publications and was constructed on top of a Fiat 500 that I then owned. While it provided a waterproof enclosure, it would have been unusable without insulation and illegal to use outside a camping ground. So, what would be the urban equivalent? If one designed a capsule to live in, where would one put it and how much space was required? I gave the subject much thought and sought a pragmatic solution.

At the RCA, students were encouraged to devise their own projects in the Furniture Design School and test them as prototypes.
If approved they could be constructed with the assistance of the craftsmen in the furniture workshop. Even though the scale of my capsule idea was considered too ambitious, I was allowed to include it among my design projects but I was also expected to produce some more orthodox furniture prototypes suitable for production.
I designed some storage systems and a range of tables and satisfied my academic requirements but continued to pursue my capsule interest. Adhocism, as defined by Charles Jencks, appealed to me and provided the stimulus for seeking an existing container of some sort which could be fitted out as a capsule home and yet not be too conspicuous in inner city London.[9]

As part of my research, I visited the Caravan & Camping Exhibition at Olympia in 1971, which showcased the actual available technologies. It also had state-of-the art prototypes on display, such as the Hoverhome and luxury motor homes of the Winnebago variety and its derivatives. While the fittings were of interest, the image they portrayed was far from what I sought. I was looking for a capsule, which did not reveal its actual use, could easily be moved in case of trouble, and could inconspicuously fit into various urban settings.

Fig. 4 Plan and cross section 3, of adaptation for habitation 1:10; Riddel at RCA, October 1972. (Drawing by © Robert Riddel)

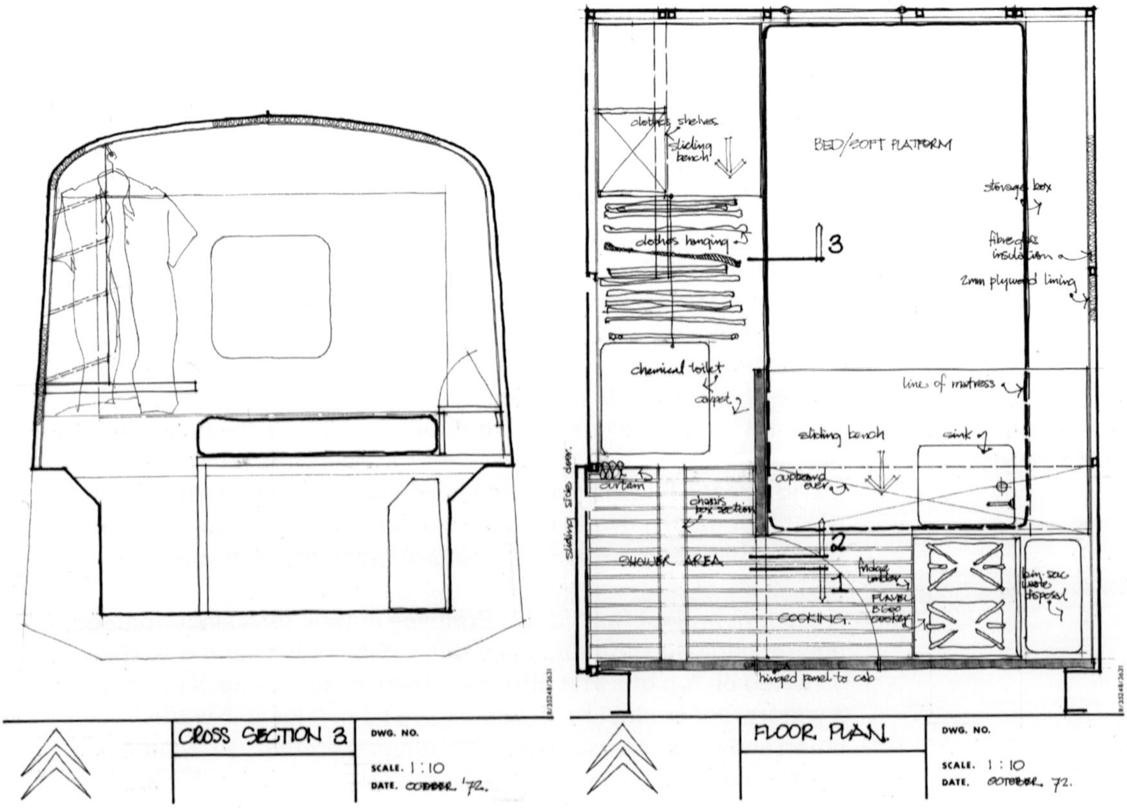

10 The VW Kombi van was manufactured from 1949 until 2013. Conversions to camping vehicles such as the Westfalia were common in the UK and Europe. The vehicle became a symbol for both the hippie and surfing generations in the US and Australia.

11 The Citroën H van was manufactured from 1949 until 1981. It had a 1.9-litre (11cv) petrol engine driving the front wheels. It was the first commercial vehicle to use monocoque construction, an ultra-low floor, a three-piece rear door, and torsion bar suspension and was technically the most advanced vehicle of its time. See Lesueur, *Les Types H de Collection.*

Over my student years in Australia, I had owned many interesting vehicles, including the Fiat 500 that I have mentioned, and the UK provided a much greater choice. The search for a suitable vehicle allowed me to pursue two key passions simultaneously – combining capsule design with an automotive interest. I considered furniture vans, which had translucent fibreglass roofs, but dismissed them as being too unwieldy to manoeuvre. They were also too high off the ground. Most of the smaller commercial vans available in the UK were too low to stand up in, as were the (then) ubiquitous VW Kombi vans, which had pop-up roofs.[10] The French equivalents, however, had front-wheel drive and much more adequate headroom in the back. They also had the floor level closer to the road as they needed no transmission shaft to the rear wheels. The Citroën H van in particular was ideal, as it was also available in different lengths **(Fig. 3)**.[11] Unfortunately, these vehicles were almost unknown in Britain, so I headed to France to find one, which proved more difficult than anticipated. While new ones were beyond my budget, second-hand examples were almost non-existent. Eventually, I struck lucky and managed to purchase one from a Belgian milk delivery service. It was the shortest wheelbase version, had only a small central window at the rear, which opened as an awning above a pair of half doors and with a single sliding windowless door just behind the cab. It was perfect and had entirely corrugated sides and roof to give the body extra strength. It also had the painted livery of its former use.

The available space for the capsule, excluding the cab, was 2.4 metres long, 1.8 metres wide, and 1.8 metres tall. In the driver's compartment were two seats, spaced apart for the gearbox, which allowed enough room between them to access the rear. The first adaptation I made was to separate the front cockpit from the rear and to create two distinct spaces. To make the intended domestic quarters private, a wall containing a flush door was built between the cab and the back and a hinged solid shutter closed off the back window. The rear compartment was now a lightproof room, and its contents and use completely undetectable from the outside. The rear quarters could be entered via the cab, the side sliding door, or the back openings. The cab, as well as having seating for the driver and one passenger, provided space for sitting/reading while parked and could be used in full view without revealing the functional aspects of the rear compartment.

The private capsule space was lined to improve the insulation and acoustic values of the metal box in which it was housed and then fitted for sleeping, sitting, cooking, washing, and storage for the necessary requisites of an adequate but simple life. The bed took up most of the space and was fixed in position so that it was used for both sleeping and sitting. The mattress was placed on a platform to allow storage below it and horizontal work and dining surfaces could be slid and secured in different positions above it. Gas cooker, sink, shower, and chemical toilet were located within a tolerable but minimum space informed by yacht design. Storage on shelves and hanging rails or clothes hooks had to be designed

Fig. 5 Full-scale prototype, London, May 1972. (Photograph by © Phil Griffin)

12 The Belgian five-digit number plates that were attached to the vehicle had been cancelled on its export, but not removed.

to cope with movement when the vehicle was driven so that the contents were not to finish up on the floor **(Fig. 4)**.

The technology used was quite conventional but depended on a freshwater tank for drinking and cooking and a grey water tank with heater of recycled water for washing. This was filtered and pumped to a holding tank for reuse. Better filters are available now but at that time, the grey tank water could be used four or five times before being replaced. Soap could be removed, but shampoo was not tolerated. The vehicle's battery was sufficient for the lighting, water pump, and heater while a small gas cylinder was carried for cooking on a two-burner stove. As soon as the prototype became sufficiently useable, I began living in it. I initially parked it close to where friends lived so I could use their bathroom facilities until mine was perfected. Central London was my preferred location and I explored areas as diverse as Camden and Wandsworth. Parking restrictions were the only consideration, and I moved location often **(Fig. 5)**.

The capsule provided the freedom that I sought, and my first long trip was up the east coast of England as far as Whitby in Yorkshire. Then, in the summer of 1972, I travelled with a girlfriend across the channel to Ostend, intending to drive to Athens. We planned a route through Belgium, France, Switzerland, Italy, and Yugoslavia to Greece. On arrival in Belgium on the first evening, we found a good central parking spot for the night. When we emerged from the vehicle the next morning, it was evident that we were parked in the middle of a produce market and in a position where we could not drive out until the market had finished. Later that day we were escorted out of Belgium by the highway police for not having valid Belgium licence plates.[12] These were attached to the vehicle when it was purchased and were not a problem anywhere else but in Belgium. Travelling through France and Italy was uneventful and we were able to park and sleep almost anywhere without being noticed. The hundreds of Australians driving through Europe at that time were usually travelling in VW Kombi vans with pop-up roofs. If they stopped for the night outside of a camping ground, they were quickly moved on. Because our vehicle did not look like a motorhome, we had no such restrictions and could stop anywhere with discretion. In rural Yugoslavia, when parked on a deserted road, some travellers on horseback, not realising the vehicle was occupied, tried to force entry into the cab. A loud sudden shout from within was enough to send them on their way at considerable speed, without their pausing long enough to investigate the source.

We drove back to London via Brindisi. A memorable stop on the return journey was Le Corbusier's chapel in Ronchamp, built in 1955. We even spent a night parked on the Champs-Élysées in central Paris without incident. We returned to Britain via France to avoid any difficulties in Belgium. Back in London, I began my final year at RCA, which culminated in the degree show in the summer of 1973. After consultation with my tutors and an inspection of the prototype vehicle, I was advised to exhibit a 1:10 model of my project rather than the full-sized version. So, prior to graduation, I sold the van, which had performed so well as my secret home for over a year.

Today, forty-five years later, the Citroën H van has become somewhat of a cult vehicle. They are available in restored condition to be fitted out as mobile coffee shops or food carts. There is also a motorhome conversion that can be rented, but its use is no longer subversive as the nature of its function is obvious.[13] At the time, I considered that my project, while a successful experiment, had little chance of commercial success. It was however a serious and pragmatic attempt at evolving a capsule lifestyle, which allowed greater freedom than hostel living, subverted conservative concepts of capital gains through land acquisition, was less troublesome than squatting, and, because it was under the radar of urban regulation, had an added dimension of satisfaction.

13
A motorhome conversion of the Citroën H is currently available in France from Camping Moulin de Lacombe. In Britain two companies specialise in conversion of restored H vans as food vehicles.

The experiment taught me, as an aspiring architect, to value a more generous space for living that could allow flexibility of both use and interpretation. The minimum space standards for public housing determined in the 1961 Parker Morris report was adopted as the norm by public housing providers in the UK. It proposed designing rooms or spaces that were determined by standard furniture layouts, but inevitably could only be arranged in a single configuration. This in my view was counterproductive to ensuring the viable life of new buildings by designing rooms or spaces that were too small to be used any other way. Older buildings, by contrast, which often had larger rooms and more generous ceiling heights, offered considerably more amenity and flexibility in the way they were inhabited and therefore could be reinterpreted by each new occupant. An appreciation for adaptability and flexibility which, as a result of my experiencing first-hand the limitations of the minimal living space determined by the vehicle during my student years, was one of the reasons that I became more committed to conservation and adaptive reuse in my later practice as an architect.

Bibliography

Architectural Design (AD), no. 2 (1970): 63.

Dawson, C., and A. Stanton. 'Another Alternative'. *Architectural Design (AD)*, no. 7 (1969): 374.

Greene, David. 'Instant City Children's Primer'. *Architectural Design (AD)*, no. 5 (1969): 274–5.

Gosseye, Janina, and John Macarthur, 'Angry Young Architects: Counterculture and the Critique of Modernism, 1967–72'. In *Hot Modernism, Queensland Post-War Architecture*, edited by John Macarthur, Deborah Van der Plaat, Janina Gosseye, and Andrew Wilson, 30–45. London: Artifice, 2015.

Jencks, Charles, and Nathan Silver. *Adhocism: The Case for Improvisation*, Cambridge, MA: MIT Press, 1972.

Lesueur, Patrick. *Les Types H de Collection*. Vanves: Hachette, 2012.

Rabeneck, Andrew. 'Hier Today'. *Architectural Design (AD)*, no. 8 (1970): 389.

Tickner, Lisa. *The Art School Revolution*. London: Francis Lincoln, 2008.

Critical Retrospection and Moving Forward: Questions that persist

Isabelle Doucet and Janina Gosseye

In discussing activist aspects of the architect's own home through a number of themes and productive tensions, there are several aspects pertaining to the nexus resistance–domesticity that a case-based book like *Activism at Home* leaves unaddressed.

First, the politicisation of the home beyond the specificity of the architect's house is addressed only to a limited extent in this volume; even if historically, the home, and particularly the right to housing, have been at the heart of activist action and, consequently, also scholarship. The eighteenth- and nineteenth-century social reformers, industrial philanthropists, and social utopianists; the modernist and post-war efforts towards mass housing; and the struggles that emerged in the 1960s to save historical inner-city working-class neighbourhoods from demolition all place the home at the centre of wider social, economic, and cultural struggles and debates. In recent times, advanced neoliberalisation of (urban) space, the privatisation of the housing market, and the diminution of socioeconomic support services place the home, and notably the *loss* of one's home, at the heart of housing activism.

Questions of domesticity and the role of the home in connection to gender, class, race, ethnicity, sexual orientation, and the intersections between these are also not explicitly addressed in this book. Holding the capacity to oppress but also to protect and to provide safety, to liberate as well as constrain, the home has been studied extensively within cultural, gender, queer, and feminist studies, to mention only a few relevant fields. Scholars in these fields have produced refined understandings of the complex workings of domesticity and the relationship between the home and activism. In these fields, discussions of domesticity open up important questions related to social, sexual, and racial liberation and oppression, domestic labour, violence, and broader challenges with regards to diversity and equality in society. Discussions within these fields also show how the home can become a site of intense struggle for recognition of one's sexual orientation, gender, race, ethnicity, and the intersections between these, and caution against making generalising claims about liberations or oppressions from domesticity. As Black feminists and feminists of colour, among others, have argued, emancipation – domestic or otherwise – may liberate some but not all women and can even come at the expense of other women.[1] Also within architectural history and theory, a wealth of scholarship exists that addresses specific questions related to gender, architecture, and domesticity,[2] or offers critical feminist perspectives as a way of studying the intrinsic relationship between social struggle, action, and the production of space and the built environment.[3] Unfortunately, it is beyond the scope of this book to engage with such important debates with the degree of rigour they deserve.

Another topic that *Activism at Home* does not explicitly address is why the various events that led up to the publication of this book did not yield more examples of women architects designing their own homes. *Activism at Home* includes only four such examples.

1
For instance, the professional careers of emancipated (often white middle class) women have been known to rely on the household support provided by other women, often women of colour. Among a wealth of scholarship the work of bell hooks (e.g. *Feminism is for Everybody: Passionate Politics*. London: Pluto Press, 2000); Sara Ahmed (e.g. *Living a Feminist Life*. Durham, NC: Duke University Press, 2017); and Cinzia Arruzza, Tithi Bhattacharya, and Nancy Fraser (*Feminism for the 99%: A Manifesto*. London and New York: Verso, 2019) comes to mind.

2
Groundbreaking works include Beatriz Colomina (ed.), *Sexuality and Space* (New York: Princeton Architectural Press, 1992) and Jane Rendell, Barbara Penner, and Iain Borden (eds.), *Gender Space Architecture: An Interdisciplinary Introduction* (London and New York: Routledge, 2000). In connection to the gendered use and design of domestic spaces, we refer to Dolores Hayden, *The Grand Domestic Revolution: A History of Feminist Design for American Homes, Neighbourhoods, and Cities* (Cambridge and London: The MIT Press, 1981); Alice T. Friedman, *Women and the Making of the Modern House: A Social and Architectural History* (New Haven: Yale University Press 2006, originally published in 1998 by Harry N. Abrams, Inc.), and Hilde Heynen and Gülsüm Baydar (eds.), *Negotiation Domesticity: Spatial Productions of Gender in Modern Architecture* (Abingdon and New York: Routledge, 2005).

To cite Despina Stratigakos: 'Where are the Women Architects?'[4] Studies dedicated to women in architecture have shown that architectural professional practice – that is, 'the office' – often offers fewer career opportunities for women than men. With this in mind, one might expect the home to be an ideal vehicle to launch a woman's career in private practice.[5] As this does not seem to be the case, one might ask whether the career paths of women in architecture do not offer the financial, social, or professional stability to pursue a prestigious own home design, let alone one that assumes a critical or resistant stance. Or perhaps it means that when women design their own homes, these do not enjoy the same visibility as those designed by their male counterparts? This is a question also of architectural authorship. Women architects have not always received credit for the buildings they designed. Furthermore, while women have been actively involved in the creation of homes, they have not always done so in a professional capacity (that is, as architects) and have consequently not been credited
for their work as it often falls outside the narrowly defined confines of authorship. We therefore ask: Is the relative absence of women architects in this book merely a result of the discipline's well-known and ongoing struggle to foreground and recover the contributions by women in architecture, both in architectural practice and its historiography, or are other factors at play?

Finally, we recognise scope for further research in the different meanings that are attached to the terms 'home' and 'activism' in different parts of the world. Giving voice to such diversity requires a broader geographical distribution and a more diverse representation of both the architects studied and the scholars writing about them. Our ambition was to encourage such diversity by organising two open calls for conferences in two different corners of the globe (Brisbane and Manchester), and by offering support with travel. While this approach allowed us to include refreshing appraisals of canonised works alongside critical examinations of lesser-known projects, the cases gathered in this book still predominantly originate in Europe and North America.

In discussing some of these 'trims' of *Activism at Home*, we wanted to give an honest appraisal of not just what we think the book *does*, but also to point to what we believe it may have done or done differently. Doing so prompts us to also look ahead. The staggering number of people who are currently in transition, refuge, migration, and exile reveals that the home remains a troubled entity. Add to this the current changes affecting the domestic sphere as a result of COVID-19 whereby the home is invaded by work and stripped of its role as a place for social encounter, and it becomes clear that the (right to a) home should not be taken for granted and deserves our ongoing critical scrutiny. Although it is yet to be seen how current conditions and future threats – for example, climate change – will affect the architecture of the home, we believe that *Activism at Home* shows that architectural practitioners and scholars have the capacity to provide analyses of and design solutions for tackling such threats in various and innovative ways.

3
We here limit ourselves to sharing a few recent works: Lori A. Brown (ed.), *Feminist Practices: Interdisciplinary Approaches to Women in Architecture* (Farnham: Ashgate, 2011); Meike Schalk, Therese Kristiansson, and Ramia Maze (eds.), *Feminist Futures of Spatial Practice: Materialisms, Activisms, Dialogues, Pedagogies, Projections* (Baunach: AADR Art Architecture Design Research, and imprint of Spurbuchverlag, 2017); Hélène Frichot, Catarina Gabrielsson, and Helen Runting (eds.), *Architecture and Feminisms: Ecologies, Economies, Technologies* (Abingdon and New York: Routledge 2018).

4
Despina Stratigakos, *Where are the Women Architects?* (Princeton and Oxford: Princeton University Press in association with Places Journal, 2016).

5
Indeed, houses that women built for themselves as sites of experimentation and innovation have featured in anthologies dedicated to women architects such as Susana Torre's *Women in American Architecture: A Historic and Contemporary Perspective* (New York: Whitney Library of Design, an imprint of Watson-Guptill Publications, 1977).

Biographies

Paola Ardizzola

is an associate professor in the history and theory of architecture at the German University in Cairo. She is a founder of the architecture department at the Antalya International University, where she served as executive dean and department chairperson until 2017. Ardizzola is an active member of AGORA, a network of forty-four universities in the Euromed region, in the Heritage and Vernacular section. She is the recipient of the Bruno Zevi International Prize for her research on Bruno Taut's work in Turkey and is currently completing a book on Zvi Hecker's oeuvre as architect and artist.

Inge Bertels

is a full professor in architectural history at the University of Antwerp and teaches both architecture and heritage students. Her research focusses on the intersection of nineteenth- and twentieth-century construction history, architectural history, and urban history. As an architectural historian and heritage specialist she feels it is important to participate both in architectural and academic debates. As such she is a member of the board of the Vlaams Architectuurinstituut (VAi) and of the editorial committee of the *International Journal of Construction History*.

Nicholas Boyarsky

is a founder and director of the London-based studio Boyarsky Murphy Architects and professor of architecture at RMIT University, where he is involved in the creative practice research PhD programme. His research interests include contested monuments, visual urbanism and ephemera, micro-urbanism and the Asian city, and ludic practices.

Thea Brejzek

is a professor of spatial theory at the University of Technology Sydney. Her research engages with the history and theory of scenography and performative environments at the intersection of theatre and architecture. She is a member of the scientific advisory board of the Bauhaus Dessau and co-editor of the Routledge journal, *Theatre and Performance Design.* Recent publications include *The Model as Performance: Staging Space in Theatre and Architecture* (Bloomsbury, 2017).

Oscar Andrade Castro

is an associate professor of architecture at the Pontificia Universidad Católica de Valparaíso. His research and practice are situated at the crossing of architectural pedagogy and collective building experiences. His work includes contributions in several international exhibitions, academic journals and book chapters, most recently at the art exhibition Documenta 14 and in the book *Architecture 68: International Panorama of the Renewal of Education* (2020).

Pierre Chabard

is an architect, critic, and historian of architecture and urbanism. He is currently associate professor of history and theory at the School of Architecture Paris-la Villette, Hesam University. Author of a PhD about Patrick Geddes' Cities Exhibitions (2008), his current research deals with social and cultural history of architectural mediations. He is the author and editor of various books and founding member of the French journal *Criticat* (2008–18); he now runs the Éditions de la Villette.

Scott Colman

is an assistant professor at the Rice University School of Architecture in Houston, Texas, where he teaches architectural and urban history, theory, and design. He is concerned about the fate of progressivism in contemporary architecture and is currently completing a book on the anarcho-socialist architect and planner Ludwig Hilberseimer.

Irina Davidovici

is a senior researcher at the gta Institute, ETH Zurich, where she leads the doctoral programme in the history and theory of architecture. She is the author of *Forms of Practice: German-Swiss Architecture 1980–2000* (2012 and 2018) and editor of *Colquhounery: Alan Colquhoun, from Bricolage to Myth* (2015). She has also written numerous scientific articles and anthology contributions that straddle urban and housing studies and architectural theory and criticism.

Els De Vos

is an associate professor at the University of Antwerp, where she chairs the interior architecture programme. A commercial edition of her PhD dissertation on home culture in 1960s Flanders was published. She has edited several volumes, including *Reuse of Modernist Buildings: A Case Study Handbook* (2019). She has co-curated several exhibitions, most recently *Female Symbols and Urban Space* (Brussels, 2020). Currently, she is involved in the COST-action on Middle Class Mass Housing in Europe.

Isabelle Doucet

is a professor of theory and history of architecture at Chalmers University of Technology, Sweden. Through a focus on resistant practices and conceptual-methodological inquiries, her research centres on the relationship between architecture, (urban) politics, and social/environmental responsibility. She is the author of *The Practice Turn in Architecture: Brussels after 1968* (2015) and her recent editorial work includes the thematic issue with Hélène Frichot 'Resist Reclaim Speculate: Situated Perspectives on Architecture and the City' (Architectural Theory Review 2018).

Valeria Federighi

is an architect and assistant professor at Politecnico di Torino. Her research work focusses on analysing mechanisms of innovation in architecture as expanding practice. She is on the editorial board of the journal *Ardeth* and she is part of the China Room research group. She is the author of *The Informal Stance: Representations of Architectural Design and Informal Settlements* (2018) and co-editor of *The Eyes of the City: Architecture and Urban Space after Artificial Intelligence* (2021).

Selin Geerinckx

is an academic assistant at the interior architecture programme of the University of Antwerp. She investigated the work of architect Jul De Roover and builds on the genealogy of the discipline of interior architecture by scrutinising the bodily and mental effects of modernist housing through modern dance theory and methodologies. Selin co-curated the exhibition *Living in Color* in Antwerp (2019) and is an appointed tutor in the International Student Workshop DOCOMOMO 2020+1 in Tokyo.

Michele Gentile

studied architecture at University G. D'Annunzio of Chieti-Pescara, Italy, where he graduated with a dissertation entitled 'Space Systems For a Second Welfare', which explored the social, political, and economic significance of the domestic space and investigated possible dwelling alternatives inside and against the neoliberal system. Having completing the Reading the Neoliberal City masters of research programme at the University of East London (UEL), he is currently based in Sheffield, UK, where he combines professional practice with architectural research.

Stylianos Giamarelos

is a lecturer in architecture at UCL's Bartlett School of Architecture and the executive editor of *The Journal of Architecture*. In 2008, he co-curated *ATHENS by SOUND*, the Greek pavilion in the eleventh Biennale of Architecture in Venice. In 2018, his research on the cross-cultural authorship of critical regionalism was a runner-up finalist for the biannual Publication Award of the European Architectural History Network.

Janina Gosseye

is an associate professor of urban architecture at TU Delft. Her research is situated at the nexus of twentieth-century architectural and urban history on the one hand, and social and political history on the other. Janina's work has been published in leading academic journals; and she has edited and authored several books, most recently, *Speaking of Buildings: Oral History in Architectural Research* (with Naomi Stead and Deborah van der Plaat, 2019).

Christina Gray is a postdoctoral fellow in the School of Architecture and Landscape Architecture at the University of British Columbia. Her research is focussed on the intersection of late twentieth-century architectural history and the role of the architectural client. She completed her PhD in architectural history at the University of California, Los Angeles in 2019.

Richard W. Hayes is an architect and architectural historian educated at Columbia University and Yale University. His publications include *The Yale Building Project: The First 40 Years* (Yale University Press, 2007), a comprehensive history of an influential educational programme founded by Charles W. Moore. He has also published articles on Moore in *Journal of Architectural Education, Scroope: Cambridge Architectural Journal,* and *Arris*. Recipient of numerous grants and awards, Hayes was a visiting fellow at the University of Cambridge in 2009 and 2013 and is now a life member of Clare Hall.

Farhan Karim is an associate professor of architecture at the University of Kansas. His research focusses on architecture and the politics of development in South Asia. He is the author of *Of Greater Dignity than Riches* and edited *The Routledge Companion to Architecture and Social Engagement*.

Helena Mattsson is a professor in history and theory at KTH School of Architecture. Her research deals with contemporary architectural history with a special focus on the interdependency between politics, aesthetics, and spatial organisations. She has published extensively in journals and edited books; she is the editor and author of several books, the most recent is *Neoliberalism on the Ground: Architecture and Transformation from the 1960s to the Present* (with K. Cupers and C. Gabrielsson, 2020). She is currently working on a book on the neoliberalisation of the 1980s welfare state (Bloomsbury Publishing).

Cathelijne Nuijsink is a Marie Sklodowska-Curie Postdoctoral Fellow at the Institute for the History and Theory of Architecture (gta) at ETH Zürich. Her research focusses on cross-cultural knowledge exchange in architecture culture in the post-war era and aims to contribute to a more dynamic and inclusive crossed history of architecture. Cathelijne's current postdoctoral research project explores the potential of 'contact zones' as a general historiographic method in the field of architecture, using as her case study a long-running ideas competition from Japan. 'Another Historiography: The Shinkenchiku Residential Design Competition, 1965–2020', as the project is titled, will result in a book, travelling exhibition, and website.

Max Ott

is an architect, independent urban researcher, and housing activist. His research and writings are focussed on the mutual relationship between ethics, urban politics, and architectural space, and are informed by an interest to illustrate how ethical discourses and practices function as social strategies to negotiate conflictual urban transformation processes. Currently, Max is a guest lecturer at the University of Applied Sciences in Munich and works for the development cooperative urban coop berlin.

Giacomo Pala

is an architect and research assistant at the Institute of Architectural Theory at Innsbruck University. He was a visiting lecturer at the Institute of Urban Design at the University of Innsbruck in 2016, directed by Peter Trummer (who supervises his PhD on Giovanni Battista Piranesi) and an external lecturer at the CUINDA programme at Chulalongkorn University in Bangkok (2020). Pala has published several articles and book chapters on his research, and presented his working hypotheses in various institutions including the ETH Zurich, the Calouste Gulbenkian Foundation in Lisbon, and the ETSAM University in Madrid.

Eliana Perotti

trained as an art historian and has worked in the field of the history of town planning since 1998. Perotti works on topics of history of urban design theory, highlighting the history of ideas, social and cultural aspects, with focus on aspects of urban sustainability, colonial urbanism, as well as on the impact of representative technologies on urban design. Her current foremost interest is the discourse on city and gender. Perotti is an initiator of the interest group Gender in Architecture and Urban Design (EAHN), and has conducted several research projects, including 'Flora Ruchat-Roncati at ETH Zurich, 1985–2002: Professor, Architect, Theorist', and 'Saffa 1958' (Swiss Women's Work Exhibition).

Linsy Raaffels

is an architectural engineer and conducts doctoral research into the architectural value of architects' houses built between 1830–1970 in the Brussels Capital Region and links her results to future valorisation perspectives. The research project 'Architects' Houses in Brussels: Strategies for Valorisation' is carried out part-time in the department of architectural engineering at the Vrije Universiteit Brussel and part-time in the office of Barbara Van der Wee Architects.

Xiang Ren

is a lecturer in architecture at the University of Sheffield School of Architecture, where he leads the MA Architectural Design programme. His research is centred around the conservation and regeneration of built heritage in traditional settlements and contemporary cities. Shortlisted twice for RIBA President's Research Awards in 2014 and 2016, his articles appeared in leading refereed journals including *Architectural Research Quarterly, Journal of Architecture, Architecture and Culture, AA Files*, and *The China Journal*.

Robert Riddel

had an architectural practice in Brisbane Australia (Riddel Architecture) for thirty years before it merged with Conrad Gargett in 2012. The practice had a reputation for conservation and adaptive reuse and worked on many public buildings. Riddel completed a PhD at the University of Queensland in 2008, on the architecture of RS Dods, which was published as a monograph in 2012. He now lives in Antwerp.

Isabel Rousset

is an architectural historian. Her research investigates the intersections between architecture, housing politics, and the social sciences in Central Europe in the nineteenth and early twentieth centuries. She is currently preparing a book on the theory and politics of housing design in modern Germany. Her work on this topic has appeared in *Journal of Architecture, Journal of Urban History*, and *Architectural Theory Review*.

Silvana Rubino

has a PhD in Social Sciences (Unicamp) and conducted postdoctoral studies at EHESS, Paris. She edited the publications *Lina por escrito* (2009) and co-edited *Domesticidade, gênero e cultura material* (2017). She also was a curator for the exhibition *Ocupação Mario de Andrade* (São Paulo, 2013) and was curator-assistant for the exhibition *Lina Bo Bardi 1914 in Rom geboren* (Lina Bo Bardi born in Rome in 1914) (Johann Jacobs Museum, Zurich, 2014). She has published many articles and book chapters on modern architecture, cultural heritage, and intellectual history. A book on women and architecture is forthcoming in 2021.

Patricio Cáraves Silva

is a full professor of architecture at Pontificia Universidad Católica de Valparaíso. He is a founding member of Ciudad Abierta, where he currently lives and has dedicated himself to think, build, and inhabit an architecture from hospitality. He has participated in more than thirty crossings of the American continent and built several projects in Ciudad Abierta.

Lee Stickells

is an associate professor in architecture at the University of Sydney. His historical research on international countercultural and ecological design experimentation has been published widely across scholarly, professional, and popular media. He contributes to the *Architectural Theory Review* editorial committee and the international advisory board for *Counterculture Studies*. Most often, though, he can be found riding bikes.

Eva Storgaard

is a lecturer at the Faculty of Design Sciences at the University of Antwerp. She holds a PhD in architecture, publishing a dissertation entitled 'The Architecture of Danish Modern: Empiricism. Craft. Organicism' (2019). Eva teaches in the masters programme of interior architecture at the Faculty of Design Sciences (University of Antwerp). She has published in academic journals such as *OASE*, *Interiors: Design, Architecture, Culture*, and *Joelho: Journal of Architectural Culture*.

Peter Swinnen

is a Brussels-based architect. After his apprenticeship at Luc Deleu/T.O.P. Office (1994–96) he founded 51N4E space producers, which he spearheaded until 2013. Between 2010 and 2015, Swinnen enrolled as a Flemish state architect, a public mandate empowering architecture as a policy-making discipline. Since 2015 he has been partner-in-chief at CRIT. Swinnen has taught at the Architectural Association, KU Leuven, Lacambre, and ETH Zürich, and is currently guest professor at UNILU.

Luke Tipene

is a lecturer and course director at the School of Architecture, University of Technology Sydney. His research centres on the history, theory, and practice of architectural drawing and how questions of accuracy and uncertainty in images affect knowledge production in spatial design. He has recently published in *The Journal of Architecture*, *IDEA Journal*, and *Cubic Journal*. He is on the editorial board of *IDEA Journal* and co-guest-editor for the 2021 issue '(Extra)ordinary Interiors: Practicing Critical Reflection'.

Stephanie Van de Voorde

teaches architectural and construction history and heritage at the department of architectural engineering of the Vrije Universiteit Brussel, Belgium. Breaking away with traditional perspectives in architectural history and heritage studies, her main research topics are related to twentieth-century building materials and building culture, as well as young heritage.

Barbara Van der Wee
is the architect-in-chief of Barbara Van der Wee Architects – Studio for Architecture and Conservation (Brussels) and is specialised in the conservation and restoration of nineteenth- and twentieth-century built heritage, including many art nouveau buildings. She teaches at the Raymond Lemaire International Centre for Conservation (University of Leuven), is a member of the Koninklijke Vlaamse Academie van België, and is an expert consultant for Europa Nostra and UNESCO World Heritage.

Kirsty Volz
is a lecturer in architecture at the Queensland University of Technology. She is codirector of emerging architecture practice Toussaint and Volz. She is currently completing her PhD at the University of Queensland and her research on interior design and scenography has been published in the *IDEA Journal, TEXT Journal, Lilith: A Feminist History*, and the *International Journal of Interior Architecture and Spatial Design*.

Lawrence Wallen
is an architect, visual artist, and professor in the School of Architecture, University of Technology Sydney. Lawrence's research operates across a range of modes employing scenographic strategies and performative readings resulting in an extensive collection of books, drawings, performances, and architectures. He exhibits and publishes widely including recent publications with *Architectural Design* (AD), *Leonardo Journal* and Bloomsbury.

Sarah Wigglesworth
is director of her London-based architectural practice which she founded in 1994. Her work is acknowledged as a pioneering influence in British architecture, and it focusses on exploring ecological building solutions. Interested in practice-based research and with over thirty years in academia, Sarah writes and speaks extensively about her and the practice's work. She was granted the title Royal Designer for Industry in 2012 and awarded an MBE in 2003.

Andrew Wilson
is an architect and senior lecturer at the School of Architecture, University of Queensland, principal of NMBW Queensland Office, and member of Total Collective. He researches twentieth-century architectural and urban history and design research with a focus on architecture and the city. He has contributed to a forthcoming book on Karl and Gertrude Langer and is currently researching the transformation of Brisbane as a consequence of the Second World War.

Acknowledgements

This book would not have been possible without the generous financial support from our respective home academic institutions: the Department of Architecture and Civil Engineering (ACE) and the Chalmers Architectural Research Initiative (C-ARC) at Chalmers University of Technology in Sweden, and the Faculty of Architecture and the Built Environment at Delft University of Technology in the Netherlands. We are extremely grateful for their support.

We would like to thank all the contributors to this book. Without their eminent scholarship, *Activism at Home* would not exist. We are grateful for their intellectual input as well as for their patience, commitment, and collegiality that made this ambitious editorial project a joy and honour to complete.

Activism at Home originates in a research collaboration that began in 2017 and that, before becoming a book, took the shape of two jointly organised events at our previous academic institutions. Along the way we have received indispensable institutional and collegial support. A first symposium hosted at the University of Queensland in Brisbane (Australia) in July 2017 was made possible thanks to the support received from the Centre for Architecture Theory Criticism History (ATCH) at the University of Queensland, which included a visiting fellowship that allowed Isabelle's stay in Brisbane to coincide with the event. A second, two-day international conference titled 'Activism at Home: Architects' Own Houses as Sites of Resistance' was hosted at the University of Manchester, UK, in 2018, where support came, among others, through a Social Responsibility in the Curriculum Fund, which allowed for embedding an international research event in a pedagogical setting and for productive exchanges between architectural research and education. Isabelle is grateful for the support received from colleagues at the School of Environment Education and Development, the Manchester School of Architecture, and the Manchester Architecture Research Group, where the book project received feedback in its early stages. Stephen Walker and Léa-Catherine Szacka helped in facilitating contacts for interviews and conference speakers. Regrettably, not all of the conference contributions made it into this book for reasons beyond the speakers' or our control. We would therefore like to take this occasion to thank all the speakers, including the keynote speakers Philip Goad, Russell Hall, Hilde Heynen, and Sarah Wigglesworth for sharing their expertise with us. An additional thank you to Sarah for honouring the book with a foreword. We would like to thank Jon Broome, Sean Griffiths, Rod Hackney, and Patty Hopkins, for their most insightful conversation with Isabelle together with her students, and for making it possible to include their voices, and images of their houses, in this book.
We are grateful for the opportunity to discuss specific aspects of the project with Torsten Lange and, in the earlier stages, for the publication in the professional magazine *Architecture Australia*, which allowed us to test the ground.

Finally, we would like to thank Doris Kleilein at JOVIS for providing a platform for our project, and the editorial and production teams at JOVIS, including Theresa Hartherz, Charlotte Blumenthal and Christen Jamar, for their excellent work and professionalism. We are thrilled to see *Activism at Home* published. We enjoyed every step in its making and we hope that our enthusiasm comes across to the readers of this book.

Isabelle Doucet and Janina Gosseye

Imprint

Cover design:
Joana Katte, Hamburg, and Torsten Köchlin, Leipzig

Cover image: House X
© Alvin Boyarsky Archive

Copy-editing:
Christen Jamar, London

Design and setting:
Joana Katte, Hamburg, and Torsten Köchlin, Leipzig

Lithography:
Bild1Druck, Berlin

Printed in the European Union

Bibliographic information published by the Deutsche Nationalbibliothek
The Deutsche Nationalbibliothek lists this publication in the Deutsche Nationalbibliografie; detailed bibliographic data are available on the Internet at http://dnb.d-nb.de

jovis Verlag GmbH
Lützowstraße 33
10785 Berlin

www.jovis.de

jovis books are available worldwide in select bookstores. Please contact your nearest bookseller or visit www.jovis.de for information concerning your local distribution.

ISBN 978-3-86859-633-5